Lecture Notes in Computer Science   10468

Commenced Publication in 1973
Founding and Former Series Editors:
Gerhard Goos, Juris Hartmanis, and Jan van Leeuwen

More information about this series at http://www.springer.com/series/7408

Bronis R. de Supinski · Stephen L. Olivier
Christian Terboven · Barbara M. Chapman
Matthias S. Müller (Eds.)

Scaling OpenMP for Exascale Performance and Portability

13th International Workshop on OpenMP, IWOMP 2017
Stony Brook, NY, USA, September 20–22, 2017
Proceedings

 Springer

Editors
Bronis R. de Supinski
Lawrence Livermore National Laboratory
Livermore, CA
USA

Barbara M. Chapman
Stony Brook University
Stony Brook, NY
USA

Stephen L. Olivier
Sandia National Laboratories
Albuquerque, NM
USA

Matthias S. Müller
RWTH Aachen University
Aachen
Germany

Christian Terboven (iD)
RWTH Aachen University
Aachen
Germany

ISSN 0302-9743   ISSN 1611-3349   (electronic)
Lecture Notes in Computer Science
ISBN 978-3-319-65577-2   ISBN 978-3-319-65578-9   (eBook)
DOI 10.1007/978-3-319-65578-9

Library of Congress Control Number: 2017949171

LNCS Sublibrary: SL2 – Programming and Software Engineering

Printed on acid-free paper

This Springer imprint is published by Springer Nature
The registered company is Springer International Publishing AG
The registered company address is: Gewerbestrasse 11, 6330 Cham, Switzerland

Preface

OpenMP is a widely accepted, standard application programming interface (API) for high-level shared-memory parallel programming in Fortran, C, and C++. Since its introduction in 1997, OpenMP has gained support from most high-performance compiler and hardware vendors. Under the direction of the OpenMP Architecture Review Board (ARB), the OpenMP specification has evolved up to and beyond version 4.5. The 4.5 version includes several refinements to existing support for heterogeneous hardware environments, many enhancements to its tasking model including the task-loop construct, and support for doacross loops. As indicated in the technical report previewing version 5.0, it will include additional new features such as a tools interface and task reductions.

The evolution of the standard would be impossible without active research in OpenMP compilers, runtime systems, tools, and environments. OpenMP is important both as a standalone parallel programming model and as part of a hybrid programming model for massively parallel, distributed memory systems built from multicore, manycore, and heterogeneous node architectures. In fact, most of the growth in parallelism of the upcoming exascale systems is expected to come from increased parallelism within a node. OpenMP offers important features that can improve the scalability of applications on such systems.

The community of OpenMP researchers and developers is united under the cOMPunity organization. This organization has held workshops on OpenMP around the world since 1999: the European Workshop on OpenMP (EWOMP), the North American Workshop on OpenMP Applications and Tools (WOMPAT), and the Asian Workshop on OpenMP Experiences and Implementation (WOMPEI) attracted annual audiences from academia and industry. The International Workshop on OpenMP (IWOMP) consolidated these three workshop series into a single annual international event that rotates across Europe, Asia-Pacific, and the Americas. The first IWOMP workshop was organized under the auspices of cOMPunity. Since that workshop, the IWOMP Steering Committee has organized these events and guided development of the series. The first IWOMP meeting was held in 2005, in Eugene, Oregon, USA. Since then, meetings have been held each year, in Reims, France; Beijing, China; West Lafayette, USA; Dresden, Germany; Tsukuba, Japan; Chicago, USA; Rome, Italy; Canberra, Australia; Salvador, Brazil; Aachen, Germany; and Nara, Japan. Each workshop has drawn participants from research and industry throughout the world. IWOMP 2017 continues the series with technical papers and tutorials. The IWOMP meetings have been successful in large part due to generous support from numerous sponsors.

The IWOMP website (www.iwomp.org) provides information on the latest event, as well as links to websites from previous years' events. This book contains proceedings of IWOMP 2017. The workshop program included 23 technical papers, two keynote talks, and a tutorial on OpenMP. The two-part paper by Leopold Grinberg, Carlo Bertolli, and Riyaz Haque was selected for the Best Paper Award. All technical papers were peer reviewed by at least three different members of the Program Committee.

September 2017   Christian Terboven
                                                         Bronis R. de Supinski
                                                          Stephen L. Olivier

Organization

Program Committee Co-chairs

Bronis R. de Supinski   Lawrence Livermore National Laboratory, USA
Stephen L. Olivier   Sandia National Laboratories, USA

General Chair

Abid Malik   Brookhaven National Laboratory, USA

Publication Chair

Christian Terboven   RWTH Aachen University, Germany

Publicity Chair

Delafrouz Mirfendereski   Stony Brook University, USA

Local Chair

Tony Curtis   Stony Brook University, USA

Program Committee

Eduard Ayguadé	BSC and Universitat Politecnica de Catalunya, Spain
James Beyer	Nvidia, USA
Taisuke Boku	University of Tsukuba, Japan
Mark Bull	EPCC, University of Edinburgh, UK
Nawal Copty	Oracle Corporation, USA
Alejandro Duran	Intel, Spain
Deepak Eachempati	Cray, USA
Nasser Giacaman	University of Auckland, New Zealand
Oscar Hernandez	Oak Ridge National Laboratory, USA
Chunhua Liao	Lawrence Livermore National Laboratory, USA
Meifeng Lin	Brookhaven National Laboratory, USA
Lawrence Meadows	Intel, USA
John Mellor-Crummey	Rice University, USA
Masahiro Nakao	RIKEN AICS, Japan
Mitsuhisa Sato	RIKEN AICS, Japan
Dirk Schmidl	RWTH Aachen University, Germany
Thomas R.W. Scogland	Lawrence Livermore National Laboratory, USA
Eric Stotzer	Texas Instruments, USA

| Priya Unnikrishnan | IBM Toronto Laboratory, Canada |
| Michael Zingale | Stony Brook University, USA |

IWOMP Steering Committee

Steering Committee Chair

| Matthias S. Müller | RWTH Aachen University, Germany |

Steering Committee

Dieter an Mey	RWTH Aachen University, Germany
Eduard Ayguadé	BSC and Universitat Politecnica de Catalunya, Spain
Mark Bull	EPCC, University of Edinburgh, UK
Barbara Chapman	Stony Brook University, USA
Bronis R. de Supinski	Lawrence Livermore National Laboratory, USA
Rudolf Eigenmann	Purdue University, USA
William Gropp	University of Illinois, USA
Michael Klemm	Intel, Germany
Kalyan Kumaran	Argonne National Laboratory, USA
Federico Massaioli	CASPUR, Italy
Lawrence Meadows	Intel, USA
Stephen L. Olivier	Sandia National Laboratories, USA
Ruud van der Pas	Oracle, USA
Alistair Rendell	Australian National University, Australia
Mitsuhisa Sato	University of Tsukuba, Japan
Sanjiv Shah	Intel, USA
Josemar Rodrigues de Souza	SENAI Unidade CIMATEC, Brazil
Christian Terboven	RWTH Aachen University, Germany
Matthijs van Waveren	KAUST, Saudi Arabia

Contents

Advanced Data Management with OpenMP

Best Paper

Hands on with OpenMP4.5 and Unified Memory: Developing Applications for IBM's Hybrid CPU + GPU Systems (Part I)

Leopold Grinberg[1(✉)], Carlo Bertolli[1], and Riyaz Haque[2]

[1] IBM Research, Yorktown Heights, USA
{leopoldgrinberg,cbertol}@us.ibm.com
[2] LLNL, Livermore, USA
haque1@llnl.gov

Abstract. High Performance Computing is steadily embracing heterogeneous systems for supporting a wide variety of workloads. Currently there are two main sources of heterogeneity in compute nodes: (a) different compute elements such as multicore CPUs, GPUs, FPGAs, etc. and (b) different types of memory including DDR, HBM, SSDs. Multiple compute elements and memory types present many opportunities for accelerating applications featuring stages characterized by different compute intensity, sequential or parallel execution, cache sensitivity, etc. At the same time programmers are facing multiple challenges in making necessary adaptations in their codes. In this study we employ IBM's OpenMP 4.5 implementation to program hybrid nodes with multiple CPUs and GPUs and manage on-node memories and application data. Through code samples we provide application developers with numerous options for memory management and data management. We consider simple functions using arrays and also complex and nested data structures.

Keywords: OpenPOWER · HPC · Offloading · Directive based programming

1 Introduction

Over the years computer systems for High Performance Computing (HPC), and more recently High Performance Analytics (HPA), have become a back-bone for businesses and research organizations. Modernization of such resources typically occurs in three- to six-year cycles, requiring application developers to quickly adapt their codes to new systems. Transition from one system to another often requires considerable code restructuring and optimization. While taking advantage of new system features like multiple compute elements is important, it is equally necessary to ensure a speedy and cost-effective transition of applications. Besides refactoring applications due to system evolution, addressing code (and library) portability across disparate systems is often a major consideration as

© Springer International Publishing AG 2017
B.R. de Supinski et al. (Eds.): IWOMP 2017, LNCS 10468, pp. 3–16, 2017.
DOI: 10.1007/978-3-319-65578-9_1

well. To this end, while actual programming strategies vary from one organization to another, they are broadly defined by two metrics: (a) the path of least disruption for porting applications from one system to another (portability) and (b) the time-to-solution (performance) on each system. Hardware and system-software vendors attempt to provide developers ways to achieve both with a reasonable balance.

From a software perspective, the two major requirements for achieving performance portability are: (a) readiness of applications to support data layouts, data structures and parallelism suitable for various compute devices and memory pools; and (b) programming models permitting compilers to generate codes for multiple compute devices from a single source. From a hardware perspective, support for features such as Unified Memory (UM), low latency in switching execution from one device to another, high memory-bandwidth between all elements of a heterogeneous node are needed for applications that can benefit from using heterogeneous resources.

In this paper, our specific contribution is in providing software developers with guidance on managing memory and data onto heterogeneous memory subsystems using IBM's OpenMP®4.5 implementation. We are focusing not only on the semantics of individual OpenMP4.5 constructs or API calls, but also how these can be productively combined together in a larger, production-level, application scenario. To our knowledge, this is the first paper that gives a detailed programming-oriented description of these OpenMP4.5 features.

This paper is structured as follows: in Sect. 2 we briefly review the evolution of the OpenMP standard from supporting threading on multi-core CPUs to providing tools for programming hybrid nodes with multiple compute elements and memories. In Sects. 3 and 4 we provide a number of scenarios for managing data starting with a simple application using array pointers and then moving on to more complex data structures based on object inheritance and nested classes. In Sect. 5 we conclude with a brief summary and outlook.

Related prior work includes a discussion on *deep copy* as part of a technical report of the OpenACC standard [3]. The report shows how the base language can be extended to natively support complex class hierarchies and structures, including objects containing pointers to dynamically allocated arrays or other objects. Unlike the conclusions of that report, we do not propose extensions to the OpenMP language in this paper but instead demonstrate mapping of complex data structures using current OpenMP specifications. Automatic deep copy support is also the subject of [2] where the authors take an experimental approach.

The study presented here will be extended in *Hands on with OpenMP4.5 and Unified Memory: Developing applications for IBM's hybrid CPU + GPU systems (Part II)*, where we will provide guidance on how programmers can take advantage of specific features present in OpenPOWER®systems.

2   Evolution of OpenMP to Accelerator Programming

OpenMP is a standard adopted and implemented by most HPC vendors as a programming language based on a shared memory model. Before the OpenMP4 era the standard focused on expressing parallelism in multicores, and starting with OpenMP4, it evolved to support special architectural combinations that couple common multicore processors (*host*) and accelerators (*devices*). Standard versions for OpenMP4 and beyond focus not only on expressing parallelism in a shared memory programming model, but also on nested parallelism, switching execution between *host* and *device* and managing disjoint physical memories. OpenMP4 allows programmers to use a single programming language, and design applications that run on *host* (CPUs) and *devices* (such as GPUs).

A full description of OpenMP4.5 data and programming constructs is beyond the scope of this paper (see [1,4,5] for details and examples). In this study we will only focus on a subset of OpenMP4.5 functionality.

3   Porting Simple Kernels to GPUs with OpenMP4.5

In this section we describe ways for allocating *device* memory and transferring data between *host* and *device*. To illustrate the techniques we consider two simple functions called in sequence and using the same arrays. Specifically, we consider (1) a simple daxpy operation (line 9, Fig. 1) executed in parallel; and (2) data initialization function initialize_x_and_y (line 11, Fig. 1) which can also be executed in parallel.

```
 1  int main () {
 2      double *x, *y;
 3      double alpha = 2.0;
 4      int N=1024*1024*10;
 5      x = (double *) malloc(N*sizeof(double));
 6      y = (double *) malloc(N*sizeof(double));
 7      initialize_x_and_y(x,y,N);
 8      #pragma omp parallel for
 9      for (int i = 0; i < N; i++) y[i] = alpha*x[i]+y[i];
10  }
11  void initialize_x_and_y(double *x, double *y, int N) {
12      #pragma omp parallel for
13      for (int i=0; i<N; ++i) {x[i] = i*0.001;    y[i] = i*0.03;}
14  }
```

Fig. 1. Code for illustrating data management strategies

In order to offload the daxpy kernel and the array initialization kernel to the *device* we need to perform two operations: (1) make the data visible to the *device*; and (2) to specify that execution of the loops should be on the *device*. The rest of the section describes several options developers can employ for managing data.

```
1  int main() {
2      double *x, *y;
3      double alpha = 2.0;
4      int N=1024*1024*10;
5      x = (double *) malloc(N*sizeof(double));
6      y = (double *) malloc(N*sizeof(double));
7      initialize_x_and_y(x,y,N);
8      #pragma omp target teams distribute parallel for map(to:x[0:N]) map(
           tofrom:y[0:N])
9      for (int i = 0; i < N; i++) y[i] = alpha*x[i]+y[i];
10 }
11 void initialize_x_and_y(double *x, double *y, int N) {
12     #pragma omp target teams distribute parallel for map(from:x[0:N], y[0:
           N])
13     for (int i=0; i<N; ++i) {x[i] = i*0.001;      y[i] = i*0.03;}
14 }
```

Fig. 2. Mapping data: code for illustrating Option 1

Option 1: The initial conditions here are that all the memory for arrays x and y have been allocated in the *host* memory using calls to `malloc`. The simplest way to make the data available to threads running on the *device* is to use the `map` clause available in OpenMP4.5.

The OpenMP4.5 specification for the `map` clause states: *"... The original and corresponding list items may share storage such that writes to either item by one task followed by a read or write of the other item by another task without intervening synchronization can result in data races..."* [5]. Thus, the specification allows implementations to choose between providing a shared storage or replicating list items on a *device*. IBM's implementation of the `map` clause for an NVIDIA GPU *device* (considered in this study) avoids creating a shared storage and instead allocates memory on the *device*, and if required, also copies data between *host* and *device*.

In the example presented in Fig. 2, the implementation of the `map(to:x[0:N])` clause leads to three operations: (1) allocating memory on the *device*; (2) copying data from the *host*; (3) deallocating *device* memory after the computations are completed. The *device*'s threads will operate on the mapped array x. The implementation of the clause `map(tofrom:y[0:N])` leads to the following operations: (1) allocating memory on the *device*; (2) copy data from the *host* to the *device* before the start of the target region; (3) copy data from the *device* to the *host* after completion of the computations in the target region; (4) deallocation of *device* memory after the copying data to the *host*. Similarly, the `map(from:x[0:N],y[0:N])` clause used in the `initialize_x_and_y` function will allocate memory on the *device*, copy the data from *device* to *host* memory after the initialization performed in the target region, and deallocate the *device* memory. Memory allocations and copying data between *host* and *device* are time consuming operations and they should be minimized in order to achieve good overall performance. We next show a way of reducing the cost associated with memory management.

Option 2: The main idea here is to allocate/deallocate *device* memory only once, and eliminate data transfer between the two code regions executed on the *device*.

Here we make use of OpenMP4.5 directive `target enter/exit data` as an alternative way of managing data. In the algorithm of Fig. 3 we present an implementation using these data directives. The memory buffers x and y are mapped when the run-time control flow reaches the invocation of the `target enter data` directive (i.e. the call inserted by the compiler in its place). Mapping with `map(alloc:)` only results in allocation in *device* memory of the space indicated by the array sections, and it does not incur any data transfer. As the data is initialized and consumed on the *device* there is no need for data transfer between *host* and *device*. Device memory allocated by `target enter data` will not be released until a corresponding `target exit data` is encoutered. In our example buffer x is discarded (`release`) without requiring any data transfers between *host* and *device*, while y, the result of the computation on the device, is copied back from *device* to *host* memory following by *device* memory deallocation. Note that in the function `initialize_x_and_y` as well as in the daxpy kernel we make an assumption that arrays x and y have already been mapped. Due to this assumption, calling function `initialize_x_and_y` without prior mapping of x and y will result in a run-time failure.

A somewhat better approach for managing data in the `initialize_x_and_y` function would be to probe if x and y have already been mapped to the device memory and then use the `if` clause to enable or disable memory operations.

```
 1  int main() {
 2      double *x, *y;
 3      double alpha = 2.0;
 4      int N=1024*1024*10;
 5      x = (double *) malloc(N*sizeof(double));
 6      y = (double *) malloc(N*sizeof(double));
 7      #pragma omp target enter data map(alloc:x[0:N], y[0:N])
 8      initialize_x_and_y(x,y,N);
 9      #pragma omp target teams distribute parallel for
10      for (int i = 0; i < N; i++) y[i] = alpha*x[i]+y[i];
11      #pragma omp target exit data map(release:x[0:N]) map(from:y[0:N])
12  }
13  void initialize_x_and_y(double *x, double *y, int N) {
14      #pragma omp target teams distribute parallel for
15      for (int i=0; i<N; ++i) {x[i] = i*0.001;    y[i] = i*0.03;}
16  }
```

Fig. 3. Mapping data: code for illustrating Option 2

```
 1  void initialize_x_and_y(double *x, double *y, int N) {
 2      int is_x_mapped = omp_target_is_present(x, omp_get_default_device());
 3      int is_y_mapped = omp_target_is_present(y, omp_get_default_device());
 4      #pragma omp target enter data map(alloc:x[0:N]) if(!is_x_mapped)
 5      #pragma omp target enter data map(alloc:y[0:N]) if(!is_y_mapped)
 6
 7      #pragma omp target teams distribute parallel for
 8      for (int i=0; i<N; ++i) {x[i] = i*0.001;y[i] = i*0.03;}
 9
10      #pragma omp target exit data map(from:x[0:N]) if(!is_x_mapped)
11      #pragma omp target exit data map(from:y[0:N]) if(!is_y_mapped)
12  }
```

Fig. 4. Code for illustrating Option 2, where function `initialize_x_and_y` can be called with or without prior mapping of arrays x and (or) y

The algorithm in Fig. 4 contains an alternative code for the `initialize_x_and_y` function. For deeply nested functional calls the approach presented in this algorithm allows us to make sure that data needed inside the target region executed on the *device* will be mapped and on exit the *host* copy will be updated and memory will be deallocated unless the memory management has already been taken care of in the preceding code sections; in another words the function `initialize_x_and_y` now can be called from anywhere in the program and it will automatically allocate and deallocate *device* memory and update the *host* copy or skip memory allocation and data copy depending whether the arrays x and y are already present on the *device*.

Option 3: OpenMP4.5 provides a runtime function for allocating device memory with the API call `omp_target_alloc`. It also provides an API for associating a pointer to memory allocated on a *device* memory with a *host* pointer through a call to `omp_target_associate_ptr` as shown in the algorithm of Fig. 5. This method for allocating memory on a *host* and a *device* gives greater flexibility when memory pools for temporary arrays are used. Note that the directives applied to the `for` loop executing daxpy and the `initialize_x_and_y` function are exactly the same as in the previous examples.

Option 4: The code in previous examples requires allocating *host* and *device* memories for both arrays, even though *host* memory allocation is not actually needed. OpenMP 4.5 provides opportunity to avoid unnecessary memory allocations by allowing the use of valid *device* memory pointers in the target regions executed on the *device* as shown in Fig. 6. Note that in the function

```
 1  double *x, *y;
 2     double *d_x, *d_y;
 3     double alpha = 2.0;
 4     int N=1024*1024*10;
 5     x = (double *) malloc(N*sizeof(double));
 6     y = (double *) malloc(N*sizeof(double));
 7     omp_set_default_device(0);
 8     d_x = (double*) omp_target_alloc(sizeof(double)*N,
            omp_get_default_device());
 9     d_y = (double*) omp_target_alloc(sizeof(double)*N,
            omp_get_default_device());
10     omp_target_associate_ptr( (void*) x, (void*) d_x, sizeof(double)*N, 0,
            omp_get_default_device());
11     omp_target_associate_ptr( (void*) y, (void*) d_y, sizeof(double)*N, 0,
            omp_get_default_device());
12     initialize_x_and_y(x,y,N);
13     #pragma omp target teams distribute parallel for
14     for (int i = 0; i < N; i++)
15        y[i] = alpha*x[i]+y[i];
16     #pragma omp target update from(y[0:N])
17     omp_target_disassociate_ptr((void*) x, omp_get_default_device());
18     omp_target_disassociate_ptr((void*) y, omp_get_default_device());
19     omp_target_free((void*) d_x, omp_get_default_device());
20     omp_target_free((void*) d_y, omp_get_default_device());
21     free(x);
22     free(y);
```

Fig. 5. Mapping data: code for illustrating Option 3

```
1  int main() {
2    double *y, *d_x, *d_y;
3    double alpha = 2.0;
4    int N = 1024 * 1024 * 10;
5    y = (double *) malloc(N*sizeof(double));
6    omp_set_default_device(0);
7    d_x = (double*) omp_target_alloc(sizeof(double)*N,
           omp_get_default_device());
8    d_y = (double*) omp_target_alloc(sizeof(double)*N,
           omp_get_default_device());
9    initialize_x_and_y(d_x,d_y,N);
10   #pragma omp target teams distribute parallel for is_device_ptr(d_x,d_y)
11   for (int i = 0; i < N; i++)
12     d_y[i] = alpha*d_x[i]+d_y[i];
13
14   omp_target_memcpy((void *) y, (void *) d_y, sizeof(double)*N,  0, 0,
15     omp_get_initial_device(), omp_get_default_device() );
16   omp_target_free((void*) d_x, omp_get_default_device());
17   omp_target_free((void*) d_y, omp_get_default_device());
18   free(y);
19 }
20 void initialize_x_and_y(double *x, double *y, int N) {
21   #pragma omp target teams distribute parallel for is_device_ptr(x,y)
22   for (int i=0; i<N; ++i) {x[i] = i*0.001; y[i] = i*0.03;}
23 }
```

Fig. 6. Mapping data: code for illustrating Option 4

initialize_x_and_y (Fig. 6) we make an assumption that input arguments x and y are valid *device* pointers, execution will fail otherwise.

3.1 Performance Assesment: Data Streaming Kernel

In this section we report on performance of a simple kernel presented in Fig. 7 on a GPU (P-100) and on a CPU (POWER8). We focus on achieved memory bandwidth (BW) utilization as the performance metric. Kernel execution time is measured by means of the omp_get_wtime() API and by using NVIDIA's profiling tool - nvprof; the size of each array was set to 64E+07 bytes. Data from our experiments are presented in the table below. Columns two and three correspond to code using OpenMP4.5 directives for offloading, while column four corresponds to results obtained using CUDA.

```
1   int nthreads = 256;
2   int nteams = (N + nthreads - 1) / nthreads;
3   t_start = omp_get_wtime();
4   #pragma omp target teams distribute parallel for thread_limit(nthreads
        ) num_teams(nteams) if(target:USE_DEVICE)
5   for (i = 0; i < N; ++i){
6     c[i] = a[i]+b[i];
7     d[i] = a[i]-b[i];
8   }
9   t_end = omp_get_wtime();
```

Fig. 7. Data streaming kernel used for performance evaluation

	OpenMP timer	nvprof timer	CUDA
Timing	5.06 ms	4.91 ms	4.96 ms
Achieved BW	471 GB/s	485 GB/s	480 GB/s

The data presented here shows comparable performance for CUDA and OpenMP4.5. Both programming models achieve about 65% of the GPU peak memory BW (732 GB/s). The small differences in timings obtained with codes using OpenMP4.5 and CUDA are in the range of normal time variation. The difference in the timings measured with `omp_get_wtime()` API and nvprof is composed of: (i) the kernel launch overhead (about 0.046 ms, measured with nvprof); and the OpenMP4.5 overhead associated with the search for device pointers corresponding to arrays a, b, c and d. Performance of the kernel presented in Fig. 7 was also measured on a ten-core POWER8 CPU, using one thread per core; switching execution from the GPU to the CPU was obtained by setting *USE_DEVICE=0*, without modifications to the code (including the OpenMP4.5 directives). The achieved kernel memory BW on the POWER8 CPU is 64 GB/s. Considering that the achievable write memory BW is about 39 GB/s (half of the achievable read BW) we can claim that about 82% of the achievable BW has been reached. We can note that the overhead due to creating a parallel region is included in the timing and it is effectively reducing the measured BW utilization.

Overall our experiments show that for data streaming kernels, like the one presented in Fig. 7, performance portability is obtained.

4   Mapping of Complex Data Structures

The OpenMP4.5 `map` clause is used for managing memory and data across *host* and *device* address spaces. While usually straightforward for native and simple POD types, mapping C++ objects is more involved especially in the presence of member data types like pointers and other objects. In this section we will present different ways to deal with complex C++ class structures.

4.1   Mapping class/struct Member Pointers

Let us start by considering a simple `struct A` (Fig. 8) that contains a pointer to an array of integers and a scalar of a type `int`. In order to make the data associated with an object of type `struct A` available on a *device*, the following operations must be performed in the *device* memory: (1) memory allocation for object of type `struct A`; (2) constructor call for `struct A`; (3) copying the value of the scalar struct member of a type `int` from *host* to *device*; (4) *device* memory allocation for the array of integers y and, if desired, copying the content of the *host* y buffer into the allocated device memory; and (4) updating the *device* copy of the object's member pointer y to the appropriate *device* memory address. Current OpenMP4.5 standard does not natively support this set of operations

```
1  struct A {
2      int* y;
3      int size;
4      A(const int* y, const long size) : y(y), size(size)  {}
5  };
6
7  int n = 100;
8  int *y = (int*) malloc(n*sizeof(int));
9  A* a = new A(y,n);
10
11  // Map array y and object a to the device using the map clause
12  #pragma omp target map(to:a[0:1]) map(to:y[0:n])
13  {
14      // Incorrect because a->y still holds the host address
15      a->y[3] += ...;
16  }
```

Fig. 8. Mapping member pointers (improper)

in a single construct, often referred to as *deep copy*. Hence if an object contains a member data pointer that is required on the *device* then, explicit mapping of the data pointed to by this pointer is required. In Fig. 8 we illustrate a possible mapping of an object of a type struct A to the *device*. The operation defined by map(to:a[0:1]) fulfills the requirements (1), (2) and (3), while the operation map(to:y[0:n]) fulfills the requirement (4). However, the code does not work because a->y on the *device* (line 15) still refers to the original host address, i.e. the requirement (5) has not been fulfilled. Mapping only the object merely copies the member pointer's host address. It is also necessary to set a->y within a's *device* copy to the appropriate *device* address.

Figure 9 shows three ways to set the member pointer a->y to the correct *device* address. For option 1 in this example, line 2 fulfills requirements (1), (2) and (3), while line 3 fulfills the remaining requirements (4) and (5). According to the OpenMP4.5 specification, mapping the same memory address more than once results in undefined behavior. Hence, for option 1 to work correctly, it is important that requirement (4) is not fulfilled prior to line 2 i.e. the address range referred to by a->y is not already mapped when line 2 executes. In the same example, operations map(to:a[0:1]) and map(to:y[0:n]) fulfill the requirements (1) through (4) on lines 11 (for option 2) and 21 (for option 3). The last requirement (5) is then fulfilled on lines 14 and 27 respectively for options 2 and 3. Option 2 utilizes an extra target region for updating the member pointer (line 15). Option 3 performs an update on line 27 with the device address obtained at line 21 through the use_device_ptr clause.

Mapping an object from the *device* to the *host* requires caution to avoid overwriting pointer y to *host* memory in the object resident in *host* memory. For options 2 and 3 in Fig. 9 if the map type tofrom is used instead of to (enter data directive used in option 1 does not allow tofrom), then upon exiting the target data region (lines 19 and 33), the object a is copied back from the *device* to the *host* as expected. But as a result of this, a->y's *host* copy is updated with the *device* address, which is not valid on the *host*. Worse still, the original (*host*) address is lost during the copy making it impossible to even retrieve the correct

```
 1  // Option 1 : Map object   a followed by mapping of a->y
 2  #pragma omp target enter data map(to:a[0:1])
 3  #pragma omp target enter data map(to:a->y[0:n])
 4  #pragma omp target
 5    a->y[3] += ...;
 6
 7  #pragma omp target exit data map(delete:a->y[0:n])
 8  #pragma omp target exit data map(delete:a[0:1])
 9
10  // Option 2 : Map array y and object a
11  #pragma omp target data map(to:y[0:n]) map(to:a[0:1])
12  {
13      // Update a->y using a target region
14      #pragma omp target
15      a->y = y;
16
17      #pragma omp target
18          a->y[3] += ...;
19  }
20  // Option 3 : Map array  y and object a, and obtain the device address
        of array y
21  #pragma omp target data map(to:y[0:n]) map(to:a[0:1]) use_device_ptr(y)
22  {
23      int* temp = a->y;
24      // Temporarily assign the device address of y to a->y
25      a->y = y;
26      // Update pointer a->y on the device to the device pointer
27      #pragma omp target update to(a->y)
28      // Reset pointer a->y on the host to the original host address
29      a->y = temp;
30
31      #pragma omp target
32          a->y[3] += ...;
33  }
```

Fig. 9. Mapping member pointers (proper)

address. This can be avoided by storing the *host* pointer value in another member pointer (leads to object bloating), updating data members individually (leads to many fine-grained updates and may be limited by object access qualifiers), or using a transparent host-device memory addressing scheme. We discuss the last alternative in detail in the second part of this paper, on integrating CUDA Unified Memory with OpenMP4.5.

Lastly, the need for updating pointers inside mapped objects also implies that virtual inheritance does not work correctly for mapped objects since this would require appropriately setting virtual-table pointers; something not allowed explicitly in C++. It should be noted that this applies only to objects created on the *host* and accessed on the *device* (and vice-versa). Objects created—and exclusively used—on the *device* can use virtual inheritance normally, albeit at the cost of performance. Moreover, correctly mapped objects comprising of, but not using virtual functions on the *device* also work.

4.2 Mapping Base and Member Classes

OpenMP 4.5 standard provides stand-alone `enter/exit data` directives to map (unmap) data independent of syntactical scope. A possible strategy for mapping (unmapping) objects to the *device* is to put these constructs in the object

```
 1  struct C {
 2    double y;
 3    C(double y) : y(y) {
 4    C* this_ = this;
 5    #pragma omp target enter data map(to:this_[0:1])
 6    }
 7  };
 8  struct B {
 9    int n;
10    double* x;
11    B(int n) : n(n) {
12      x = (double*) malloc(n*sizeof(double));
13      for (int i = 0; i < n; ++i) x[i] = i;
14    B* this_ = this;
15      #pragma omp target enter data map(to:this_[0:1])
16      #pragma omp target enter data map(to:x[0:n])
17    }
18  };
19  struct A : public B {
20    int n;
21    double y;
22    C c;
23    A(int n, double y) : B(n), n(n), y(y), c(y*y) {
24    A* this_ = this;
25    #pragma omp target enter data map(to:this_[0:1])
26    }
27  };
28  // Create object of type A. Undefined behavior
29  A a(10, 20.0);
30
31  #pragma omp target
32  { printf("a.n = %d, a.y = %d\n", a.n, a.y);//Undefined behavior }
```

Fig. 10. Mapping C++ objects (improper)

constructors (destructors) in order to hide the complexity of mapping objects from users. While this is a valid approach, for general C++ objects this requires an abundance of caution. To illustrate the advantages and issues with such a mapping strategy let us consider the following two examples (Figs. 10 and 12).

Creating object a (line 29, Fig. 10) triggers a cascade of events including initialization of class A's bases and members and attempts to map *host* memory segments to a *device*. Before the *host* memory associated with the object a can be mapped (line 25, Fig. 10) the constructor for base class B is invoked (line 11, Fig. 10). This constructor maps a memory segment associated with type B to the *device* (line 15, Fig. 10). Since this memory segment is a subregion of the segment allocated for object a (B being the base class), and that subregion has been already mapped, the effect of trying to map object a later on line 25 is undefined. The map directive for member class C (line 5) also poses the exact same problem.

Clearly, trying to hide the complexity of mapping from a user (who may only need to create a and treat the constructor of A as a black box) results in an incorrect initialization order where an object's constituents (base and member) end up getting mapped before the object itself. In the next example we demonstrate a technique that enforces the proper mapping order and resolves this issue.

First we introduce a templated class Mapper as shown in Fig. 11. Note the variable Mapper<T>.iMapped which is initialized before seeking to map the

```
1  template<typename T>
2  class Mapper {
3    private:
4      T* ptr;
5      bool iMapped;
6    public:
7      Mapper(T* ptr) : ptr(ptr) {
8        iMapped = !omp_target_is_present(ptr, omp_get_default_device());
9        // map only if the target is not already present
10       #pragma omp target enter data map(to:ptr[0:1]) if(iMapped)
11     }
12     ~Mapper() {
13       // unmap only if this mapper mapped it
14       #pragma omp target exit data map(delete:ptr[0:1]) if(iMapped)
15       ptr = NULL;
16     }
17 };
```

Fig. 11. Mapper class for mapping C++ objects

memory associated with a class T (line 8, Fig. 11). This variable evaluates to true if the corresponding memory segment has not been mapped, allowing the map clause to succeed. On the other hand, if a memory segment associated with the object has already been mapped, the variable evaluates to false precluding any attempt to map the same memory (or its subregion) again. More importantly, during object destruction, the memory unmapping will only occur if the mapping was done within the object constructor. Note the similarity of this approach to the technique presented in Fig. 4 to locally control mapping and unmapping of arrays within a function.

Next we modify the code presented in Fig. 10 to extend the classes to be mapped such that the Mapper class is declared as their first base class (Fig. 12). Being the first base class of A, Mapper<A>'s constructor gets invoked prior to any other action of A's constructor (line 22, Fig. 12), and it correctly maps an object of size A to the *device*. Any subsequent calls to map a slice of A (e.g. through Mapper<B> and Mapper<C> on lines 11 and 3, Fig. 12) are prevented as explained above. Conversely, during object destruction, only the destructor for Mapper<A> is allowed to unmap the object preventing a constituent slice of the object from being unmapped prematurely. Note that all the previous map directives for the object (lines 5, 15 and 25, Fig. 10) are replaced with corresponding update clauses (lines 5, 14 and 24, Fig. 12). However, map directives specific to data members (e.g. B.x on line 15 and 14 in Figs. 10 and 12 respectively) remain unchanged. This idiom of enforcing the correct map/unmap sequence using the order of object construction allows creating and mapping of objects of type B and C as stand alone objects (i.e., not being members of A). While the classes B and C need not necessarily extend the Mapper themselves, it is still necessary to predicate their map and unmap directives with a guard condition similar to the variable Mapper.iMapped. In case of virtual bases, the Mapper needs to be made a virtual base itself.

Finally, we want to emphasize that placing data directives (such as map and update) inside a constructor prohibits using that constructor inside a target

```
1  struct C : public Mapper<C> {
2    double y;
3    C(double y) : Mapper<C>(this), y(y) {
4      C* this_ = this;
5      #pragma omp target update to(this_[0:1])
6    }
7  };
8  struct B : public Mapper<B> {
9    int n;
10   double* x;
11   B(int n) : Mapper<B>(this), n(n) {
12     x = (double*) malloc(n*sizeof(double));
13     for (int i = 0; i < n; ++i) x[i] = i;
14     #pragma omp target update to(this->n)
15     #pragma omp target enter data map(to:x[0:n])
16   }
17 };
18 struct A : public Mapper<A>, public B {
19   int n;
20   double y;
21   C c;
22   A(int n, double y) : Mapper<A>(this), B(n), n(n), y(y), c(y*y) {
23     A* this_ = this;
24     #pragma omp target update to(this_[0:1])
25   }
26 };
27
28 // Create object of type A. OK
29 A a(10, 20.0);
30
31 #pragma omp target
32 { printf("a.n = %d, a.y = %d\n", a.n, a.y);//OK }
```

Fig. 12. Mapping C++ objects using the Mapper class presented in Fig. 11

region executed on a *device*. In that case, it would be required to provide a constructor version without the directives. Alternatively we can apply the directives separately from the constructor. This, however needs programmer discipline to ensure that a class is mapped/updated/unmapped in a manner consistent with its creation/destruction. It might also require persisting hitherto local constructor data for later use by the directives increasing the overall object size.

5 Summary

Programming systems with multiple memories and compute devices using OpenMP 4.5 demand careful architecting data and memory management schemes. The pay off for adding extra code lines and additional complexity in code design is in code portability, i.e., opportunity to deploy applications on architecturally different systems. Having a portable application based on a single source code is a first step for achieving the ultimate goal - performance portability.

Acknowledgement. This work was performed under the auspices of the U.S. Department of Energy by Lawrence Livermore National Laboratory under contract DEAC52-07NA27344 (LLNL-CONF-730677) and supported by Office of Science, Office of Advanced Scientific Computing Research.

References

1. Chapman, B., Jost, G., van der Pas, R.: Using OpenMP: Portable Shared Memory Parallel Programming (Scientific and Engineering Computation). The MIT Press, Cambridge (2007)
2. Chen, T., Sura, Z., Sung, H.: Automatic copying of pointer-based data structures. In: Ding, C., Criswell, J., Wu, P. (eds.) LCPC 2016. LNCS, vol. 10136, pp. 265–281. Springer, Cham (2017). doi:10.1007/978-3-319-52709-3_20
3. Complex data management in OpenACC® programs. Technical report, OpenACC-Standard.org, November 2014. http://www.openacc.org/sites/default/files/inline-files/TR-14-1.pdf
4. OpenMP standard webpage. http://openmp.org/
5. OpenMP Language Committee: OpenMP Application Program Interface, version 4.5 edn. July 2013. http://www.openmp.org/mp-documents/openmp-4.5.pdf

Hands on with OpenMP4.5 and Unified Memory: Developing Applications for IBM's Hybrid CPU + GPU Systems (Part II)

Leopold Grinberg[1(✉)], Carlo Bertolli[1], and Riyaz Haque[2]

[1] IBM Research, Yorktown Heights, USA
{leopoldgrinberg,cbertol}@us.ibm.com
[2] LLNL, Livermore, USA
haque1@llnl.gov

Abstract. Integration of multiple types of compute elements and memories in a single system requires proper support at a system-software level including operating system (OS), compilers, drivers, etc. The OS helps in scheduling work on different compute elements and manages memory operations in multiple memory pools including page migration. Compilers and programming languages provide tools for taking advantage of advanced architectural features. In this paper we encourage code developers to work with experimental versions of compilers and OpenMP standard extensions designed for hybrid OpenPOWER nodes. Specifically, we focus on nested parallelism and Unified Memory as key elements for efficient system-wide programming of CPU and GPU resources of OpenPOWER. We give implementation details using code samples and we discuss limitations of the presented approaches.

Keywords: OpenPOWER · HPC · Offloading · Directive based programming · Nested parallelism

1 Introduction

Programming applications for specific hardware components as well as taking advantage of specific system software typically have a two-fold effect: (a) achieving higher performance and productivity on a given class of systems; and (b) adversely affecting the application portability and/or performance portability to other systems. In addition to these considerations, taking advantage of hardware and system software innovations available in a subset of emerging systems sets a tone and directions for developing future systems for High Performance Computing and Analytics. It also fuels advances in language features and standard evolution.

In the first part of this two-part paper (*Hands on with OpenMP4.5 and Unified Memory: Developing applications for IBM's hybrid CPU + GPU systems (Part I)* [3] we discussed how node memory and application data can be managed

© Springer International Publishing AG 2017
B.R. de Supinski et al. (Eds.): IWOMP 2017, LNCS 10468, pp. 17–29, 2017.
DOI: 10.1007/978-3-319-65578-9_2

using OpenMP4.5 directives. In this *Part II* we introduce methodologies taking advantage of hardware and software features which are more advanced and in part not fully supported by the OpenMP4.5 standard. Specifically, we will discuss three advanced topics: nested parallelism, use of Unified Memory and use of GPU's on-chip memory.

Our scope here is limited to programming IBM's system containing multiple POWER®CPUs and NVIDIA®GPUs with a directive based programming model. Here we employ the OpenMP4.5 standard [5] and IBM®extensions to the standard (supported in the open source CLANG®and IBM's proprietary XL®compilers) to program CPUs (*host*) and GPUs (*device*) and manage on-node memories. IBM's current hybrid CPU-GPU nodes, such as two-socket Minsky®nodes containing two ten-core POWER8®CPUs and four P-100 GPUs interconnected with NVLink 1.0 provide many opportunities for nested parallelism and concurrent execution on all compute elements. These nodes also support Unified Memory (UM) that provides a pool of memory accessible on the CPU and the GPU using a single pointer. To take advantage of UM at the present time, we rely on interoperability between OpenMP4.5 and CUDA®, and use of CUDA Managed Memory [7,8]. Use of UM substantially simplifies managing application data on heterogeneous systems. However, whereas the OpenMP4.5 standard encompasses UM support, current implementations do not support it. Pointers to buffers allocated using CUDA Managed Memory can be treated as valid device pointers inside OpenMP4.5 `target` regions, but the OpenMP compiler and runtime implementations considered in this paper do not support the concept of replacing the explicit data transfers between the *host* and *device* with features provided by the UM. Consequently, porting codes based on UM and OpenMP4.5 to systems not supporting UM may require some adaptations.

This paper makes the following contributions:

- In Sect. 2 we describe a scheme allowing nested parallelism and simultaneous execution of codes on *host* and *devices* using OpenMP4.5 directives.
- In Sect. 3 we show how architecture-specific memory support can be integrated in the codes programmed with OpenMP4.5. Specifically, we present an example making use of a section of the GPU's L1-cache which can be explicitly managed by compilers in order to host application data.
- In Sect. 4 we describe ways to develop applications using OpenMP4.5 directives and UM on systems with adequate hardware and software support. We also discuss the advantages and limitations of this approach.

To our knowledge, this is the first paper that exposes the integration of advanced system-software and hardware features in codes programmed using OpenMP4.5. Use of Unified Memory in conjunction with directive-based programming of NVIDIA GPUs is not new. For example, the PGI compiler supporting OpenACC [6] can intercept all calls to host memory allocation/de-allocation, replacing them with appropriate calls to the UM interface and rendering all data mapping operations as no-ops. UM support is an optional feature of the PGI compiler and is enabled through a compiler option. Use of UM within the

Kokkos programming framework has also been reported in [2]. Unlike these techniques, in this paper we show how programmers can make explicit use of the UM interface for memory management and still write correct code using OpenMP4.5 device constructs.

2   Concurrent Executions on CPUs and GPUs via OpenMP Nested Regions

Multiple compute resources in IBM's hybrid CPU + GPU nodes offer a range of choices for execution policies. For example a single MPI task can perform operations in parallel (using OpenMP) on the CPU cores (a model that has been widely adopted on the multicore CPUs) and it can also offload work to one or more GPUs. Each GPU can concurrently (or sequentially) support offloading work from a number of MPI tasks. In another scenario, a subset of OpenMP threads running on the *host* can offload work to one or more *devices* concurrently, while another subset of OpenMP threads can start nested parallel regions on the *host*.

2.1   Parallel Regions on *device*: Correspondence Between CUDA and OpenMP4.5

Before diving into the topic of nested parallelism we would first like to explain the correspondance between expressing parallelism using CUDA and using OpenMP4.5 directives. The OpenMP4.5 implementation on GPU maps parallelism abstractions which are exposed to OpenMP users, to lower-level GPU programming mechanisms. target regions are compiled into PTX (or GPU) kernels when NVIDIA GPUs are selected as OpenMP device type. The OpenMP runtime will invoke the kernels when encountering a target pragma. When a target region contains a teams region, the GPU kernel is started with multiple CUDA threadblocks and threads. Each OpenMP team is mapped to a single CUDA threadblock and two teams cannot be mapped to the same threadblock. OpenMP threads within each team are mapped to CUDA threads (one OpenMP thread is one CUDA thread). When target does not contain a teams construct, only one threadblock is started. The execution of a team (or threadblock) inside a target and outside of parallel regions is sequential - a single thread (team master) within each threadblock executes the region and all other threads are waiting to be recruited for parallel work. When a parallel region is encountered by the team master, all necessary threads within each threadblock are activated and participate in the parallel region.

Control of CUDA grid and threadblock sizes is critical to performance tuning in GPU kernels, whenever the OpenMP runtime chosen default values can be improved. Control is exposed at the OpenMP level through clauses of the teams construct. num_teams can be used to instruct the OpenMP runtime to start a specific number of teams (threadblocks). thread_limit tells the OpenMP runtime not to start more than the specified number of threads. To limit the amount of threads to be recruited to execute a parallel region, users can employ the **num_threads** clause of `parallel`. Note that the OpenMP4.5 constructs **num_teams**, **thread_limit** and **num_threads** are valid on both *host* and *device*. In the following section we will make use of those constructs for execution on a *host* and on a *device*.

2.2   OpenMP4.5 and Nested Parallelism Across a Node

In this section we discuss how a certain work load can be subdivided and executed concurrently across CPU and GPU threads using all the compute resources of a node. For this purpose we will use a schematic illustration provided in Fig. 1. Here a parallel region with three OpenMP threads is created on the *host*, and threads with IDs 0 and 1 will offload work to the *devices* 0 and 1 correspondingly, while the third thread will create an inner parallel region of 4 threads on the *host*.

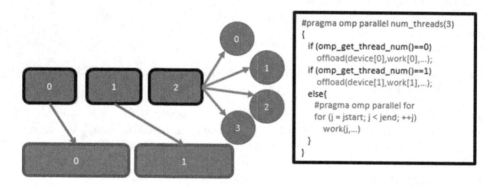

Fig. 1. Nested parallel regions with concurrent execution on *host* and *devices*. Outer parallel region contains three CPU threads. CPU threads 0 and 1 launch kernels on devices 0 and 1 correspondingly, while CPU thread 2 creates a parallel region with four CPU threads on a *host*.

A more detailed and specific example is provided in Fig. 2. In this example we first enable nested parallelism by calling OpenMP API `omp_set_nested(1)` (line 9) and then acquire the number of visible devices (**num_devices**) by calling the OpenMP API `omp_get_num_devices()` (line 11). In the next step a parallel region with up to **num_devices**+1 threads is created on the *host*. The first **num_devices** iterations of the main for loop will offload work to the *devices* with IDs 0, ... , **num_devices**-1, and in the last iteration a parallel region will be created on the *host* and the remaining work will be executed in parallel using at most (MAX(1,`omp_get_max_threads()`-**num_devices**)) threads. In this example we require that 90% of the work be executed on the *devices*, while the remaining work be executed on the *host*. In general, work distribution between *host* and *device(s)* may be determined (at run time) by taking into account the *host* and *device* hardware characteristics (e.g. ratio of *device/host* memory bandwidth, FLOP rate, etc.), expected execution time and even the availability of *device* memory.

```
 1  int main(){
 2    double *x, *y;
 3    int num_devices, i, chunk, j_start, N=1024*1024*10;
 4    double DEVICE_FRACTION = 0;
 5    bool USE_DEVICE;
 6    x = (double *) malloc(N*sizeof(double));
 7    y = (double *) malloc(N*sizeof(double));
 8    //enable nested parallel regions
 9    omp_set_nested(1);
10    //get number of devices
11    num_devices = omp_get_num_devices();
12    //90% of work done on device(s)
13    if (num_devices > 0)    DEVICE_FRACTION = 0.9;
14    #pragma omp parallel for num_threads(num_devices+1) \
15     private(chunk,j_start,USE_DEVICE)
16    for (i = 0; i < (num_devices+1); ++i){
17      //divide work, set default device
18      if (i < num_devices){ //use device
19        omp_set_default_device(i);
20        chunk = DEVICE_FRACTION*N / num_devices;
21        j_start = chunk*i;
22        USE_DEVICE = true;
23        printf("using DEVICE No %d, j_start = %d, chunk = %d\n",i,j_start,
               chunk);
24      }
25      else {      // use host
26        chunk = N; //default
27        j_start = 0; //default
28        USE_DEVICE = false;
29        if (num_devices > 0){
30          j_start = (DEVICE_FRACTION*N / num_devices) * num_devices;
31              chunk = N - j_start;
32        }
33        printf("using HOST:  j_start = %d, chunk = %d\n",j_start,chunk);
34      }
35      initialize_x_and_y(x+j_start,y+j_start,chunk,j_start,USE_DEVICE);
36    }
37    free(x);    free(y);
38    return 0;
39  }
40
41  void initialize_x_and_y(double *x, double *y, int N, int offset, bool
        USE_DEVICE)
42  {
43    #pragma omp target   map(from:x[0:N],y[0:N])  if(USE_DEVICE)
44    #pragma omp teams distribute parallel for  if(target:USE_DEVICE)
45    for (int i=0; i<N; ++i){
46      x[i] = (offset+i)*0.001;
47      y[i] = (offset+i)*0.003;
48      if ( (!USE_DEVICE) && (i == 0))
49        printf("num_threads = %d, num_teams=%d\n",omp_get_num_threads(),
               omp_get_num_teams());
50    }
51  }
```

Fig. 2. Nested parallelism: concurrent execution on *host* and *devices*

```
1 export  OMP_NUM_THREADS=20
2 export  OMP_PLACES={0;20;8}
3 ./a.out
4 using  DEVICE No 0, j_start = 0, chunk = 2359296
5 using  DEVICE No 1, j_start = 2359296, chunk = 2359296
6 using  DEVICE No 2, j_start = 4718592, chunk = 2359296
7 using  DEVICE No 3, j_start = 7077888, chunk = 2359296
8 device: CPU:   j_start = 9437184, chunk = 1048576
9 num_threads = 1, num_teams=16
```

Fig. 3. Concurrent execution on *host* and *devices*; nested parallelism: output of code from Fig. 2.

3　Clang's Extension for OpenMP4.5 for *device* On-chip Memory Allocation

NVIDIA GPUs allow developers to take advantage of allocating relatively small buffers in an "on-chip memory", also referred to as the *shared memory* in CUDA terminology. While there are multiple reasons for using shared memory, here we skip the discussion on use cases and refer readers to NVIDIA's programming guide [4] and NVIDIA's devblog describing using shared memory [1].

OpenMP4.5 standard does not provide developers with the means of specifically taking an advantage of the GPU's shared memory. However, IBM's extension to the OpenMP4.5 specification implemented for the Clang supports the use of shared memory. It is expected that future versions of IBM's XL compiler will also support shared memory for NVIDIA GPUs. Furthermore, OpenMP is also evolving towards incorporating special memory types as first-class citizens in the standard.

In this section we illustrate (see Fig. 4) use of shared memory in a matrix-transposition code that uses OpenMP4.5 directives. Currently, in order to allow compiler to allocate buffers in the GPU's shared memory, developers should use static memory allocation and place the corresponding code after the directive `#pragma omp target teams` but before the directive `#pragma omp distribute` (see Fig. 4, line 29). If the compiler determines that the size of the requested buffer (`VAL[BLK_SZ][BLK_SZ+1]`) is small enough to fit into the GPU's shared memory it places it there; otherwise the buffer is allocated in the global *device* memory. Note the use of the `if` clause in the code presented in Fig. 4: setting the value of the variable `USE_DEVICE` to 1 or to 0 results in code execution on the *device* or on the *host* respectively. Whether the target region is executed on a *device* or on a *host*, the buffer `VAL[BLK_SZ][BLK_SZ+1]` is designated as team-private, which eliminates race conditions between different teams. On the GPU *device* each `team` will be mapped to a different CUDA threadblock, and on *host* teams will be mapped to CPU threads.

At this stage of compiler development, IBM's implementation limits the size of the GPU's shared memory available to application's data to 800 bytes per team, and consequently we set `BLK_SZ=8`. In tests performed on IBM's Minsky nodes with offloading the matrix transposition to the P-100 GPU we observe effective memory BW utilization of 243 GB/s, while the achievable memory BW is in the 480–500 GB/s range. A simple (two-loop) kernel for matrix transposition not using shared memory achieves only 83 GB/s, which is expected due to non-coalesced memory access.

4   Use of Unified Memory and OpenMP4.5 Directives

The OpenMP4.5 memory model is based on the notion of heterogeneous memory address spaces (*host* and *device*) with directives for explicitly managing data movement and coherence between them. Under this model, coding is complicated by two factors. First, using OpenMP4.5 directives correctly in the presence of class member pointers is non-trivial and may involve considerable code changes to work (as illustrated in the first part of this paper). Secondly, explicitly managing coherence between two address spaces can be highly error-prone except in the simplest of cases.

Starting with the OpenMP4.5 standard, using native memory management mechanism (e.g. CUDA memory allocators) is also supported by special clauses to enable architecture-specific data allocation. For example, pointers to memory allocated using `cudaHostAlloc`, `cudaMallocHost`, `cudaMallocManaged` and `cudaMalloc` can now be used inside OpenMP4.5 `target` regions. Here we focus on the use of CUDA Managed Memory, and specifically on eliminating the need for explicit data transfers between the *host* and *devices*. Currently implicit data transfer between *host* and *devices* is not supported by the OpenMP standard, and methodology required for such a support is a considered as a research topic.

Employing CUDA Managed Memory substantially reduces the complexity of managing deep copies and also resolves the coherency issues. This is achieved by allocating data in a Unified Memory space [7,8] which is accessible on both the *host* and *device* using a single pointer.

Memory buffers associated with the Managed Memory automatically migrate between the *host* and *device* when a memory fault is encountered. The exact mechanism responsible for buffer migration is outside the scope of this paper. In this section we illustrate how to work with arrays, classes and common data structures like `std::vector` using UM and OpenMP4.5 directives. Considering that the OpenMP4.5 standard has been designed to also work with *devices* not supporting UM, we also discuss concerns with the integration of UM and OpenMP4.5 from the standpoint of code portability.

It is also important to note that for correct behavior of a code mixing OpenMP directives and CUDA API, especially on nodes with multiple visible *devices*, setting default *device* must be done twice: once using the OpenMP4.5 API `omp_set_default_device` (device_ID) and then using the CUDA API `cudaSetDevice` (device_ID).

4.1   Eliminating Explicit Deep Copies

In Fig. 5, we consider a UM-based version of code described in the first part of this paper.

```
1  #define MIN(a,b) (a < b ? a : b)
2  #define BLK_SZ 32
3  int main(){
4
5    omp_set_default_device(0);
6
7    int Nr = 1024*8, Nc = 1024*8;
8    double *U = new double[Nr*Nc];
9    double *UT = new double[Nr*Nc];
10   bool USE_DEVICE=1;
11
12   //allocate U and UT in device memory
13   #pragma omp target enter data map(alloc:U[0:Nr*Nc],UT[0:Nr*Nc]) if(
        target:USE_DEVICE)
14
15   //initialize U
16   #pragma omp target teams distribute thread_limit(512) if(target:
        USE_DEVICE)
17   for (auto col = 0; col < Nc; ++col){
18     #pragma omp parallel for if(USE_DEVICE)
19     for (auto row = 0; row < Nr; ++row){
20       U[row*Nc+col] = row*0.001 + col*0.0003;
21     }
22   }
23   int nteams = (Nr*Nc + BLK_SZ*BLK_SZ - 1)/(BLK_SZ*BLK_SZ);
24   int  nthreads = BLK_SZ;
25   #pragma omp target teams num_teams(nteams) thread_limit(nthreads) if(
        target:USE_DEVICE)
26   {
27     // sufficiently small array VAL will be allocated in GPU's shared
          memory
28     // otherwise in device memory
29     double VAL[BLK_SZ][BLK_SZ+1];
30
31     #pragma omp distribute collapse(2)
32     for (auto rstart = 0; rstart < Nr; rstart += BLK_SZ){
33       for (auto cstart = 0; cstart < Nc; cstart += BLK_SZ){
34
35         auto rend = MIN(Nr,rstart+BLK_SZ);
36         auto cend = MIN(Nc,cstart+BLK_SZ);
37
38         //fill in temporary buffer (shared memory)
39         #pragma omp parallel if(USE_DEVICE)
40         {
41           #pragma omp for collapse(2)
42           for (auto row=rstart; row < rend; ++row){
43             for (auto col=cstart; col < cend; ++col)
44               VAL[row-rstart][col-cstart] = U[row*Nc + col];
45           }
46           //transpose and write data from shared memory to device memory
47           #pragma omp for collapse(2)
48           for (auto row=cstart; row < cend; ++row){
49             for (auto col=rstart; col < rend; ++col)
50               UT[row*Nr + col] = VAL[col-rstart][row-cstart];
51           }
52         }
53       }
54     }
55   }
56
57   // copy data from the device to host memory and deallocate device
        memory
58   #pragma omp target exit data map(from:U[0:Nr*Nc],UT[0:Nr*Nc]) if(
        USE_DEVICE)
59 }
```

Fig. 4. Code illustrating use of NVIDIA's GPU shared memory and OpenMP4.5 directives. Currently only IBM's extensions to OpenMP4.5 spec implemented in CLANG compiler allow use of GPU's shared memory.

```
1  struct A {
2     int* y;
3     int size;
4     A(const int* y_, const long size_) : y(y_), size(size_)  {}
5  };
6
7  int n = 100;
8  int* y; cudaMallocManaged(&y, n*sizeof(int)); // Allocate in UM
9  A* a = new A(y,n);
10
11 // Only map object a to the device using the map clause
12 #pragma omp target map(to:a[0:1])
13 {
14    // OK because a->y holds the unified address
15    a->y[3] += ...;
16 }
```

Fig. 5. Deep copy of a data structure using Managed Memory

Let us start by comparing this example to the codes presented in [3] (Figs. 7 and 9). First, the call to `malloc` on line 8 (Fig. 7 of [3]) is replaced with `cudaMallocManaged`. Second, the operation `map(to:y[0:n])` on line 12 (Fig. 7 of [3]) has been removed since UM automatically moves data between the two address spaces. Most importantly, compared to the version of this example in Fig. 7 in [3], our UM-based example in Fig. 5 works correctly. This is because being allocated in Managed Memory, the *host* address referred by `a.y` is valid on the *device* as well. This eliminates the need to update `a`'s *device* copy with the correct address. Note however, that since object `a` itself is not UM-allocated, it is still required to map it before use inside the target region (line 12, Fig. 5). In the next Sect. 4.2 we show how to allocate objects like `a` in Managed Memory.

4.2   Mapping Classes Using UM

For mapping a class using UM, we follow the approach described in [7]. We first define a class that overrides the `new` and `delete` operators as shown in Fig. 6.

Second, we further modify the code presented in Fig. 5 to make class `A` UM-allocated as shown in Fig. 7. In this example, we extend class `A` with the class `UMMapper` overriding the former's default `new` and `delete` operators with the latter's. With this change, object `a` is now allocated in UM (line 9, Fig. 7). Third, we correspondingly replace the map clause `map(to:a[0:1])` with the `is_device_ptr(a)` clause in Fig. 7 (line 12). Since `a` is allocated in the UM the map clause is not required; at the same time, however, it is necessary to inform the OpenMP4.5 runtime that `a` is a valid *device* pointer. If that is not done, the OpenMP4.5 runtime will attempt (and fail) to find the device mapping for `a`. Therefore the `is_device_ptr` clause is critical for correct execution. Note that the `is_device_ptr` clause is not required for the member pointer `a.y`; member pointers are simply moved to the *device* as part of enclosing object and no attempt is made to find their device address. If however, the pointer `y` is used directly inside a target region, that region would have to be predicated with a `is_device_ptr(y)`

```
 1  class UMMapper {
 2    public:
 3      void* operator new(size_t len) {
 4        void* ptr; cudaMallocManaged(&ptr, len); return ptr;
 5      }
 6      void* operator new[](size_t len) {
 7        void* ptr; cudaMallocManaged(&ptr, len); return ptr;
 8      }
 9      void operator delete(void* ptr) noexcept (true) {
10        cudaFree(ptr);
11      }
12      void operator delete[](void* ptr) noexcept (true) {
13        cudaFree(ptr);
14      }
15  };
```

Fig. 6. Overriding **new** and **delete** operators: objects derived from UMMapper will be allocated using Managed Memory

```
 1  struct A : public UMMapper {
 2    int* y;
 3    int size;
 4    A(const int* y_, const long size_) : y(y_), size(size_)  {}
 5  };
 6
 7  int n = 100;
 8  int* y; cudaMallocManaged(&y, n*sizeof(int)); // Allocate y using UM
 9  A* a = new A(y,n);
10
11  // "a" is a valid device pointer
12  #pragma omp target is_device_ptr(a)
13  {
14    // OK because a->y holds the unified address
15    a->y[3] += ...;
16  }
```

Fig. 7. Using unified memory: accessing class object and its members on *host* and *device*

clause. Note that this strategy for creating UM-based classes does not work for objects allocated outside the **new** operator, e.g. stack-allocated objects.

4.3   Working with std::vector, UM and OpenMP4.5

In this section let us consider a code section using `std::vector` (Fig. 8). Here offloading the two code loops (lines 5 and 9, Fig. 8) to the *device* would require mapping the vectors x and y to the *device* memory and deep-copying their data; something not possible using OpenMP4.5 directives alone. A way to overcome this limitation and to allow the use of `std::vector` inside target regions executed on a *device*, is to allocate the data for these vectors using UM and avoiding the deep-copy altogether. The `std::vector` can be made UM-based by specializing its memory allocator to use Managed Memory [7] as shown in Fig. 9. Accordingly, we modify the example in Fig. 8 by specializing the allocators for vectors x and y to use the `UMAllocator` as shown in Fig. 10.

The class `UMAllocator` ensures that the vector data is allocated in Managed Memory and that the data will be migrated between the *host* and *devices* upon

```
 1 double alpha = 2.0;
 2 int N=1024*1024*10;
 3 vector<double> x(N);
 4 vector<double> y(N);
 5 for (int i = 0; i < N; ++i) {
 6    x[i] = i*0.01;
 7    y[i] = i*0.03;
 8 }
 9 for (int i = 0; i < N; ++i) {
10    y[i] = alpha*x[i] + y[i];
11 }
```

Fig. 8. Using std::vector in daxpy

```
 1 template <class T>
 2 class UMAllocator<T> {
 3   public:
 4     typedef T value_type;
 5     typedef const T& const_reference;
 6     template <class U> UMAllocator(const UMAllocator<U>& other);
 7     T* allocate(std::size_t n) {
 8       T* ptr;
 9       cudaMallocManaged(&ptr, sizeof(T)*n);
10       return ptr;
11     }
12     void deallocate(T* p, std::size_t n) {
13       cudaFree(p);
14     }
15 };
16 template <class T, class U>
17 bool operator==(const UMAllocator<T>&, const UMAllocator<U>&) {
18   return true;
19 }
20 template <class T, class U>
21 bool operator!=(const UMAllocator<T>&, const UMAllocator<U>&) {
22   return false;
23 }
```

Fig. 9. Specialized managed memory allocator for std::vector

```
 1 double alpha = 2.0;
 2 int N=1024*1024*10;
 3 vector<double, UMAllocator<double> > x(N);
 4 vector<double, UMAllocator<double> > y(N);
 5 #pragma omp target teams distribute parallel for map(to:x,y)
 6 for (int i = 0; i < N; ++i) {
 7    x[i] = i*0.01;
 8    y[i] = i*0.03;
 9 }
10 #pragma omp target teams distribute parallel for map(to:x,y)
11 for (int i = 0; i < N; ++i) {
12    y[i] = alpha*x[i] + y[i];
13 }
```

Fig. 10. Using std::vector with specialized managed memory allocator

encountering page faults. The `map` clauses on lines 5 and 10 perform a bitwise copy of the structure of the vectors x and y to the *device* (including the data pointer to UM) allowing both loops to work correctly on *host* and *device*.

Conceivably, one might similarly want to create an "OpenMP-mapped" `std::vector` by using an allocator with additional `enter/exit data` clauses for mapping the vector's data to the *device*. This will, however, not work since mapping the vector structure (e.g. lines 5 and 10, Fig. 10) would then additionally require updating the underlying vector data pointer to the correct *device* address; something not allowed directly for the `vector` class. We further emphasize that in the code presented in the Fig. 10, although vectors x and y are used exclusively on the *device*, their initial allocation will always be on the *host*. This is because the C++ specification requires the vector data to be default constructed; there is no way to circumvent this default initialization behavior. For the same reason, any attempt at present to write a "*device*-only" allocator (e.g. one using `cudaMalloc` instead of `cudaMallocManaged`) will also fail.

4.4   Limitations of Integrating UM and OpenMP4.5

Although the techniques described above for using UM within OpenMP4.5 target regions are both convenient and elegant, it should be emphasized that mixing OpenMP4.5 and CUDA Managed Memory would require specific hardware and system-software support. For systems with NVIDIA GPUs this approach will not work with devices prior to Pascal GPUs and with versions of CUDA prior to CUDA 8.0.

5   Summary and Outlook

OpenMP is further evolving into version 5 with performance and usability critical changes. First, it will include an interface for performance profiling tools (OMPT). This defines a set of events generated by the runtime that can be intercepted by a profiling tool, and a set of hooks that can be used to inspect the internal state of the library. Second, it includes the concept of implicit declare target, which requires compilers to make function definitions available for devices even if these were not explicitly marked by the user for device compilation. This simplifies building existing host libraries for devices, including some basic STL patterns that are extensively used in technical computing applications. Lastly, the OpenMP committee is working on a set of memory-related constructs that will enable users to express different kind of storage in their program and that are currently under study as a vehicle to express non-volatile memory buffers on CPU and shared memory buffers on GPUs.

Acknowledgement. This work was performed under the auspices of the U.S. Department of Energy by Lawrence Livermore National Laboratory under contract DEAC52-07NA27344 (LLNL-CONF-730616) and supported by Office of Science, Office of Advanced Scientific Computing Research.

References

1. Using shared memory in CUDA C/C++, April 2017. https://devblogs.nvidia.com/parallelforall/using-shared-memory-cuda-cc/
2. Edwards, H.C., Trott, C., Sunderland, D.: Kokkos, a manycore device performance portability library for C++ HPC applications, March 2014. http://on-demand.gputechconf.com/gtc/2014/presentations/S4213-kokkos-many core-device-perf-portability-library-hpc-apps.pdf
3. Grinberg, L., Bertolli, C., Haque, R.: Hands on with openmp4.5 and unified memory: developing applications for IBM'S hybrid CPU + GPU systems (part I). Submitted for IWOMP 2017
4. CUDA C/C++ programming guide - shared memory section, April 2017. http://docs.nvidia.com/cuda/cuda-c-programming-guide/#shared-memory
5. OpenMP Language Committee: OpenMP Application Program Interface, version 4.5 edn., July 2013. http://www.openmp.org/mp-documents/openmp-4.5.pdf
6. Sakharnykh, N.: Combine OpenACC and unified memory for productivity and performance, September 2015. https://devblogs.nvidia.com/parallelforall/combine-openacc-unified-memory-productivity-performance/
7. Unified memory in CUDA 6, April 2017. https://devblogs.nvidia.com/parallelforall/unified-memory-in-cuda-6/
8. Beyond GPU memory limits with unified memory on Pascal, April 2017. https://devblogs.nvidia.com/parallelforall/beyond-gpu-memory-limits-unified-memory-pascal/

Advanced Implementations
and Extensions

Leveraging OpenMP 4.5 Support in CLANG for Fortran

Hyojin Sung$^{(\boxtimes)}$, Tong Chen, Zehra Sura, and Tarique Islam

IBM Research, Yorktown Heights, USA
hsung@us.ibm.com

Abstract. Modern computer systems are increasingly parallel and heterogeneous, and the demand for high-level programming interfaces for such systems is rapidly growing. OpenMP 4.0 extended its CPU-based directives to support device offloading. Programmers can now simply insert directives to identify computations and data to be offloaded. Compilers/runtime with OpenMP support then manage code translation and data transfers. While there are various ongoing efforts to support OpenMP device offloading for Fortran as well as C/C++, the most widely used open-source compiler, LLVM, supports C/C++ only. In this paper, we describe our project, XLFLANG, that aims to build an OpenMP Fortran compiler by bridging an existing Fortran front-end and LLVM C/C++ front-end (CLANG). We translate output from IBM XL Fortran front-end into CLANG AST and feed it to CLANG where OpenMP directives are lowerized to LLVM IR. This approach allowed us to reuse CLANG code generation and LLVM optimizations while handling Fortran-specific features in our XLFLANG. However, language dependences of CLANG AST especially with OpenMP directive representations pose unique challenges both in correctness and performance aspects. We addressed these challenges to generate CLANG AST, taking care to expose possible optimization opportunities. We were able to map all major OpenMP offloading directives/clauses from Fortran to CLANG AST, and our evaluation shows the resulting AST does not add significant overheads or interfere with later optimizations.

1 Introduction

Modern computer systems are increasingly parallel and heterogeneous, and parallel programming to exploit available parallelism has become the norm for programming itself. However, parallel programming is historically known to be error-prone and difficult to maintain, and there has been continuous effort to make parallel programming more accessible and tractable. Providing high-level abstractions and structured control for parallelism is one of the successful approaches to improve the programmability and portability of parallel programs. Especially with heterogeneous systems that commonly have a general-purpose host offloading computations to special-purpose accelerators, high-level interfaces can efficiently hide low-level details of host-device communications. It also

© Springer International Publishing AG 2017
B.R. de Supinski et al. (Eds.): IWOMP 2017, LNCS 10468, pp. 33–47, 2017.
DOI: 10.1007/978-3-319-65578-9_3

improves code portability so that the same program can run on systems with different accelerators.

As the demand for high-level programming interfaces for heterogeneous systems grows, various attempts have been made in academia and industry. OpenMP is one of the popular parallel programming models that extends its CPU-based interfaces to support device offloading. OpenMP provides high-level directives that programmers can insert at appropriate points to identify computations and data to be offloaded to devices. Then compilers/runtime with OpenMP support translate these directives to actual codes that transfer data and manage offloaded computations.

OpenMP currently provides programming interfaces for C/C++ and Fortran with offloading support. Fortran is a language especially strong with numeric computation and scientific computing. It provides rich array notations that enables various array and loop based optimizations. There is a large volume of Fortran programs and libraries accumulated for decades in high-performance computing areas. Such computationally intensive Fortran programs have strong potential to scale very well on massively parallel devices such as GPUs, allowing OpenMP compilers/runtime to seamlessly map OpenMP constructs to GPU kernels. However, to our knowledge, OpenMP compilers with full offloading support exist only for C/C++, but not for Fortran yet.

In this paper, we describe our project to provide OpenMP Fortran support with full offloading features and competitive performance. Our project, XLFLANG, aims to build an OpenMP Fortran compiler by bridging an existing Fortran front-end and LLVM C/C++ front-end (CLANG). Our translator takes output from IBM XL Fortran front-end and translates it into CLANG AST but using our own semantic analyzer. Once the AST is generated, it is fed into CLANG code-generation (CodeGen) and translated into LLVM IR format. Our key observation in XLFLANG design is finding a right translation level that maximizes the reuse of existing C/C++ OpenMP support while retaining and utilizing Fortran-specific information for efficient code generation. With this approach, we can incorporate Fortran-specific handling of OpenMP directives in XLFLANG semantic analysis phase (while common codes with C/C++ are reused from CLANG) and avoid repeating low-level code generation and low-level optimizations for LLVM IR.

There were various challenges in mapping Fortran to an AST designed for a different language for OpenMP support. While Fortran and C/C++ share many common features, they are meaningfully different in user-defined type representation and address-based type handling. This poses a major challenge for XLFLANG in handling Fortran-specific data structures such as dope vectors and common blocks correctly when they appear in OpenMP data clauses. In addition, call-by-reference function call semantics, extra alias information available in Fortran only, and other base language differences from C require XLFLANG to perform additional AST node generation or modification to map Fortran to valid CLANG AST. We aimed to address these challenges in XLFLANG by generating compatible CLANG AST, taking care to expose possible optimization opportunities. We found that this task is more challenging than expected because we do not introduce any Fortran-specific changes in CLANG.

Despite some limitations, we could map all major OpenMP directives and clauses from Fortran to CLANG AST. Evaluation shows that the resulting CLANG AST from XLFLANG does not add significant overheads or interfere with LLVM back-end optimizations, providing comparable performance to equivalent C versions.

The contributions of XLFLANG translator can be summarized as follows:

- XLFLANG provides full-feature OpenMP 4.5 support for Fortran by leveraging CLANG, the first open-source compiler with full OpenMP support with offloading directives.
- XLFLANG provides comparable performance to equivalent C benchmarks tested, showing that its Fortran-to-CLANG AST translation introduces manageable overheads and does not interfere with later optimizations.
- XLFLANG revealed new use-cases of OpenMP offloading directives and clauses in Fortran and contributed to expanding the specification.

The rest of the paper is organized as follows: Sect. 3 describes the major challenges we had with translating OpenMP features in XLFLANG: OpenMP data handling clauses. Section 4 discusses how the base language differences between Fortran and C/C++ affected our implementation: handling OpenMP atomic/reduction clauses with logical equivalence operators, linking global symbols, and utilizing alias information. In Sect. 5, we present our experimental results for XLFLANG on several kernels and two benchmarks. The paper wraps up with related work (Sect. 6) and conclusion (Sect. 7).

2   XLFLANG Overview

LLVM compiler provides a robust C/C++ front-end, CLANG, with full OpenMP 4.5 support, but it currently does not have comparable solutions for processing Fortran programs. Our approach to provide the same OpenMP support for Fortran with minimal effort is bridging an existing Fortran front-end (for Fortran parsing/lexing and basic semantic analysis) and CLANG/LLVM (for code generation for OpenMP and back-end compilation). For the front-end, we leverage an existing and acknowledged, robust XL Fortran front-end (FFE) [6]. The FFE is a component of the proprietary IBM XL product compiler. It implements the full Fortran 2003 standard, and also support earlier versions including Fortran 95, Fortran 90, and Fortran 77.

Fig. 1. The Overall Design of XLFLANG

Figure 1 illustrates the compilation flow of our translator. It transforms the output of FFE (W-code IR) into CLANG AST form, then the regular C/C++ CLANG/LLVM compiler is invoked with this AST as input.

2.1   XL Fortran Front-End

The FFE takes Fortran source code as input and produce W-code files as output. W-code is the intermediate format used within XL compiler. The front-end parses the source code and performs semantic analysis. Using the semantic analysis result, it augments user-provided OpenMP directives with necessary data handling clauses (details can be found in Sect. 3). It also includes a scalarize subcomponent that transforms Fortran array operations into corresponding loops. The W-code generated by the front-end contains very few Fortran language-specific features for example, array shape descriptors and some built-in functions, but it does include embedded information derived from language-specific semantics such as, for example, aliasing information.

2.2   XLFLANG

Our W-code to CLANG AST translator takes W-code as input and produces CLANG AST as output. It utilizes the CLANG Libtooling library [14] to parse command-line arguments, create a CLANG scope with appropriate initializations, populate it with AST code corresponding to W-code, and generate an AST binary file. The translator interfaces with an IBM-internal tool that decodes W-code binaries and provides utilities to iterate over the code and invoke user-defined actions for each W-code instruction. It first processes the entire W-code stream, gathering information and program elements used in the code, including types, literals, symbols, functions, labels, and static initializers. XLFLANG then once again traverses the code to generate the corresponding AST declarations, expressions, and statements. XLFLANG performs necessary transformations to the semantics of W-code output to generate CLANG-compatible AST, but does not modify control flows or loop structures.

2.3   CLANG/LLVM

The CLANG AST binary file produced by XLFLANG is then fed into the C/C++ CLANG/LLVM compiler to produce an object file or executable binary. XLFLANG relies on CLANG driver for compiling and linking the AST files with both Fortran and C/C++ libraries. Several XL Fortran libraries including Fortran I/O are linked by default. To link binaries and libraries with and without device support together, XLFLANG again relies on CLANG driver that allows linking a separate set of libraries for host and device objects.

3   OpenMP Data Handling Clauses with Common Block and Dynamic Variables

XLFLANG faced unique challenges in translating OpenMP features in the context of Fortran programs into CLANG AST. In many cases, translation is mechanical simply mapping an IR entry for an OpenMP directive/clause into a CLANG AST node of the same type. Unfortunately, we encountered numerous exceptions to this simple scenario due to differences between language features and IR specifications. In this and following sections, we focus on describing the major challenges addressed in XLFLANG for correct and efficient OpenMP support.

3.1   Background: Memory Objects in Fortran

The most common way to reference a memory object in Fortran is to use a variable name. Sometimes, scope, field, or subscript can be added. Unlike C/C++, pointer arithmetic with "address of" operator (&) or "dereference" operator (*) is not allowed. OpenMP data handling clauses specify how memory objects in the program should be allocated/freed, and how their value should be initialized for the program scope of constructs. These clauses include private, firstprivate, lastprivate, threadprivate, copyin, copyprivate, map, and reduction. CLANG performs semantic analysis to generate AST nodes for these clauses, but the semantics for Fortran variables in these clauses are not straightforward in some cases to simply reuse CLANG. With a simple example using a private clause for a scalar variable in Fig. 2, we illustrate how this clause requires different kinds of variables in Fortran to be treated.

| `integer a` | `subroutine mysub(a)`
`integer a` | `integer s, a(100)`
`common /blk1/ a,s` | `integer, allocatable :: a` |

(a) Local variable   (b) Dummy parameter   (c) Common variable   (d) Allocatable/pointer variable

Fig. 2. Different Variable Types in Fortran

Local Variable. In Fig. 2(a), the variable, a, is a local variable in Fortran, which is the counterpart of automatic variable in C/C++. The data handling clause can be directly translated into corresponding CLANG AST.

Dummy Parameter. In Fig. 2(b), the variable, a, is a dummy parameter of the procedure. Since parameters are passed by reference in Fortran (while by value in C), the access to parameter variable is a dereference from the pointer. In the W-code IR, there is a pointer, say `.a`, for the address passed through the parameter, and the references for s is actually `*.a` in IR. Consequently, the clause, `private(a)`, is actually `private(*.a)` in internal representation.

Common Variable. In Fig. 2(c), the variable, s, appears in a common block. In Fortran, variables in a common block are allocated contiguously and the common block with the same block names are linked across procedures. Common blocks in different procedures can have different layout of the variables. Therefore, variables in a common block are not independent variables, and are treated as array sections of the owner common block variable. In this example, the semantics of clause `private(s)` is `private(blk1[400, 4])`, where blk1 is the character array for the common block, 400 is the offset in the common block for variable s and 4 is the length. The array section is in C/C++ format, i.e., [start index : length] instead of [start index : end index].

OpenMP 4.0 standard does not allow array section in private clauses or copyin clauses for threadprivate. Such clauses in Fortran can not be directly translated into CLANG AST. Even though array sections are allowed in map clauses, we may still have issues when more than one variable in the same common block appears in the map clauses at the same construct. We do not want to map the whole common block for correctness and efficiency reason, but mapping each variable individually may result in multiple sections from one root variable, like `map(tofrom:a[0, 100], a[200, 50])`. This is currently not allowed by the OpenMP standard, requiring XLFLANG to find its own solution.

Dynamic Variable. There are three kinds of dynamic variable in Fortran, allocatable, pointer and assumable size array. Their size and shape are determined at runtime. To correctly access them, metadata about these variables are stored in a data structure, called "dope vector". Dope vector contains a pointer pointing to the data, a field for the status and fields for boundary of each dimension when the dynamic variable is allocated. Figure 2(d) shows an example of allocatable variable. When allocatable variables appear in a data handling clause, the action requested by the clause (data transfer, privatization, etc.) needs to be performed both on the dope vector itself and the data pointed by it. As a result, they cannot be mechanically mapped to CLANG AST.

In summary, the data handling clauses in Fortran require additional logic in XLFLANG to correctly initialize and transfer data, depending on the kind of the variable. In the following sections, we discuss our solution for the two major issues as identified above, array section and deep copy.

3.2 Transformation for Array Section

Example shown in Fig. 3(a) has a map clause for common variable a and c. XLFLANG translates variables a and c into array sections for the common block, and generates a map clause, `map(tofrom: blk[0, 100], blk[300, 400])`. There are two sections from a single root pointer blk. Such map clause is not allowed by OpenMP standard 4.0.

Our solution is to use separate temporary reference-type variables to represent each array section in the clause and in the enclosed code. Fortran allows such transformation, since all the data references are through the original variable, and can be easily identified for code transformation. In C/C++, the possible use of a pointer makes it difficult, if not impossible, to track the origin of each dereference. Moreover, overlapping may happen with pointer expressions. With the reference-type variable, different common variables are no longer referenced from the same root pointer. Each variables can be privatized or mapped individually. The transformation of the example is shown in Fig. 3(b).[1] Similarly, if a common variable is used in a private clause, we create temporary reference variables for each common variable and access them as an array (Fig. 4).

```
integer a(100), b(200), c(400)
common /blk/a, b, c
!$omp target map(tofrom: a, c)
do i = 1, 100
  c(i) = a(i)
enddo
```

(a) Original code

```
char (&c_ref)[1600] = *&blk + 1200UL;
char (&a_ref)[400] = *&blk;
#pragma omp target map(from: c_ref) map(to: a_ref) firstprivate(i)
{
    for (i = 1; i <= 100; i += 1) {
        ((int *)c_ref)[i] = ((int *)a_ref)[i];
    }
}
```

(b) Translated code

Fig. 3. Common Variable in `map` Clauses

```
integer a(100), b(200), c(400)
common /blk/a, b, c

!$omp parallel private(a, c)
  a(1) = 0
  c(1) = 2
```

(a) Original code

```
char (&c_ref)[1600] = *&blk + 1200UL;
char (&a_ref)[400] = *&blk;
#pragma omp parallel private(c_ref) private(a_ref)
{
    ((int *)a_ref)[0L] = 0;
    ((int *)c_ref)[0L] = 2;
}
```

(b) Translated code

Fig. 4. Common Variables in `private` Clauses

---

[1] The output is cropped from the result of CLANG ast-dump. Please be aware that the output of ast-dump from CLANG is in C format and may miss some necessary parenthesis. We use it in the paper because it is more readable than printing raw CLANG AST node information.

3.3   Transformation for Dynamic Variables

Because of the wide use of allocatable/pointer variable for dynamic data size in Fortran, handling dynamic variables correctly with deep copy is critical. As discussed above, "dope vectors" are used in Fortran to represent a pointer and other metadata about dynamic variables. When a dynamic variable appears in a map clause, we need to copy the dope vector and the data as well ("deep copy"), and fix the data pointer in the dope vector to point to the address of the newly mapped data. This may involves recursive traversal of multiple levels of pointers. The similar issue occurs for private clauses. When an allocatable variable appears in the private clause, first the data for the variable needs to be privatized. Secondly, the dope vector should be privatized so that each thread can allocate different size for the allocatable variable. More precisely, the dope vector should be firstprivate so that metadata can be customized per OpenMP thread. Therefore, XLFLANG needs to extends its deep copy mechanism for map clauses to the other data handling clauses too. Even though the problem is similar for map and private clause, they are handled differently with the interface provided in CLANG. Examples of map and private are shown in Fig. 5.

```
integer, allocatable :: mya(:), myb(:)

!$omp target map(to:mya) map(from:myb)
...
```

(a) Original code

```
char d_mya[56];
char d_myb[56];
char *_3, *_4, *_5, *_6;
#pragma omp target map(from: _5[0:_6]) map(to: d_myb)
         map(to: _3[0:_4])
{
    *&d_myb = _5;
    *&d_mya = _3;
}
```

(b) Translated code

Fig. 5. Allocatable Array in `map` Clause

In the example of Fig. 5(a), d_mya and d_myb are the dope vector for the allocatable array mya and myb in W-code IR, respectively. In the translated code, temporary pointers, _3 and _5, are initialized with the data pointer in the dope vector if the variable is allocated, otherwise null value is the default (the null value is not used in runtime). The size of the array section, variable _4 and _6, are also initialized from the dope vector. The references inside the target region still retrieve the information from dope vector to construct the access expression: the data pointer and the lower bound of the array.

Deep copy is a challenging issue in general for both Fortran and C/C++. OpenMP 4.0 supports only the most simple form of deep copy, array section with a pointer. More recent OpenMP 4.5 adds the support for pointer as a field, and as a result, temporary pointer and the assignments are no longer needed. XLFLANG implementation will be simplified once support for the latest standard is fully implemented. For private clauses, OpenMP standard the array section is not allowed. Therefore, we have to use reference-type variable for the data.

3.4 Combined Cases

In the example shown in Fig. 6, the variable mya is a parameter for allocatable array, which is passed in to the subroutine as a pointer to the dope vector. In our translator, we have to handle both the deep copy and array section. Consequently, one private clause in Fortran is actually translated into three private clauses in CLANG, as shown in the example.

```
subroutine test(mya)
integer, allocatable :: mya(:)

!$omp parallel private(mya)
...
```

(a) Original code

```
char (&d_mya_ref)[56] = *.d_mya;

char (&mya_ref)[*d_mya_ref + 48 * (*d_mya_ref + 40)] = *(*(d_mya_ref + 0));
#pragma omp parallel private(mya_ref) firstprivate(d_mya_ref)
        firstprivate(.d_mya)
{
   .d_mya = d_mya_ref;
  *d_mya_ref + 0 = mya_ref;
```

(b) Translated code

Fig. 6. Parameter Allocatable Array in **private** Clause

3.5 Limitations

We found that not all the cases of data handling clauses can be represented with CLANG AST. One example is copyin for threadprivate. When an individual common variable, instead of the common block name, appears in the copyin clause, there is no way to express this case with CLANG AST. This is a case of array section. However, neither array section nor referenced-type variables are allowed for copyin. The underlying reason is that the copyin needs the original symbol to find the corresponding threadprivate copy. Clang has to be extended to handle this case.

4   Challenges from Language Differences

In this section, we discuss how differences between Fortran and C/C++ at the language specification level influenced XLFLANG design and implementation.

4.1   Fortran-Only Operators in OpenMP Atomic and Reduction Directives

Fortran provides logical equivalence/non-equivalence operators (`.EQV.` and `.NEQV.`) that return true/false if and only if both operands have the same value respectively. C/C++ equality/non-equality operators (`==` and `!=`) offer the same logic. While these relational operators can replace `.EQV.` and `.NEQV.` in the plain non-OpenMP Fortran context, they cannot be used in OpenMP atomic or reduction clauses. Therefore, we emulate them with `XOR` operator (for `.NEQV.`) and the negation of `XOR` (for `.EQV.`) on arithmetic values. When `.EQV.` is used in OpenMP atomic and reduction clauses, additional code needs to be generated to perform the negation. In case of reduction, XLFLANG generates the reduction clause with `XOR` operator, and adds post-processing codes to perform the negation on the reduced result. Handling `.EQV.` in atomic clauses is more complicated than reduction clauses, since OpenMP atomic clauses have restrictions on the type of operations allowed. We exploit a mathematical property about `XOR` and `XNOR` to solve the issue; The result of `XNOR` on two operands is equivalent to the result of `XOR` on one operand and the negative of the other operand. In summary, we can implement an OpenMP atomic clause with `v = v XNOR exp` as `v = v XOR (!exp)`.

4.2   Linking Global Symbols

The common practice for declaring and defining global symbols is different in Fortran and C/C++. In Fortran, symbols for module variables do not appear in its object file, but .mod file is generated in addition to include metadata on module variables and functions. When the module variable is "used" by another module or function, the corresponding .mod file is referred and the variable appears in the using module's object file as a weak symbol. In summary, there does not exist a single object file with a strong symbol for module variables, but there can be multiple object files with weak or common symbols. When linked together, the final binary will resolve these weak symbols to point to the same storage. Globals can be linked in the same way in C/C++ by adding "weak" attribute ($\_\_attribute\_\_((weak))$) to each declaration/definition, but a much more common way is declaring it as "extern" in a header file and defining once in a source file.[2] In link time, one strong definition will generate a strong symbol in the binary (multiple definitions are not allowed).[3]

---

[2] Weak symbols are not mentioned by the C/C++ language standards.

[3] The symbol will be weak if uninitialized in C, or initialized to 0 in C++.

This different linkage style of globals caused an issue with compiling and linking module variables in `omp declare target` construct in XLFLANG. If a variable is `declare target` as shown in Fig. 7, the variable is automatically initialized on device as the program starts and can be accessed without explicit data transfer. It is useful when a variable is reused across multiple OpenMP target constructs.

```
module globals
...
!$omp declare target (mya, myb)
end module
```
globals.f

```
...
use globals
!$omp target
      mya = myb
!$omp end target
```
test.f

Fig. 7. Globals in `omp declare target`

When a module variable is `declare target` and accessed in other modules, the variable appears as a weak symbol (not an external reference) in each referring object file. OpenMP code-gen implementation in CLANG assumed each instance as a strong symbol and generated additional strong metadata symbols in each object file, causing multiple definition errors. Also, CLANG code-gen records all variables in `omp declare target` in a table and passes the table to OpenMP runtime to initiate data transfers. With multiple weak symbols from different object files, the table creates duplicate entries, and OpenMP runtime failed as it assumed a unique entry for each symbol. These cases in CLANG code-gen and OpenMP runtime are allowed by rare in C/C++, and the findings by XLFLANG drove fixes in CLANG that made OpenMP support and runtime more robust.

4.3   Intrinsic Aliasing Information in Fortran

Unlike C/C++, Fortran does not allow pointer arithmetic. Pointers in Fortran are just variables with the POINTER attribute, not a distinct data type. This leads to an important corollary that address aliasing through pointer arithmetic does not exist in Fortran. For XLFLANG to utilize the guarantee for non-aliasing addresses with minimal to no changes to other components, we used the `noalias` attribute for variables in CLANG AST. The keyword is originally for marking variables with `restrict` keyword in source codes. It later helps the alias analysis and other optimization passes in LLVM to build strong alias sets and determine the applicability of a given optimization. XLFLANG adds this keyword to function arguments for OpenMP outlined functions that capture code sections within OpenMP constructs. Alias information are often lost during the function outlining process if inter-procedural alias analysis cannot recover it, leading to many disabled common optimizations such as common subexpression elimination and LICM. Using the strong non-aliasing guarantee from Fortran, XLFLANG can safely add `noalias` attribute to arguments of OpenMP outlined functions, which cannot be trivially done for C/C++ programs.

5 Experimental Result

We evaluate the performance of XLFLANG by comparing the execution time of the "same" kernels written in Fortran and C compiled by XLFLANG and CLANG respectively. The evaluation was done on an OpenPower node using two Power 8 sockets (model PowerNV 8247-42L) and two NVIDIA Kepler GPUs K40m. The operating system run by the host processor is a bare-metal Linux distribution (Ubuntu version 14.04.1). The Fortran and C versions of the "same" kernel are intended to have the same operations to our best effort. There could be slight differences inevitably introduced by using different languages. We report the execution time of the computation kernels only to exclude possible differences in language libraries and setup.

We measure both the sequential performance of the kernels and parallel performance with OpenMP pragma to evaluate the performance on basic Fortran statements as well as OpenMP directives. We also gather data for the performance of kernels with gcc and gFortran as a control group. Since the gcc and gFortran share the same back-end optimization as CLANG and XLFLANG share LLVM back-end, the comparison can provide further insight of the performance of our system.[4]

All the reported execution times are normalized to the corresponding CLANG C performance for sequential or parallel version respectively. Wall time is measured for the sequential execution, while the data transfer time and kernel execution time acquired from nvprof are used for the parallel version.

The first kernel we used is simple vector_add. This kernel is used to evaluate XLFLANG for different variable types in Fortran, as discussed in Sect. 3. The second kernel we used is jacobi-2d from Polybench. Polybench provides both C and Fortran version, which is convenient for our experiment. We modified the kernels to add OpenMP directives for GPU offloading. It is straightforward for vector_add. For jacobi_2d, we add the `target data map` outside the nested loop and add `target teams distribute parallel do collapse(2)` to the two inner loop nests, as described in [10].

The execution time of sequential code is shown in Table 1. The performance for Fortran and C are almost the same when simple variables or parameter arrays are used. The difference between *c-simple* and *f-simple*, and *jacobi-2d-c* and *jacobi-2d-f* for CLANG/XLFLANG shows that the compilation overheads introduced by XLFLANG is minimal. There is a quite significant slowdown for common variables because the code is less efficiently scheduled due to the shared root pointer for the arrays. Allocatable array performs slightly better because it

---

[4] It is not the purpose of this paper to compare the sequential and the parallel performance. We did not aggressively optimize how the loops are parallelized for GPU. Nor is it the focus of this paper to compare the performance of CLANG and gnu compiler. For both compilers, we used -O3 for the sequential version only.

Table 1. Sequential execution time

kernels	CLANG/XLFLANG	gcc/gfortran
c-simple	1.00	1.5
f-simple	1.01	1.19
f-common	1.61	1.3
f-allocatable	0.88	1.07
f-parameter	1.01	1.06
jacobi-2d-c	1.00	1.38
jacobi-2d-f	1.05	1.38

Table 2. Parallel execution time

kernel time	HtoD time	DtoH time
1.00	1.00	1.00
1.03	1.00	1.00
1.03	1.0	1.00
2.69	1.02	1.00
1.26	1.03	0.99
1.00	1.00	1.00
1.01	1.00	0.93

triggered loop unrolling and doubled the unroll factor from 8 to 16. In the result for gcc/gFortran, it can be observed that similar trend for better performance on f-allocatable and worse performance on f-common. For the jacobi-2d kernel, XLFLANG introduced 5% slowdown while gcc and gFortran have the same performance on both versions of the code.

The result for offloading to GPU with OpenMP is reported in Table 2. The kernel execution time, the data transfer time for host to device (HtoD) and device to host (DtoH) are shown. Most of the Fortran code have the similar performance for kernel computation and data transfer, except for the vector_add_alloc. vector_add_alloc is more than 2.5 times slower than the other kernels. It is because the handling of the pointer in the dope vector disabled optimizations in CLANG code generation for OpenMP. When we move to the new OpenMP runtime interface, the dope vector will be handled directly with the support for pointer field in a struct. There will be no extra assignments in GPU code and the code can be optimized.

In summary, the experiments showed that XLFLANG is able to generate correct and comparably efficient binary for different Fortran variables, and with or without OpenMP directives.

6   Related Work

Many researchers and industry programmers proposed automatic conversion tools from Fortran to other modern languages such as C/C++, Matlab, and Python [1,4,8,9,12], and many of the projects are still active.

F2C [8] is one of the first Fortran to C source-to-source translator published in 90's. F2C prints out a C representation of the intermediate C parse tree by a Fortran 77 compiler. As a source-to-source converter, the tool uses C struct (and union of struct) and #define macros to represent Fortran common blocks and equivalence, which may significantly increase the resulting C code size. XLFLANG also takes intermediate IR (W-code) as input, but its translation takes place between intermediate language levels both for input and output. Translating to AST allows more efficient and succinct translation, circumventing various source-level limitations. Also, F2C works only for Fortran 77 files while XLFLANG is tested up to Fortran 2003 and much more robust with regard to Fortran specification changes as FFE lowerizes new features to common W-code IR.

FABLE [9] is a recent effort on automatic Fortran to C++ conversion. It is influenced by prior work [1,8], but applies various techniques to improve performance and readability of its C/C++ output including translating global variables and SAVE variables to C++ struct. It also supports a subset of Fortran 90 as well as Fortran 77. It requires iterative re-converting, compiling, and testing and manual code changes to improve performance and code quality of the final output. XLFLANG does not need iterative compilation and testing to get working AST, relying on LLVM for performance optimizations. Some of their optimization techniques including using C++ struct for global variables for modular binaries could be applied to future XLFLANG design.

Rose source-to-source compiler infrastructure [11] provides source-to-source compilation with various source-level optimization support for many languages including Fortran and C/C++ with OpenMP. It bears similarity to XLFLANG and even more so to CLANG in that it implements various transformations and optimizations including OpenMP 3.0 support by manipulating its internal AST. XLFLANG focuses mainly on efficiently translating a high-level IR to another high-level IR while minimizing overheads from language differences. Also XLFLANG and CLANG/LLVM combined provides up-to-date OpenMP 4.5 support, compared to OpenMP 3.0 support in Rose.

More recently, an open-source development project for Fortran front-end for LLVM, FLANG [13], has launched. Since the project is still ongoing, there is not enough information to compare with XLFLANG.

7   Conclusions

Rapidly evolving parallel architectures and programming models led to the reduced cycle of compiler and runtime development. We believe our approach to XLFLANG is in line with such trend, minimizing redundant effort while augmenting existing compiler infrastructure. Bridging one IR to another IR with completely different assumptions and backgrounds was not without challenges, but our work showed that it could be done with proper understanding of the base languages, Fortran and C/C++, and OpenMP requirements. Our future work includes adding AST-level optimizations to XLFLANG, interfacing with CLANG/LLVM to convey alias information from Fortran, and extending its support to more recent Fortran family.

Acknowledgement. This work was supported in part by the United States Departmnet of Energy CORAL program (contract B604142). We thank the IBM XL compiler team for their help and support for this work.

References

1. F2cpp: a python script to convert fortran 77 to C++ code. http://sourceforge.net/projects/f2cpp
2. OpenMP homepage. http://www.openmp.org/
3. Antao, S.F., Bataev, A., Jacob, A.C., Bercea, G.T., Eichenberger, A.E., Rokos, G., Martineau, M., Jin, T., Ozen, G., Sura, Z., Chen, T., Sung, H., Bertolli, C., O'Brien, K.: Offloading support for OpenMP in Clang and LLVM. In: LLVM-HPC 2016 (2016)
4. Barrowes, B.: F2matlab. http://engineering.dartmouth.edu/~d30574x/consulting/consultingIndex.html
5. Chen, T., Sura, Z., Sung, H.: Automatic Copying of Pointer-Based Data Structures (2017)
6. IBM Corporations: Xl fortran for linux. http://www-03.ibm.com/software/products/en/xlfortran-linux
7. Dietrich, R., Juckeland, G., Wolfe, M.: Open ACC programs examined: a performance analysis approach. In: 2015 44th International Conference on Parallel Processing, pp. 310–319, September 2015
8. Feldman, S.I., Gay, D.M., Maimone, M.W., Schryer, N.L.: A Fortran to C converter (1990)
9. Grosse-Kunstleve, R.W., Terwilliger, T.C., Sauter, N.K., Adams, P.D.: Automatic Fortran to C++ conversion with fable. Source Code for Biology and Medicine (2012)
10. JamesBeyer, J.L.: Targeting GPUs with OpenMP 4.5 device directives. http://on-demand.gputechconf.com/gtc/2016/presentation/s6510-jeff-larkin-targeting-gpus-openmp.pdf
11. Liao, C., Quinlan, D.J., Panas, T., Supinski, B.R.: A ROSE-based OpenMP 3.0 research compiler supporting multiple runtime libraries. In: Sato, M., Hanawa, T., Müller, M.S., Chapman, B.M., Supinski, B.R. (eds.) IWOMP 2010. LNCS, vol. 6132, pp. 15–28. Springer, Heidelberg (2010). doi:10.1007/978-3-642-13217-9_2
12. Peterson, P.: F2py: Fortran to Python interface generator. http://cens.ioc.ee/projects/f2py2e
13. L.F. Team. Flang. https://github.com/llvm-flang
14. T.C. Team. Clang 5 documentation: Libtooling. https://clang.llvm.org/docs/LibTooling.html

Compiling and Optimizing OpenMP 4.X Programs to OpenCL and SPIR

Marcio M. Pereira$^{(\boxtimes)}$, Rafael C.F. Sousa, and Guido Araujo

Institute of Computing, University of Campinas—UNICAMP, Campinas, Brazil
{mpereira,guido}@ic.unicamp.br, rafael.cardoso@students.ic.unicamp.br

Abstract. Given their massively parallel computing capabilities heterogeneous architectures comprised of CPUs and accelerators have been increasingly used to speed-up scientific and engineering applications. Nevertheless, programming such architectures is a challenging task for most non-expert programmers as typical accelerator programming languages (e.g. CUDA and OpenCL) demand a thoroughly understanding of the underlying hardware to enable an effective application speed-up. To achieve that, programmers are usually required to significantly change and adapt program structures and algorithms, thus impacting both performance and productivity. A simpler alternative is to use high-level directive-based programming models like OpenACC and OpenMP. These models allow programmers to insert both directives and runtime calls into existing source code, thus providing hints to the compiler and runtime to perform certain transformations and optimizations on the annotated code regions. In this paper, we present *ACLang*, an open-source LLVM/Clang compiler framework (http://www.aclang.org) that implements the recently released *OpenMP 4.X Accelerator Programming Model*. *ACLang* automatically converts OpenMP 4.X annotated program regions into OpenCL/SPIR kernels, while providing a set of polyhedral based optimizations like tiling and vectorization. OpenCL kernels resulting from ACLang can be executed on any OpenCL/SPIR compatible acceleration device, not only GPUs, but also FPGA accelerators like those found in the Intel HARP architecture. To the best of our knowledge and at the time this paper was written, this is the first LLVM/Clang implementation of the OpenMP 4.X Accelerator Model that provides a source-to-target OpenCL conversion. Experiments using ACLang on the Polybench benchmark reveal speed-ups of up to $30x$ on an Exynos 8890 Octacore CPU with a ARM Mali-T880 MP12 GPU, up to $62x$ on a 2.4 GHz dual-core Intel Core i5 processor equipped with an Intel Iris GPU unit, and up to $112x$ on a 2.1 GHz 32 cores Intel-Xeon processor equipped with a Tesla K40c GPU.

1 Introduction

With the advent of heterogeneous computing many parallel programming models have emerged seeking to improve the performance of sequential code by *offloading* computation *kernels* from a *host* machine (e.g. CPU) to an acceleration

© Springer International Publishing AG 2017
B.R. de Supinski et al. (Eds.): IWOMP 2017, LNCS 10468, pp. 48–61, 2017.
DOI: 10.1007/978-3-319-65578-9_4

device (e.g. GPU). Kernels are typically designed using specialized libraries and languages like CUDA [3] which has demonstrated high-performance execution on NVIDIA GPUs. On the other hand, for FPGA accelerators (e.g. Intel HARP) integrated mobile (e.g. ARM Mali) and laptop GPUs (e.g. Intel Iris), OpenCL [1] has been the language of choice as it offers flexibility and platform portability.

Although OpenCL provides a library that eases the task of offloading kernels to accelerator devices, its function calls are complex, have many parameters and require the programmer to have a good knowledge of the device architecture's features in order to enable a correct and effective usage of its hardware (e.g. block size, memory model, etc.). In this sense, OpenCL can still be considered a somehow low-level library for heterogeneous computing.

Introduced through OpenMP 4.0 the new *OpenMP Accelerator Model* [4, 10] proposes a number of new clauses aimed at speeding up the task of programming heterogeneous architectures. This model extends the concept of offloading and enables the programmer to use dedicated directives to define offloading target regions and control data movement between host and devices. Although most OpenMP directives used for multicore hosts can also be used inside target regions, the new accelerator model eases the tasks of identifying data-parallel computation.

This paper describes *ACLang*, an open source (http://www.aclang.org) LLVM Clang based compiler that implements the OpenMP Accelerator Model. The main contributions of this paper to the Clang/LLVM OpenMP community are: (i) it adds a new *runtime library* to LLVM/CLang that supports OpenMP offloading to accelerators like GPUs and FGPAs (not described in this paper). Kernel functions are extracted from OpenMP annotated regions and are dispatched as OpenCL or SPIR [2] code to be loaded and compiled by OpenCL drivers before being executed by the device; (ii) it leverages on the ISL [11] implementation of the polyhedral model to implement a multilevel tiling optimization on the extracted kernels; (iii) it provides a vectorization pass developed specifically to exploit the vector instructions available in OpenCL. This whole process is transparent and does not require any programmer intervention.

The paper is organized as follows: Sect. 2 gives an outline of the structure of the *ACLang* compiler. Section 3 describes general design concepts of tiling and vectorization when applied to the extracted kernels. Section 4 provides performance numbers and analyzes the results when programs are compiled with *ACLang* . Related work is discussed in Sect. 5. Finally, Sect. 6 concludes the paper.

2   The Structure of the ACLang Compiler

This section describes *ACLang's* structure and execution flow. The following example shows how *ACLang* works from a programmer perspective. Listing 1.1 presents two loops from the "Matrix Vector Product and Transpose" (mvt) program of the Polybench [5] benchmark suite after they have been annotated with OpenMP 4.X pragmas.

Listing 1.1. Fragment of Polybench mvt benchmark application

```
1  // Problem size
2  #define N 8192
3
4  void mvt_gpu(float* a,  float* x1,  float* x2,
5                          float* y1,  float* y2)
6  {
7    int i,j;
8
9    #pragma omp target data device(GPU) map(to: a[:N*N])
10   {
11     #pragma omp target map(to: y1[:N]) map(tofrom: x1[:N])
12     #pragma omp parallel for simd
13     for (i=0; i<N; i++)
14       for (j=0; j<N; j++)
15         x1[i] = x1[i] + a[i*N + j] * y1[j];
16
17     #pragma omp target map(to: y2[:N]) map(tofrom: x2[:N])
18     #pragma omp parallel for simd
19     for (i=0; i<N; i++)
20       for (j=0; j<N; j++)
21         x2[i] = x2[i] + a[j*N + i] * y2[j];
22   }
23 }
```

Listing 1.2. OpenCL kernel for the first loop of mvt after vectorization

```
1  __kernel void mvt_gpu_0(__global float *a,
2                          __global float *x1,
3                          __global float *y1) {
4    int b0 = get_group_id(0);
5    int t0 = get_local_id(0);
6    __private float4 _ft0;
7    __private float4 _ft1;
8    __private float4 _ft2;
9    _ft0 = vload4(0, &x1[(4*b0) + t0]);
10   for (int c1 = 0; c1 <= 8191; c1 += 4){
11     _ft1 = vload4(0, &a[((32768*b0) + (8192*t0)) + c1]);
12     _ft2 = vload4(0, &y1[c1]);
13     _ft0 = _ft0 + (_ft1 * _ft2);
14   }
15   x1[(4*b0) + t0] = (((_ft0.x + _ft0.y) + _ft0.z) + _ft0.w);
16 }
```

In the first loop the program computes the matrix vector multiplication followed by the transpose between a and y1 storing the result into vector x1. The second loop does a similar task for a, y2 and x2. As shown in Listing 1.1, the `target` clause defines the portion of the program that will be executed by the device (GPU in the example). The `map` clause details the mapping of the data between the host and the target device. For example in the first kernel of Listing 1.1 inputs (a and y1) are mapped *to* the GPU, and array x1 is mapped *to/from* the GPU. This means that array x1 is read and written during the kernel execution in the GPU. This strategy offers maximal flexibility to the developer to decide which part of the code is profitable to run on which architecture.

Host code to perform data offloading in *ACLang* is handled automatically during the LLVM/IR generation phase and occurs in between the begin and end scopes of pragmas "omp target [data] map". Also, during this phase *ACLang* extracts annotated loops from the compiler AST and transforms them into OpenCL kernels in source code format (Listing 1.2).

Moreover, *ACLang* also optimizes the extracted OpenCL kernels. For example as shown in Listing 1.2 it tiles and vectorizes the first loop of the code in Listing 1.1 transforming it to OpenCL kernel with blocks and threads suitable to run on any GPU containing vector instructions, like the ARM Mali-T880 MP12 GPU (preferred vector size is 4). The generated kernel can also go through a SPIR generation pass to produce the kernel bit code in SPIR format.

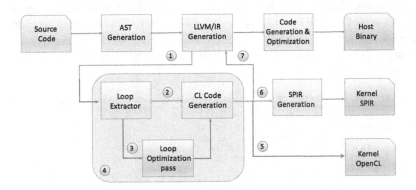

Fig. 1. *ACLang* Compiler pipeline

Figure 1 shows the *ACLang* execution flow pipeline. The LLVM IR generation phase of *ACLang* handles the conversion of the AST nodes generated by the Semantic phase into LLVM Intermediate Representation[1]. In this phase, the annotated loops are extracted from the AST ❶, optimized ❸, and/or transformed ❷ into OpenCL kernels in source code format (see Sect. 3 for more details on the loop optimization pass). Kernels ❺ can also go through the SPIR generation pass ❻ to produce kernel bit codes in SPIR format. *ACLang*'s transformation engine ❹ provides information to the LLVM IR generation phase ❼ to produce intermediate code that calls *ACLang* runtime library functions. These functions are used to perform data offloading and kernel dispatch to the OpenCL driver. Listing 1.3 shows the LLVM intermediate code produced for the first loop of the mvt application (see Listing 1.1, lines 13–15). Lines 2–7 show the result of the tiling optimization required to carry out vector optimization. Lines 11–21 show the kernel that results for the tiling where the first and third loops (lines 2 & 4) define the number of blocks and threads used by the runtime library to dispatch the kernel (line 10).

The *ACLang* runtime library has two main functionalities: (i) it hides the complexity of OpenCL code from the compiler; and (ii) it provides a mapping from OpenMP directives to the OpenCL API, thus avoiding the need for device manufacturers to build specific OpenMP drivers for their GPUs or FPGAs.

The offloading mechanism implements the OpenMP 4.X **target data**, **target** and **declare target** constructs. The compiler generates calls to the

---

[1] Historically, this was referred to as *codegen*.

AClang runtime library whenever a `target data` or `target` directive is encountered. The `declare target` construct will result in the extraction of the appropriate code to be stored inside the kernel.

The compiler also generates calls to the *AClang* runtime library, at the beginning and at the end of the C/C++ main function. At the beginning, the library determines the availability of an OpenCL driver and identifies the accelerator devices connected to it. After that, the *AClang* runtime library initialize the data structures that handle the devices and the context and command queues for each device. In addition it creates the necessary data structures to store the handles for the kernels and the buffers to offload data to the accelerator devices memories. The call at the end of the main function promotes the cleanup of these data structures.

Listing 1.3. Fragments of the transformation of `mvt` benchmark application

```
1  // Performing tile optimization with tile-size = 4
2  for (int c0 = 0; c0 <= 8191; c0 += 4)
3    for (int c1 = 0; c1 <= 8191; c1 += 4)
4      for (int c2 = 0; c2 <= 3; c2 += 1)
5        for (int c3 = 0; c3 <= 3; c3 += 1)
6          x1[c0 + c2] += (a[8192 * c0 + c1 + 8192 * c2 + c3] *
7                          y1[c1 + c3]);
8
9  /* Converting to OpenCL kernel where
10    global_work_size = 8192, and block_size = 4 */
11  __kernel void mvt_gpu_0(__global float *a,
12                          __global float *x1,
13                          __global float *y1) {
14    int b0 = get_group_id(0);
15    int t0 = get_local_id(0);
16    for (int c1 = 0; c1 <= 8191; c1 += 4) {
17      for (int c3 = 0; c3 <= 3; c3 += 1)
18        x1[4 * b0 + t0] += (a[32768 * b0 + 8192 * t0 + c1 + c3] *
19                            y1[c1 + c3]);
20    }
21  }
```

3   Tiling and Vectorization

Automatic loop transformations is a complex and cumbersome task which is hard to generalize. To address this problem, *ACLang* leverages on the ISL [11] implementation of the polyhedral model to transform the OpenMP annotated loops and create opportunities for loop tiling and vectorization. This is achieved in two steps.

First, annotated loop statements at the AST representation of the complier are transformed to a polyhedral linear-algebraic representation [14]. This model consists of an iteration domain, access relations, and a schedule. A standard dependence analysis is then performed using ISL. This step takes the iteration domain, access relations, and the schedule as inputs and determines which iteration statements depend on which other iteration statements. Second, the polyhedral engine selects a new execution order by using a reordering function (a *schedule*). The core transformation in this step finds a set of affine transformations that tile the loops so that they can be mapped to the blocks and threads in the OpenCL kernel code [13]. Tiling is a key transformation for GPUs. It has been studied from two perspectives: data locality and optimization and parallelization. The focus here is to partition the iteration space into tiles that can concurrently run on different GPU cores with a reduced inter-core communication[2]. This transformation is also instrumental in limiting the amount of memory used inside a block, to better exploit local memory resources. One of the key goals of our transformation framework is to find good ways of performing tiling. An important parameter in tiling is the size of the tiles, as its size affects the performance of the resulting code. Clearly there is an optimal tile-size that depends on the characteristics of the GPU being used and the actual code being tiled. *ACLang* uses the polyhedral engine to implement a multilevel tiling strategy tailored to the multiple levels of parallelism and to the memory hierarchy of the accelerator. As an example, tiling can be directly applied to the loops of Listing 1.1, as the outermost loops can be executed in parallel because their iterations update disjoint parts of the x1 and x2 arrays.

ACLang also provides a vectorization pass developed to exploit the short-vector instructions available in OpenCL. Automatic vectorization for modern short-SIMD instructions has been a popular topic in compiling technology with implementations for ARM Neon, Intel AVX and SSE, etc. Exploring vector computations in GPUs, however, suffers from several limitations involving alignment, redundant loads and stores, etc. GPUs use different schemes to expose vector computations: current NVIDIA GPUs use multiple levels of fine-grain threads, while others use explicit short-vector instructions. Other manufacturers like AMD have been using a combination of both [7]. In view of this non-uniformity and the availability of short-vector instructions in the OpenCL model, we decided to restrict the vectorization pass of *ACLang* to the use of these short-vector instructions. Although automatic vectorization can be extended to handle more sophisticated control-flow restructuring including outer-loop vectorization [19], at this time, we focus only on inner loops.

Kernels are vectorized in a two step process. First, *ACLang* uses the polyhedral optimization engine to re-structure loop nests so as to determine the innermost loops that can be vectorized. Second, *ACLang* vector optimization engine replaces the appropriate statements in the inner loops by short-vector instructions. Listing 1.2 presents the extracted kernel of the first loop from the mvt program (see Listing 1.1) after it has been vectorized.

State-of-the-art vectorizing compilers incorporate a cost model to decide whether vectorization is expected to be profitable [20]. These models are typically applied to a single loop, and do not consider potential combination of transformations at the loop-nest level. The *ACLang* optimization engine does not yet include a profitability heuristic. This will be addressed in future work.

By default *AClang* performs tiling on kernels whenever possible. Compiling flag -opt-poly=none can be used to disable this if needed (notice that such option disables both tiling and vectorization). *AClang* also performs vectoriza-

---

[2] A tile is atomically executed on a GPU core with communication required only before and after execution.

tion whenever possible on loops annotated with pragma `parallel for simd` or explicitly via command line (`-opt-poly=vectorize`) for all annotated loops.

4   Experimental Evaluation

AClang has been evaluated using three heterogeneous CPU-GPU architectures: (i) a mobile Exynos 8890 Octa-core CPU (4×2.3 GHz Mongoose & 4×1.6 GHz Cortex-A53) integrated with an ARM Mali-T880 MP12 GPU (12×650 MHz), and running Android OS, v6.0 (Marshmallow) (ii) a laptop with 2.4 GHz dual-core Intel Core i5 processor integrated with an Intel Iris GPU containing 40 execution units, and running MacOS Sierra 10.12.4; and (iii) a desktop with 2.1 GHz 32 cores Intel Xeon CPU E5-2620, NVIDIA Tesla K40c GPU with 12 GB and 2880 Cuda cores, and running Linux Fedora release 23. The results presented in all experiments are averaged over ten executions. Variance is negligible; hence, we will not provide error intervals. The experiments use a set of programs from the well-known Polybench benchmark suite [5] and the Parboil benchmark suite [6] with standard input sizes. The programs have been re-written in OpenMP 4.X. For the sake of simplicity we refer to this set of modified programs as the *Unibench* suite.

Figures 2(a), (b) and (c) show detailed speed-ups normalized to the sequential execution, compiled with $-O3$. Three optimization flavours are represented by bars in the figures: (a) *GPU* (green bar), the basic *ACLang* OpenCL kernel execution; (b) *GPU+tiling* (orange bar) when using *ACLang* tiling optimization; and (c) *GPU+vector* (blue bar) when combining *ACLang* tiling and vectorization. The experimental evaluation indicates that the implemented optimizations can yield significant performance benefits for most of programs. A thorough analysis of the final program performance is done in the section below.

4.1   Performance Analysis

Overall, the experiments revealed that *ACLang* can speed-up the execution of Unibench programs up to $30x$ when running on the Exynos/ARM-Mali, up to $62x$ on the Intel/Iris and up to $112x$ on the Intel Xeon/Tesla K40c. Also, as shown in the figures, when tiling followed by vectorization can be applied, application performance improve, with *syrk* application revealing the best relative performance improvement ($6x$) with respect to the tiled optimized code on Exynos/-Mali, and *3mm* application, $2.5x$ on Intel/Iris.

As one can notice in Fig. 2(c), performance improvement has been measured on the Tesla K40c when using tiled followed by vectorization even though that architecture does not have vector instructions. This can be explained by the fact that vectorization helps the OpenCL driver to improve memory throughput at run time. Tesla K40c hardware can do stores and loads for 64 and 128 bit types in a single transaction on each multiprocessor what reduces overall latency and increases effective throughput. The hardware can process 256 and 512 byte transaction sizes per warp, so a suitably aligned float4 load/store request for a

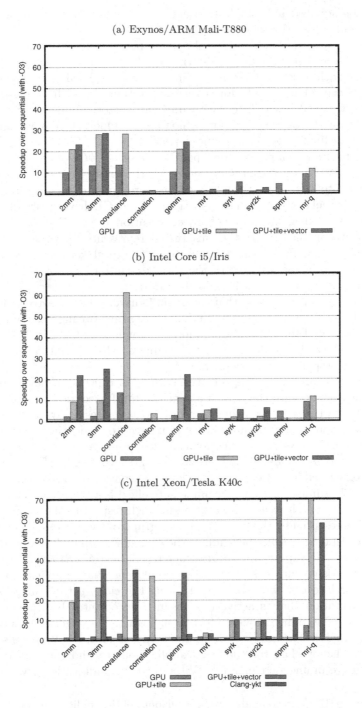

Fig. 2. Unibench Benchmark programs (Color figure online)

warp can be serviced in a single transaction. This can result in higher global memory bandwidth utilization at any given level of occupancy.

We also observed that substantial speed-ups have been produced in some of the programs that run the longest times. The slowdowns observed in some benchmarks such as mvt, occur mainly in the mobile (ARM Mali-T880) device and in instances that execute for a very short time. In such cases, the extra parallelism achieved by *AClang* with tiling and vectorization is not enough to compensate for the overhead of data offloading or OpenCL management tasks which are coordinated by the runtime library.

To account for the impact of the OpenCL overhead, *AClang*'s runtime library was instrumented to measure the percentage of the total program execution time corresponding to each one of the following tasks, represented as bars, in Figs. 3(a) and (b): (a) kernel computation (blue bar); (b) OpenCL driver tasks like context creation, queue management, kernel objects creation and GPU dispatch (orange bar). As shown in the graphs, the purple bar represents the time to offloading the data and is an important component of the total kernel execution time; for example approximately 40% of the total execution time of *3dconv* on the Intel/Iris architecture is spent in offloading data.

Figures 3(a) and (b) reveals that the OpenCL driver takes an astonishing share of the total execution time on most *Unibench* programs (orange bar plus purple bar). We also noted that this effect is more pronounced in the ARM/Mali architecture (not shown here) meaning that the OpenCL driver used in this architecture needs some performance improvement.

In order to evaluate the impact of the OpenCL runtime, a new experiment was designed to measure the percentage of the total execution time due to the OpenCL+Offloading overhead when varying the data sizes. Only programs which exhibit low speedups or even slowdown with respect to sequential code were used.

The bars in Fig. 3(c) represent for each program the percentage of execution time due to OpenCL+Offloading (coral) and the kernel useful computation (blue). As expected, Fig. 3(c) shows that longer executions times can amortize the OpenCL+Offloading overhead. The immediate effect is a decrease in the program slowdown or even an increase in the speed-up with respect to the sequential execution, as represented by the points and lines graph of Fig. 3(c) and its right-side y-axis. For instance, *2dconv* benchmark shows a slowdown of *0.35x* for data size equals to *2048* and a speed-up of *1.90x* when the data size is *8192*.

For comparison purposes, we ran the same benchmark applications on the Intel Xeon architecture with Tesla K40c using the *clang-ykt*, a Clang OpenMP 4.5 implementation that is actively being introduced into the Clang compiler trunk as part of an industry-wide effort to support the next generation of supercomputers [15, 17]. The only caveat we make in our initial comparisons against *clang-ykt* is that we had to modify all applications to find the best code performance as recommended in [17][3]. Without such modifications, we achieved

---

[3] According to [17], it is essential to collapse all loops of the application, and parallelize the critical loops using the combined construct target teams distribute parallel for.

(a) The breakdown of total execution time on ARM/Mali

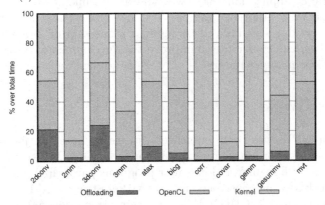

(b) The breakdown of total execution time on Intel/Iris

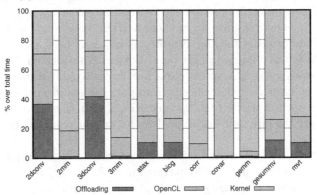

(c) OpenCL overhead variation with data set size on Intel/Iris

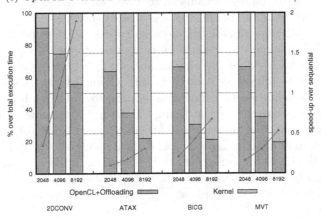

Fig. 3. Total execution time breakdown when using *AClang* with tile optimization (Color figure online)

slowdowns with respect to sequential execution for all applications. For instance, in the `covariance` application, the slowdown was $2x$ while we obtained a speedup of $66x$ with *AClang*. Another example was the classical matrix multiplication ($2\,mm$) that showed a slowdown of $6x$ against a speedup of $20x$ with *AClang*. We hope *AClang* can contribute to improve the development of of the *clang-ykt* compiler and *libomptarget* library.

5   Related Work

Compiling for GPUs has been extensively studied. Lee et al. [9] developed a compiler framework for automatic translation from OpenMP to CUDA. Their system handles both regular and irregular programs parallelized using OpenMP directives. Work sharing constructs in OpenMP are translated into distribution of work across threads in CUDA. However their system does not optimize data access and is restricted to NVIDIA GPUs. Baskaran et al. [8] developed a source-to-source transformation framework that can take an arbitrarily nested affine input C program and generate an efficient CUDA program. To generate tiled code, their affine transformations produce a band of fully permutable loops, that are automatically formed. This band is then transformed into tiled code. Their system optimizes data access costs for access to global memory and also makes use of on-chip shared memory. However, the solution does not explore other types of optimizations (e.g. vectorization), and is restricted to NVIDIA GPUs. Moreover the end user has to deal with two sources: the original one and the CUDA code.

Many efforts have been done to develop source-to-source compilers using the polyhedral framework to perform loop transformations. For instance, PPCG [12] introduces some advanced algorithms which can expose much more parallelism than other methods. It also introduces affine partition heuristics and code generation algorithms to improve locality in registers and shared memory. *ACLang* complements and enhances the effectiveness of such systems with additional optimization passes (e.g., vectorization), and a source-to-end solution that reaches a broad range of heterogeneous systems by using the support of OpenCL drivers.

Antao et al. [16] describes their initial work to fully support code generation for OpenMP device offloading constructs into Clang/LLVM. They describe a new driver implementation to handle compilation for multiple host and device types, which generalizes the current Clang CUDA implementation and supports OpenMP. They claim that the solution can be extended to any offloading based language including OpenCL and OpenACC. They describe an implementation of the OpenMP offloading constructs in the runtime library, giving details of how data mapping is implemented and how different device code sections in the binaries are handled to enable application execution on different devices without recompilation.

Tian et al. [18] proposes a small set of extensions to the LLVM IR to support explicit parallel, SIMD, and offloading constructs, thus enabling the transformation of these constructs in the LLVM middle-end. They also propose a unified framework for parallelization, offloading and vectorization compiler transformations. Unlike Tian, we made a design decision to quickly have a tiling and vectorization optimization engine focused on extracted kernels so as to deliver the best possible performance on target devices.

Leading optimizing compilers recognize the importance of devising a cost model for vectorization, but have so far provided only partial solutions. The most advanced cost model for loop transformations-enabled vectorization was proposed by Trifunovic et al. [20]. It is based on polyhedral compilation, and is capable of capturing from the polyhedral representation itself the main factors that contribute to the profitability of vectorization.

Our offloading implementation has many parts in common with the current OpenMP offloading support based on *libomptarget* that is present in *clang-ykt*. However, it was tailored for the specifics of the OpenCL model and contains some limitations that are not compatible with a fully functional OpenMP implementation. Currently, our library is used to enable the direct communication between host and an OpenCL driver, thus covering a whole range of GPUs from different vendors. On the other hand, *libomptarget* enables the communication between host and a target-independent offload library which, in turn, is used for communication between the host (read, *libomptarget*) and the target devices, thereby enabling the support of different programming models.

6 Future Directions

For the sake of compatibility with the OpenMP 4.X standard our next step is to replace our current offloading mechanism for the new mechanism present in *clang-ykt* and integrate our runtime library to *libomptarget*. However, we will preserve our kernel extraction, transformation and optimization engines.

We are also planning to design and implement a cost model algorithm for heterogeneous computing that takes into consideration processor's characteristics and data transfer time. The goal of this model is to help developers to effectively exploit the target device. Moreover, we are working on new OpenMP 4.X runtime libraries for the Microsoft SMARTNIC [21] and Intel HARP2 [22] architectures in order to easy the task of offloading computation to FPGA accelerators.

Acknowledgments. The authors would like to thank the anonymous reviewers for the insightful comments.

This work is supported by Samsung (grant 4716.08) and FAPESP Center for Computational Engineering and Sciences (grant 13/08293-7).

References

1. OpenCL: The Open Standard for Parallel Programming Language of heterogeneous Systems. Khronos Group (2010). http://www.khronos.org/opencl
2. SPIR: An OpenCL Standard Portable Intermediate Language for parallel compute and graphics. Khronos Group (2014). https://www.khronos.org/spir

3. CUDA – Compute Unified Device Architecture. NVIDIA. http://www.nvidia.com/object/cuda_home_new.html
4. OpenMP API Specification for Parallel Programming. Version 4.5, OpenMP ARB (2015). http://openmp.org/wp/openmp-specifications/
5. PolyBench/GPU: Implementation of PolyBench codes for GPU processing. http://web.cse.ohio-state.edu/~pouchet/software/polybench/GPU/
6. Parboil Benchmarks. http://impact.crhc.illinois.edu/parboil/parboil.aspx
7. OpenCL Optimization Guide: AMD Developer Central. http://developer.amd.com/tools-and-sdks/opencl-zone/amd-accelerated-parallel-processing-app-sdk/opencl-optimization-guide
8. Baskaran, M.M., Ramanujam, J., Sadayappan, P.: Automatic C-to-CUDA code generation for affine programs. In: Gupta, R. (ed.) CC 2010. LNCS, vol. 6011, pp. 244–263. Springer, Heidelberg (2010). doi:10.1007/978-3-642-11970-5_14
9. Lee, S., Min, S.-J., Eigenmann, R.: OpenMP to GPGPU: a compiler framework for automatic translation and optimization. In: PPoPP 2009, pp. 101–110 (2009)
10. Liao, C., Yan, Y., Supinski, B.R., Quinlan, D.J., Chapman, B.: Early experiences with the OpenMP accelerator model. In: Rendell, A.P., Chapman, B.M., Müller, M.S. (eds.) IWOMP 2013. LNCS, vol. 8122, pp. 84–98. Springer, Heidelberg (2013). doi:10.1007/978-3-642-40698-0_7
11. Verdoolaege, S.: isl: an integer set library for the polyhedral model. In: Fukuda, K., Hoeven, J., Joswig, M., Takayama, N. (eds.) ICMS 2010. LNCS, vol. 6327, pp. 299–302. Springer, Heidelberg (2010). doi:10.1007/978-3-642-15582-6_49
12. Verdoolaege, S., Carlos Juega, J., Cohen, A., Ignacio Gómez, J., Tenllado, C., Catthoor, F.: Polyhedral parallel code generation for CUDA. ACM Trans. Archit. Code Optim. 9(4), 1–23 (2013)
13. Bastoul, C.: Code generation in the polyhedral model is easier than you think. In: Proceedings of the 13th International Conference on Parallel Architectures and Compilation Techniques - PACT 2004. IEEE Computer Society (2004)
14. Grosser, T., Verdoolaege, S., Cohen, A.: Polyhedral AST generation is more than scanning polyhedra. ACM Trans. Program. Lang. Syst. 37(4), 50 (2015). Article No. 12. http://dx.doi.org/10.1145/2743016
15. Bertolli, C., Antao, S.F., Bercea, G.-T., Jacob, A.C., Eichenberger, A.E., Chen, T., Sura, Z., Sung, H., Rokos, G., Appelhans, D., O'Brien, K.: Integrating GPU support for OpenMP offloading directives into Clang LLVM-HPC2015, Austin, Texas USA, 15–20 November 2015 (2015)
16. Antao, S.F., Bataev, A., Jacob, A.C., Bercea, G.-T., Eichenberger, A.E., Rokos, G, Martineau, M, Jin, T., Ozen, G., Sura, Z., Chen, T., Sung, H., Bertolli, C., O'Brien, K.: Offloading support for OpenMP in Clang and LLVM. In: 2016 Third Workshop on the LLVM Compiler Infrastructure in HPC (2016)
17. Martineau, M., McIntosh-Smith, S., Bertolli, C., Jacob, A.C., Antao, S.F., Eichenberger, A., Bercea, G.-T., Chen, T., Jin, T., O'Brien, K., Rokos, G., Sung, H., Sura, Z.: Performance analysis and optimization of Clang's OpenMP 4.5 GPU support. In: 7th International Workshop on Performance Modeling, Benchmarking and Simulation of High Performance Computing Systems, pp. 54–64. IEEE Press (2016)
18. Tian, X., Saito, H., Su, E., Gaba, A., Masten, M., Garcia, E., Zaks, A.: LLVM framework and IR extensions for parallelization, SIMD vectorization and offloading. In: 2016 Third Workshop on the LLVM Compiler Infrastructure in HPC (2016)
19. Nuzman, D., Zaks, A.: Outer-loop vectorization revisited for short SIMD architectures. In: International Conference on Parallel Architecture and Compilation Techniques, PACT 2008 (2008)

20. Trifunovic', K., Nuzman, D., Cohen, A., Zaks, A., Rosen, I.: Polyhedral-model guided loop-nest auto-vectorization. In: International Conference on Parallel Architecture and Compilation Techniques, PACT 2009 (2009)
21. Firestone, D.: SmartNIC: FPGA innovation in OCS servers for Microsoft Azure. In: OCP U.S, Summit (2016)
22. Hussain, W., Airoldi, R., Hoffmann, H., Ahonen, T., Nurmi, J.: HARP2: an X-scale reconfigurable accelerator-rich platform for massively-parallel signal processing algorithms. J. Sig. Process. Syst. **85**(3), 341 (2016)

Extending OpenMP SIMD Support for Target Specific Code and Application to ARM SVE

Jinpil Lee[1]([⊠]), Francesco Petrogalli[2], Graham Hunter[2], and Mitsuhisa Sato[1]

[1] RIKEN Advanced Institute for Computational Science, Kobe, Japan
{jinpil.lee,msato}@riken.jp
[2] ARM Ltd., Cambridge, UK
{Francesco.Petrogalli,Graham.Hunter}@arm.com

Abstract. Recent trends in processor design accommodate wide vector extensions. SIMD vectorization is more important than before to exploit the potential performance of the target architecture. The latest OpenMP specification provides new directives which help compilers produce better code for SIMD auto-vectorization. However, it is hard to optimize the SIMD code performance in OpenMP since the target SIMD code generation mostly relies on the compiler implementation. In this paper, we propose a new directive that specifies user-defined SIMD variants of functions used in SIMD loops. The compiler can then use the user-defined SIMD variants when it encounters OpenMP loops instead of auto-vectorized SIMD variants. The user can optimize the SIMD performance by implementing highly-optimized SIMD code with intrinsic functions. The performance evaluation using a image composition kernel shows that the user can optimize SIMD code generation in an explicit way by using our approach. The user-defined function reduces the number of instructions by 70% compared with the auto-vectorized code generated from the serial code.

Keywords: OpenMP · SIMD vectorization · VLA programming - Vector Length Agnostic programming

1 Introduction

Recent trends in processor design accommodate wide vector extensions and many-core architectures. We expect that these trends will continue to improve the flops per watt ratio. Current Intel Xeon Phi processors have the 512-bit vector instruction set, Advanced Vector eXtensions (AVX-512), and more than 60 cores. ARM released a new vector instruction set for high performance computing, named Scalable Vector Extension (SVE) [2], which allows up to 2048-bit wide vector registers. Parallel programming is getting more important when using these architectures to exploit the potential performance. OpenMP (OMP) is widely used to describe node-level parallelism on shared-memory architectures. The directives such as *parallel* and *for* can describe thread-level parallelism on many-core architectures.

© Springer International Publishing AG 2017
B.R. de Supinski et al. (Eds.): IWOMP 2017, LNCS 10468, pp. 62–74, 2017.
DOI: 10.1007/978-3-319-65578-9_5

On the other hand, SIMD vectorization has been done automatically by compilers. Compilers analyze code structures such as loop statements and find parallelism. When the target structures are safe to be vectorized, the compiler generates SIMD instructions. The latest OMP specifications provide new directives which help this auto-vectorization process. The *simd* directive specifies vectorizable loops (SIMD loops) in the serial code. The *declare simd* directive can be given to function definitions in the serial code to specify that the target functions are vectorizable in the SIMD loop. These directives ensure that target constructs are safe to be vectorized so that compilers can skip some hard analysis such as pointer alias analysis and avoid generating runtime checks to prevent aliasing.

The OMP directives reduce the burden of compiler analysis for SIMD vectorization. However, it is hard to optimize the SIMD code performance in OMP since the target SIMD code generation mostly relies on the compiler implementation. In this paper, we propose a programming interface connecting user-defined SIMD functions and SIMD loops. To this end, we introduce the *alias simd* directive which specifies the user-defined SIMD variant of the target function. The compiler uses the specified function in the SIMD loop instead of vectorizing the target function. By using this interface, we can split the loop iteration translation and the SIMD code generation for the loop body. Code translation for controlling loop iterations remains architecture-independent by using the OMP *simd* directive. The user can write highly optimized SIMD code with architecture-dependent programming methods such as intrinsic functions.

The main target architecture of our proposal is ARM SVE. SVE is a vector length agnostic instruction set. Most instructions use a predicate mask. Our proposal includes a way of handling predicate masks and optimization in the SVE instruction set. We also consider fixed-length vector instruction sets such as Intel AVX to make the proposal to cover traditional SIMD extensions. The user-defined SIMD function can be implemented in the various ways since our proposal only relies on the function declaration and the vector ABI. In this paper, we use intrinsic functions provided by processor vendors to implement SIMD variant functions.

The rest of the paper is organized as follows: Sect. 2 shows related works proposing explicit SIMD programming models. In Sect. 3, we briefly introduce the new ARM vector instruction set, SVE, and its intrinsic functions as preliminary knowledge. In Sect. 4, we introduce the *alias simd* directive in OpenMP, which allows explicit SIMD implementations in OMP SIMD loops. In Sect. 5, some sample code and preliminary results of the performance evaluation are given to show the effectiveness of our proposal. Finally, we discuss the future work and conclude the paper in Sect. 6.

2   Related Work

There have been many attempts to establish an explicit SIMD programming model [11]. ARM C Language Extensions (ACLE) [1], which is only available on ARM architecture, provides a type-generic interface to program ARM SVE instructions. Thanks to its vector-length agnostic design, the iteration of the SIMD loop can be controlled without considering target architecture's vector length. ispc (Intel SPMD Program Compiler) [10] defines new programming language to describe SIMD-level parallelism. It covers various Intel SIMD instruction sets such as SSE, AVX, and AVX-512 in the Xeon Phi architecture. The language-based approach such as ispc, Intel array notation [7], Sierra [8], and Terra [3] require a dedicated implementation in compilers. [4] takes compiler-independent approach using C++ template. Cyme [5] and Vc [6] are implemented as a library. While these models provide high-level interface for SIMD programming, they assume a fixed vector length so that the SIMD loop iteration step should be modified manually when targeting an extension with a different vector register size.

3   Overview of ARM Scalable Vector Extension

SVE is a new vector extension to the A64 instruction set of the ARMv8-A architecture designed to exploit increases in hardware capability without requiring software recompilation.

The vector length in SVE can be configured dynamically in the range from 128 to 2048 bits, in multiples of 128. Although the value can be obtained through system registers, the SIMD instruction set is designed to be *Vector Length Agnostic (VLA)*.

Most instructions take a predicate register to mask available elements in the operand vector registers.

The following are some of the key features of SVE.

- 32 vector registers (Z0-Z31).
- 16 predicate registers (P0-P15).
- Configurable vector length: 128 to 2048-bit (maximum is processor-dependent).
- Enables the VLA programming model – the same program can run on machines with different vector register length, without requiring recompilation.

3.1   The Vector Length Agnostic Programming Model

Listing 1 shows an example of a vector addition in C and its equivalent SVE assembly code. The operand p0 is a predicate register which is used to mask active and inactive lanes of the vector registers z0 and z1.

```
1   ; for (i = 0; i < N; i++) { C[i] = A[i] + B[i]; }
2   ; x9, x10, x11 and x12 hold N, A, B, and C, respectively
3         mov      x8, xzr
4         b        .Lcond
5   .loop:
6         ld1d     z0.d, p0/z, [x10, x8, lsl #3]
7         ld1d     z1.d, p0/z, [x11, x8, lsl #3]
8         fadd     z0.d, z0.d, z1.d
9         st1d     z0.d, p0, [x12, x8, lsl #3]
10        incd     x8              ; increase i
11  .Lcond:
12        whilelo  p0.d, x8, x9    ; set p0.d[i] = (i < N)
13        b.first  .loop           ; execute the loop iteration
14                                 ; if the first lane is active
```

Listing 1: Vector Add Example in SVE

Figure 1 shows how SVE instructions modify register values in Listing 1. Here, we assume that the data type of A, B, and C is double *, and the data type of i and N is unsigned long int.

After setting the loop induction variable (i, carried by x8) to zero, the code branches directly to the instruction whilelo, which compares the current iteration value i and the last iteration value (N in this case, carried by x9). The instruction sets the loop predicate register, p0, as p0.d[i] = (i < N) ? 1 : 0, for each one of the logical lanes implied by a SIMD loop iteration.

If at least the first logical lane of the predicate vector is active (b.first), the branch is taken back to the start of the loop.

The predicate register is then used in the loop body to mask out the inactive lanes. In Listing 1, the loads (ld1d), and the store (st1d) instruction use the predicate register to process only the active lanes, effectively removing the need

256-bit SVE

Iter	x8 (i)	whilelo p0.d, x8, x9 $(i < N)$
0	0	1|1|1|1
1	4	1|1|1|1
2	8	1|1|1|1

384-bit SVE

Iter	x8 (i)	whilelo p0.d, x8, x9 $(i < N)$
0	0	1|1|1|1|1|1
1	6	1|1|1|1|1|1

512-bit SVE

Iter	x8 (i)	whilelo p0.d, x8, x9 $(i < N)$
0	0	1|1|1|1|1|1|1|1
1	8	1|1|1|1|0|0|0|0

Fig. 1. Vector loop control using the predicate generated by the whilelo instruction, for different SVE implementations. N is 12. Notice that the same code in Listing 1 works independently on the vector size thanks to the incd x8 instruction. In the predicate representation, logical lane numbering is intended left-to-right.

of introducing a scalar loop tail to fix up the last elements of the computation that do no fill a full vector register length.

The logical iteration of the loop is then advanced using the incd instruction, which is used to increase the iteration variable i by the number of double elements a scalable vector register can hold.

The, another whilelo instruction is issued and the branch condition in .Lcond is checked again.

For the interested reader, other examples showing how to use SVE for VLA programming are available in the white paper [9].

3.2 Intrinsic Programming Interface

Like most SIMD instruction sets, SVE has an intrinsic programming interface which can be used in high-level programming languages such as C and C++. ARM C Language Extensions (ACLE) has been extended to support SVE. Listing 2 shows the ACLE version of the vector addition given in Listing 1. Because of its VLA approach, the loop is written using the *while* construct. *svbool_t* is the data type for predicate registers. *svfloat64_t* is the data type for double precision FP registers.

```
1    unsigned long i = 0;
2    svbool_t p = svwhilelt_b64_s64(i, N);
3    svbool_t tp = svptrue_b64();
4    while (svptest_first(tp, p)) {
5      svfloat64_t vec_a = svld1(p, &(A[i]));
6      svfloat64_t vec_b = svld1(p, &(B[i]));
7      svfloat64_t vec_c = svadd(p, vec_a, vec_b);
8      svst1(p, &(C[i]), vec_c);
9      i += svcntd();
10     p = svwhilelt_b64_s64(i, N);
11   }
```

Listing 2: Vector Add Example in ACLE

The predicate variable is created by *svwhilelt_b64_s64()* which do the same process in Listing 1. *svtrue_b64()* generates a predicate in which all elements are active. At the beginning of every iteration, *svptest_first()* checks the head of the predicate register to see if the next iteration has an active predicate element to process. The load and store instructions in Listing 1 are equivalent to *svld1()* and *svst1()*. *svadd()* calculates SIMD addition of the double data type. *svcntd()* returns the number of 64-bit elements in a vector register. It is then used to increase the loop iteration variable for the next SIMD execution.

Note that many routines in Listing 2 are given without specifying the element data type. It is because ACLE provides a type generic programming interface implemented using templates in C++, or _Generic in C11.

4   Explicit Programming Interface for Vectorizing Functions

As discussed in Sect. 1, the current OMP specification cannot specify the SIMD implementation of functions used in SIMD loops. Although the directives can help the compiler check that the target code can be vectorized, the SIMD code generation is a transparent part to the user. In this section, we propose an explicit programming interface to expose user-defined SIMD functions available in OMP SIMD loops.

4.1   Overview of the Proposed Programming Model

The basic concept of our proposal is that we provide SIMD variants of existing functions instead of using auto-generated SIMD functions. To this end, we add a new directive, named *alias simd*, in the OpenMP specification. Listing 3 shows an example code of the *alias simd* directive. Vector data types ($int4\_t$, $int8\_t$) and intrinsic functions (e.g. *intrinsic_add4*) in the listing are pseudo code.

```
1   #pragma omp declare simd notinbranch          // A
2   int add(int a, int b) {
3      return a + b;
4   }
5   #pragma omp alias simd to(add) simdlen(4)     // B
6   int4_t add_vec4(int4_t a, int4_t b) {
7      return intrinsic_add4(a, b);
8   }
9   #pragma omp alias simd to(add) simdlen(8)     // C
10  int8_t add_vec8(int8_t a, int8_t b) {
11     return intrinsic_add8(a, b);
12  }
13
14  #pragma omp simd simdlen(VL)  // VL is 4 or 8
15  for (i = 0; i < n; i++) {
16     z[i] = add(x[i], y[i]);
17  }
```

Listing 3: Explicit SIMD Variant in OMP SIMD Loop

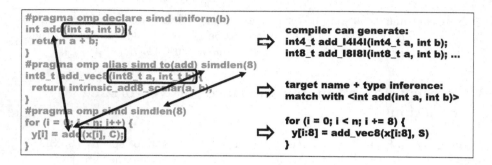

Fig. 2. Code Translation OverviewCode Translation Overview

The purpose of the *alias simd* directive is mapping SIMD variant functions defined by the user to the original functions in the serial code. In *B* and *C* in Listing 3, the function name or declaration is given by the *to* clause for the mapping process. We need the full declaration when functions with different argument types have the same name by using template (in C++) or *_Generic* (in C11). *alias simd* has the *simdlen* clause to distinguish SIMD variants by the vector length. These variants can be defined at the same time. We do not expect that Intel AVX and ARM SVE SIMD variants are available at the same time since we assume that portability among vendors is maintained by using some guard macros (e.g. *__AVX__*, *__ARM_NEON__*).

The mapping process is independent from *declare simd* so that the SIMD function is generated from the scalar function even if SIMD variants are given. SIMD variants have priority over the compiler-generated SIMD function when translating the OMP *simd* directive. The compiler will select a SIMD variant by the proper vector length (or the vector length can be given explicitly by the *simdlen* clause). We may need the scalar function definition and the *declare simd* directive in case that the loop is not vectorizable, or no proper SIMD variant is given.

Figure 2 shows how the compiler translates a OMP loop and replace functions with the SIMD variant by the *alias simd* directive. The *simd* directive specifies that the following loop should be vectorized and the vector length is 8. Function *add()* is used in the loop body. To vectorize the loop, the compiler needs to generates the SIMD code of *add()*.

The *declare simd* directive is given with the scalar code of *add()*. Since *simdlen* is not given, SIMD functions with any vector length can be generated from the compiler. In this example, the SIMD function with vector length 8 (*add_I8I8I()*) can be generated for the loop body.

On the other hand, a user-defined SIMD function is given with the *alias simd* directive. *add_vec8()* is implemented by using (pseudo) SIMD intrinsic functions. The function adds a scalar value to a vector register. On most architectures, each SIMD intrinsic function is specific to a vector length. The *simdlen* clause is given in the *alias simd* to tell the compiler that the following function can be used to execute 8 iterations of int operations in parallel. The *to* clause specifies the original scalar function. It tells the compiler that *add_vec8()* is a SIMD variant of *add()*. The compiler infers data types of arguments in (add()) to complete the function declaration. The process follows the architecture's vector ABI. In this example, the compiler infer *int* from *int8_t*.

When the compiler translates the OMP loop in Fig. 2, two SIMD functions are available, compiler-generated *add_I8I8I()* and user-defined *add_vec8()*. In our proposal, user-defined functions have higher priority to allow the user to optimize the SIMD performance by implementing fast SIMD algorithms.

4.2   Syntax of the Alias Simd Directive

Figure 3 shows the syntax of the *alias simd* directive. The directive is given along with the complete definition of a SIMD variant. We do not assume any specific programming model for the implementation. Therefore, any kind of programming model can be used to implement SIMD variants if they adhere to the proper argument types and vector length. At first, we explain the syntax for the fixed-length SIMD architecture, and then extend it for SVE's VLA approach.

```
#pragma omp alias simd to(name_or_decl) [clause_list]
function_definition

name_or_decl := function_name
              | function_declaration
clause := simdlen(integer_expr)
        | inbranch
        | notinbranch
        | linear(linear_list [: linear_step])
```

Fig. 3. Definition of Alias Simd Directive

The *to* clause comes with either the name or declaration of the target function. When a function name is given, the compiler would infer the scalar type of each vector/scalar argument in the SIMD variant. The type reference follows target architectures's vector ABI. Multiple types can be mapped to the same vector type (e.g. generic programming model). In that case, the complete declaration should be given to choose the correct target function. The *to* clause cannot be omitted.

The *simdlen* clause specifies the SIMD length used in the SIMD variant. By the *simdlen* clause given in the *simd* directive, the SIMD loop may require several SIMD variants for the same function. The *simdlen* clause in *alias simd* is used to link the correct SIMD variant to a function call in the SIMD loop. The compiler registers the SIMD variant as the default SIMD implementation for the architecture when *simdlen* is omitted. When the target instruction set is SVE, *simdlen* is omitted by default. However, we can still use *simdlen* for SVE. This can be useful when there are highly-optimized SVE SIMD functions for a specific vector length.

The *inbranch/notinbranch* clause specifies whether the target function is called in a conditional statement or not. For example, the SIMD variant have additional arguments when *inbranch* is given. This clause is used to choose the correct SIMD variant, and infer the scalar types of the target argument (with *inbranch*, mask/predicate argument will be excluded in type inference).

The *linear* clause specifies the linear step of the target scalar variable increased in SIMD lanes. Regardless of the step value, the corresponding argument would have the original (scalar) data type. Since the privatization and linear increment should be implemented inside the SIMD function, multiple variants with different steps look the same from the compiler. The *linear* clause in *alias simd* should be given to distinguish the multiple SIMD intrinsic variants in the source code so that the compiler can choose the correct one. The syntax of *linear_list* and *linear_step* is the same as for the already existing OpenMP constructs.

5   Preliminary Evaluation

In this section, we introduce a use case of our proposal and perform a preliminary evaluation. We use the *alias simd* directive to optimize a simple image composition code. ALCE intrinsic functions are used to implement a SIMD function in SVE. Since the proposal has not been implemented yet, we compare the auto-vectorized code, which is equivalent to OMP SIMD vectorization in the current LLVM implementation, and the hand-written SIMD code simulating the behaviour of the *alias simd* directive. Both the serial and ACLE code are compiled by the SVE LLVM compiler and the binaries are executed on the instruction simulator, which has been provided by ARM.

5.1   Vectorization of Image Composition Kernel

Listing 4 shows the serial implementation of the composition code and the main loop. All color values are stores in the *unsigned char* type which has a range from 0 to 255. Each image has four channels, *red*, *green*, *blue*, and *alpha*. The image composition is done by a loop statement. In each iteration, function *add_filter()* is called for the *red*, *green*, and *blue* channel.

```
1   typedef unsigned char uchar;
2   typedef unsigned short ushort;
3
4   #pragma omp declare simd
5   uchar add_filter(uchar a2, uchar in1, uchar in2) {
6     if (a2 > 0) {
7       ushort temp = (ushort)in1 + (ushort)in2;
8       if (temp > 255) return 255;
9       else return (uchar)temp;
10    }
11    else return in1;
12  }
13
14  uchar out_r[N]; uchar out_g[N]; uchar out_b[N];
15  uchar in1_a[N]; uchar in1_r[N]; uchar in1_g[N]; uchar in1_b[N];
16  uchar in2_a[N]; uchar in2_r[N]; uchar in2_g[N]; uchar in2_b[N];
17
18  void loop() {
19  #pragma omp simd
20    for (int i = 0; i < N; i++) {
21      out_r[i] = add_filter(in2_a[i], in1_r[i], in2_r[i]);
22      out_g[i] = add_filter(in2_a[i], in1_g[i], in2_g[i]);
23      out_b[i] = add_filter(in2_a[i], in1_b[i], in2_b[i]); }}
```

Listing 4: Image Composition Code

add_filter() returns the sum of the two input images when the alpha mask value of the second image is not 0. When the value is 0, it returns the color value of the first image. Since the summation may overflow the maximum value (255), the code stores the temporary data in the *unsigned short* type, and checks the value range. Therefore, the serial code contains type conversion and branching.

Listing 5 shows the ACLE implementation of the composition code. Note that the function has additional argument p. It is because the compiler generates a predicate value to process the remainder loop as shown in Sect. 3. We assume that SVE vector functions always have a predicate variable as a first argument. It is not used in type inference shown in Sect. 4.

```
1   #pragma omp alias simd to(add_filter)
2   svuint8_t add_filter_acle(svbool_t p, svuint8_t a2,
3     svuint8_t in1, svuint8_t in2) {
4     svuint8_t zero = svdup_n_u8_x(p, 0);
5     svbool_t alpha_mask = svcmpgt_u8(p, a2, zero); // a2 > zero
6     svuint8_t temp = svand_u8_z(alpha_mask, in2, in2);
7     return svqadd_u8(in1, temp);
8   }
```

Listing 5: Vectorization of Image Composition Code using Alias Simd

The ACLE version uses *svqadd_u8()*, saturating integer addition, to calculate the summation. When the summation is outside the range, *svqadd_u8()* ensures that the value will be the maximum (255). This can avoid type conversion shown in the serial version and therefore increase performance. In SVE, branches can be replaced by SIMD instructions with predicate registers. The alpha mask values are checked in parallel by *svcmpgt_u8()*, which generates a predicate value. It can be used to generate the second operand of the summation to avoid the branch. The values are set to zero when the corresponding predicate value is inactive. As a result, the ACLE implementation can exploit the SIMD-level parallelism for *unsigned char* (8-bits) on the target hardware.

Listing 6 shows the main loop code written in ACLE. Even though ACLE provides a generic programming interface, porting to ACLE requires manual transformation including rewriting loops, generating predicates, and adding vector load/store instructions. As shown in Listing 4, this transformation is transparent and portable in our approach since it is programmed by the OMP *simd* directive.

```
 1   void loop() {
 2     int i = 0;
 3     svbool_t p = svwhilelt_b8_s32(i, N);
 4     svbool_t tp = svptrue_b32();
 5     while (svptest_first(tp, p)) {
 6       svuint8_t vin1_r = svld1_u8(p, in1_r+i);
 7       // loads for vin1_{g, b}, vin2_{a, r, g, b}
 8       svuint8_t vout_r = add_filter_acle(p,vin2_a,vin1_r,vin2_r);
 9       svuint8_t vout_g = add_filter_acle(p,vin2_a,vin1_g,vin2_g);
10       svuint8_t vout_b = add_filter_acle(p,vin2_a,vin1_b,vin2_b);
11       svst1_u8(p, out_r+i, vout_r);
12       // stores for vout_{g, b}
13
14       i += svcntb();
15       p = svwhilelt_b8_s32(i, N); }}
```

Listing 6: Main Loop in ACLE

5.2   Evaluation Results

Figure 4 shows the performance of the auto-vectorized serial code and the hand-written ACLE code. Since we do not assume any specific hardware implementation, the performance is measured by counting the number of instructions issued during the execution of the loop. We have evaluated the performance with two dataset sizes, 32×32 and 320×320 pixels, using two simulated hardware implementations, with 256-bit and 1024-bit wide vectors.

The results show that the hand-written code simulating *alias simd* executes less instructions compared with the auto-vectorized code. In most cases, the auto-vectorized code executes $3.7 \sim 3.8$ times more instructions than the hand-written code. When increasing the vector length in the small data set (32×32 with 1024-bit SIMD), the ratio is decreased to 3.4 because the total instruction number is small and instructions for loop control becomes significant.

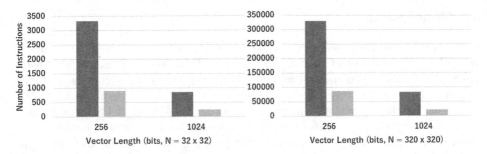

Fig. 4. Performance of Image Composition Kernel, as number of total instructions issued when executing the loop

The serial version includes the type conversion from *unsigned char* to *unsigned short* to calculate summation of two pixels. In auto-vectorization, the compiler generates SIMD addition instructions for *unsigned short*, which doubles the number of SIMD add instructions per iteration compared to the intrinsic code. Before the calculation, the compiler generates type conversion instructions. It also adds extra calculations which do not exist in the intrinsic code.

The branch used for color clamping to the maximum value is translated to SIMD compare and selection instructions in auto-vectorization. There are type conversion to *unsigned short* since the calculated values are stored in the *unsigned short* type. After the calculation, the data type is converted into *unsigned char*. The check for alpha mask is translated in the same way.

On the other hand, the intrinsic version calculates the summation using *unsigned char* type instructions. Since it uses the saturating addition instruction, *svqadd_u8()*, the range check and clamping is unnecessary. The optimization is intended to avoid the unnecessary type conversion to reduce the number of instruction executed, and improve the instruction throughput by using *unsigned char* type SIMD instructions.

It should be emphasized that our approach provides an explicit way of programming SIMD instructions. The performance result shows that our approach can successfully change the way how the code uses the SIMD instructions, which cannot be done with existing OMP SIMD directives. This is important even for a product-level compiler since it cannot always generate the optimal SIMD code. And there may be a gap between high-level languages and hardware instruction sets which make it difficult to describe the optimal SIMD code. We have used the saturating addition instruction in SVE, which cannot be described directly in the C language without using a wider type.

Our proposal is designed to be independent from instruction sets. If we implement the code transformation of *alias simd* for a specific SIMD instruction set and the vector ABI, we can describe user-defined SIMD functions to optimize the SIMD performance on the target architecture. For example, we can optimize the SIMD performance using Intel AVX intrinsic functions on Intel processors (e.g. generating a histogram using Intel AVX512-CD).

6   Conclusion

In this paper, we proposed a new OMP directive, *alias simd*. It specifies user-defined SIMD variants of functions called in SIMD loops. The compiler uses the SIMD variant when translating OMP loops instead of auto-vectorized SIMD variants. The user can optimize the SIMD performance by implementing highly-optimized SIMD variants with intrinsic functions. Even for a product-level compiler, it is difficult to generate optimal SIMD code for every case. Our proposal provide an explicit way to program SIMD-level parallelism while keeping common and trivial parts (e.g. loop iteration transformation) portable. For the next step, we will implement our proposal in the LLVM compiler so that we can try various examples and instruction sets.

References

1. ARM C Language Extensions for SVE. https://developer.arm.com/docs/100987/latest/arm-c-language-extensions-for-sve
2. ARM Scalable Vector Extension. https://developer.arm.com/products/architecture/a-profile/docs
3. DeVito, Z., Hegarty, J., Aiken, A., Hanrahan, P., Vitek, J.: Terra: a multi-stage language for high-performance computing. In: Proceedings of the 34th ACM SIG-PLAN Conference on Programming Language Design and Implementation, PLDI 2013, NY, USA, pp. 105–116 (2013). http://doi.acm.org/10.1145/2491956.2462166
4. Estérie, P., Gaunard, M., Falcou, J., Lapresté, J.T., Rozoy, B.: Boost.simd: generic programming for portable simdization. In: Proceedings of the 21st International Conference on Parallel Architectures and Compilation Techniques, PACT 2012, NY, USA, pp. 431–432 (2012). http://doi.acm.org/10.1145/2370816.2370881
5. Ewart, T., Delalondre, F., Schürmann, F.: Cyme: a library maximizing SIMD computation on user-defined containers. In: Kunkel, J.M., Ludwig, T., Meuer, H.W. (eds.) ISC 2014. LNCS, vol. 8488, pp. 440–449. Springer, Cham (2014). doi:10.1007/978-3-319-07518-1_29
6. Kretz, M., Lindenstruth, V.: VC: A C++ library for explicit vectorization. Softw. Pract. Exper. **42**(11), 1409–1430 (2012). http://dx.doi.org/10.1002/spe.1149
7. Krzikalla, O., Zitzlsberger, G.: Code vectorization using intel array notation. In: Proceedings of the 3rd Workshop on Programming Models for SIMD/Vector Processing, WPMVP 2016, NY, USA, p. 6:1–6:8 (2016). http://doi.acm.org/10.1145/2870650.2870655
8. Leissa, R., Haffner, I., Hack, S.: Sierra: a SIMD extension for C++. In: Proceedings of the 2014 Workshop on Programming Models for SIMD/Vector Processing, WPMVP 2014, NY, USA, pp. 17–24 (2014). http://doi.acm.org/10.1145/2568058.2568062
9. Petrogalli, F.: A sneak peek into SVE and VLA programming. https://developer.arm.com/hpc/a-sneak-peek-into-sve-and-vla-programming
10. Pharr, M., Mark, W.R.: ispc: a SPMD compiler for high-performance CPU programming. In: 2012 Innovative Parallel Computing (InPar), pp. 1–13, May 2012
11. Pohl, A., Cosenza, B., Mesa, M.A., Chi, C.C., Juurlink, B.: An evaluation of current SIMD programming models for C++. In: Proceedings of the 3rd Workshop on Programming Models for SIMD/Vector Processing, WPMVP 2016, NY, USA, pp. 3:1–3:8 (2016). http://doi.acm.org/10.1145/2870650.2870653

OpenMP Application Studies

OpenMP Tasking and MPI in a Lattice QCD Benchmark

Larry Meadows[1](✉) and Ken-ichi Ishikawa[2]

[1] Intel Corporation, Hillsboro, OR, USA
lawrence.f.meadows@intel.com
[2] University of Hiroshima, Hillsboro, USA
ishikawa@theo.phys.sci.hiroshima-u.ac.jp

Abstract. Beginning with an existing well-optimized lattice quantum chromodynamics solver using OpenMP+MPI, we develop two task-based implementations, one with OpenMP tasking and one with hand-coded "untasking". We achieve better overlap of MPI communication and computation with both methods, and expose some performance issues in OpenMP tasking. Both task-based implementations outperform the original implementation when strong scaling.

Keywords: Openmp · Tasking · MPI

1 Introduction

Overlapping MPI communication with computation is a key optimization technique for many HPC applications. MPI provides asynchronous send and receive calls, but there is still code inside the MPI library that needs to execute on the processor. To hide the largest amount of MPI time, this code needs to be executed in parallel with computation.

The CCS-QCD benchmark [1] offloads MPI to dedicated cores using a simple shared-memory synchronization mechanism. This mechanism works well but has some limitations:

- The dedicated cores are idle when not running MPI code.
- The list of dedicated cores must be communicated to the application, and the application must be run in such a way that those cores are not included in the cores used for computation. This may be a challenge in many job launching systems.
- There is overhead associated with the synchronization mechanism used to perform the offload.
- The number of MPI ranks per node is limited by the number of dedicated cores.

In this paper we present two alternative versions of CCS-QCD that use tasks to multiplex MPI with computation on the same set of cores. In Sect. 2 we

© Springer International Publishing AG 2017
B.R. de Supinski et al. (Eds.): IWOMP 2017, LNCS 10468, pp. 77–91, 2017.
DOI: 10.1007/978-3-319-65578-9_6

describe the hardware and software used for the performance results. Section 3 describes CCS-QCD. Sections 4 and 5 present a OpenMP tasking implementation. Section 6 presents an alternate task-based implementation. Section 7 analyzes performance and compares the three implementation. Section 8 is conclusions and future work.

2   Hardware and Software

We used the following hardware and software for the results presented in this paper:

Processor: Intel® Xeon Phi™ 7250 processor with 68 cores, 1.4 GHz, 96 GiB DDR, 16 GiB MCDRAM.

Fabric: Intel® Omni-Path Architecture cards, cables, and switches with 100 Gb/sec theoretical bi-directional bandwidth.

Compilers: Intel® C++ Composer XE and Intel® Fortran Composer XE version 17.0.2.174.

OS: Linux 3.10.0-327.36.3.el7.xppsl_1.4.3.3482.x86_64, a Centos 7.2 kernel with patches for Intel® Xeon Phi™ processor support. The OS is booted with `nohz_full=1-271` which allows all OS CPUs except for CPU 0 to enter tickless mode, reducing the frequency of OS timer interrupts.

All runs were made using only 64 cores for compute and avoiding the first two cores for compute threads.

3   The CCS-QCD Benchmark

The CCS-QCD quark solver benchmark was developed at the Center for Computational Sciences (CCS) at the University of Tsukuba, Japan. It solves the Wilson-Clover quark propagator using a single precision BiCGStab solver.

The full solver consists of calls to the Wilson-Clover Dirac hopping matrix multiplication (called Mult in this paper), calls to BLAS-like routines, and calls to `MPI_Allreduce`. In this paper we discuss only the Mult routine, which takes approximately 65% of the total solver time.

Mult is a 4-dimensional 9-point stencil on a matrix of fermion sites. Each iteration of the nested stencil loop operates on a site, combining the fermion sites with the gauge links for each dimension. The data structures have been optimized for SIMD, so each site in the program consists of several sites from the lattice. The inner loop is highly optimized using AVX-512 intrinsics [3]. Similar techniques are described in the references from [1] and in [4].

We exploit the reuse inherent in the stencil by tiling the 4-dimensional loop nest to improve L2 locality. Thus the loop nest consists of four outer loops over the blocks followed by 4 inner loops over each tile.

MPI decomposition simply divides the iteration space in one or more dimensions. Boundaries in each distributed dimension are exchanged during each call to the Mult routine. We do not use explicit halo regions. Rather, the buffer for each surface is packed and sent, and the receive side applies the buffer to the corresponding surface in the post and final computations as described below.

Since the stencil is only ± 1 in each dimension, all of the inner sites can be computed without needing any data from other ranks. In other words, the interior computation can progress in parallel with the MPI data transfer. Figure 1 illustrates a three-dimensional 8^3 lattice.

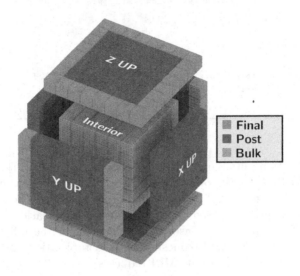

Fig. 1. 8^3 3d lattice showing interior (Interior), surfaces (Final+Post), post-computation (Post), and final computation (Final).

We therefore implement Mult in six phases:

1. Post asynchronous receives (`MPI_Irecv`)
2. Pack data for each surface into a buffer.
3. Send buffers to neighbors (`MPI_Isend`)
4. Compute the interior
5. Wait for the receives (and sends) to complete
6. Apply each recieve buffer to its corresponding surface.

In the initial implementation of the benchmark we assumed that the asynchronous MPI calls could progress independently of the interior computation, thus hiding some or all of the MPI time. We found two problems with this approach: First, the asynchronous MPI calls themselves take a noticable amount of time, and this time is completely serial. Second, MPI implementations often require calls into MPI in order to make progress; in this approach there are no calls into MPI while the interior computation is occurring.

We therefore decided to offload the MPI calls to a separate thread. The baseline version of the benchmark described in this paper uses this offload implementation. It turned out to be a relatively simple modification, using a simple

Listing 1. Taskloop replacement code

```
template<typename T> void
for_recursive(int low, int high, int grain, T body) {
tail_recurse:
    int count = high - low;
    if (count > grain) {
    int mid = low + count / 2;

    #pragma omp task for_recursive<T>(low, mid, grain, body);

    low = mid; goto tail_recurse;
    }
    body(low, high);
}
...
#pragma omp taskgroup for_recursive(0, n, 1, [=](low,high) {
for (int i = low; i < high; ++i)
    loop_body(i);
});
```

queue; the application puts requests on a queue and the offload thread executes them. Each MPI rank has its own offload thread. This thread is explicitly created with `pthread_create` and bound to the first two cores. The first two cores are excluded from the cores used by the rest of the application. This gives us a dedicated MPI "engine". We ensure MPI progress in the offload engine by alternately polling for new MPI requests from the application and polling MPI with `MPI_Test` calls for outstanding MPI requests.

4   Tasking Implementation

Because of the issues mentioned in the introduction we decided to explore an alternate approach to overlapping MPI and communication. Measurement shows that the offload MPI threads do relatively little work. If, instead, we can borrow one of the application threads when we need to perform MPI calls, and also use that thread to perform work while waiting for MPI to complete, we can avoid the awkwardness and overhead of MPI offload and also gain more flexibility in running multiple ranks per core.

As described in the previous section, the existing implementation has 6 phases. Phases 2, 4, and 6 are parallel regions. Phases 1 and 5 are serial regions. If we analyze the dependences between computations and MPI sends or receives, we can create a finer-grained dependence graph that allows more available parallelism without synchronization, as described below.

Note: The `taskloop` construct has not been optimized in the compiler we used, so instead we used a recursive divide-and-conquer construct as shown in Listing 1.

(1) The MPI send buffer for a given dimension and direction depends only on the corresponding surface. We call these surface computations the precomputations. In this step the surface consists of the full surface (Final+Post

in Fig. 1). The code for the pre-computation and send for each distributed dimension and direction DIR is:

```
#pragma omp task
{
    #pragma omp taskgroup
    for_recursive(0, DIR_nblocks, 1, [=](int low, int high) {
    for (int block = low; block < high; ++block) {
        pre_compute(DIR, block);
    }
    });        // for_recursive
    // implicit wait for taskgroup
    MPI_Isend(DIR_buf, ..., &req);
    MPI_Wait(&req);
} // task
```

(2) The interior computation is completely independent of both the pre- and post-computations, and is implemented with a single taskloop:

```
#pragma omp task
{
    for_recursive(0, nblocks, 1, [=](int low, int high) {
    for (int block = low; block < high; ++block) {
        bulk_compute(block);
    }
    });
}
```

(3) Each application of a received MPI buffer to its corresponding surface depends only on the receive for that dimension and direction. We call these surface computations the post-computations. The code for the receive and post-computation for distriibuted dimension and direction DIR is:

```
#pragma omp task
{
    // DIR_req is from irecv for dimension and direction DIR
    // posted outside of parallel region
    MPI_Wait(DIR_req);
    for_recursive(0, DIR_nblocks, 1, [=](int low, int high) {
    for (int block = low; block < high; ++block) {
        // post compute using buffer for DIR
        post_compute(DIR, block);
    }
    });        // for_recursive
}
```

We express these independent computations inside a single parallel region. The master thread spawns tasks for step (1) for each distributed dimension and direction, then spawns a task for step (2), then finally spawns tasks for step (3) for each distributed dimension and direction.

There is a minor problem in this revised formulation: It turns out that the post-computations are not completely independent. The post-computation iterations at the edges depend on buffers for more than one dimension. We handle this by constraining all the post-computations to the interiors of the surfaces, labelled as "Post" in Fig. 1. We then enclose all the post-computations in a taskgroup. When the taskgroup completes we spawn tasks to execute the final cleanup iterations for the edges, labelled as "Final" in the figure. The code modifies step (3) and adds an additional step as follows:

```
#pragma omp master
{
    #pragma omp taskgroup
    {
        // code from step (3) for each distributed direction and dimension
        ...
    }
    // implicit wait for taskgroup
    for (each final edge E) {
        #pragma omp task
        postcompute(E);
    }
}
```

The `postcompute` function takes the array bounds for the particular block to be computed. Note that the iterations for the post-computations themselves are blocked, as seen in the code for step (3); however, the final computations are not blocked. The extra code to block the final computations slowed the program down.

Finally, rather than calling the MPI functions directly as shown in the psuedo code, we instead poll the MPI library to allow other tasks to progress while waiting for MPI completions. We use an OpenMP lock to serialize access to the MPI library.[1] We poll on the lock and use the `taskyield` directive to execute other work while waiting for it to become available. Also, rather than calling `MPI_Wait` we poll on `MPI_Test` when waiting for completions.

5   Initial Performance Results

We ran the application on a 32^4 problem (distributed in up to 3 dimensions) using both the original version and the tasking version. Since the original version requires one extra core per MPI rank we ran it on only 1 and 2 MPI ranks per node.[2] We ran the tasking version on 1, 2, 4, and 8 ranks. We used one thread per core (in this and all runs).

The baseline version uses the static workstealing scheduler described in [2].

The data in Fig. 2 shows that there is negligible penalty for replacing the bulk Mult loop with tasks, even with two ranks per node. At 8 nodes, tasking with 8 ranks per node is faster than baseline, and with 4 ranks per node is equal to baseline. However, on fewer than eight nodes the performance is worse. To understand why, we profiled the 32^4 8 rank single node run. The data shows 89.5% of the time in the application code and 10.1% of the time in the OpenMP runtime. Much of the OpenMP runtime is in routines for task scheduling. We therefore initially assumed that part of the slowdown is due to overhead in the OpenMP task scheduling. This motivated us to rewrite the code to use our own tasking system, which we call *untasking*. This is described in the next section.

---

[1] The quality and even availablity of `MPI_THREAD_MULTIPLE` varies between implementations, and it is a good place for `taskyield`.

[2] Since there are 68 cores, we should have been able to run up to 4 MPI ranks per node, but we were unable to persuade the MPI implementation to avoid the first 4 cores.

Nodes	Ranks/Node	Baseline (seconds)	Tasking (seconds)
1	1	16.46	16.91
1	2	17.18	16.75
1	4		17.07
1	8		18.24
2	1	9.20	9.22
2	2	9.24	9.72
2	4		9.84
2	8		9.55
4	1	5.77	8.69
4	2	7.00	8.89
4	4		6.16
4	8		6.06
8	1	7.03	11.26
8	2	5.98	7.87
8	4		5.99
8	8		4.48

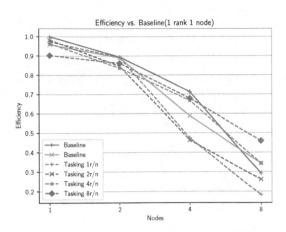

Fig. 2. Baseline vs. Tasking

6 Tasking by Hand, or Untasking

Careful consideration of the Mult algorithm reveals that the OpenMP tasking implementation can perform more work than is needed. The matrix sizes are determined by the problem size, which does not change during the run, and therefore the number of iterations for each computation phase is constant for the duration of the program. Also, we can describe each iteration with only three values: the iteration number, the phase (pre-computation, bulk, post-computation, final), and the direction (T, Z, Y, X up and down for pre- and post-computation phases).

Therefore, the only task type we need be concerned with is an iteration, which we describe with the following data structure:

```
enum { TaskPre = 0, TaskBulk = 1, TaskPost = 2, TaskFinal = 3 };
struct Task {
    unsigned int kind:2;      // phase
    unsigned int dir:3;       // direction
    int iter:27;              // iteration
};
```

We precompute several arrays of Task structs: one for each direction for each distributed dimension, which is used by both the pre- and the post-computation for that dimension and direction; one for the bulk computation; and one for the final computation. We also precompute a static distribution per thread for each of the arrays.

We use the Intel® Threading Building Blocks (Intel® TBB) concurrent queue class to implement a task stealing scheduler. There is one concurrent queue (declared as tbb::concurrent_queue<Task>) for each OpenMP thread. The task scheduling loop for a thread dequeues Tasks (iterations) from the thread's queue until the queue is empty, then searches all the queues looking for a task to steal.

Listing 2. Untask Master Thread

```
do {     // wait for pre-computations
  predone = 1;
  for (int dir = 0; dir < 8; ++dir) { // (up,down) for T,Z,Y,X direction
    if (dirDone(dir, pre)) continue;
    while (!dirDone(dir, pre) && taskQ[tid].pop(task))
      doTask(task)
    if (dirDone(dir, pre))
      MPI_Isend(buffer[dir], ...)
    else predone = 0;
  }
} while (!predone);
do {     // wait for receives and enqueue post-computations
  recvdone = 1;
  for (int dir = 0; dir < 8; ++dir) {
    if (dirDone(dir, recv)) continue;
    recvdone = 0;
    if (MPI_Test(req[dir],...))
      for (int j = 0; j < nthreads; ++j) {      // add post for this dir
        start = surfacedist[j][dir].start; n = surfacedist[j][dir].end;
        for (int i = start; i < start+n; ++i)
          taskQ[j].push(taskBuf[dir][i]);
      }
  }
} while (!recvdone);
do {     // wait for post-computations
  postdone = 1;
  for (int dir = 0; dir < 8; ++dir) { // (up,down) for T,Z,Y,X direction
    if (dirDone(dir, post)) continue;
    while (!dirDone(dir, post) && taskQ[tid].pop(task))
      doTask(task)
    else postdone = 0;
  }
} while (!postdone);
for (int j = 0; j < nthreads; ++j) {      // enqueue final iterations
  start = finaldist[j][dir].start; n = finaldist[j][dir].end;
  for (int i = start; i < end; ++i)
    taskQ[j].push(finalBuf[i])
} // fallthrough to execute tasks
```

The master thread posts all the receives with `MPI_Irecv` before entering the parallel region. This adds to the serial time but it is important to post the receives before the matching sends whenever possible to avoid extra overhead. Then, after entering the parallel region, each thread first enqueues all of its iterations from the static distribution for the pre-computations and the bulk computation. Then, the master thread enters the region in Listing 2, while the worker threads enter the task scheduling loop.

The master thread has a special role in the untasking implementation. It is used to enforce required dependences on MPI buffers, as well as executing tasks while waiting for dependences to be satisfied.

When enqueuing the pre-computations and bulk iterations, we make sure to enqueue the pre-computations first, since we want to get the MPI sends posted as quickly as possible to avoid delaying other ranks. The first loop in the master region repeatedly loops through the directions and checks to see if a direction is finished. If the direction is not finished the master thread executes iterations from its own queue until the iterations for that direction are finished, then calls `MPI_Isend` with the buffer for that direction. The loop continues until all pre-computations are complete.

To check that a given pre-computation direction is complete we maintain an atomic counter for each direction. As a thread completes an iteration for that direction, it increments the corresponding counter. The master thread reads the counter and compares it to the total number of iterations required for that direction.

After the master thread notes that all pre-computations are complete, it goes into another loop waiting for the receives for each direction to complete. We choose to execute no tasks during this loop so that we complete the receives as early as possible and so that we always have a thread active in the MPI library to ensure progress. As each receive completes, the master thread enqueues the iterations for the matching post-computation for all the threads.

Once the receives are all complete, the master thread loops waiting for each direction's post-computations to complete, as well as executing its own iterations while waiting.

Finally, when all the post-computations are complete, the master thread enqueues all the final iterations for all the threads, and then exits the master region to participate in completing all the remaining tasks.

7   Revised Performance Results

Figure 3 is a copy of Fig. 2 with the untasking results added. The untasking result with 8 ranks per node is the winner after two nodes. Strong scaling to 8 nodes is 55% efficient, vs. 46% for tasking and 34% for baseline.

Nodes	Ranks/ Node	Baseline (seconds)	Tasking (seconds)	Untasking (seconds)
1	1	16.46	16.91	16.18
1	2	17.18	16.75	16.18
1	4		17.07	16.34
1	8		18.24	17.36
2	1	9.20	9.22	8.59
2	2	9.24	9.72	8.61
2	4		9.84	9.22
2	8		9.55	8.80
4	1	5.77	8.69	6.10
4	2	7.00	8.89	6.61
4	4		6.16	5.34
4	8		6.06	5.29
8	1	7.03	11.26	6.73
8	2	5.98	7.87	5.53
8	4		5.99	4.55
8	8		4.48	3.73

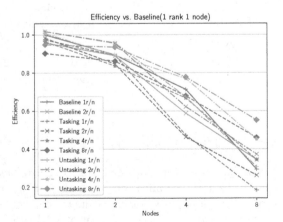

Fig. 3. Baseline, tasking, and untasking

It is useful to analyze strong scaling in more detail. As we double the number of nodes, the computational work per node is cut in half. The MPI traffic also changes, but the progression is more complicated and depends on the total number of ranks, not just the number of nodes. Further, some MPI traffic is internode and some is intranode and the ratio changes with the number of nodes and ranks. The general trend is toward more and smaller messages as the number of ranks increases, but the total message volume also gets larger since there is more exposed surface area.

When strong scaling, at some point the MPI time exceeds the computation time, and from there on the MPI time becomes an increasingly large portion of the total time. Performance analysis will help us to understand how the MPI time varies as we increase the number of nodes and change the number of ranks per node, how effective we are at hiding the MPI time, and how much time is spent not doing useful work (parallel overhead and load imbalance).

Table 1 shows one method of time accounting on the three different implementations on 2 and 8 nodes. The following three subsections describe the method used to analyze each implementation and the meanings of the table entries, then a final subsection has our interpretation of the results.

Table 1. Time accounting

Metric	Baseline		Tasking		Untasking	
	2×2	8×2	2×2	8×8	2×2	8×8
Work/thread (10^6 cycles)	10,680	3,684	9,416	2,709	10,759	3,554
MPI time (10^6 cycles)	3,760	5,281	3,870	3,881	3,992	1,611
Elapsed time (10^6 cycles)	12,938	8,379	13,276	6,390	11,885	5,006
MPI MB/node	31,394	12,558			31,394	18,837
MPI GB/sec/node	11.69	3.33			11.01	16.37
Work %	82.55	43.97	70.92	42.39	90.53	71.00
MPI %	0.36	34.96	4.35	27.47		
Overhead %			2.58	5.51	8.77	28.08
Unaccounted %	17.10	21.07	22.15	24.63	0.70	0.92
Imbal %	6.28	11.03	2.80	4.37	1.24	4.23

7.1 Baseline Timing Data

In the baseline code, the MPI work is performed asynchronously by the offload thread, and the application waits in a serial region for the offload thread to report completion. We measure the time spent in the application waiting for the offload thread. This is the amount of MPI time that was not hidden by the bulk computation. We estimate the work time using event-based sampling and count the samples in the Mult routine. Since this data is per-thread we can also use it to estimate imbalance.

work time	average over threads in Mult from event-base sampling
MPI time	total time in MPI offload thread
elapsed time	time in Mult on master thread
work %	work time / elapsed time
MPI %	exposed MPI time / elapsed time
unaccounted %	(elapsed time - (work time + exposed MPI time)) / elapsed time
imbal %	(max work time - min work time) / elapsed time

Some of the unaccounted time is explained by this load imbalance. More of the unaccounted time is due to OpenMP fork-join overhead; the baseline code has three separate parallel regions.

7.2   Tasking Timing Data

The tasking code was a challenge to instrument. The usual trick of estimating fork-join overhead and overall load imbalance by timing the threads inside the parallel region does not work here, because the threads are executing OpenMP tasks while waiting in the barrier. We ended up using two methods. First, each computational task is timed; the timing points are equivalent to those in the untasking code. Second, we used the OMPT `ompt_callback_idle` callback to measure the idle time.

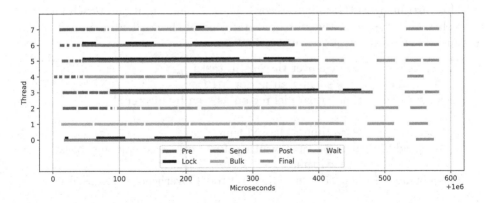

Fig. 4. Execution timeline for tasking

work	average over threads in computational tasks
MPI time	maximum time any thread spent waiting for MPI
elapsed time	time in parallel region as seen by master thread
work %	work time / elapsed time
MPI %	average MPI time per thread / elapsed time
overhead %	average idle time per thread / elapsed time
unaccounted %	(elapsed time - (work time + MPI time + overhead)) / elapsed time
imbal %	(max work time - min work time) / elapsed time

The unaccounted time is quite high, so to better understand the behavior we instrumented both the tasking and the untasking code to collect begin and end timestamps for the tasks and for the MPI communication. Figure 4 shows data for one Mult call at about one second into the computational portion of the benchmark for one MPI rank. We plot durations for each instance of the different task types as well as the total MPI send and wait (for receive) duration for each MPI instance. The time spent in the MPI lock routine (recall that it tests an OpenMP lock and issues `taskyield` if the lock is busy) is overlaid on the MPI operation in which it occurs.

7.3   Untasking Timing Data

We instrumented the untasking code to count the cycles spent executing tasks, waiting for work, and enqueing tasks. We also measured the time for each thread inside the parallel region, and the time on the master thread to execute each parallel region. This gives us a measure of OpenMP fork-join time. We also instrumented the master thread to measure MPI wait time. As with tasking, we also instrumented the code to record the start and duration of each instance of each untask type and the start and duration of the MPI wait loop (refer to Listing 2). This data is plotted in Fig. 5.

work	average over threads in tasks
MPI time	time spent waiting for MPI
elapsed time	time in parallel region as seen by master thread
work %	work time / elapsed time
overhead %	average time waiting for work + enqueuing tasks / elapsed time
unaccounted %	(elapsed time - (work time + overhead)) / elapsed time
imbalance %	(max work time - min work time) / elapsed time

We have high confidence in the untasking time accounting because of the tiny unaccounted time. The additional data in Fig. 5 helps us to understand where the idle portion of the overhead occurs.

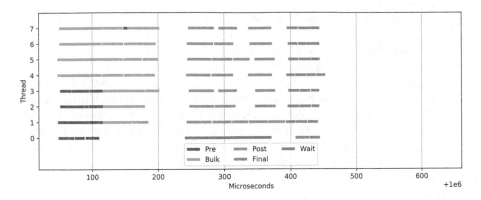

Fig. 5. Execution timeline for untasking

7.4   Comparison

Referring to Table 1 we can see that the amount of work performed by the baseline and untasking versions is very similar, as expected. When going from 2 to 8 nodes, we would hope for the work to decrease by a factor of 4, but it decreases by closer to a factor of 3. This is explained by the increased surface to volume ratio obtained by using more ranks.

The amount of work performed by the tasking code is about 10% less for 2 nodes and about 15% less for 8 nodes. This is not understood. The work measurement was confirmed by comparison with event sampling results, so the difference is real. More detailed analysis is required. Unfortunately, this reduced work does not lead to better performance.

We see that the MPI time increases from 2 to 8 nodes in the baseline case, even though the number of bytes per node decreases. In the untasking case, even though we are transferring more bytes per node, the MPI time decreases dramatically. This is explained by the increased parallelism afforded by 8 ranks per node.

In the tasking case, the MPI time as measured from within the code does not decrease as expected from 2 to 8 nodes. To see why we must refer again to Fig. 4. There are three long-duration send instances, and two long-duration wait instances. The expectation was that the lock calls, which include `taskyield`, would allow those threads to execute other tasks while waiting for the MPI lock. In practice the timeline data shows that even though several long-duration lock waits (with accompanying `taskyields`) occurred, no other tasks were executed during that time, thus only about half the threads were doing non-MPI work for much of the interval. Further, the MPI time, which includes the time waiting for the lock, is artificially inflated.

The MPI bandwidth numbers are somewhat misleading, as they do not distinguish between inter- and intra-node transfers, and also include any load imbalance that shows up as MPI wait time. However, they are a perfectly valid metric to compare different implementations, node counts, and rank layouts. The numbers are absent for the tasking code because we cannot measure MPI time accurately.

The poor scaling of the baseline case from 2 to 8 nodes is largely explained by the exposed MPI time of 34.96%.

In the untasking case we turn again to Fig. 5. There is almost a 100us gap from the time the last pre-iteration completes until the master thread starts waiting for receives to start the post-iterations. Careful examination of the code in Listing 2 reveals that the master thread does not call into the MPI library for every iteration of the send loop. We therefore suspect that some of this gap is due to delayed MPI progress. Some of it may also be due to the cost of the atomic counters used for synchronization.

Gaps in the post-iteration portion of the chart are expected due to delay in receiving messages from other ranks; this also leads to delay in starting the final iterations which are dependent on all the receives. There is about $10 \mu s$ of load imbalance because of the granularity of the post iterations (thread 1 is the laggard).

8 Conclusions and Future Work

With 8 nodes and 8 ranks per node, both the OpenMP tasking implementation and the untasking implementation outperform the baseline implementation, by 1.3x in the tasking case and 1.6x in the untasking case. The untasking implementation is 1.2x faster than the tasking implementation.

The detailed timeline of the OpenMP tasking implementation in Fig. 4 reveals that `taskyield` does not function as we expected it to. This is under investigation. Inspection of the figure suggests that the tasking implementation would perform much better if this were resolved.

We found that it was essential to collect not only summary times but traces of task execution in order to understand (and debug) the behavior. Because of the very fine granularity of the tasks in this benchmark (from 1000 to 50,000 cycles), collection overhead must be kept very low. We used inline hand instrumentation with the RDTSC instruction and stored all timestamps in memory, then dumped them to a file for each MPI rank. We continue to explore methods for incorporating such find-grained low-overhead instrumentation into more general-purpose tools. A high-quality interactive viewer for general timeline data would have been welcome.

The baseline implementation is able to use cooperative hierarchical threading, where threads on a core cooperate on the same tiled loop iteration (described by Meadows et al. in [2]). We did not use this method in the OpenMP tasking implementation, and therefore used only one thread per core. For fair comparison we used only one thread per core in the baseline and untasking runs. Running with only one thread per core reduced the performance of the baseline code. In the untasking implementation it would be possible to add hierarchical threading, since we have complete control over threading and task execution. In the OpenMP tasking implementation, we would have to use nested OpenMP within each task, and the overhead is prohibitive at this granularity.

CCS-QCD is still somewhat slower than the best LQCD implementations (Peter Boyle's Grid in [5] and QphiX in [4]) on Intel® Xeon Phi^{TM} processors, and falls short of the processor's best micro-architectural performance for this code. An alternative implementation that uses a different tiling strategy and better prefetching should allow us to improve performance when using one thread per core while also making the tasks larger, reducing the impact of task scheduling overhead.

References

1. Boku, T., Ishikawa, K.I., Kuramashi, Y., Meadows, L., D'Mello, M., Troute, M., Vemuri, R.: A performance evaluation of CCS QCD Benchmark on the COMA (Intel(R) Xeon Phi^{TM}, KNC) system. In: PoS LATTICE 2016, vol. 261 arXiv:1612.06556 [hep-lat] (2016)
2. Meadows, L., Pennycook, S.J., Duran, A., Wilmarth, T., Cownie, J.: Workstealing and nested parallelism in SMP systems. In: Maruyama, N., Supinski, B.R., Wahib, M. (eds.) IWOMP 2016. LNCS, vol. 9903, pp. 47–60. Springer, Cham (2016). doi:10.1007/978-3-319-45550-1_4
3. Intel Corporation: Intel® Advanced Vector Extensions 512 (Intel® AVX-512), Intel® 64 and IA-32 Architectures Software Developer's Manual, Order Number 325462–061US, Intel Corporation, Section 5.19., December 2016
4. Kalamkar, D.D., Smelyanskiy, M., Farber, R., Vaidyanathan, K.: Quantum chromodynamics (QCD). In: Intel Xeon Phi Processor High Performance Programming Knights Landing Edition, chap. 26, pp. 581–598. Morgan Kaufmann (2016)
5. Boyle, P.: Grid: data parallel C++ mathematical object library. https://github.com/paboyle/Grid

On the Performance of Parallel Tasking Runtimes for an Irregular Fast Multipole Method Application

Patrick Atkinson$^{(\boxtimes)}$ and Simon McIntosh-Smith

Merchant Venturers Building, Woodland Road, Bristol BS8 1UB, UK
{p.atkinson,simonm}@bristol.ac.uk

Abstract. This paper will present our work on optimising and comparing the performance of an irregular algorithm for the increasingly important fast multipole method with the use of tasks. Our aim is to provide insight into how different methods of synchronisation can affect the performance of tree-based particle methods, finding that performance can be improved by 21% on some platforms. We also compare the performance of the chosen application between different OpenMP implementations and to other task-parallel programming models, finding that significant performance differences can be observed on both NUMA and Many Integrated Core architectures.

Keywords: OpenMP · Tasks · Mini-apps · Locks · Atomics

1 Introduction

Introduced in 2007, OpenMP tasks have allowed for the simplification of expressing parallel execution of irregular problems, such as divide and conquer algorithms. The mapping of tasks to threads is non-deterministic and the scheduling efficiency is highly dependant on the underlying runtime. The availability of different OpenMP implementations and other similar task-parallel programming models, such as OmpSs [1], Intel Threading Building Blocks [2], and Cilk [3], has given application developers many options to choose from, whilst differences in scheduling techniques and the features provided has lead to differences in performance.

As the tasks constructs in the OpenMP standard have been expanded and matured in the past 10 years, the level of parallelism in current architectures has increased dramatically. Non-unified Memory Access (NUMA) architectures are now commonplace in high performance systems, with current generation Intel architectures comprising of as many as 22 cores per socket. In addition to NUMA architectures, the introduction of many integrated core architectures, such as the 72 core Intel Knights Landing chip, has demonstrated the need for low-overhead and scalable parallel runtimes.

In addition to simplifying the expression of irregular problems, task-parallelism has the potential to increase performance on systems with large

© Springer International Publishing AG 2017
B.R. de Supinski et al. (Eds.): IWOMP 2017, LNCS 10468, pp. 92–106, 2017.
DOI: 10.1007/978-3-319-65578-9_7

numbers of cores. Using fine-grained parallelism by way of task dependencies, tasks are only executed when the specific data they operate on is available. This is in contrast to conventional OpenMP programs that make use of fork-join constructs whereby steps of an algorithm are executed in a series of parallel for-loops, whilst a task-based approach would allow for each step to overlap and correctness assured through the programmer's use of task-dependencies.

OpenMP has become the de facto standard for thread-parallelism in HPC, with a large range of different implementations from groups such as Intel, GNU, and Cray; it has become a simple and powerful way to parallelise both existing and new applications. It is not the only parallel programming model that offers task-parallelism however. Cilk [3], TBB [2], StarPU [4], OmpSs [1], Kokkos [5], and even the C++11 standard all now offer task constructs, giving an application developer a wide range of options. However, there is also great uncertainty in which models provide both the richest and the most convenient APIs, while also offering the greatest performance on modern, highly parallel architectures.

This paper will present a comparison of a range of different programming models and OpenMP implementations using a representative application, known as a 'mini-app'. Mini-apps are scaled-down applications that capture the performance characteristics of real scientific codes; they are commonly used to rapidly compare and test both programming models and architectures [6]. Currently however, few mini-apps exist that can make good use of tasks and can be used to assess current tasking programming models. Hence, the comparison will be performed using a new Fast Multipole Method mini-app, MiniFMM[1], developed at the University of Bristol. The method works primarily around a tree traversal algorithm and can exhibit high load imbalance, thus providing an interesting real application to compare and test tasking performance.

The outline of the paper is as follows: Sect. 3 briefly describes the FMM and details of the particular variant used, Sect. 4 gives details of the OpenMP implementation and discusses the challenges faced using the tasking model with FMM, Sect. 5 gives an overview of differences in OpenMP implementations and similar programming models, Sect. 6 provides a comparison and discussion of the different programming models, and Sect. 7 concludes the paper describing how the results can be generalised and applied to other task-based methods to improve performance.

2 Background and Related Work

Previous work has shown the significant design and performance differences between OpenMP implementations. Most work has focused on comparing the performance and runtime execution characteristics of micro-benchmarks, such as computing Fibonacci numbers and sorting arrays. Olivier et al. [7] had previously compared the parallel performance of OpenMP tasks using the BOTS benchmark suite [8], finding that the overhead costs and idle thread times varied greatly between benchmarks. This work was then extended by Virouleau et al.

---

[1] https://github.com/uob-hpc/minifmm.

who looked at the KASTORS benchmark suite from BSC [9], which examined the performance of tasks with data dependencies, finding that the performance of some of the benchmarks could be impacted by the OpenMP runtime used. Whilst these benchmarks have provided key insights, the aim of this paper is to examine how the performance of a representative application is affected by both parallel overheads and runtime decisions.

Previous efforts to parallelise the fast multipole method (FMM) have shown that task-based approaches provide large performance benefits. The tree-traversal algorithm designed by Yakota et al. [10] was initially implemented with tasking features from Intel TBB and large performance improvements were gained over similar methods. Following on from this, Pericas et al. [11] extended this work by implementing the tree-traversal step using tasks with data-dependencies in OpenMP, finding only minor performance improvements could be gained. Making use of extra data-dependency constructs available in StarPU, Agullo et al. [12], found that performance could be improved over OpenMP.

3 Method Overview

The FMM has many uses in the fields of physics and computational mathematics, including calculating gravitational/electrostatic forces, fluid dynamics, plasma simulation, and acoustics [13]. Fundamentally, the algorithm provides a linear time approximation to $O(n^2)$ problems and allows for tunable precision of results. It works by grouping particles via a space partitioning tree (such as an octree), where groups of particles are located at each tree node. As in the N-body problem, each particle will need to calculate the force due to all other particles in the system. The difference using the FMM is that particles are compared group to group; each target group of particles is compared to all other nodes in the tree, resulting in two outcomes:

1. If the two nodes are far enough away, the force contribution for a source node can be approximated for the target node.
2. Else the forces for each particle will be calculated directly.

If the force contribution can be approximated, then the target doesn't need to consider any tree node below that source node. This has the very important property of the application's control flow not being known until runtime; the control flow is data-dependant. It is also of note that the application is compute-bound due to the high FLOP/byte ratio of directly computing the forces of particles in nodes that are close together.

The Dual Tree Traversal method for FMM, devised by Yakota and Dehnen [10], has been shown to be an efficient tree traversal method that also allows user control over the distance required to approximate node interactions, hence greater control over the precision of the final results. It is worth noting that other FMM implementations exist that do not allow for control over the distance at which approximations are made; this affects the implementation when using tasks and is outlined further in Sect. 4.1. Pseudo-code for the tree traversal is shown in Listing 1.1.

```
dtt(node source, node target)
{
  // calculate distance between source and target
  ...

  if (source and target well separated)
    approximate_force(source, target)

  else if (is_leaf(source) && is_leaf(target))
    direct_force(source, target)

  else
  {
    if (source.radius > target.radius)
      for (child in target)
        dtt(child, source)

    else
      for (child in source)
        dtt(target, child)
  }
}
```

Listing 1.1. Dual Tree Traversal

All of the results collected in this paper are run with an input of $O(10^6)$ particles uniformly distributed inside a box. At the finest level of the tree structure, the maximum number of particles per node is set to 300. These input parameters were selected to match those seen in previous work [10, 11]. Unless stated, all tests are performed using double precision values.

4   Implementation Overview

As the method evaluates all pairs of nodes in the tree, it is possible for two threads to be calculating the force contribution for the same target node. In OpenMP, task dependencies, atomics, and locks can all be used to ensure correctness. This section will detail efforts to increase performance of synchronisation in a task-based application using the architectures listed in Table 1 and using the Intel C Compiler (17.0).

4.1   Task Dependencies

Using task dependencies introduced in the OpenMP 4.0 standard, we can avoid memory read/write conflicts. However, optimal performance won't be achieved for two reasons. Firstly, task dependencies are resolved in the order in which tasks are created, hence an unnecessary ordering on tasks is enforced; the fast multipole method permits updating particle values in any order. Secondly, the work of finding the distance between nodes and deciding whether to approximate or calculate the force directly and creating a task to do so, is too great for a single thread to perform whilst issuing enough tasks to saturate the other threads with work, hence the entire computation is stalled by the thread issuing tasks. With large numbers of threads this can cause a severe bottleneck; running on 256 threads of a KNL and using data-dependencies in this way results in performance that is ~22x slower than alternatives and as such a parallel traversal is required. However, using a parallel traversal with data-dependencies has the issue of task dependencies only being enforced for the immediate child tasks of the current task, hence data conflicts would not be enforced across threads.

4.2   Atomics

An alternative to task dependencies would be to make the accumulations within a task be atomic operations. Hence, for both the direct and approximate calculations, the force updates are applied atomically for each particle. As the force calculations are over all particles in a node, this can mean many atomic operations are required. In addition, the method requires complex numbers (added to C standard in ISO C99) and built-in complex data-type atomic operations are not supported within OpenMP, hence separate arrays of real and imaginary types are required instead.

4.3   Locks

Another option would be to create a lock for every node in the tree, then lock and unlock a node to update the entire group of particles inside a node.

Which of these two options (locks or atomics) performs better depends entirely on the execution of the method. Atomically updating the forces for each particle introduces a fixed overhead compared to locks, however, high lock contention will cause large amounts of idle thread time. As can be seen in Fig. 1a, using atomics results in superior performance on Broadwell for both single and double precision data. However, on Intel Xeon Phi Knights Landing (KNL), Fig. 1b shows that double precision performance is roughly equivalent, whilst locks outperform atomics for single precision.

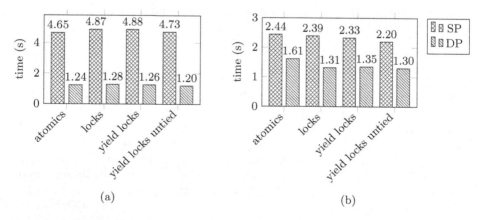

Fig. 1. Comparison of synchronisation methods on (a) two sockets of 22-core Broadwell (b) 64-core Xeon Phi Knights Landing

It is also possible to improve the performance of locks when combined with task constructs in OpenMP. Introduced by Chalk [14], the use of `taskyield` when a task cannot acquire a lock, shown in Fig. 1.2, as opposed to using `omp_set_lock`, can dramatically improve performance. Essentially, a thread executing a task tries to acquire a lock and if it is unsuccessful, a task scheduling point is reached, allowing for the runtime to suspend the execution of the current task. This allows the executing thread to do other work in the hope that when the task execution is resumed, the lock can now be acquired. In Figs. 1a and b, this method is referred to as 'yield lock' and, as can be seen, this alone has little effect when compared to `omp_set_lock`. However, when combined with untied tasks, i.e. `pragma omp task untied`, the performance difference is noticeably improved. The use of the **untied** keyword allows for any thread to resume the execution of a suspended task. Whilst it was measured to have no performance impact when combined with atomics or `omp_set_lock`, using untied tasks in conjunction with `taskyield` and locks leads to a performance increase ('yield locks untied' in Figs. 1a and b). This is due to threads being able to resume tasks that were suspended by another thread when a lock could not be acquired; overall this leads to better load balance of tasks.

```
int locked = 0;
while (!locked)
{
    locked = omp_test_lock(&target->lock);
    if (!locked)
    {
        #pragma omp taskyield
    }
}
```

Listing 1.2. Locking with taskyield

Instead of using a single lock per tree node, two locks could also be used. One to prevent a race condition on the approximate force accumulation and one to prevent the race condition on the direct force accumulation. Using two locks, the same synchronisation methods were tested and the results are displayed in Figs. 2a and b. Overall, this results in the best performance as lock contention was reduced, however some interesting effects were observed. Firstly, there is little benefit gained from the use of #taskyield lock variant on Broadwell. This is because as lock contention is lower, the #taskyield is less likely to be encountered. Whilst on KNL, higher thread counts result in high enough lock contention that the use of #taskyield is still marginally beneficial when using double-precision values. The use of **untied** tasks generally results in worse performance when using two locks.

From these results it was concluded that if you have highly contended locks, as in the case where a single lock was used per tree node, then there are performance benefits from using 'yield locks' and **untied** tasks. In contrast, with locks that have lower contention, these keywords aren't needed and can result in the same or even worse performance.

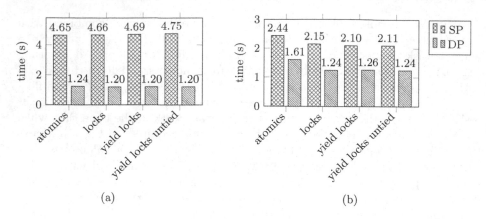

Fig. 2. Comparison of synchronisation methods using two locks per tree node on (a) two sockets of 22-core Broadwell (b) 64-core Xeon Phi Knights Landing

Another attempt to optimise lock performance was to specify the lock implementation via the `omp_init_lock_with_hint` function added in OpenMP 4.5. This allows a user to request a lock optimised for high contention (`uncontended/contended`) and/or speculative locks. It was found that in all cases `uncontended` locks performed worse than `contended`, and whilst speculative locks are supported on Intel Xeon CPUs (but not Xeon Phi), the use of the hint had no effect. The ability to specify the lock implementation was only available in the Intel OpenMP implementation, whilst the Cray compiler and GCC lacked this feature.

Whilst this alternative to task dependencies, referred to as 'conflicts' in Chalk [14], could be added to the OpenMP standard as a task clause, it can be seen that in this application, there is not a definitive method to implementing 'conflicts'; as seen in Fig. 1a, atomics still outperform the alternatives when using double precision values in the mini-app, whilst locking with `taskyield` and untied tasks perform better in other cases.

4.4   Extensions to Task Dependencies

Programming models such as OmpSs and StarPU have the ability to declare commutative task dependencies. This feature allows for the specified data locations to be updated in any order, regardless of the order the tasks were issued. This is in contrast to data dependencies in OpenMP, where for a data dependency, the order in which tasks are created is the order in which the tasks have to be executed. Hence, commutative task dependencies provide benefits to applications such as fast multipole; however, due to having to perform a parallel tree traversal, the data dependencies won't be enforced for all threads (as in Sect. 4.1).

4.5   Comparison Baseline

In contrast to a task-based approach, the algorithm can also be implemented in a thread-parallel fashion. This is done by recursing down the tree and instead of issuing tasks, we record whether to perform the direct or approximate force calculation for the current node. Then, each node can be iterated over in a `parallel for` loop, performing the required operations. A dynamic schedule was found to be optimal due to the high load imbalance between the number of operations each node needed to perform. This has the advantage of avoiding the race condition in that no two threads will write to the same target node. However, using tasks still has a number of advantages. Firstly, there's an overhead cost of initially building the list of nodes needing to be operated on per thread; a small cost in performance, which can dramatically increase memory usage; in the worst case each node will store a list of all other nodes in the tree. When implemented, this thread-parallel version tripled the number of lines of code compared to the task-based approach of the tree traversal. Therefore, whilst it is possible that the task-based approach may not offer a significant performance increase over this approach, a runtime that is able to match the performance of a thread-parallel implementation will be deemed a success, demonstrating tasking can reduce code size without impacting performance. However, due to the overhead of initially finding the lists of interactions, it was hoped that tasking implementations could be slightly faster than the thread-parallel equivalent. This thread-parallel implementation of the algorithm is referred to as the 'loop' implementation of the algorithm for the remainder of the paper.

To compare to other FMM implementations we profiled the task-parallel method, observing that 96% of the runtime was spent calculating the forces directly. Counting the number of interactions between particles and knowing the number of FLOPs per interaction tells us the compute performance achieved in the direct force calculation, which was measured to be approximately 882 DP GFLOPs on the dual socket Broadwell CPU. Comparing this to previous work [10] (and to the peak FLOPs) would indicate that the mini-app was both representative of larger FMM applications and achieved reasonable performance.

5   Programming Models

This section briefly introduces each of the programming models used in the comparison and discusses key features identified in each.

OmpSs - OmpSs provides a testing ground for new OpenMP features, and has previously motivated changes to the OpenMP standard, such as task data-dependencies. The OmpSs programming model is syntactically similar to OpenMP and provides both a compiler that allows for additional task extensions as well as a runtime system. For our tests we are using the Intel compiler backend (17.0) for OmpSs [1].

BOLT - BOLT stands for 'BOLT is OpenMP over Lightweight Threads'. From Argonne National Laboratory, the BOLT project aims to provide a lightweight threading runtime based on the LLVM OpenMP runtime [15]. In contrast to current OpenMP implementations based on OS-level threads, BOLT aims to use light-weight threads, provided by Argobots [15], to improve performance.

Intel Cilk Plus - Built as an extension to Cilk++, Cilk plus provides a simple interface of three keywords that enable task and data parallelism. The scheduling policy has been shown to provide load balance close to optimal [3].

Intel TBB - An object-oriented C++ runtime library, Intel TBB maintains a double-ended queue per thread, retrieving new tasks from the back of its queue to exploit temporal locality. If a thread has finished its work, it steals from the front of another thread's queue [2].

OpenMP - Previous work has highlighted some of the implementation decisions of each of the OpenMP runtimes finding that, depending on the architecture, significant performance differences can be observed. For example, the Intel implementation maintains a task queue per thread as opposed to a single task queue for all threads (as in GNU OpenMP). This has the effect of improving data locality by allowing threads to enqueue tasks on each thread's own queue first, in the hope that data can be reused from recently executed tasks.

Table 1. Target machines

	Broadwell	KNL
Processor	Xeon E5-2699 v4	Xeon Phi 7210
Sockets	2	-
Total cores	22	64
Total threads	44	256
Total TFLOPS	1.54	2.66

6   Results

The performance evaluation was conducted on two of the most recently released architectures. This was done to both reflect current devices in some of the largest supercomputers and to examine the performance characteristics of different task-parallel runtimes with both high numbers of threads and NUMA architectures. The details of the target machines appear in Table 1. The results were obtained with both Hyper-Threading turned on and off for Broadwell, whilst on KNL three different configurations were tested with 1, 2, or 4 threads per core.

For the results, the Intel Compiler (17.0) was used for OpenMP, TBB, Cilk, and the OpenMP parallel loop version of the algorithm. GCC 6.3 and Cray CCE 8.5.8 were used for the OpenMP GNU and Cray results respectively. The OmpSs version used was 16.06.3.

6.1   Broadwell

Figures 3 and 4 show the parallel speedup when increasing the number of cores and, as can be seen, the different programming models and runtimes exhibit similar scaling performance. The GNU and Cray OpenMP implementations exhibit

Table 2. Serial and fastest runtimes achieved using Broadwell

	OpenMP					OmpSs	Cilk	TBB
	Intel	GNU	Cray	BOLT	Loop			
Serial (s)	156.057	157.365	154.120	156.170	156.721	157.855	156.100	156.825
Parallel (s)	4.654	4.843	4.871	4.656	4.654	4.719	4.632	4.745

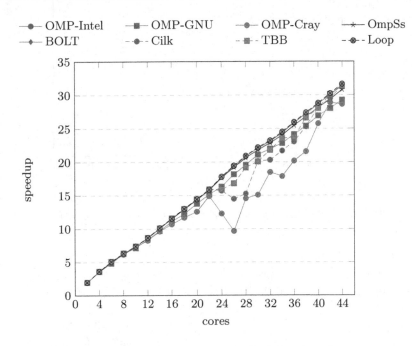

Fig. 3. Parallel speedup on Broadwell with 1 thread per core

the poorest parallel times, whilst the serial times do not differ from the other frameworks. The Intel OpenMP runtime performs well however and was consistently measured, along with Cilk, to give the best performance (Table 2).

The BOLT OpenMP implementation exhibits very similar performance to the Intel OpenMP implementation. This could be due to the Intel OpenMP runtime being open-sourced and used as the OpenMP backend for LLVM, on which BOLT is based. Cilk exhibits good performance on both Broadwell and KNL, being the fastest on both architectures - this is impressive because of its relatively small feature-set. Intel TBB achieves reasonable performance on both targets, but slightly lags behind other Intel runtime implementations.

The majority of the runtimes compete with the baseline parallel loop implementation (as described in Sect. 4.5) when using tasking, hence for this CPU architecture, tasks provide a scalable and efficient way to parallelise the mini-app whilst reducing the amount of code.

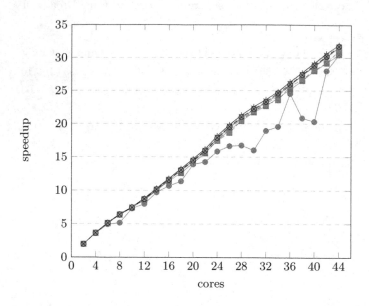

Fig. 4. Parallel speedup on Broadwell with 2 threads per core

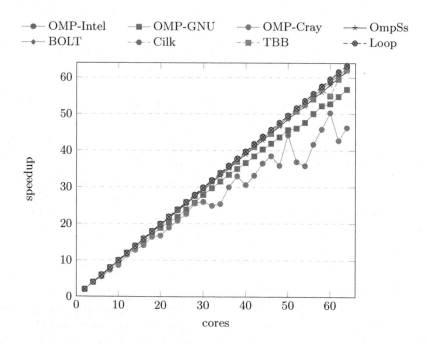

Fig. 5. Parallel speedup on KNL with 1 thread per core

Table 3. Serial and fastest runtimes achieved using KNL

	OpenMP							
	Intel	GNU	Cray	BOLT	Loop	OmpSs	Cilk	TBB
Serial (s)	181.385	199.271	185.728	181.401	175.975	190.622	181.272	181.371
Parallel (s)	2.059	3.508	3.224	2.054	1.949	2.192	2.010	2.533

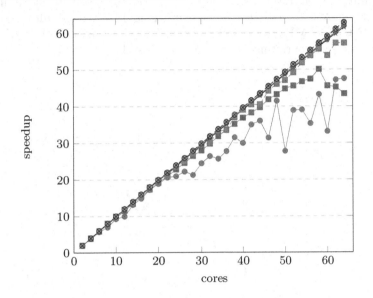

Fig. 6. Parallel speedup on KNL with 2 threads per core

6.2 Knights Landing

On KNL the performance of tasks in all frameworks were slightly worse than the parallel loop implementation. The Intel and Bolt OpenMP runtimes performed the best when running the task parallel approach, yet the parallel loop method was 1.05x faster. Most runtimes achieved similar performance when running with a single thread per core, however, running 2 and 4 Hyper-Threads per core highlighted the weakness in some of the other runtimes. The Intel implementation of OpenMP and Cilk both exhibited good scaling with high numbers of threads whilst TBB lagged slightly behind. However, the Cray OpenMP implementation exhibited poor scaling with all three thread configurations and gave poorer performance as the number of threads per core increased (Table 3).

The GNU OpenMP runtime actually results in a degradation in performance as more threads are added. Whilst initially showing good performance in Fig. 5, it can be seen that performance starts to degrade when using two Hyper-Threads per core (Fig. 6). Then finally with 4 Hyper-Threads per core (Fig. 7), the runtime of the application becomes severely limited when the number of threads used increases.

Initially the performance of OmpSs on KNL was extremely limited and with 256 threads was roughly 10x slower than the parallel loop implementation of the method. This is due to the default scheduler being unsuitable for many-integrated core architectures as it maintains a single global ready queue for tasks, which causes high contention on this data-structure when utilising large numbers of threads. Instead, the distributed breadth-first scheduler was used. This scheduler maintains a task queue per thread and work-steals, resulting in performance similar to the other implementations. Like the default scheduler in OmpSs, GNU OpenMP also maintains a single task queue for all threads, thus explaining the poor performance seen in Figs. 6 and 7.

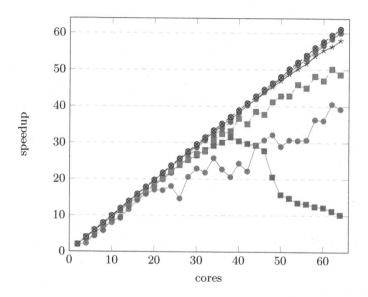

Fig. 7. Parallel speedup on KNL with 4 threads per core

7 Conclusion

The OpenMP tasking constructs were designed to allow users to easily express the parallelism of recursive and irregular algorithms. In terms of productivity, OpenMP task features were a simple and powerful way to parallelise the mini-app, drastically reducing the code required compared to the parallel loop implementation.

Using our FMM mini-app, we have looked at how task synchronisation can be improved for particle methods by comparing atomics and various ways of using locks in OpenMP, finding that performance can be improved by up to 21% on KNL whilst also bringing improvements on Xeon CPUs.

A common pattern in N-body, finite element, and unstructured mesh applications is to have data locations receiving multiple, unordered contributions. Hence, the work done on examining synchronisation features in OpenMP could be generalised and applied to a wide range of applications.

In addition to examining language features, we also compared OpenMP implementations to each other and to other task-parallel programming models. We found that on Broadwell, most programming models and OpenMP implementations performed well, competing with an equivalent parallel loop implementation. However, on KNL we found that a parallel loop implementation outperformed all task implementations of the method. Therefore, future work will focus on understanding this difference and investigating solutions to improving task performance on this platform.

This work builds upon the success of previous mini-app work within the HPC group at the University of Bristol [16], demonstrating that mini-apps are powerful tools to both compare and test different programming models, as well as investigate different language features that can lead to increased performance for a more general set of applications.

Acknowledgements. The authors would like the thank EPSRC for funding this work, as well as Bristol's Intel Parallel Computing Centre (IPCC) for access to the KNL platform. We would also like to thank GW4 for access to the Isambard supercomputer for Broadwell results.

References

1. Duran, A., Ayguad, E., Badia, R.M., Labarta, J., Martinell, L., Martorell, X., Planas, J.: OMPSS: a proposal for programming heterogeneous multi-core architectures. Parallel Process. Lett. **21**(02), 173–193 (2011). http://www.worldscientific. com/doi/abs/10.1142/S0129626411000151
2. Kim, W., Voss, M.: Multicore desktop programming with intel threading building blocks. IEEE Softw. **28**(1), 23–31 (2011)
3. Blumofe, R.D., Leiserson, C.E.: Scheduling multithreaded computations by work stealing. J. ACM **46**(5), 720–748 (1999). http://doi.acm.org/10.1145/324133. 324234
4. Augonnet, C., Thibault, S., Namyst, R., Wacrenier, P.-A.: StarPU: a unified platform for task scheduling on heterogeneous multicore architectures. Concurr. Comput. Pract. Exp. **23**(2), 187–198 (2011). http://dx.doi.org/10.1002/cpe.1631
5. Edwards, H.C., Sunderland, D.: Kokkos array performance-portable manycore programming model. In: Proceedings of the 2012 International Workshop on Programming Models and Applications for Multicores and Manycores (PMAM 2012), pp. 1–10. ACM (2012)
6. Heroux, M.A., Doerfler, D.W., Crozier, P.S., Willenbring, J.M., Edwards, H.C., Williams, A., Rajan, M., Keiter, E.R., Thornquist, H.K., Numrich, R.W.: Improving Performance via Mini-applications, Sandia National Laboratories, Technical report SAND2009-5574 (2009)

7. Olivier, S.L., de Supinski, B.R., Schulz, M., Prins, J.F.: Characterizing and mitigating work time inflation in task parallel programs. In: Proceedings of the International Conference on High Performance Computing, Networking, Storage and Analysis, ser. SC 2012, pp. 65:1–65:12. IEEE Computer Society Press, Los Alamitos (2012). http://dl.acm.org/citation.cfm?id=2388996.2389085

8. Duran, A., Teruel, X., Ferrer, R., Martorell, X., Ayguade, E.: Barcelona openMP tasks suite: a set of benchmarks targeting the exploitation of task parallelism in openMP. In: 2009 International Conference on Parallel Processing, pp. 124–131, September 2009

9. Virouleau, P., Brunet, P., Broquedis, F., Furmento, N., Thibault, S., Aumage, O., Gautier, T.: Evaluation of OpenMP Dependent Tasks with the KASTORS Benchmark Suite, pp. 16–29. Springer, Cham (2014). http://dx.doi.org/10.1007/978-3-319-11454-5_2

10. Yokota, R.: An FMM based on dual tree traversal for many-core architectures **7**(3), 301–324. http://journals.sagepub.com/doi/abs/10.1260/1748-3018.7.3.301

11. Miquel, P., Abdelhalim, A., Keisuke, F., Naoya, M., Rio, Y., Satoshi, M.: Towards a dataflow FMM using the OMPSS programming model **12** (2012). http://id.nii.ac.jp/0606/00073141

12. Agullo, E., Aumage, O., Bramas, B., Coulaud, O., Pitoiset, S.: Bridging the gap between openMP and task-based runtime systems for the fast multipole method. IEEE Trans. Parallel Distrib. Syst. **PP**(99) 1 (2017)

13. Greengard, L.F.: The Rapid Evaluation of Potential Fields in Particle Systems (ACM Distinguished Dissertation). The MIT Press, Cambridge (1988)

14. Aidan Chalk, A.M.E., Mason, L.: Task-based parallelism in DL POLY 4 (2017). http://staging.ixpug.org/documents/1491984172IXPUG_Spring_2017_paper_13(1).pdf

15. Argonne National Laboratory: Bolt is openMP over lightweight threads. http://www.bolt-omp.org/

16. Martineau, M., McIntosh-Smith, S., Gaudin, W.: Evaluating openMP 4.0's effectiveness as a heterogeneous parallel programming model. In: 2016 IEEE International Parallel and Distributed Processing Symposium Workshops (IPDPSW), pp. 338–347, May 2016

Porting VASP from MPI
to MPI+OpenMP [SIMD]
Optimization Strategies, Insights and Feature Proposals

Florian Wende[1]([✉]), Martijn Marsman[2], Zhengji Zhao[3], and Jeongnim Kim[4]

[1] Zuse Institute Berlin, Berlin, Germany
wende@zib.de
[2] University of Vienna, Vienna, Austria
martijn.marsman@univie.ac.at
[3] National Energy Research Scientific Computing Center, Berkeley, USA
zzhao@lbl.gov
[4] Intel Corporation, Hillsboro, USA
jeongnim.kim@intel.com

Abstract. We describe for the VASP application (a widely used electronic structure code written in FORTRAN) the transition from an MPI-only to a hybrid code base leveraging the three relevant levels of parallelism to be addressed when optimizing for an effective execution on modern computer platforms: multiprocessing, multithreading and SIMD vectorization. To achieve code portability, we draw on MPI parallelization together with OpenMP threading and SIMD constructs. Combining the latter can be challenging in complex code bases. Optimization targets are combining multithreading and vectorization in different calling contexts as well as whole function vectorization. In addition to outlining design decisions made throughout the code transformation process, we will demonstrate the effectiveness of the code adaptations using different compilers (GNU, Intel) and target platforms (CPU, Intel Xeon Phi (KNL)).

1 Introduction

Computational electronic structure (ES) methods are indispensable tools in materials research, in search of novel materials for battery energy storage and quantum computing as well as in understanding fundamental materials properties. The *Vienna Ab-initio Simulation Package* (VASP) [1,2] is a state-of-the-art parallel ES code, supporting a wide range of electronic structure methods, from Density-Functional-Theory (DFT), Hartree-Fock (HF) and hybrid (HF/DFT) functionals, to the many-body-perturbative approaches based on the random-phase-approximation (GW and ACFDT) [3–5]. Distributed parallel computers and the MPI programming model have been critical from the beginning for VASP to solve bigger and complex materials problems faster.

The recent increase in computing power is largely driven by the parallelism on a shared-memory processor (SMP) through many cores and (hardware) threads, and wide SIMD vector units. For instance, the second generation Intel® Xeon Phi™

© Springer International Publishing AG 2017
B.R. de Supinski et al. (Eds.): IWOMP 2017, LNCS 10468, pp. 107–122, 2017.
DOI: 10.1007/978-3-319-65578-9_8

processor, formerly code named Knights Landing (KNL) [6], has up to 72 cores, 4 hardware threads and two 512-bit wide SIMD units per core, and up to 16 GB of high bandwidth memory. However, treating each core as a distributed memory node and relying on MPI only can incur high overhead in terms of memory use and communication, leaving a lot of performance on the table. OpenMP, the standard SMP parallel programming model, provides attractive solutions for VASP to increase the performance through multithreading and SIMD vectorization, all enabled by optimizing compilers and runtime.

Transforming VASP to better exploit modern processors by introducing additional levels of parallelism is challenging: the organically grown VASP contains 100 k lines of code spread across hundreds of FORTRAN (90) source files. Adapting the code base to meet modern computer platform requirements, we have to ensure the portability, extensibility and maintainability as well. This work summarizes our efforts to extend the parallelism on a node by adopting OpenMP multithreading and vectorization standards, including the integration of threaded libraries, which itself is critical to performance. We apply SIMD optimizations at various levels and focus on two specific examples of OpenMP 4 SIMD constructs in FORTRAN codes to highlight its power and limitations.

2   Core Computations in VASP

In essence, VASP solves a set of Schrödinger-like eigenvalue equations

$$H[\{\psi\}]\psi_n = \epsilon_n\psi_n, \qquad n = 1, .., N \tag{1}$$

for N eigenvalue/-function pairs $\{\epsilon_n, \psi_n\}$, where N is of the order of the number of electrons in the simulation box (typically $N < 10^3$). The operator $H[\{\psi\}]$, the Hamiltonian, depends on the set of solutions $\{\psi\}$, requiring iterations until the self-consistency is achieved in terms of the total energy and electron density. These equations are solved by means of iterative matrix diagonalization algorithms, e.g., Blocked-Davidson or RMM-DIIS [1,2]. The set of solutions $\{\psi\}$ to Eq. 1 must be explicitly kept orthonormal:

$$\int \psi_n^*(\mathbf{r})\psi_m(\mathbf{r})d\mathbf{r} = \delta_{nm}. \tag{2}$$

This is done by means of Gram-Schmidt orthogonalization.

The eigenfunctions ψ_n are basically expressed in a plane wave basis set, i.e., VASP stores their Fourier coefficients. The last statement is a bit of a simplification since in reality VASP uses a Projector-Augmented-Wave (PAW) basis. A description of the PAW method, however, is beyond the scope of this paper. For details, we refer the reader to the paper by Kresse and Joubert [7]. Here it suffices to know that a key ingredient of the PAW method is the projection of the eigenfunctions onto a set of localized functions p_α centered on the atomic sites in the simulation box:

$$c_{\alpha n} = \int_{\Omega_\alpha} p_\alpha(\mathbf{r})\psi_n(\mathbf{r})d\mathbf{r}, \tag{3}$$

where Ω_α is a certain volume around the atomic site on which p_α is localized.

Computationally speaking, an N-electron VASP calculation consists of many independent 3d FFTs, matrix-matrix multiplications, matrix diagonalizations, and other linear algebra methods. The Gram-Schmidt orthogonalization of the eigenfunctions involves Cholesky decomposition and inversion of $N \times N$ matrices and requires all-to-all communication. Ideally, VASP can be expressed as a sequence of optimized library calls, reaping the benefits of highly optimized parallel numerical libraries (FFT, BLAS and LAPACK/ScaLAPACK) on each platform. In practice, achieving a high fraction of the peak FLOPS on a node and scaling towards hundreds of nodes is challenging because of the following: (i) $N_{\mathbf{G}}$ the basis size (number of plane-wave coefficients) is much larger than N, leading to skinny-tall matrix shapes; (ii) the number of 3d FFTs grows as N or higher, but each 3d FFT is small, typically $100 \times 100 \times 100$; and (iii) computations in multiple libraries and user codes and "collective" communications have to be coordinated.

2.1   MPI Parallelization

In order to handle a wide range of ES methods and problem sizes, VASP implements parallelization schemes which distribute data and work over MPI-ranks at two levels:

1. *High-level:* the eigenfunctions ψ_n are distributed over the MPI-ranks in a round-robin fashion. Large parts of the work can be distributed similarly in a natural way. For instance, solving Eq. 1 using the RMM-DIIS algorithm can in principle be done on a pure by-function basis, i.e., each MPI-rank works solely on the functions it owns locally. This is the default level of parallelization under MPI.
2. *Low-level:* in addition to the distribution of data and work over eigenfunctions, data and work may be further distributed over the Fourier components that make up a single eigenfunction. VASP implements its own MPI-enabled 3d FFT based on a series of 1d FFTs and `MPI_Alltoall(v)`.

P 2.1. Blocked evaluation of the action of H on ψ: Schematically, the blocked evaluation of the action of the Hamiltonian H onto the eigenfunctions is made up of the following elemental steps:

Algorithm 1. For each ψ_i, $i \in \{N_b\}_{\mathrm{loc}}$: in blocks of n_b

---

1: Fourier transforms $\psi_j(\mathbf{r}) = \mathrm{FFT}\{\psi_j(\mathbf{G})\}(\mathbf{r})$ for $j \in \texttt{block}$
2: PAW projections $c_{\alpha j} = \sum_{\mathbf{r} \in \Omega_\alpha} p_\alpha(\mathbf{r})\psi_j(\mathbf{r})$, $j \in \texttt{block}$, $\forall\, \alpha$
3: Local potential $[V\psi]_j(\mathbf{r}) = V(\mathbf{r})\psi_j(\mathbf{r})$, $j \in \texttt{block}$, $\forall\, \mathbf{r}$
4: Non-local potential $[V_{\mathrm{NL}}\psi]_j(\mathbf{r}) = \sum_{\alpha\beta} p_\alpha(\mathbf{r})V_{\alpha\beta}^{\mathrm{NL}}c_{\beta j}$ $j \in \texttt{block}$, $\mathbf{r} \in \Omega_\alpha$
5: Kinetic energy $[T\psi]_j(\mathbf{G}) = T(\mathbf{G})\psi_j(\mathbf{G})$, $j \in \texttt{block}$, $\mathbf{G} \in \{\mathbf{G}\}_{\mathrm{loc}}$
6: Total action $[H\psi]_j(\mathbf{G}) = [T\psi]_j(\mathbf{G}) + \mathrm{FFT}\{[V\psi + V_{\mathrm{NL}}\psi]_j(\mathbf{r})\}(\mathbf{G})$, $j \in \texttt{block}$, $\mathbf{G} \in \{\mathbf{G}\}_{\mathrm{loc}}$

$\{N_b\}_{loc}$ denotes the set of eigenfunctions owned locally by a certain MPI-rank (*high-level*), and $\{\mathbf{G}\}_{loc}$ is the set of Fourier coefficients of these eigenfunctions owned by that MPI-rank (*low-level*). We name the kinetic energy operator $T(\mathbf{G})$, the local potential $V(\mathbf{r})$, and the non-local potential $V_{\alpha\beta}^{NL}$ without additional explanation.

The Fourier transforms (steps 1 and 6) are either 3d FFTs or 1d FFTs + MPI_Allto allv. The latter is used if Fourier components of an eigenfunction are distributed over multiple MPI-ranks (as well). Steps 2 and 4 invoke BLAS3 DGEMM. The element wise products (steps 3 and 5) and sum (step 6) are done by means of BLAS1 calls.

P 2.2. Global contractions: With global contractions we denote, for instance, computing $H_{ij} = \int \psi_i^*(\mathbf{r})H\psi_j(\mathbf{r})d\mathbf{r}$ with $i,j = 1,..,N$, where N denotes all eigenfunctions (not only those local to a particular MPI-rank). These operations are done as follows:

1. *Action:* compute the action of the Hamiltonian H onto the eigenfunctions owned locally by each (group of) MPI-rank(s). See the previous paragraph.
2. *Redistribute the data:* VASP redistributes the Fourier components of the eigenfunctions from a situation where each MPI-rank holds part of the coefficients of part of the eigenfunctions ψ and the action $H\psi$ (i.e., a combination of the parallelization levels mentioned at the top), to a situation where it holds a certain part of the coefficients of all eigenfunctions and the corresponding coefficients of the action.
3. *Local contraction:* each MPI-rank computes

$$H_{ij} = \sum_{\{\mathbf{G}\}_{red}} \psi_i^*(\mathbf{G})\,[H\psi]_j\,(\mathbf{G}), \quad \forall\, i,j. \tag{4}$$

4. *Global sum:* A global sum across all MPI-ranks is taken over $H_{ij}, \forall\, i,j.$
5. *Back distribution:* the eigenfunctions are redistributed back to the original situation where each MPI-rank held a certain part of the Fourier coefficients of part of the eigenfunctions.

Steps 2, 4 and 5 involve global MPI communication: the data redistribution and back-distribution (steps 2 and 5) are done by means of MPI_Alltoall calls and the global sum invokes MPI_Allreduce across all MPI-ranks. The local contractions (step 3) are done with BLAS3 ZGEMM calls.

3   MPI+OpenMP Threading

3.1   OpenMP Threading Strategy

Similar to the MPI parallelization strategy, explicit OpenMP threading was added at two levels as well:

1. *High-level:* many algorithms that work on the eigenfunctions locally owned by a particular MPI-rank $\{N_b\}_{loc}$ process these in blocks of n_b functions (see Paragraph P 2.1.). Blocking increases data reuse and allows certain operations to be done by means of BLAS3 (matrix×matrix) instead of BLAS2 calls. At the highest level, OpenMP threading was introduced by distributing the work on these blocks of n_b eigenfunctions over threads by straightforward loop-level parallelism (`!$omp parallel do`) over the functions within a block.

2. *Low-level:* many elemental steps involve point-by-point computations on the Fourier components or the real-space grid points. The distribution of work over OpenMP threads was achieved (i) by the introduction of loop-level parallelism using "`!$omp parallel do`" over $\{r\}$ and $\{G\}$ (steps 3, 5 and 6 of Algorithm [1]); (ii) by explicit domain decomposition of $\{\Omega_\alpha\}$ over threads (steps 2 and 4); and (iii) by use of threaded versions of FFT and BLAS/LAPACK.

When the library calls are made within the user-level parallel constructs, they are executed serially. SclaLAPACK or ELPA utilizes the threaded BLAS.

At present we do not allow for nesting of OpenMP parallel regions, and the combination of high- and low-level threading has not been extensively explored until now. The combination of parallelization under MPI and OpenMP threading is subject to some constraints as well. Currently, we avoid MPI communication inside OpenMP parallel regions completely and choose `MPI_THREAD_SINGLE` at the MPI initialization. As a consequence the combination of low-level MPI parallelization and high-level OpenMP threading can be troublesome: many algorithms involve loops over the eigenfunctions in a block (potential candidates for OpenMP loop parallelism) that contain local reductions of quantities over the MPI-ranks that share the Fourier coefficients of an eigenfunction, e.g.,

```
do i = 1,n_b
    call some_work(psi(i),result(i))
    call MPI_Reduce(MPI_comm_low_level,result(i))
enddo
```

These constructs have to be restructured to avoid communication within OpenMP parallel loops:

```
!$omp parallel do
do i = 1,n_b
    call some_work(psi(i),result(i))
enddo
!$omp end parallel do
call MPI_Reduce(MPI_comm_low_level,result(1:n_b))
```

which looks trivial here, but is not always easily achievable. The upside of the high-level OpenMP threading strategy is that the OpenMP parallel regions tend to contain a fair amount of work, and that it in principle constitutes an additional level of parallelism. The low-level OpenMP parallelization strategy supplants the low-level MPI parallelization (distribution of Fourier coefficients over MPI-ranks) and consists of many small OpenMP parallel regions.

Somewhat surprisingly, the combination of high-level MPI parallelization plus low-level OpenMP threading, is the most efficient: the combination of the distribution of individual eigenfunctions (data and work) over MPI-ranks and the use of threaded 3d FFT, BLAS3 and explicit parallel loop constructs. We attribute this to the improved OpenMP runtimes: "hot teams" in case of Intel OpenMP, for instance. Any modern implementation of the latter maintains a pool of OS threads that once created helps avoid the cost of newly creating and destroying threads whenever they are needed. This significantly reduces the overhead of fine-grained fork-join operations, some of which are necessary to use the threaded libraries.

Figure 1 illustrates the LOOP+ execution times—total program execution time excluding the pre- and post-processing, which becomes negligible for realistic computations—of the hybrid VASP version for three different inputs and combinations of MPI/OpenMP (we use high-level MPI and low-level OpenMP).[1]

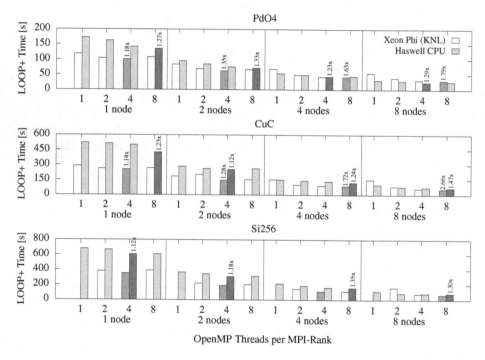

Fig. 1. LOOP+ execution times of the hybrid VASP version for three different inputs and with different combinations of MPI/OpenMP (we use high-level MPI and low-level OpenMP). The colored bars denote the fastest executions, and the numbers on top of these bars refer to the performance gain over an MPI-only execution for the given node count (if present). (Color figure online)

---

[1] Benchmarks were done on Cori, a Cray XC40 system at NERSC. It has over 9300 Intel Xeon Phi 7250 (KNL) nodes with 68 CPU cores (272 threads) @1.4 GHz and 96 GB DDR4 main memory per node. In addition, Cori has over 2000 dual-socket 16-core Intel Xeon E5-2698v3 ("Haswell") nodes, each with 32 CPU cores (64 threads) @2.3 GHz, a 256-bit wide vector unit per CPU core, and 128 GB DDR4 memory. Cori's nodes are interconnected with Cray's Aries network with Dragonfly topology. A comprehensive study of the different kinds of parameters and options when building and running VASP on Cori is given in [8].

In all cases we use 32 CPU cores per Haswell node and 64 CPU cores per Xeon Phi (KNL) node. Using 8 OpenMP threads per MPI-rank then means, that there are 4 and 8 MPI-ranks per node, respectively. We use three different inputs to cover important use cases: (PdO4) DFT calculation of oxygens on Pd surface; (CuC-vdW) van Der Waals DFT calculation of di-carbon on Cu surface, and (Si256) HSE hybrid calculation of a vacancy in bulk silicon. They differ in problem sizes, constituent ionic types and ES methods, exercising various code paths in VASP. They represent medium production runs and are chosen to evaluate the performance and the scalability from a node to 8 nodes.

For all inputs, the transition from MPI-only to hybrid MPI+OpenMP results in an improved overall program performance when using up to 8 and 4 OpenMP threads per MPI-rank on the Haswell CPU and the Xeon Phi, respectively. The colored bars denote the fastest executions, and the numbers on top of these bars refer to the performance gain over an MPI-only execution for the given node count (if present). Hybrid VASP executes up to 1.47x and 2.66x faster than the MPI-only version on Haswell and KNL, respectively. A major benefit of hybrid runs is the reduced memory footprint, which impacts KNL performance more than Haswell. All the hybrid runs fit into 16 GB and thus can take advantage of the high-bandwidth MCDRAM on KNL. The missing Si256 data on KNL in Fig. 1 are due to the allocation of enough 2 MB huge pages on the Cori system failed with 64 tasks per node.

Going beyond 8 threads per MPI-rank, the performance drops—significantly more distinct on the Xeon Phi. This is attributed to the limited scalability of the low-level OpenMP parallelization including both the user-level constructs and threaded "smallish" 3d FFTs—being performed for many VASP inputs. Another important factor is the change in communication patterns. The collective communication of large messages typically scales as $(M/n_p) \log_2 n_p$ for n_p tasks. Larger message sizes of the collectives over fewer communication channels can lead to an increased communication time and cancel out the performance gains in computations through OpenMP parallelization.

4   SIMD Vectorization

Modern CPUs increasingly draw on the Single-Instruction Multiple-Data (SIMD) execution model as a third level of parallelism beside conventional multi-processing and multithreading to achieve high compute performance. The Intel Xeon Phi (KNL), for instance, features 512-bit wide vectors to operate eight 64-bit words at once by executing the same instruction on each of its eight SIMD lanes. Only a single (vector) instruction needs to be fetched and decoded, resulting in a largely increased arithmetic throughput over scalar execution at the cost of only a bit more logic on the chip.

4.1   OpenMP 4 SIMD Constructs

For the programmer to approach SIMD vectorization in the code, OpenMP 4.0 introduced compiler directives [9] for (i) loop vectorization via !$omp simd, and (ii) function vectorization via !$omp declare simd. Both of the two can be extended using additional clauses like simdlen(x) to specify the number x of data elements to be processed throughout SIMD execution, or aligned(varlist[:alignment]) to tell the compiler about data alignment of variables in the list. The uniform(varlist) clause instructs the compiler to broadcast the values of variables in varlist across all SIMD lanes. A comprehensive outline of the available clauses in the OpenMP 4.0 and the current 4.5 standard can be found in [10,11].

SIMD vectorization in VASP happens either implicitly through and within library calls or explicitly in the user code on the loop-level using compiler directives. For complex loops, however, the effectiveness of the compiler generated SIMD code strongly depends on the loop structure. Math function calls like exp, log and pow, or control flow divergences can even prevent the compiler from SIMD vectorization at all. Subsequently, we focus on two techniques we found very useful when tackling even complex codes: whole function vectorization and manual loop splitting, both using high-level vector data types and OpenMP 4 compiler directives.

Combining multithreading and SIMD vectorization in VASP is realized via the !$omp parallel do simd construct, enabling both at the same time for a single loop or a loop nest. It also allows for (implicit) context dependent switching between "multithreading+SIMD" and "SIMD" if nested parallelism is disabled, which is usually the case in the HPC field.

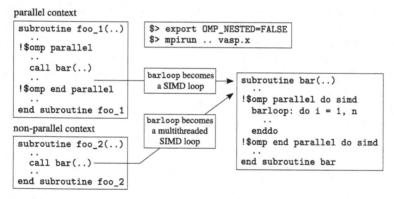

As many VASP subroutines and functions are used in different calling contexts, this way it is always guaranteed that SIMD parallelism is addressed. However, depending on the loop trip count, chunks can be distributed among threads in an unfortunate way so that the chunk size is not a multiple of the native SIMD width of the target platform. As a consequence, data alignment issues might result in loading unaligned data, and for short loops loop peeling and remainder loop execution might be dominant. To approach that issue, OpenMP 4.5 introduced the schedule(simd:static) clause to automatically match the chunk size with the width of the SIMD registers. With the current GNU compiler[2] not supporting

---

[2] At the time of the writing of this paper, we used the GNU compiler gfortran-6.3. This version does not fully support OpenMP 4.5 for Fortran (the same seems to be true for gfortran- 7.1—tested on a local workstation). For remarks on that, see the text below.

the full OpenMP 4.5 standard, one can use `schedule(static, x)` instead with some x that is a multiple of the SIMD width.

4.2 Whole Function Vectorization in VASP

Among the compute intensive code sections in the user-level part of VASP is those using hybrid functionals. For certain classes of workloads a non-negligible amount of time is spent within the `ggaall_grid` routine containing the hotspot loop

```
subroutine ggaall_grid(x_1,..,x_k,e)
  ..
!$omp simd
  do i = 1,n
    call ggaall(x_1(i),..,x_k(i),y_1(i),..,y_l(i),c_1)
    e = e+f(y_1(i),..,y_l(i))
  enddo
  ..
end subroutine ggaall_grid
```

with "large" **n**. Inside `ggaall` a nest of subroutine calls is implemented with runtime dependent control flow. One such hierarchy looks as follows:

```
ggaall
  +-> calc_expchwpbe_sp
  |     +-> ex
  |     +-> ex_sr
  |     +-> vx
  |     +-> vx_sr
  |     +-> wpbe_spline
  |           +-> wpbe_splin2
  +-> corunsppbe
        +-> gcor2
```

Within any of these routines loops with small trip counts are mixed with scalar code. SIMD vectorization thus can be effective only along the calling hierarchy. Staying entirely within OpenMP 4 without adapting the code base too much, we modified each of the above listed subroutines as follows:

```
subroutine foo(..[,c_1])
  !$omp declare simd (foo) simdlen(VL) [uniform(c_1)]
  ..
end subroutine foo
```

The uniform clause applies only to the top-level function `ggaall` in the hierarchy with c_1 affecting the branching in `ggaall`. Compiling the modified code base, only the Intel compiler was capable of generating an executable.[3] According to its optimization report, subroutine and function arguments in all cases are transferred using gather and scatter operations because Fortran passes dummy arguments by reference. While on the caller side the information that these references are pointing to addresses that are consecutive in main memory is

---

[3] `gfortran-6.3` found fault with the `!$omp declare simd (foo)` directive for subroutine definitions within Fortran modules (not so for functions): it states that `foo` has been host associated already. Working around by moving subroutines outside the module causes conflicts with variable scoping. We did not implement that workaround, as subroutine vectorization fails only with the GNU compiler, and only in the module context.

present, on the callee side the compiler has to assume they are not, hence generating vector gather and scatter operations. To fix that issue, we use the `ref` modifier together with the `linear` clause: `!$omp declare simd (foo) linear(ref(x_1,..,x_k,y_1,..,y_l))..` (not supported by `gfortran-6.3`).

The performance improvements over executing the hotspot loop in `ggaall_grid` sequentially are quite different for the considered target platforms. The execution on the Haswell CPU seems to benefit only slightly from SIMD vectorization. About a factor 1.35 gain can be measured opposed to a factor 4.36 on the Xeon Phi (see Table 1). For the Haswell CPU, the assembly contains both SSE and AVX SIMD instructions, despite building with `-xcore-avx2` and specifying the `simdlen(VL)` clause with `VL=4` for execution with AVX(2)—all these specifics are reported by the Intel compiler within its optimization report. Currently, the Fortran `!$omp declare simd` construct seems to be a tripping hazard when heading for code portability and effective SIMD vectorization at the same time.

To get rid of these limitations, we integrated into VASP a high-level vector coding scheme combining real vectors with OpenMP 4 compiler directives to promote SIMD vectorization when looping over the vector elements [12,13]. Figure 2 contains the definition of the Fortran `simd` module. For the GNU compiler, we provide an interface to access vector math calls through `libmvec` [14] (we use `glibc-2.25`).

```
module simd
  type,public :: simd_real8
    real*8 :: x(0:SIMD_WIDTH-1)
  end type simd_real8
  type,public :: simd_mask8
    logical :: x(0:SIMD_WIDTH-1)
  end type simd_mask8
  ..
  !GNU-only (in all other cases 'simd_foo' is replaced by 'foo')
  interface
    function simd_exp(x) bind(c,name="__exp_finite")
!$omp declare simd (simd_exp)
      real*8 :: simd_exp
      real*8,value,intent(in) :: x
    end function simd_exp
    ..
  end interface
end module simd
```

Fig. 2. Fortran `simd` module. `SIMD_WIDTH` is defined as a constant in a separate file `simd.inc`. For the GNU compiler, we provide an interface to access vector math calls through `libmvec`.

Using these high-level vectors means to manually split the relevant loops into chunks of size `SIMD_WIDTH` (defined in a separate file `simd.inc` in a generic way), pack and unpack data to vectors, and then to apply the scalar-to-vector code expansion, including subroutine and function definitions. The scheme is illustrated in Fig. 3—the overhead of vector un-/packing and mask creation becomes negligible in case of complex loops. At the cost of more or less intensive code

```
subroutine foo(..)                    subroutine foo(..)
   ..                                    ..
   do i = 1,n                            do i = 1,n,SIMD_WIDTH
                                      !$omp simd
                                         do ii = 0,SIMD_WIDTH-1
                                            vmask%x(ii) = .false.
                                            if ((i+ii) <= n) then
                                               vmask%x(ii) = .true.
                                               vx%x(ii) = x(i+ii)
                                            endif
                                         enddo
   call bar(x(i),y(i))                   call vbar(vx,vy,vmask)
                                      !$omp simd
                                         do ii = 0,SIMD_WIDTH-1
                                            if (vmask%x(ii)) x(i+ii) = vx%x(ii)
                                         enddo
   enddo                                 enddo
   ..                                    ..
end subroutine foo                    end subroutine foo

subroutine bar(x,y)                   subroutine vbar(x,y,mask)
   real*8 :: x,y                         type(simd_real8) :: x,y
                                         type(simd_mask8) :: mask
                                         integer :: ii
                                      !$omp simd
                                         do ii = 0,SIMD_WIDTH-1
   y = log(x)                            if (mask%x(ii)) y%x(ii) = simd_log(x%x(ii))
                                         enddo
end subroutine bar                    end subroutine vbar
```

Fig. 3. Manual scalar-to-vector (left to right) expansion of a simple Fortran code snippet.

adaptations, the advantages of using this coding scheme comprise dealing with vectors and masks in a natural way as well as a straightforward mixing of scalar and vector code, e.g., if there is library calls or print statements throughout the SIMD execution. With the SIMD_WIDTH parameter, vector lengths can be adapted to any meaningful value, matching at least the native SIMD vector length.

Code compilation with the Intel compiler resulted in the above listed calling tree (comprising 20 loops after the adaptations) could be effectively vectorized, with the (compiler-)estimated performance gains close to the theoretical expectations (4x and 8x for computations on 64-bit words with AVX(2) and AVX512, respectively). Additionally, we used the optimization report to further tune the computation by removing unnecessary divides and re-computations of intermediate values, for instance—all these optimizations have been back-ported to the other code versions for a fair comparison. The GNU compiler, however, achieved success in vectorizing only 5 out of the 20 loops, missing the most compute intensive ones. Among these 5 loops are two with calls to log, exp and pow, supporting our interface definitions to libmvec (we verified the respective calls in the assembly). The remaining 15 loops contain control flow divergences and "smallish" loop nests. However, it is not totally clear to us why gfortran failed vectorizing them, as for similar loop structures gcc achieves success [13].

Considering the execution times for the hotspot loop in ggaall_grid, listed in Table 1, the relevance of an effective SIMD vectorization is evident. With the Xeon Phi behind the Haswell CPU in the reference case, switching to SIMD execution, it goes ahead significantly when using the Intel compiler. The almost 3x gain over the execution on the Haswell CPU to a large fraction results from twice the SIMD vector width and the fact that on KNL there is two SIMD units per CPU core, together with native support for vector masks. For the GNU compiler, we only see that our high-level vector scheme is working at least in the sense that it improves data locality.

Table 1. Execution time (in seconds) of the hotspot loop in `ggaall_grid` on a Haswell CPU and an Intel Xeon Phi (KNL). The "reference" refers to the optimized scalar code, while the other two are for SIMD vectorized code via OpenMP 4 directives only, and with high-level vectors.

	gfortran-6.3		ifort-17 (update 2)	
	Haswell	Xeon Phi KNL	Haswell	Xeon Phi KNL
reference	93 s	168 s	80 s	96 s
`!$omp declare simd`	–	–	59 s (1.35x)	22 s (4.36x)
high-level vectors	74 s (1.26x)	98 s (1.71x)	42 s (1.90x)	14 s (6.86x)

4.3   Loop Splitting

Another kind of computation with a significant amount of time spent in the user code is the integration of the dynamically screened two electron integrals over frequency

$$\sigma(\omega) = \frac{i}{2\pi} \int_{-\infty}^{+\infty} \frac{W(\omega')}{\omega + \omega' - \epsilon_2 + i\,\Delta \text{sign}(\epsilon_2 - \mu)}\, d\omega'. \tag{5}$$

It is implemented as an interpolation using those n satisfying $\omega'_n < n\Delta \leq \omega'_{n+1}$. Determining these n introduces loop depencenes, as going for ω'_{n+1} happens faster with ω'_n known already. The loop structure for this computation is shown in Fig. 4.

```
n = 1
do i = 1,n_omega_interpolate
  if ((i*delta) > omega(n+1)) then
    do
      n = n+1
      if (omega(n+1) > (i*delta)) exit
    enddo
  endif
  tmp = some_func_of(screened_2e_int(n),screened_2e_int(n+1))
  ..  !computation using 'tmp'
enddo
```

Fig. 4. Structure of the reference code for the integration of the dynamically screened two electron integrals over frequency according to Eq. 5.

SIMD vectorization of the i-loop suffers from the above mentioned loop dependencies introduced by determining the n-values. All computation starting at line "tmp = ..," however, is independent of the other iterations. We therefore split the i-loop into chunks of size SIMD_WIDTH, and further decompose the resulting inner loop over ii, ranging from 0 to SIMD_WIDTH - 1, into 3 parts l_k (see Fig. 5): l_1, the pre-computation of the n-values, l_2, gathering all needed data into vtmp indexed through n (this results in gather loads), and l_3, the actual computation using vtmp.

```
n = 1
do i = 1,n_omega,SIMD_WIDTH
   ii_max = min(SIMD_WIDTH-1,n_omega-i)
   l1: do ii = 0,ii_max
      if (((i+ii)*delta) > omega(n+1)) then
         do
            n = n+1
            if (omega(n+1) > ((i+ii)*delta)) exit
         enddo
      endif
      vn%x(ii) = n
   enddo
   l2: do ii = 0,ii_max
      idx = vn%x(ii)
      vtmp%x(ii) = some_func_of(screened_2e_int(idx),screened_2e_int(idx+1))
   enddo
!$omp simd
   l3: do ii = 0,ii_max
      .. !computation using 'vtmp'
   enddo
enddo
```

Fig. 5. Loop splitting applied to the code listed in Fig. 4 using high-level vectors.

Both, the second and third inner most loop are candidates for SIMD vectorization. However, we annotate only the third one using OpenMP 4 directives, and let the compiler decide about vectorization of the second loop. Depending on whether the target platform supports vector gather operations, the latter will be vectorized or not. As the loop splitting into parts requires to store (or "back up") those intermediate values computed in l_q and needed in at least one other $l_{q' \geq q}$ (e.g. vn and vtmp in Fig. 5), our high-level vector approach is the natural way for an effective implementation.

We also considered using the !$omp ordered simd construct for l_1 (determining the n-values) (see Fig. 6). According to the OpenMP 4.5 standard [11], the execution of the block enclosed by the ordered simd construct happens exactly in the order given by the sequential execution of the surrounding loop using a single SIMD lane. However, there seems to be no guarantee that intermediate results of the serialized execution are kept for subsequent SIMD executions. In our sample it is the per-loop-iteration n-values that are needed subsequent to the ordered block to access the right data in each iteration of the i-loop. We found with the Intel Fortran compiler (gfortran-6.3 did not vectorize the code with the ordered construct) a non-deterministic behavior regarding what is kept

```
n = 1
!$omp simd
do i = 1,n_omega
  !$omp ordered simd
    if ((i*delta) > omega(n+1)) then
      do
        n = n+1
        if (omega(n+1) > (i*delta)) exit
      enddo
    endif
    !it seems to be not guaranteed that intermediate values n_{i=1}, n_{i=2},.. are
    !available hereafter → results might be wrong
  !$omp end ordered
    tmp = some_func_of(screened_2e_int(n),screened_2e_int(n+1))
    .. !computation using 'tmp'
enddo
```

Fig. 6. SIMD version of the code listed in Fig. 4 using the `ordered simd` construct. The computation when executed in SIMD mode might give faulty results (see the text for explanation).

and what is not kept, resulting in wrong simulation results. Assuming our observation is correct, we propose to extend the `!omp ordered simd` construct by a `keep(varlist)` clause to instruct the compiler to move intermediate values of any of `varlist` to the corresponding SIMD lane of a vector equivalent which then can be accessed thereafter.

In the above loop, we would extend the line containing `!$omp ordered simd` by the `keep(n)` clause. We would expect the compiler to transform the code (in its intermediate representation) into something similar to what is shown in Fig. 5, but with l_2 and l_3 merged.

Table 2 summarizes the execution times spent in the integration procedure on a Haswell CPU and an Intel Xeon Phi. Both the GNU and the Intel compiler achieved success when vectorizing the high-level vector code, eventhough the Intel compiler generates the faster executable for the Xeon Phi.

Table 2. Execution time (in seconds) of the integration of the dynamically screened two electron integrals over frequency on a Haswell CPU and an Intel Xeon Phi (KNL).

	gfortran-6.3		ifort-17 (update 2)	
	Haswell	Xeon Phi KNL	Haswell	Xeon Phi KNL
reference	12.8 s	44 s	11.1 s	29 s
high-level vectors	6.9 s (1.86x)	6.8 s (6.47x)	6.6 s (1.68x)	4.2 s (6.90x)

5   Insights and Proposals

Extending large codes so as to address all levels of parallelism needed to fully utilize modern CPU's compute capabilities was and is a very challenging task. For the VASP application, we gave a brief overview of the transition from an MPI-only to a hybrid MPI+OpenMP [SIMD] code, and pointed out relevant design decisions related to, for instance, what level of granularity OpenMP actually should be located at to complement with the already existing MPI parallelism. We found the most efficient way to achieve that in VASP is placing MPI and OpenMP at the different ends of the workload partitioning. More precisely, MPI is the means for work distribution at the outer most level of parallelism, whereas OpenMP sits at a very low-level of the calling hierarchy, either within library calls (e.g., threaded FFT and BLAS/LAPACK calls) or on the loop level within the user code.

Interchanging both of the two, so that MPI happens from within OpenMP, or raising OpenMP to the same level as MPI, however, is difficult to handle due to some VASP-internal constraints but more importantly due to poor interoperability between MPI and OpenMP. The current MPI standards and limited support for MPI_THREAD_MULTIPLE narrow our design space and force unnecessary barriers and synchronization points. Few MPI libraries provide optimized implementations that take advantage of the shared memory on a node and the available thread pool and communication channels. While computations may be greatly improved through thread-level parallelization, new communication paths can become bottlenecks and diminish the performance gain. A prime example is the reduction of large messages that can be "parallelized" by segments and multiple message queues. The thread scaling of the current VASP hybrid thus solely relies on the effectiveness of (OpenMP) threading within the libraries and loop parallelization and runtimes. Improved interoperability of MPI and OpenMP and flexible library APIs is critically needed to extend the thread scalability and in turn, the overall scalability. Nevertheless, for a set of representative workloads, we demonstrated on both a Haswell CPU and a Xeon Phi (KNL) system an overall improved execution with up to 8 OpenMP threads per MPI-rank compared to running MPI-only.

Additionally, at the low-level end of the calling hierarchy, SIMD vectorization by means of OpenMP 4 SIMD constructs complements OpenMP threading. We illustrated two kinds of optimizations that apply to different sections in the VASP code: whole function vectorization and loop splitting, both for complex loop structures. A direct comparison of the vectorization capabilities of the GNU gfortran-6.3 and the Intel ifort-17 (update 2) compiler showed that the GNU Fortran compiler and support for OpenMP 4.5 lags behind significantly. As in complex codes mixing scalar and SIMD vector code is unavoidable, we propose, for reasons discussed in Sect. 4.3, to extend the ordered simd construct by a keep(varlist) clause to make per-loop-iteration intermediate results available to subsequent SIMD execution.

Acknowledgements. This work is (partially) supported by Intel within the IPCC activities at ZIB, by the ASCAR Office in the DOE, Office of Science, under contract number DE-AC02-05CH11231. It used the resources of National Energy Scientific Computing Center (NERSC).

References

1. Kresse, G., Furthmüller, J.: Efficient iterative schemes for ab initio total-energy calculations using a plane-wave basis set. Phys. Rev. B **54**, 11169–11186 (1996)
2. Kresse, G., Furthmüller, J.: Efficiency of ab-initio total energy calculations for metals and semiconductors using a plane-wave basis set. Comput. Mater. Sci. **6**(1), 15–50 (1996)
3. Marsman, M., Paier, J., Stroppa, A., Kresse, G.: Hybrid functionals applied to extended systems. J. Phys. Condens. Matter **20**(6), 064201 (2008)
4. Kaltak, M., Klimeš, J., Kresse, G.: Cubic scaling algorithm for the random phase approximation: self-interstitials and vacancies in Si. Phys. Rev. B Condens. Matter Mater. Phys. **90**(5), 054115–054115 (2014)
5. Liu, P., Kaltak, M., Klimeš, J., Kresse, G.: Cubic scaling *GW*: towards fast quasi-particle calculations. Phys. Rev. B: Condens. Matter **94**(16), 165109 (2016)
6. Sodani, A., Gramunt, R., Corbal, J., Kim, H.S., Vinod, K., Chinthamani, S., Hutsell, S., Agarwal, R., Liu, Y.C.: Knights landing: second-generation Intel Xeon Phi product. IEEE Micro **36**(2), 34–46 (2016)
7. Kresse, G., Joubert, D.: From ultrasoft pseudopotentials to the projector augmented-wave method. Phys. Rev. B **59**, 1758–1775 (1999)
8. Zhao, Z., Marsman, M., Wende, F., Kim, J.: Performance of hybrid MPI/OpenMP VASP on Cray XC40 based on Intel Knights landing many integrated core architecture. In: CUG Proceedings (2017)
9. Klemm, M., Duran, A., Tian, X., Saito, H., Caballero, D., Martorell, X.: Extending OpenMP* with vector constructs for modern multicore SIMD architectures. In: Chapman, B.M., Massaioli, F., Müller, M.S., Rorro, M. (eds.) IWOMP 2012. LNCS, vol. 7312, pp. 59–72. Springer, Heidelberg (2012). doi:10.1007/978-3-642-30961-8_5
10. OpenMP Architecture Review Board: OpenMP Application Program Interface, Version 4.0. (2013). http://www.openmp.org
11. OpenMP Architecture Review Board: OpenMP Application Program Interface, Version 4.5. (2015). http://www.openmp.org/
12. Wende, F., Noack, M., Schütt, T., Sachs, S., Steinke, T.: Application performance on a Cray XC30 evaluation system with Xeon Phi coprocessors at HLRN-III. In: Cray User Group (2015)
13. Wende, F., Noack, M., Steinke, T., Klemm, M., Zitzlsberger, G., Newburn, C.J.: Portable SIMD performance with OpenMP* 4.x compiler directives. In: Euro-Par 2016, Parallel Processing, 22nd International Conference on Parallel and Distributed Computing (2016)
14. Senkevich, A.: Libmvec (2015). https://sourceware.org/glibc/wiki/libmvec

OpenMP* SIMD Vectorization and Threading of the Elmer Finite Element Software

Mikko Byckling[1], Juhani Kataja[2], Michael Klemm[3(✉)], and Thomas Zwinger[2]

[1] Intel Finland, Tampere, Finland
mikko.byckling@intel.com
[2] CSC - IT Center for Science, Espoo, Finland
{juhani.kataja,thomas.zwinger}@csc.fi
[3] Intel Deutschland GmbH, Feldkirchen, Finland
michael.klemm@intel.com

Abstract. We describe the design and implementation of hierarchical high-order basis functions with OpenMP* SIMD constructs in the Elmer Finite Element software. We give rationale of our design decisions and present some of the key challenges encountered during the implementation. Our numerical results on a platform supporting Intel® AVX2 show that the new basis function implementation is **3x** to **4x** faster when compared to the same code without OpenMP SIMD in use, or **5x** to **10x** faster when compared to the original Elmer implementation. In addition, our numerical results show similar speedups for the entire finite element assembly process.

Keywords: Finite elements · Basis functions · Implementation · OpenMP · SIMD

1 Introduction

Numerical solution of partial differential equations with the Finite Element Method (FEM) is theoretically well-established and understood [5]. Numerical solutions of high accuracy can be attained with the hp-version of the finite element method, which allows varying local polynomial orders and mesh refinement for the elements (see [16,17] and references thereof).

The main caveat of hp-FEM is the complexity of its implementation, at least when compared to the standard FEM. Nowadays several software packages and libraries exist which implement, either partially or fully, the hp-finite element method. In addition to Elmer, such software packages include, among others, deal.II [2], 3Dhp [6,7], and NGsolve [13,14]. For a fully automated framework approach based on a special purpose compiler, we refer the reader to FeniCS [10].

The aim of this paper is to describe the implementation of higher-order basis functions using the OpenMP* SIMD constructs. To our knowledge, this is the first attempt to SIMD vectorize such an application with OpenMP SIMD directives. In addition, recent multi-threading improvements in Elmer are discussed.

© Springer International Publishing AG 2017
B.R. de Supinski et al. (Eds.): IWOMP 2017, LNCS 10468, pp. 123–137, 2017.
DOI: 10.1007/978-3-319-65578-9_9

For multi-threading in the finite element assembly process, we describe the design decisions made to achieve a parallel efficiency similar to the existing MPI implementation. As we focus on OpenMP SIMD constructs in this work, we do not investigate the parameter space to determine the effect of altering the number of MPI ranks versus the number of OpenMP threads.

The structure of the paper is as follows. Section 2 introduces the multi-physical finite element solver Elmer [11], highlights some of its capabilities, and shortly describes its existing MPI parallelization scheme. Section 3 gives an overview of the design choices for multi-level parallelism in Elmer, followed by a description of the OpenMP multi-threading. The basic structure and the implementation of high-order finite element basis functions using OpenMP SIMD constructs is described in Sect. 4. Performance results are given in Sect. 5. Finally, Sect. 6 concludes the paper and presents future work.

2   Elmer FEM

Elmer is a multi-physics, finite element software package that has its origins in the Finnish national CFD technology program from 1995 funded by the Finnish agency of technology and innovation. Since September 2005, Elmer is open source under the GNU Public License (GPL) with a later extension to LGPL (2012) for its library functionality. The official Elmer repository is hosted at GitHub at https://github.com/ElmerCSC/elmerfem.

Elmer contains a multitude of physical models [12], starting from the traditional engineering disciplines of elastic body deformation (Navier equation) and fluid problem (Navier-Stokes equations), reaching over from heat transfer to the recent improvements in electrodynamics, currently under active development under the support of the Finnish agency of technology (TEKES). An important scientific application field of Elmer is numerical Glaciology, i.e., numerical simulation of ice-sheets and glaciers in the context of climate change and paleo-climate reconstructions. Combining elements from fluid flow, heat transfer, and solid body deformation, Elmer/Ice [9] (http://elmerice.elmerfem.org) is a good example of utilizing multi-physics and apply it to an important topic for the wider public, as the melting of land-based ice masses is suspected to directly contribute to sea-level rise.

Elmer's solvers are written in Fortran 2003 with parts of the core routines in C. The Elmer package contains additional programs, such as a simple graphical user interface, ElmerGUI, and a mesh/CAD translation tool, ElmerGrid. The solver utilizes shared object libraries and provides optional interfaces to common linear algebra packages, such as Trilinos, Hypre, and MUMPS.

The solver modules are either library or user code, both of which are dynamically loaded during run-time. The solver to use is defined in the solver input file. A typical run of a solver consists of the following steps:

1. read input files and populate internal data structures, including mesh data and other model definitions, and
2. call the solver's entry function and passing it the model data as a handle.

Apart from decomposing the mesh for MPI ranks, no further mesh pre-processing is needed for the solver.

The steps taken by a typical solver module are:

1. Finite element assembly (loops over active elements):
   (a) Evaluate right hand side functions and material data at the nodes of the element.
   (b) Loop over integration points on the element (numerical integration).
       i. Evaluate the basis functions at the integration points (library call).
       ii. Interpolate the load functions and material data to integration points
       iii. Loop over the evaluated basis functions and evaluate the contribution of the bilinear forms, associated with the problem, to the *local stiffness matrix*.
   (c) *Glue* the local stiffness matrix to the sparse structure representing the *global stiffness matrix* (library call).
2. Linear system solve (solves the arising linear system through a library call).

Normally only the problem specific parts of a solver code, such as defining the used load function, are implemented by the end-user. The problem non-specific parts, such as evaluation of the basis functions or solution of the linear system, are implemented as library calls.

In a typical finite element computation, there are $N = 10^4 \ldots 10^9$ elements, each of which has $K = 10^0 \ldots 10^2$ basis functions, where K depends on the element polynomial degree p and its type.

For numerical integration, the basis functions need to be evaluated at integration points. The number of integration points depends on the polynomial degree of the integrands. Denote by d the element dimension. As Elmer uses a scaled composite Gaussian quadrature rule for high order elements, to accurately integrate a product of two degree p polynomials

$$N_I = \left(\lceil \frac{2p+1}{2} \rceil \right)^d \tag{2.1}$$

integration points are needed. Thus, as the number of basis functions scales linearly to the element degree, the amount of computational work needed for basis function evaluation via direct computation scales as $O(p^{d+1})$.

The main parallelization method utilized by Elmer is implemented via domain decomposition and the Message Passing Interface (MPI) [15]. The mesh is partitioned into different domains which are distributed to different MPI ranks. The processes mutually communicate by exchanging messages when needed. Figure 1 shows a horizontally, partitioned vertically extruded mesh for a typical run of Elmer/Ice on the Antarctic ice sheet.

By the nature of the finite element method, the assembly part—the main loop over the elements in the pseudo code above—contains local operations within elements. As elements are fully contained in only one of the mesh partitions, the assembly does not require communication across tasks. On the other hand, the solution of the resulting linear system is a global operation and thus requires

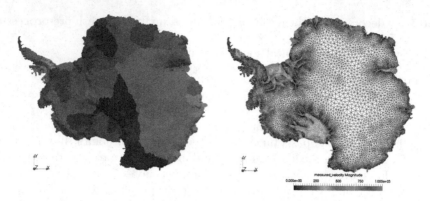

Fig. 1. Typical partition pattern (left) and mesh (right) for an Elmer/Ice application of the Antarctic ice sheet obtained with Gmsh/YAMS/ElmerGrid. The mesh consists of 10 internally extruded wedge-prism layers (3×10^4 elements in one layer) with horizontal refinements according to the gradient of the measured surface velocities (range from 0–≈4000 m a^{-1}, with a cut-off at 1000 m a^{-1} in the picture).

the processes to communicate. In Elmer, the solution of the linear system is typically achieved by an externally linked linear algebra package specialized for the solution of sparse matrix systems in parallel.

In the example shown in Fig. 1, the solution of the Stokes equations as well as the heat transfer equation is needed. Consequently, the finite element computation needs stabilization to satisfy the LBB-condition (see, e.g., [3], Chap. 3, Sect. 4). In Elmer stabilization can be achieved either using the residual based stabilized finite elements method [8] or the residual-free bubbles method [1]. For the work described in this paper, the latter method is a strong motivator: as the residual free bubbles are generally of high polynomial degree p, by Eq. 2.1 a large amount of integration points is needed, making the assembly of the stiffness matrix a computationally intensive operation.

3   Implementation of Multi-level Parallelism

In this section, we describe the design choices and implementation of the multilevel parallelism in Elmer with OpenMP threading. As described in Sect. 2, Elmer is currently mostly parallelized through MPI and domain decomposition.

The two main computational components of Elmer are the finite element assembly and the resulting (sparse) linear solve. The focus of our work is on adding SIMD and multi-threaded parallelism to the finite element assembly. For having multi-threading in the linear solver part, threading has been previously added to its key computational kernels, such as sparse matrix-vector products, vector additions, and vector dot products. In case the linear solve is implemented through a library call, the library is assumed to support multi-threading in a proper fashion.

```
INTEGER :: nzlocal, nzglobal
INTEGER :: ind(nzlocal)
REAL(KIND=dp):: lval(nzlocal), gval(nzglobal)
! Construction of ind index vector omitted
DO i=1,nzlocal
  gval(ind(i)) = gval(ind(i)) + lval(i)
END DO
```

Listing 1. Innermost loop of the finite element gluing process.

Algorithmically the finite element assembly is nearly trivially parallel, with access conflicts arising only where the entries of the local stiffness matrix is summed, or glued, to the entries of a global stiffness matrix. The innermost loop of this gluing process is described in Listing 1, where gval denotes the array of global stiffness matrix values, lval the local stiffness matrix values, ind the local matrix indices corresponding to the entries in the global matrix, and nzlocal and nzglobal the number of global and local entries, respectively. For a single element the values of ind are unique. For two or more neighboring elements values of ind overlap and thus synchronization is needed to guarantee atomicity of the update.

Let N_T denote the number of threads. For the design of multi-threaded concurrency in the finite element assembly process, the following algorithmic options were considered:

- *Sub-domain decomposition:* Decompose elements in each domain into N_T sub-domains. Then first process the elements in each sub-domain with a single thread in parallel and then process the internal boundaries either serially or in parallel by using ATOMIC and CRITICAL constructs for synchronization.
- *Coloring:* Perform a lightweight decomposition of domains into fully independent units of work by multi-coloring the finite element mesh. Process elements one color at a time in parallel with N_T threads.
- *Concurrent access:* Process elements in each domain with N_T threads. In the case of concurrent access, use ATOMIC and CRITICAL-constructs for synchronization.

Although initially considered attractive, use of the sub-domain decomposition approach was rejected due to its limited scalability arising from the decreasing volume-to-surface ratio. That is, as the size of the sub-domains gets smaller, the size of the internal boundaries, which require either serial computations or synchronization, tends to increase rapidly. The same argument for avoiding synchronization holds for the straightforward model with concurrent access as well. In addition, the use of ATOMIC prevents SIMD vectorization of the loops requiring synchronization, i.e., the loop in Listing 1 becomes a scalar operation.

Coloring was selected as the method of choice. Using coloring allows to completely avoid the use of synchronization constructs and thus will not suffer from any locking overhead. Such atomicity arises from the definition of coloring: in a colored mesh two adjacent elements are of different color by construction, i.e., elements of the same color are independent. In terms of Listing 1, it follows that the index vectors `ind` for elements of the same color do not overlap. Thus no `ATOMIC` construct is needed and SIMD vectorization of the gluing process is attainable.

The downside of using coloring is that it requires an additional loop over the colors. With coloring, the finite element assembly process described in Sect. 2 becomes:

1. Finite element assembly (loops over colors):
   (a) Finite element assembly (loops over active elements of the current color):
       i. Evaluate right hand side functions and material data at the nodes of the element.
       ii. Loop over integration points on the element (numerical integration).
          A. ...

Deactivating coloring needs no special treatment as it is equivalent to performing the assembly over a single color. The coloring itself is also an additional, although inexpensive, step which needs to be added to the mesh read-in process.

To avoid a serial bottleneck due to the coloring process, we adopted a multi-threaded coloring algorithm from [4]. To make the change as transparent as possible, and to avoid adding coloring loops to all element assembly loops, we implemented coloring on the Elmer solver core level such that the Elmer solver core performs the assembly over a single color at a time.

4   Implementation of SIMD Basis Functions

In this section, we describe the design and implementation of high-order basis functions with OpenMP SIMD constructs in Elmer. Elmer has existing implementations for high-order elements for all supported element types, i.e., line (1D), triangle and quadrilateral (2D), tetrahedral, pyramidal, prismatic, and hexahedral elements (3D). The nodal basis functions of line, triangular, and tetrahedral elements are linear, whereas quadrilaterals and hexahedrals have a bilinear nodal basis, and prismatic elements are a mix between the two.

4.1   Algorithmic Background

The implementation found in Elmer uses the definitions of high-order finite element basis functions defined in the literature (see [17] and also [16]) and automatically enforces the continuity of the basis functions in the global mesh. This is sometimes also referred to as *enforcing parity*. Due to processing only one integration point at time, the existing implementation of high-order basis functions in Elmer is purely scalar and difficult to turn into an efficient SIMD code because of the conditional constructs used for enforcing parity.

Denote the polynomial degree of the basis functions by p. In the following we describe the low-level structure of the high-order basis functions used in Elmer, and show how to map the structure to an efficient OpenMP SIMD implementation.

To ensure that the resulting discretization is well-conditioned, high-order finite element basis functions are typically based on some class of orthogonal polynomials. The implementation in Elmer is based on Legendre polynomials $P_j(x)$, defined recursively as

$$P_0(x) = 1, \qquad P_1(x) = x,$$
$$P_{j+1}(x) = \frac{2j+1}{j+1} x P_j(x) - \frac{j}{j+1} P_{j-1}(x). \tag{4.1}$$

With Legendre polynomials $P_j(x)$, we define an integrated Legendre polynomial $\phi_j(x)$ as

$$\phi_j(x) = \sqrt{\frac{1}{2(2j-1)}} \int_{-1}^{x} P_{j-1}(x') dx'$$
$$= \sqrt{\frac{1}{2(2j-1)}} (P_j(x) - P_{j-2}(x)), \tag{4.2}$$

and $\varphi_j(x)$ as

$$\varphi_j(x) = \frac{4\phi_j(x)}{1-x^2}, \tag{4.3}$$

with $j \geq 2$ for both Eqs. 4.2 and 4.3[1]. For instance, for $j = 2, \ldots, 4$, we have $\phi_2(\xi) = \frac{\sqrt{6}}{4}(\xi^2 - 1)$, $\phi_3 = \frac{\sqrt{10}}{4}\xi(\xi^2 - 1)$, $\phi_4 = \frac{\sqrt{14}}{16}(5\xi^4 - 6\xi^2 + 1)$ and $\varphi_2(x) = \sqrt{6}$, $\varphi_3(x) = -\sqrt{10}x$ and $\varphi_4(x) = -\frac{\sqrt{14}}{4}(5x^2 - 1)$.

The values of polynomials $P_j(x)$, $\phi_j(x)$, and $\varphi_j(x)$ are evaluated at points $x_k \in [-1, 1]$, with typical values of $j \leq 12$ and $k \leq 500$. When the values of $\varphi_j(x)$ are computed directly from those of $\phi_j(x)$, the endpoints of the interval, i.e., $x = -1$ and $x = 1$ are problematic as they will cause a division by zero. The approach taken in Elmer to overcome such difficulties is to simplify polynomials $P_j(x)$, $\phi_j(x)$, and $\varphi_j(x)$ up to a suitably large value and then switch by the value of j during runtime as needed. For a shortened version of the implementation of $P_j(x)$ in Elmer, see Listing 2. The functions $\phi_j(x)$ and φ_j have been implemented similarly, up to $p = 16$.

High-order finite element basis functions are defined through functions $P_j(x)$, $\phi_j(x)$, and $\varphi_j(x)$. Like normal nodal finite elements, high-order finite elements have (bi)linear basis functions of degree one associated with the element nodes. In addition, high-order elements have basis functions of degree $p > 1$ associated with their edges (edge functions in 2D and 3D), their faces (face functions in 3D), and their interior (bubble functions in 1D, 2D, and 3D). Edge and face functions are directed such that the global direction over two neighboring elements is consistent. Bubble functions have a direction in 1D or 2D if they are associated with a boundary mesh of a higher dimensional mesh.

By definition, for $p \geq 2$, edge functions are defined along one edge of an element and vanish towards the other edges. Similarly, face functions are defined along one face and vanish towards the other element faces.

---

[1] Note that $\phi_j(x)$ is a scaled $\phi_j(x)$ with its zeroes at $x = \pm 1$ removed.

```
FUNCTION LegendreP(j,x) RESULT(fval)
  INTEGER , INTENT(IN) :: j
  REAL (KIND=dp) :: x, fval
  SELECT CASE(j)
  CASE(0)
     fval = 1
  CASE(1)
     fval = x
  CASE(2)
     fval = -0.1D1 / 0.2D1 + 0.3D1 / 0.2D1 * x ** 2
  ! Rest of the cases omitted for brevity
```

Listing 2. Legendre function implementation in Elmer.

Denote by A and B the local nodes of an edge $\mathcal{E} = (A, B)$ and by A, B, and C the nodes local nodes of a face $\mathcal{F} = (A, B, C)$. Let $L_X(\mathbf{n})$ denote the *linear* function of a node n. For linear elements such as triangles and tetrahedrons, these correspond to regular nodal basis functions, but for quadrilaterals and hexahedral elements they are separately defined as having a value of 1 at the node and vanishing towards the other element nodes linearly. Figure 2 shows the parity enforcing numbering scheme used in Elmer for element edges and faces.

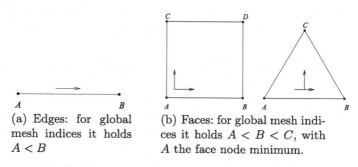

(a) Edges: for global mesh indices it holds $A < B$

(b) Faces: for global mesh indices it holds $A < B < C$, with A the face node minimum.

Fig. 2. Mesh directivity for element edges and faces.

For triangles and tetrahedral elements, the edge functions are defined as

$$N_j^{(A,B)}(\mathbf{x}) = L_A(\mathbf{x})L_B(\mathbf{x})\varphi_j(L_B(\mathbf{x}) - L_A(\mathbf{x})). \qquad (4.4)$$

Edge basis functions of other element types are defined in a similar fashion. We note that quadrilateral and hexahedral elements have some added complexity arising from the definition of the nodal basis functions. However, as the structure of the basis functions is not relevant to the subject of this paper, we refrain from discussing such technicalities any further. Definition 4.4 enables enforcing the continuity of the edge functions in the global mesh. We simply check the global indices corresponding to the endpoints of a local edge endpoints and swap the local edge endpoints if necessary.

```
INTEGER :: j, k, A, B, pmax_edge, nbasis, nbmax
REAL(KIND=dp) :: La, Lb, u(nvec), v(nvec), N(nvec,nbmax)
! Loop over element edges and
! setting A and B to enforce continuity omitted
DO j=2,pmax_edge
  !$OMP SIMD PRIVATE(La, Lb)
  DO k=1,nvec
    La = TriangleL(A,u(k),v(k))
    Lb = TriangleL(B,u(k),v(k))

    N(k,nbasis+j-1) = La*Lb*VarPhi(j,Lb-La)
  END DO
  nbasis = nbasis + pmax_edge - 1
  !$OMP END SIMD
END DO
```

Listing 3. Triangle element basis function implementation.

```
FUNCTION TriangleL(node, u, v) RESULT(fval)
  INTEGER, INTENT(IN) :: node
  REAL(KIND=dp), INTENT(IN) :: u,v
  REAL(KIND=dp) :: fval
  REAL(KIND=dp), PARAMETER :: c = 1D0/2D0, &
                              d = 1D0/SQRT(3D0)
  !$OMP DECLARE SIMD(TriangleL) UNIFORM(node) &
  !$OMP LINEAR(REF(u)) LINEAR(REF(v)) NOTINBRANCH

  SELECT CASE(node)
  CASE(1)
     fval = c*(1-u-d*v)
  CASE(2)
     fval = c*(1+u-d*v)
  CASE(3)
     fval = d*v
  END SELECT
END FUNCTION TriangleL
```

Listing 4. $L_n(x, y)$ SIMD function definition.

4.2 SIMD Implementation

The relevant part of an OpenMP SIMD implementation of a triangle basis function calculation, based on Eq. 4.4, is described in Listing 3. The functions L and φ_j, called from Listing 3 are implemented via the OpenMP DECLARE SIMD construct as shown in Listings 4 and 5.

For each edge, A and B are invariant in the SIMD loop after the global edge direction has been determined. The parameter j behaves similarly, i.e., it remains constant for each SIMD lane. Thus we can declare the input parameters node in TriangleL and j in varPhi with the UNIFORM clause, which in conjunction with NOTINBRANCH enables the compiler to generate code avoiding masking. To hint the compiler that the other function arguments are accessed in a unit stride fashion, LINEAR clause with REF modifier is used.

Bubble functions triangles and face functions tetrahedral elements are defined as

$$N_{i,j}^{(A,B,C)}(\mathbf{x}) = L_A(\mathbf{x})L_B(\mathbf{x})L_C(\mathbf{x})P_i(L_B(\mathbf{x}) - L_A(\mathbf{x}))P_j(2L_c(\mathbf{x}) - 1), \quad (4.5)$$

with $i, j = 0, 1, 2, \ldots, p - 3$, $i + j = 0, 1, \ldots, p - 3$ and where P_i denotes a Legendre function (see Eq. 4.1). Modifying Listing 2 to include DECLARE SIMD definitions analogously to Listing 5, a SIMD version of P_i can be constructed. Equation 4.5 can then be implemented similarly to Eq. 4.4: for a SIMD lane of points to evaluate, the values of A, B, and C are constant after the determining the face's direction. Values i and j are also fixed and determined by p.

```
FUNCTION VarPhi(k, x) RESULT(fval)
  INTEGER, INTENT(IN) :: k
  REAL (KIND=dp), INTENT(IN) :: x
  REAL (KIND=dp) :: fval
  !$OMP DECLARE SIMD(VarPhi) UNIFORM(k) &
  !$OMP LINEAR(REF(x)) NOTINBRANCH

  SELECT CASE(k)
  CASE(2)
    fval = -SQRT(0.6D1)
  CASE(3)
    fval = -x * SQRT(0.10D2)
  ! Rest of implementation omitted for brevity
```

Listing 5. $\varphi_j(x)$ SIMD function definition.

In Sect. 2, we described the pseudocode to compute the entries of the local element stiffness matrix by iterating over the integration points. As previously, denote by K the total number of basis functions for a single element and by N_I the total number of integration points needed, see Eq. 2.1. Let $u_i(\mathbf{x})$ denote the ith basis function of an element and let I_j denote the jth integration point.

For each element all the basis functions must be evaluated for all integration points I_j. Therefore $u_i(\mathbf{x})$ can be evaluated for all integration points at once instead of calling library functions repeatedly for a single integration point at a time. For instance, in Listing 3 the original pointwise approach corresponds to the case nvec $= 1$, whereas the new approach corresponds to the case nvec $= N_I$. In terms of the data layout, the old approach corresponds to

$$\begin{bmatrix} u_1(I_1) \ u_2(I_1) \ \cdots \ u_K(I_1) \end{bmatrix}$$

whereas the new approach is equivalent to

$$\begin{bmatrix} u_1(I_1) & u_2(I_1) & \cdots & u_K(I_1) \\ u_1(I_2) & u_2(I_2) & \cdots & u_K(I_2) \\ \vdots & \vdots & & \vdots \\ u_1(I_K) & u_2(I_K) & \cdots & u_K(I_K) \end{bmatrix}. \tag{4.6}$$

The new data layout is more favorable to the local matrix assembly. Having the number of integration points as the leading dimension leads to operations with $N_I \times K$ matrices instead of $1 \times K$ vectors. Hence the arithmetic intensity of the operations is improved and the finite element assembly process becomes computationally more efficient.

5   Performance Evaluation

In this section, we evaluate the new OpenMP SIMD basis function implementation and compare its performance to the old one. We also make a performance comparison between the new threaded implementation with mesh coloring and MPI for finite element assembly. As a test system we use a two socket Intel® Xeon® E5-2697v3 system with 14 cores per socket running at 2.60 GHz. The server contains 64 GB main memory with 2133 MHz frequency. We use the tools of Intel® Parallel Studio XE 2017, update 2 (Intel Fortran compiler, Intel MKL, and Intel MPI). As compiler flags to compile Elmer we use `-O2 -xCORE-AVX2 -vecabi=cmdtarget`.

We first evaluate the time to calculate finite element basis functions for different element types and different basis function degree p. The number of integration points was selected according to Eq. 2.1 and a composite integration rule was used, i.e., we use $N_I = 4, 9, 16, 25, 36, 49$ and $N_I = 8, 27, 64, 125, 216, 343$ integration points for $p = 1, \ldots, 6$, in 2D and 3D, respectively.

The combined time to evaluate the full basis set 100 times for triangular and hexahedral elements is given in Fig. 3. We compare the old implementation with the new implementation with OpenMP SIMD constructs disabled and enabled. We note that only a single thread was used, i.e., the timings are purely serial.

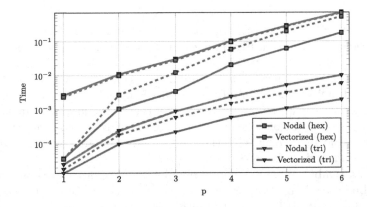

Fig. 3. Evaluation times of basis functions with OpenMP enabled (solid lines) and disabled (dashed lines) against basis function polynomial order p.

From Fig. 3, we observe that for the selected element types, the new implementation with OpenMP SIMD constructs is almost an order of magnitude faster than the old implementation for large p. Disabling OpenMP SIMD functionality negatively affects performance for large p: the new implementation is only approximately 30% better than the old one. For $p = 1$, the new implementation seems significantly more efficient than the old one (with or without OpenMP SIMD), especially for 3D elements. The difference is due to the new data layout being more SIMD friendly and the compiler being able to auto-vectorize the code without `DECLARE SIMD` constructs.

To study the performance of the FE assembly, we set up a unit cube of 125K hexahedral elements and solve a Poisson model problem. As the polynomial degree p increases, the FE assembly operation becomes more compute bound. We compare the old code and data layout with the new code on a full node with 28 threads in total. In Table 1, *novec* refers to the old implementation, *nocol* and *col* to the new implementation with and without mesh coloring.

Table 1. Average timings (in milliseconds) per thread for different phases of FE assembly for a Poisson model problem in unit cube with 125K hexahedral elements.

p	Local matrix		Update			Assembly total		
	novec	col	novec	nocol	col	novec	nocol	col
1	33.1	11.6	7.39	6.57	5.00	45.7	24.1	25.2
2	297	75.1	65.4	33.8	39.0	395	118	149
3	1155	207	192	85.4	75.6	1387	325	398
4	4667	838	398	153	97.3	5369	1020	969
5	15833	2635	714	247	133	16806	3036	2890

Table 1 shows that although the new implementation is faster for small p, the performance gains from Fig. 3 are not fully realized when the whole matrix assembly is considered, especially when p is small. A similar situation occurs when a single thread is used. Further profiling reveals that the difference is due to overhead from other solver routines called when performing the assembly, for instance, querying material parameters. For larger p, the new implementation is over **4x** faster than the old one, because of the new data layout for SIMD. The use of mesh coloring is beneficial, especially when p is large and the size of the local stiffness matrix is large.

As the assembly phase is trivially parallel when coloring is in use, the timings can be expected to be approximately equal to those obtained with domain decomposition and MPI. To verify the hypothesis, we compare the timings of assembly with mesh coloring to those of MPI. In both cases, we use the OpenMP SIMD version of the code and the new data layout. Table 2 describes the results on a full node with 28 threads or MPI ranks.

The update operation with MPI domain decomposition is similar to assembly with just one color, i.e., it avoids the use of an `ATOMIC` construct and thus vectorizes well. Timings between OpenMP and MPI are generally very similar. For large p, MPI is consistently slightly faster due to NUMA effects, that is, Elmer initializes the global stiffness matrix in a single thread during solver initialization.

Table 2. Average timings (in milliseconds) for MPI with domain decomposition vs. mesh coloring for a Poisson model problem in a unit cube with 125K hexahedral elements.

p	Local matrix		Update		Assembly total	
	MPI	col	MPI	col	MPI	col
1	10.8	11.6	4.20	5.00	19.1	25.2
2	88.0	75.1	21.8	39.0	116	149
3	217	207	46.9	75.6	272	398
4	906	838	79.1	97.3	995	969
5	2743	2635	124	133	2876	2890

6   Conclusion

We have presented an implementation of higher-order finite element basis functions in Elmer using OpenMP SIMD constructs. To our knowledge this is the first attempt of using such constructs for such computations. In addition, we presented how multi-threading of the finite element assembly process of Elmer has been implemented via multi-coloring the element mesh. Our experimental results show that the new implementation is significantly more efficient than the old one and that for the finite element assembly process, a multi-threaded implementation with coloring can match the performance of an existing MPI domain decomposition.

As a future work, with the new SIMD basis and multi-threading improvements now implemented, our intention is to modify solvers needed in computational Glaciology to support both the new OpenMP SIMD basis and multi-threading based on our experiments. We are confident that such enhancements will allow modeling of scientifically interesting problems, such as those related to climate change, more efficiently and accurately. With the shift towards OpenMP threading and SIMD, the best possible setting for the number of MPI ranks per node and the number OpenMP threads per MPI ranks needs to be determined. This exercise is also left for future work, as searching the parameter space is beyond the scope of this paper.

Acknowledgments. Thomas Zwinger was supported by the Nordic Centre of Excellence, eSTICC.

Intel and Xeon are trademarks or registered trademarks of Intel Corporation or its subsidiaries in the United States and other countries. *Other brands and names are the property of their respective owners.

Software and workloads used in performance tests may have been optimized for performance only on Intel microprocessors. Performance tests, such as SYSmark and MobileMark, are measured using specific computer systems, components, software, operations and functions. Any change to any of those factors may cause the results to vary. You should consult other information and performance tests to assist you in fully evaluating your contemplated purchases, including the performance of that product when combined with other products. For more information go to http://www.intel.com/performance.

Optimization Notice: Intel's compilers may or may not optimize to the same degree for non-Intel microprocessors for optimizations that are not unique to Intel microprocessors. These optimizations include SSE2, SSE3, and SSSE3 instruction sets and other optimizations. Intel does not guarantee the availability, functionality, or effectiveness of any optimization on microprocessors not manufactured by Intel. Microprocessor-dependent optimizations in this product are intended for use with Intel microprocessors. Certain optimizations not specific to Intel microarchitecture are reserved for Intel microprocessors. Please refer to the applicable product User and Reference Guides for more information regarding the specific instruction sets covered by this notice.

References

1. Baiocchi, C., Franca, L.P., Franca, L.P.: Virtual bubbles and the Galerkin least squares method. Comput. Methods Appl. Mech. Eng. **105**, 125–141 (1993)
2. Bangerth, W., Hartmann, R., Kanschat, G.: deal.II - a general purpose object oriented finite element library. ACM Trans. Math. Softw. (TOMS) **33**(4), 24 (2007)
3. Braess, D.: Finite Elements, 2nd edn. Cambridge University Press, Cambridge (2001)
4. Çatalyürek, Ü.V., Feo, J., Gebremedhin, A.H., Halappanavar, M., Pothen, A.: Graph coloring algorithms for multi-core and massively multithreaded architectures. Parallel Comput. **38**(10), 576–594 (2012)
5. Ciarlet, P.G.: The Finite Element Method for Elliptic Problems. North-Holland, Amsterdam (1978)
6. Demkowicz, L.: Computing with hp-Adaptive Finite Elements: Volume 1 One and Two Dimensional Elliptic and Maxwell Problems. CRC Press, Boca Raton (2006)
7. Demkowicz, L., Kurtz, J., Pardo, D., Paszyński, M., Rachowicz, W., Zdunek, A.: Computing with hp-Adaptive Finite Element Method: Volume II Frontiers: Three Dimensional Elliptic and Maxwell Problems. Chapmann & Hall/CRC, Boca Raton (2007). Applied Mathematics & Nonlinear Science
8. Franca, L.P., Frey, S.L.: Stabilized finite element methods: II, the incompressible Navier-Stokes equations. Comput. Methods Appl. Mech. Eng. **99**, 209–233 (1992)
9. Gagliardini, O., Zwinger, T., Gillet-Chaulet, F., Durand, G., Favier, L., de Fleurian, B., Greve, R., Malinen, M., Martín, C., Råback, P., Ruokolainen, J., Sacchettini, M., Schäfer, M., Seddik, J.T.H.: Capabilities and performance of Elmer/Ice, a new-generation ice sheet model. Geosci. Model Dev. **6**, 2135–2152 (2013)
10. Logg, A., Mardal, K.A., Wells, G.: Automated Solution of Differential Equations by the Finite Element Method: The FEniCS Book, vol. 84. Springer, Berlin (2012)
11. Lyly, M., Ruokolainen, J., Järvinen, E.: ELMER-a finite element solver for multiphysics. CSC-report on scientific computing 2000, pp. 156–159 (1999)
12. Råback, P., Malinen, M., Ruokolainen, J., Pursula, A., Zwinger, T.: Elmer Models Manual, March 2016
13. Schöberl, J.: C++11 implementation of finite elements in NGsolve. Technical report 30, TU Wien (2014)
14. Schöberl, J., et al.: NGsolve finite element library. http://sourceforge.net/projects/ngsolve

15. Snir, M., Otto, S.W., Huss-Lederman, S., Walker, D.W., Dongarra, J.: MPI - The Complete Reference, vol. 1, 2nd edn. MIT Press, Cambridge (1998)
16. Solin, P., Segeth, K., Dolezel, I.: Higher-Order Finite Element Methods. Chapman & Hall/CRC Press, London (2003)
17. Szabo, B.A., Babuska, I.: Finite Element Analysis. Wiley, Chichester (1991)

Analyzing and Extending Tasking

Extending OMPT to Support Grain Graphs

Peder Voldnes Langdal$^{(\boxtimes)}$, Magnus Jahre, and Ananya Muddukrishna

Department of Computer and Information Science,
Norwegian University of Science and Technology, Trondheim, Norway
pedervl@stud.ntnu.no, {magnus.jahre,ananya.muddukrishna}@ntnu.no

Abstract. The upcoming profiling API standard OMPT can describe almost all profiling events required to construct *grain graphs*, a recent visualization that simplifies OpenMP performance analysis. We propose OMPT extensions that provide the missing descriptions of task creation and parallel for-loop chunk scheduling events, making OMPT a sufficient, standard source for grain graphs. Our extensions adhere to OMPT design objectives and incur a low overhead for BOTS (up to 2% overhead) and SPEC OMP2012 (1%) programs. Although motivated by grain graphs, the events described by the extensions are general and can enable cost-effective, precise measurements in other profiling tools as well.

Keywords: OMPT · Performance analysis · Performance visualization

1   Introduction

Programmers are required to write parallelized code to take advantage of the multiple cores and accelerators exposed by modern processors. The OpenMP standard API [3] is among the leading techniques for parallel programming used by programmers. All programmers have to do is incrementally insert OpenMP directives into otherwise serial code. The directives are translated by compilers into parallel programs that are scheduled by runtime systems.

Getting OpenMP programs to perform well is often difficult since programmers work with limited information. Program translation and execution happens in the background driven by compiler and runtime system decisions unknown to programmers. Performance visualizations depict these background actions faithfully and do a poor job of connecting problems to code semantics understood by programmers.

The grain graph is a OpenMP visualization method for OpenMP that shows performance problems on a fork-join graph of *grains* – task and parallel for-loop chunk instances [15]. Problem diagnosis becomes effective since programmers can easily match the fork-join structure to the code they wrote. Insightful metrics derived from the graph guide optimization decisions. The graph is constructed post-execution using profiling measurements from the MIR runtime system [14].

We have previously found [11] that except for task creation and parallel for-loop chunk scheduling, the upcoming OpenMP Tools API (OMPT) [7,19] standard can describe all profiling events required to obtain measurements for grain

© Springer International Publishing AG 2017
B.R. de Supinski et al. (Eds.): IWOMP 2017, LNCS 10468, pp. 141–155, 2017.
DOI: 10.1007/978-3-319-65578-9_10

graphs. In the paper, we propose OMPT extensions that provide the missing descriptions. Our extensions adhere to the design objectives of OMPT and incur a low overhead for standard benchmarks and programs from EPCC [1,2] (up to 3% overhead for schedbench excluding statically scheduled loops with small chunks, 2.7% for taskbench), BOTS [6] (2%) and SPEC OMP2012 [17] (1%), when evaluated extensively with and without OMPT tools attached. Although our extensions are motivated by grain graphs, the events they describe are general and can enable cost-effective, precise measurements in other profiling tools as well.

2   Background

We explain required background information on OMPT and grain graphs in the section.

2.1   OMPT

The OpenMP Tools API (OMPT) [7,19] is an upcoming addition to the OpenMP specification to enable creation of portable performance analysis tools. OMPT supports asynchronous sampling and instrumentation-based monitoring of runtime events.

Tools based on OMPT, hereafter simply called tools, are a collection of functions that reside in the address space of the program being profiled. During startup, the runtime system calls the tool's initialization function, which in turn registers callback functions with the runtime system to be called at specific events such as starting a thread, starting a worksharing region, task creation, and task scheduling.

The foremost design objectives of OMPT [7] are:

- Tools should be able to obtain adequate information to attribute costs to application source code and the runtime system.
- OMPT support incorporated in an OpenMP runtime system should add negligible overhead when no tool is in use.

2.2   Grain Graphs

The grain graph is a recent visualization method for OpenMP that works at the level of task and parallel for-loop chunk instances, collectively called *grains* [15]. The graph captures the fork-join program progression familiar to programmers by placing parent and child grains in close proximity without timing as a placement constraint. Grains with performance problems such as work inflation, inadequate parallelism, and low parallelization benefit are pin-pointed on the graph. Example grain graphs are shown in Fig. 1.

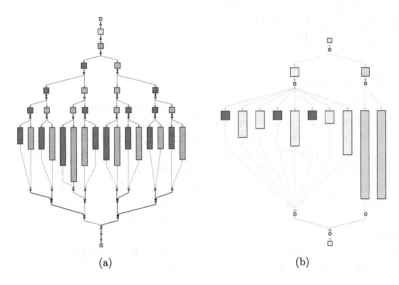

(a)   (b)

Fig. 1. Example grain graphs. (a) Graph of BOTS Fibonacci program for small input (n = 32, cutoff = 4). Grain colors encode location in source code. (b) Graph of a simple OpenMP parallel for-loop with 10 iterations executed on two threads with the dynamic schedule. Grain colors encode the worker thread. Problematic chunks (here, those with low parallel benefit) are pinpointed with a superimposed red highlight and other chunks are dimmed. (Color figure online)

The grain graph visualization is implemented in a reference prototype [16] that relies on detailed profiling measurements from the MIR runtime system [14]. Per-grain metrics from MIR such as execution time and parallelization cost are combined with the grain graph structure to derive metrics that guide optimizations.

Parallel benefit is a derived metric equal to a grain's execution time divided by its parallelization cost including creation time. Parallel benefit aids inlining and cutoff decisions by quantifying whether parallelization is beneficial. Grains with low parallel benefit should be executed sequentially to reduce overhead.

3   Extending OMPT

We propose two extensions to make OMPT a sufficient source for descriptions of profiling events required to construct grain graphs. The first extension enables measuring time spent in creating task instances. Task creation time is required to derive the parallel benefit metric of grain graphs. The second extension describes detailed parallel for-loop execution events including chunk assignment, enabling performance analysis at the chunk-level – a key feature of grain graphs. Both extensions adhere to OMPT design objectives (Sect. 2.1) and separate concerns similar to the rest of the interfaces. More details about the extensions follow.

3.1   Task Creation Duration

Creating a task instance typically involves pushing it into a task queue after allocating and initializing book-keeping data structures. This can take an uneven amount of time subject to memory allocation latencies and queue contention. An existing callback in OMPT called `ompt_callback_task_create` can notify tools that task creation is taking place. However, it does not allow measuring the duration of the process. Allowing tools to determine per-task creation time enables precise guidance about inlining and cutoffs. Also, situations where task creation duration estimates computed by tools are outdated or mismatched with the runtime system can be avoided.

To extend OMPT with the ability to inform tools about task creation duration, we considered three alternative approaches:

1. Add an endpoint parameter to the `ompt_callback_task_create` callback, and let the callback be invoked both at the start and end of task creation. This enables tools to measure the time between calls at the expense of changing the signature and the semantics of an existing callback.
2. Introduce a new callback that denotes the beginning of task creation and let the existing callback `ompt_callback_task_create` be called at the end of task creation. This approach differs from the first in that it avoids changing the signature of an existing callback but introduces a new one. An advantage of the approach is that tools can measure other metrics and not just time between the begin and end callbacks.
3. Measure the task creation duration inside the runtime system and report it to the tool as an extra parameter to `ompt_callback_task_create`. The advantage of this approach is that it avoids an additional callback invocation before each task creation event. However, it forces tools to agree on the notion of time. Some tools may require time measured in processor cycles, while others may only need microsecond precision. To complicate things further, the runtime system may decide to measure elapsed processor cycles using a hardware performance counter – a scarce resource for tools. In the case that multiple cycle counters exist, the tool would not necessarily know which counter is used by the runtime system.

We chose the third approach because it reduced callback overhead and was specific to time. The time agreement disadvantage was solved by allowing tools to register a function in tool-space that returns the current time. This function is called by the runtime system before and after task creation, and the difference between the two time values is returned as a callback parameter.

Our design for the task creation duration extension has the following new function signatures:

```
// The signature of the new ompt_tool_time callback to
// register a tool-space time function
typedef double (*ompt_tool_time_t) (void);
// The proposed new signature to ompt_callback_task_create
typedef void (*ompt_callback_task_create_t) (
  ompt_data_t *parent_task_data,
  const ompt_frame_t *parent_frame,
  ompt_data_t *new_task_data,
  ompt_task_type_t type,
  int has_dependences,
  double event_duration,      // A new addition to return duration
  const void *codeptr_ra
);
```

The event_duration parameter is typed as a double-precision float-ing point number to give tools increased precision and be consistent with omp_get_wtime. If the tool has not registered an ompt_tool_time function, the event_duration is reported as 0. We chose to return 0 instead of falling back to a low-precision timer consistent with omp_get_wtime so that no extra timing overhead is incurred if tools opt out of registering a time function. The value 0 is also returned if the runtime system or compiler decides the task cre-ation duration is lower than the overhead to call the ompt_tool_time function twice.

3.2   Extended For-loop Events

Currently, OMPT lacks interfaces to understand chunks. Parallel for-loop sup-port is also meager. The existing loop-focused callback ompt_callback_work carries little information about looping parameters. Tools can help programmers correctly diagnose parallel for-loop problems if enabled with per-chunk metrics such as creation duration, execution duration, and iteration range, as demon-strated by grain graphs [15].

We propose extending OMPT with two new callbacks, one for chunks and the other for loops, that improve the quality of information provided at loop events to tools, enabling them to measure the execution time of individual chunks and map chunks to iterations or worker threads.

The signatures for the new callbacks are shown below.

```
// The proposed ompt_callback_chunk signature
typedef void (*ompt_callback_chunk_t) (
  ompt_data_t *task_data, // The implicit task of the worker
  int64_t lower,          // Lower bound of chunk
  int64_t upper,          // Upper bound of chunk
  double create_duration, // Interval found from tool-supplied instants
  int is_last_chunk       // Is it the last chunk?
);
```

```
// The proposed ompt_callback_loop signature
typedef void (*ompt_callback_loop_t) (
  omp_sched_t loop_sched,           // Actual schedule type used
  ompt_scope_endpoint_t endpoint,   // Begin or end?
  ompt_data_t *parallel_data,       // The parallel region
  ompt_data_t *task_data,           // The implicit task of the worker
  int is_iter_signed,               // Signed loop iteration variable?
  int64_t step,                     // Loop increment
  const void *codeptr_ra            // Runtime call return address
);
```

The proposed callback ompt_callback_chunk is called before a chunk starts execution. It describes the iteration range and creation time of the chunk. Chunk creation time is calculated using a tool-space ompt_tool_time function if provided, similar to approach for tasks (Sect. 3.1). The information can be used by tools to identify chunks that execute shorter than their creation time and guide chunk size selection, as demonstrated by grain graphs.

The new loop callback ompt_callback_loop is meant to be called instead of the existing ompt_callback_work whenever a parallel for-loop is encountered. This callback provides additional loop-level information such as loop increment and the schedule type at runtime. Schedule type is not always set in the source code and can be decided by the compiler, runtime system, and environment variables. The is_iter_signed parameter is used to inform tools about the signedness of the iteration variable, so that tools can cast the iteration bounds reported by ompt_callback_chunk to the correct type.

The extensions require minimal changes to existing OMPT implementations. The ompt_callback_work callback is simply replaced by ompt_callback_loop in code that processes the for construct. Calls to ompt_callback_chunk should be made in runtime system functions that handle assignment of chunks to worker threads executing dynamically scheduled for-loops.

A relatively larger change is required to handle statically scheduled for-loops where worker threads calculate their chunk iteration ranges directly through code inserted by the compiler. In this case, compilers should additionally generate calls to ompt_callback_chunk, preferably through a call to the runtime system. Calling the runtime system for every chunk is expensive if chunk sizes are small. We avoid this overhead when there is no tool attached, or when the attached tool has not registered for the ompt_callback_chunk callback, by conditionally calling the runtime system as shown in the pseudocode snippet below.

```
bool callbackPerChunk = __omp_runtime_should_callback_per_chunk();
while (UB = min(UB, GlobalUB), idx = LB, idx < UB) {
    if (callbackPerChunk) {
        __omp_runtime_for_static_chunk(...)
    }
    for (idx = LB; idx <= UB; ++idx) {
        BODY;
    }
    LB = LB + stride; UB = UB + stride;
}
```

Notice that the snippet does not contain code to compute chunk creation time. For statically scheduled loops, we chose to return 0 as the creation duration in the ompt_callback_chunk callback since only a few simple operations are required to create a chunk. Compiler writers can instead decide to call the tool-space time function if chunk creation is more involved.

4 Evaluation

Evaluation of the proposed extensions is discussed in this section.

4.1 Experimental Setup

Our test machine has two Intel Xeon E5-2630 2.2 Ghz 10-core processors. Each core has private 32 KB L1 instruction and data caches, and a 256 KB L2 cache. Each processor has a shared 25 MB L3 cache. Hyper-threading is disabled. The system has 64 GB RAM and runs CentOS Linux with kernel version 3.10.

We selected a wide range of benchmarks to test the extensions. Our benchmark set consisted of *schedbench* and *taskbench* micro-benchmarks from the EPCC OpenMP micro-benchmark suite [1,2] and programs from BOTS [6] and SPEC OMP2012 [17].

Benchmarks from schedbench and taskbench capture overhead of supporting parallel for-loops and tasks respectively. Both sets have the following parameters: *Outer repetitions* specifies how many times to repeat the test, *test time* specifies the target time for each test, and *delay time* specifies the busy-wait duration inside loop iterations and tasks. We parameterized schedbench with 50 outer repetitions, test time 30 ms, delay time 0.1 μs, and 4096 iterations per thread to produce the same conditions on our modern test system as the original authors of schedbench [1]. We used default parameters for taskbench except for increasing the number of outer repetitions to 50 and the test time to 30 ms to significantly reduce variance. We report median measurements of 20 runs for schedbench and taskbench benchmarks.

We included all programs from BOTS and C/C++ programs from SPEC OMP2012 in our benchmark set. We used large inputs when available, medium otherwise for BOTS programs. The task creation cutoffs used with BOTS programs were 256 for FFT, 20 for Fib, 8 for N Queens, 5 for Floorplan, 3 for Strassen, and 2 for Health. For Sort, the sequential merge and quicksort cutoffs used were 2048 and the insertion sort cutoff was 20. Reference inputs were used for SPEC OMP2012 programs except 376.kdtree. This program has a bug found by grain graphs [15] that SPEC has since acknowledged and resolved to fix in a future release. Providing the reference input to the bug-fixed version of 376.kdtree lowers the parallelism exposed, so we increased the cutoff from 2 to 8. Nested parallelism in 352.nab causes high execution time variance, so we ran it with nested parallelism disabled. We report median measurements of 20 and 12 runs for BOTS and SPEC OMP2012 programs respectively.

We ran benchmarks with and without a tool attached. The setup without an attached tool is called *no tool* in the paper. The attached tool had two flavors: a *no callbacks* variant that registered no callbacks and a *with callbacks* variant that registered relevant callbacks but did not execute any code within.

All benchmarks were run on 20 threads, with each thread pinned to a core. Threads with even IDs were pinned to cores on the same processor. Those with odd IDs were pinned to cores on the other processor.

Benchmarks, tools, and different versions of the LLVM OpenMP runtime were compiled using LLVM Clang version 4.0 with $-O3$ optimization. The default OpenMP runtime system of Clang 4.0 supports an outdated OMPT specification. We refer to this runtime system as *TR2* since it supports a subset of the OMPT Technical Report 2. The group behind OMPT has augmented TR2 with support for the more recent OMPT Technical Report 4 [18]. We refer to this runtime system as *TR4*. We modified TR4 to include our extensions and called it *TR4E*. We also modified Clang to generated code that supports the chunk scheduling extension in statically scheduled for-loops. This modified compiler was used to compile benchmarks that linked with TR4E. Our modifications in TR4E and Clang are consistent with the prevailing implementation style and are publicly available for review [12].

Table 1. Callbacks registered by the *with callbacks* tool variant are runtime system specific.

Runtime system	**for** construct	**task** construct
TR2	ompt_event_loop_begin ompt_event_loop_end	ompt_event_task_begin
TR4 TR4E	ompt_callback_work ompt_callback_loop ompt_callback_chunk	ompt_callback_task_create ompt_callback_task_create

Callbacks registered by tools are shown in Table 1. These differ because the runtime systems support different versions of OMPT. TR2 did not have a direct equivalent to the ompt_callback_task_create callback of TR4. We used the TR2 callback ompt_event_task_begin, a close match called once before task execution.

4.2   Experimental Results

Overhead of supporting the extensions and attaching tools are discussed in the section. We refer to callbacks that describe parallel for-loop and chunk events as loop and chunk callbacks respectively.

The EPCC micro-benchmarks schedbench and taskbench work by first performing some work W sequentially without using OpenMP, and then doing the same amount of work W on N threads using OpenMP. The difference in execution time of the two work operations is reported as timing overhead by the micro-benchmarks. We report these timing overhead measurements relative to our baseline TR4, calling them *relative overhead* in the paper.

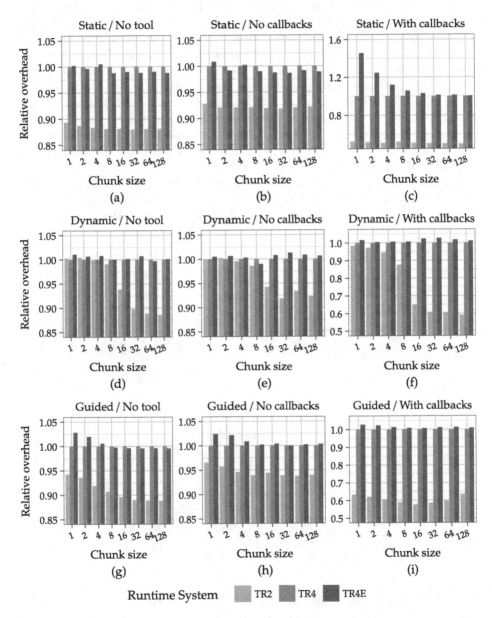

Fig. 2. Relative overhead of loop-based extensions measured with schedbench microbenchmarks are up to 3% except for statically scheduled small chunks that require a runtime system call per-chunk. TR4 is the baseline.

Results of schedbench experiments are shown in Fig. 2. TR2 has the lowest relative overhead since it supports an outdated OMPT implementation with fewer features. TR4E incurs less than 1% overhead over TR4 when no tool is attached, except for the guided schedule with chunk size 1 where the difference is 2.8%. When a tool with no callbacks is attached, the guided schedule again experiences the highest increase in overhead, up to 2.5%. The tool variant with callbacks registers the loop callback with all runtime systems, and additionally the chunk callback in TR4E. With callbacks registered, TR4E incurs up to 3% higher overhead than TR4, except for the case of statically scheduled loops with chunk sizes below 32 where enabling the conditional per-chunk runtime system call (Sect. 3.2) incurs up to 50% overhead given the fine-grained nature of iterations. The overhead of the chunk callback is low in all other scenarios. We also ran tests where only the loop callback is registered in TR4E. Results of these tests are not discussed in the paper due to space reasons and available in an external database for review [10].

Results of taskbench experiments are shown in Fig. 3. We note that performance flaws of TR2 have been rectified in the TR4. Specifically, thread synchronization needed to assign unique task IDs in parallel for OMPT callbacks in

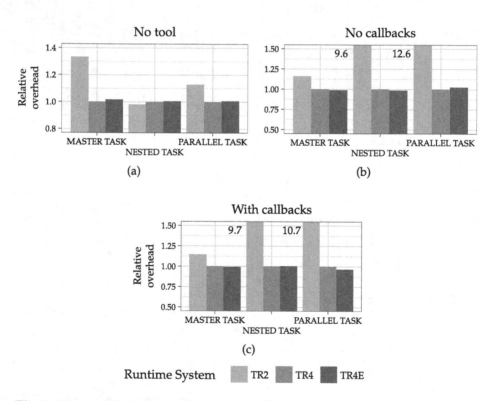

Fig. 3. The proposed task creation extension incurs up to 2.7% relative overhead for taskbench micro-benchmarks. TR4 is the baseline.

TR2 is problematic and increases overhead for NESTED TASK and PARALLEL TASK micro-benchmarks when a tool is attached. MASTER TASK generates tasks only on the master thread, and therefore is not affected. TR4E adds negligible task creation overhead over TR4 since it requires less than 1% extra instructions. With no tool attached, the highest increase in overhead is 1.7%,

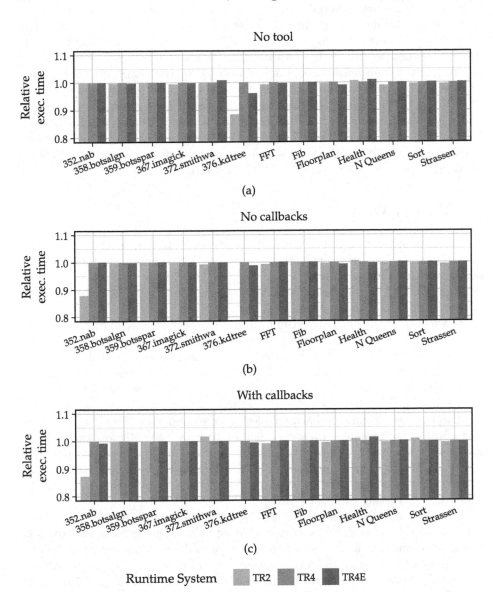

(a)

(b)

(c)

Fig. 4. SPEC OMP2012 and BOTS programs incur up to 1% and 2% overhead respectively with the proposed extensions. TR4 is the baseline. Programs with alpha-numeric names are from SPEC OMP2012.

seen with the MASTER TASK micro-benchmark. When the tool variant that does not register callbacks is attached, PARALLEL TASK incurs a 2.7% increase in overhead. Registering callbacks shown in Table 1 leads to equal overheads in TR4 and TR4E.

Results of experiments with SPEC OMP2012 and BOTS programs are shown in Fig. 4. We compare overall execution times to evaluate the overhead of the proposed extensions. Alignment and SparseLU are present in both benchmark suites. We show variants from SPEC OMP2012 since they use larger inputs. Most programs see no change in execution times. 376.kdtree runs 4% faster due to incidental optimization opportunities used by the modified Clang 4 compiler. Also, this program does not run to completion with an attached tool even after 5 h of execution due to the previously mentioned problem with parallel task ID assignment in TR2, so the results are omitted. With no tool attached, 372.smithwa and Health run 1% slower. When the tool variant that does not register callbacks is attached, no significant slowdown is observed. Registering callbacks causes Health to run 2% slower on TR4E.

5   Related Work

The main motivation for the proposed extensions is to construct grain graphs portably. However, the events described by the extensions have found use in other profiling APIs and tools.

The POMP API [13], a base for OMPT, included events to describe the start and completion of for-loop chunks.

Qawasmeh et al. [20] analyze timing and cache performance of runtime events including task creation to decide on optimal scheduling strategies in the OpenUH runtime system. They extend [21] the Sun/Oracle Collector API [9] to record the events. The task creation event in their design is described using separate start and stop events. The same two events are used by Servat et al. [22] for instrumenting the Nanos++ runtime system.

The proposed chunk callback enables tools to understand and support for-loops better. For example, Yoga et al. [23] build data race detectors that rely on structured parallelism events such as task creation and synchronization events to flag conflicting memory accesses in Intel TBB programs. Their technique can potentially be extended to OpenMP for-loop chunks by plugging in our chunk callback and treating chunks as tasks.

Drebes et al. [5] augment the LLVM OpenMP runtime system to collect parallel for-loop chunk traces. The traces are used to map chunks to worker threads in their Aftermath tool [4], enabling diagnosis of load imbalance problems. Unlike our extension, their implementation does not trace chunks of statically scheduled parallel for-loops – a dominant parallelization pattern. Excluding 367.imagick, 91/105 parallel for-loops in SPEC OMP2012 are statically scheduled.

Intel's VTune Amplifier [8] recently improved its OpenMP debugging feature set by characterizing loop schedules, chunk sizes, and time spent scheduling iterations. These are understood through source code inspection and sampling, provided profiled programs use Intel or GCC runtime systems. Our proposed OMPT extensions enable tools to portably compute similar metrics without need for source code inspection.

6   Conclusions

We presented extensions to OMPT that add a time duration parameter to the task creation callback, improve information provided by the loop callback, and introduce a new callback to describe chunk events, with the intention to construct grain graphs portably from any OMPT-compliant runtime system. Overhead incurred by the extensions with or without tools attached is low – up to 3% for EPCC micro-benchmarks, excluding the use of the chunk callback for statically scheduled chunks of sizes below 32. Programs from BOTS and SPEC OMP2012 slowdown negligibly, with only outliers slowing down by up to 2% and 1% respectively. The extensions adhere to OMPT design objectives, are implemented in a consistent, maintainable manner in a standard toolchain, and are publicly available [12]. Although motivated by grain graphs, the events described by the extensions are general and can enable cost-effective, precise measurements in other profiling tools as well.

Acknowledgment. We are grateful to anonymous reviewers for comments that helped improve the paper. One reviewer generously pointed out that our proposed chunk callback can be applied in data race detection tools as well. We thank Joachim Protze (RWTH Aachen), Jonas Hahnfeld (RWTH Aachen), Sergei Shudler (TU Darmstadt) and Harald Servat (Intel) for helpful comments and suggestions regarding the extensions. This paper is partially funded by the TULIPP project, grant number 688403 from the EU Horizon 2020 Research and Innovation programme.

References

1. Bull, J.M.: Measuring synchronisation and scheduling overheads in OpenMP. In: Proceedings of First European Workshop on OpenMP, vol. 8, p. 49 (1999)
2. Bull, J.M., Reid, F., McDonnell, N.: A microbenchmark suite for OpenMP tasks. In: Chapman, B.M., Massaioli, F., Müller, M.S., Rorro, M. (eds.) IWOMP 2012. LNCS, vol. 7312, pp. 271–274. Springer, Heidelberg (2012). doi:10.1007/978-3-642-30961-8_24
3. Dagum, L., Menon, R.: OpenMP: an industry standard API for shared-memory programming. IEEE Comput. Sci. Eng. **5**(1), 46–55 (1998)
4. Drebes, A., Pop, A., Heydemann, K., Cohen, A.: Interactive visualization of cross-layer performance anomalies in dynamic task-parallel applications and systems. In: 2016 IEEE International Symposium on Performance Analysis of Systems and Software (ISPASS), pp. 274–283, April 2016
5. Drebes, A., Bréjon, J.-B., Pop, A., Heydemann, K., Cohen, A.: Language-centric performance analysis of OpenMP programs with aftermath. In: Maruyama, N., Supinski, B.R., Wahib, M. (eds.) IWOMP 2016. LNCS, vol. 9903, pp. 237–250. Springer, Cham (2016). doi:10.1007/978-3-319-45550-1_17

6. Duran, A., Teruel, X., Ferrer, R., Martorell, X., Ayguade, E.: Barcelona OpenMP tasks suite: a set of benchmarks targeting the exploitation of task parallelism in OpenMP. In: Proceedings of the 2009 International Conference on Parallel Processing, ICPP 2009, pp. 124–131 (2009). http://dx.doi.org/10.1109/ICp.2009.64

7. Eichenberger, A.E., Mellor-Crummey, J., Schulz, M., Wong, M., Copty, N., Dietrich, R., Liu, X., Loh, E., Lorenz, D.: OMPT: an OpenMP tools application programming interface for performance analysis. In: Rendell, A.P., Chapman, B.M., Müller, M.S. (eds.) IWOMP 2013. LNCS, vol. 8122, pp. 171–185. Springer, Heidelberg (2013). doi:10.1007/978-3-642-40698-0_13

8. Intel: Intel VTune Amplifier Webpage, May 2017. https://software.intel.com/en-us/intel-vtune-amplifier-xe

9. Itzkowitz, M., Mazurov, O., Copty, N., Lin, Y., Lin, Y.: An OpenMP runtime API for profiling. OpenMP ARB as an official ARB White Paper, vol. 314, pp. 181–190 (2007). http://www.compunity.org/futures/omp-api.html, http://www.compunity.org/futures/omp-api-old.html

10. Langdal, P.V.: Extending OMPT to support grain graphs - dataset, 6 2017. https://figshare.com/articles/Extending_OMPT_to_support_Grain_Graphs_-_Dataset/5086837

11. Langdal, P.V.: Generating grain graphs using the OpenMP tools API. Technical report, NTNU (2017). https://brage.bibsys.no/xmlui/handle/11250/2434632

12. Langdal, P.V.: LLVM OpenMP TR4E Alpha Release, May 2017. https://doi.org/10.5281/zenodo.570288

13. Mohr, B., Malony, A.D., Hoppe, H.C., Schlimbach, F., Haab, G., Hoeflinger, J., Shah, S.: A performance monitoring interface for OpenMP. In: Proceedings of the Fourth Workshop on OpenMP (EWOMP 2002), pp. 1001–1025 (2002)

14. Muddukrishna, A., Jonsson, P.A., Langdal, P.: anamud/mir-dev: MIR v1.0.0, March 2017. https://doi.org/10.5281/zenodo.439351

15. Muddukrishna, A., Jonsson, P.A., Podobas, A., Brorsson, M.: Grain graphs: OpenMP performance analysis made easy. In: Proceedings of the 21st ACM SIGPLAN Symposium on Principles and Practice of Parallel Programming, PPoPP 2016, NY, USA, pp. 28:1–28:13 (2016). http://doi.acm.org/10.1145/2851141.2851156

16. Muddukrishna, A., Langdal, P.: anamud/grain-graphs: Grain Graphs v1.0.0, March 2017. https://doi.org/10.5281/zenodo.439355

17. Muller, M.S., Baron, J., Brantley, W.C., Feng, H., Hackenberg, D., Henschel, R., Jost, G., Molka, D., Parrott, C., Robichaux, J., Shelepugin, P., van Waveren, M., Whitney, B., Kumaran, K.: SPEC OMP2012 - an application benchmark suite for parallel systems using OpenMP. In: Proceedings of the 8th International Conference on OpenMP in a Heterogeneous World, IWOMP 2012, pp. 223–236 (2012). http://dx.doi.org/10.1007/978-3-642-30961-8_17

18. OMPT Tools Interface Group: LLVM OpenMP Runtime with Changes Towards TR4. GitHub (2017). https://github.com/OpenMPToolsInterface/LLVM-openmp

19. OpenMP Language Working Group: OpenMP Technical report 4: Version 5.0 Preview 1, November 2016. http://www.openmp.org/wp-content/uploads/openmp-tr4.pdf

20. Qawasmeh, A., Malik, A.M., Chapman, B.M.: Adaptive OpenMP task scheduling using runtime APIs and machine learning. In: 2015 IEEE 14th International Conference on Machine Learning and Applications (ICMLA), pp. 889–895, December 2015

21. Qawasmeh, A., Malik, A., Chapman, B., Huck, K., Malony, A.: Open source task profiling by extending the OpenMP runtime API. In: Rendell, A.P., Chapman, B.M., Müller, M.S. (eds.) IWOMP 2013. LNCS, vol. 8122, pp. 186–199. Springer, Heidelberg (2013). doi:10.1007/978-3-642-40698-0_14

22. Servat, H., Teruel, X., Llort, G., Duran, A., Giménez, J., Martorell, X., Ayguadé, E., Labarta, J.: On the instrumentation of OpenMP and OmpSs tasking constructs. In: Caragiannis, I., Alexander, M., Badia, R.M., Cannataro, M., Costan, A., Danelutto, M., Desprez, F., Krammer, B., Sahuquillo, J., Scott, S.L., Weidendorfer, J. (eds.) Euro-Par 2012. LNCS, vol. 7640, pp. 414–428. Springer, Heidelberg (2013). doi:10.1007/978-3-642-36949-0_47

23. Yoga, A., Nagarakatte, S., Gupta, A.: Parallel data race detection for task parallel programs with locks. In: Proceedings of the 2016 24th ACM SIGSOFT International Symposium on Foundations of Software Engineering, FSE 2016, NY, USA, pp. 833–845 (2016). http://doi.acm.org/10.1145/2950290.2950329

Patterns for OpenMP Task Data Dependency Overhead Measurements

Joseph Schuchart[✉], Mathias Nachtmann, and José Gracia

High Performance Computing Center Stuttgart (HLRS),
University of Stuttgart, Stuttgart, Germany
{schuchart,nachtmann,gracia}@hlrs.de

Abstract. Starting with version 4.0, the OpenMP standard has introduced data dependencies to provide a way for synchronizing the concurrent execution of task based on dataflow information. This indirect approach to fine-grained sychronization offers a convenient way for creating a task graph without having to explicitly synchronize individual tasks and can be used to parallelize both regular and irregular applications to expose a higher level of concurrency to the runtime system. However, the cost associated with task creation and management, including matching input and output dependencies, is a crucial factor in designing the granularity of individual tasks, i.e., the amount of work to encapsulate in a task. In this work, we present a set of benchmarks designed to determine the overhead associated with dependency management and give an overview of the performance characteristics of a set of compilers widely used in parallel computing. We hope to provide application developers with a way to make informed decisions on the granularity of their tasks given the dependency patterns dictated by the algorithm. Our benchmark results show varying performance characteristics of different implementations that are both interesting and important to have in mind throughout the task design process.

1 Introduction

The concept of expressing concurrency through tasks continues to gain traction among developers of thread-parallel applications. The OpenMP standard has introduced the concept of tasks to broad user community with the release of version 3.0. In contrast to traditional parallel loop constructs, the tasking concept allows users to expose irregular or unstructured concurrent patterns, e.g., tree traversal. Tasks can have arbitrary size, ranging from a few instructions to complex computations involving nested tasks.

Starting with version 4.0 of the standard, OpenMP allows users to specify data dependencies between tasks they define in their application [1]. Data dependencies provide a convenient way of controlling the order of tasks without explicit synchronization calls. Using the dependency information provided by the user, the scheduler can build a task dependency graph that contains information on the required ordering of the tasks.

© Springer International Publishing AG 2017
B.R. de Supinski et al. (Eds.): IWOMP 2017, LNCS 10468, pp. 156–168, 2017.
DOI: 10.1007/978-3-319-65578-9_11

OpenMP allows to specify two types of dependencies: output (`out` and its alias `inout`) and input (`in`) dependencies. Output dependencies signal the scheduler that the task will produce data at the specified data location for consumption by other tasks. Tasks with similar output dependencies on the same data location have to be scheduled in the order they were defined.

Input dependencies, on the other hand, inform the scheduler that the specified data point will be consumed by the task and thus the task should run after any previously defined task with a matching output dependency. Tasks with input dependencies on the same data location can be executed in parallel as they only consume data without altering it. It is up to the user to correctly specify the data dependencies of tasks to ensure correctness of the application as compilers supporting the OpenMP standard are not required to validate the defined dependencies.

Dependencies can be either *matched* or *unmatched*, e.g., an input with no corresponding output dependencies is unmatched. We consider a output dependencies to be matched if at least one corresponding input and output dependencies has or will be defined, respectively.

While task dependencies provide a convenient way for users to control task execution, their implementation is not trivial as it requires a significant amount of book-keeping needed to track the specified memory locations of dependencies and determine the order of tasks. This may have a significant impact on the time needed to create and execute tasks with data dependencies. Information on the overhead incurred by the different numbers of task dependencies is important in the design of an application using tasks with task dependencies, i.e., the minimum workload performed by a task should be large enough to compensate for the additional work needed to handle task dependencies. This paper presents our efforts to create a set of benchmarks to determine the overhead of different OpenMP implementations in handling tasks with different numbers of dependencies, both matched and unmatched.

The remainder of the paper is structured as follows: Sect. 2 presents a survey of related work, which is followed by a description of our benchmark design in Sect. 3, an outline of the measurement methodology in Sect. 4, and the results in Sect. 5. From that, we draw our conclusions in Sect. 6.

2   Related Work

Bull et al. have presented a microbenchmark suite for OpenMP tasks, which has been integrated into the EPCC OpenMP benchmark suite [3]. They showed a large variation in overhead for task creation and synchronization, dependending on the compiler, machine, and number of threads used. The current version of the benchmarks suite does not cover OpenMP task data dependencies. We decided to use this benchmark suite as the basis for our implementation presented in Sect. 3.3. A similar microbenchmark suite has been presented by Lagrone et al. in [10]. However, the set of benchmarks presented there is smaller than with the EPCC benchmark suite and does not cover data dependencies either.

Others have focused on application-based benchmarks, both for OpenMP (SPEC OpenMP [2,11], the Barcelona OpenMP Tasks Suite [8]) and Intel TBB tasks (PARSEC benchmark suite [5]). However, none of these benchmark suites cover task dependencies.

The PARSECSs benchmark suite is a task-based implementation of the PARSEC application benchmark suite using dependencies for data-flow control [4]. The KASTORS benchmark suite covers OpenMP task data dependencies through a set of micro-kernels, comparing the performance of their implementations with and without data dependencies [14]. While these approaches are useful for estimating the overall performance of task-based parallelization, they are less suitable for deciding design aspects such as the size of individual tasks.

Recent attempts have been made to perform task dependency management and scheduling in hardware rather than software to reduce the overhead. Two such designs are presented in [7] and [15], respectively. However, systematic studies of the overheads have not been presented in either work.

To the best of our knowledge, there have been no previous attempts to measuring the overhead of task data dependencies in OpenMP.

3   Benchmark Design

The main contribution of this paper is the design of a set of patterns, which characterize the performance of creating and executing tasks with data dependencies between them. We have experimented with different task graph patterns to determine the impact of the following properties to the performance of task creation in an implementation of OpenMP 4.0: (i) The number N of data dependencies defined per task, with $N \in \{1, 2, 4, 8, 16, 24, 32\}$; (ii) the overall number of memory locations referenced in dependencies; (iii) matched vs unmatched dependencies; and (iv) the dependency type (input and output dependencies).

While determining the cost associated with creating tasks with varying number of defined data dependencies has been the initial motivation for this work, we decided to also look at the other factors. The following paragraphs shortly describe the patterns together with the properties they are meant to explore.

3.1   Basic Patterns

P_1: **The Chain Pattern** is the most straight-forward pattern in our collection and forms a sequence of tasks with N dependencies (links) between two succeeding task, as depicted in Fig. 1(a). The number of distinct memory locations used as in the dependencies is fixed to N. The use of input dependencies would require the same amount of output dependencies from the previous task and would thus double the number of dependencies per task.

P_2: **The Linked List Pattern** is a modification of the Chain pattern P_1 such that only a subset of the N defined data dependencies are actually matched by previous or successive tasks. Thus, the pattern can be seen as a linked list with one link between two tasks. Pattern P_2 is depicted in Fig. 1(b) and is created by leaving $N - 1$ *input* dependencies unmatched. Since input dependencies do not cause any ordering of tasks, each task also needs to provide one output dependency. All dependencies point to different memory locations, thus ensuring that all unmatched dependencies remain as such. Incidentally, this extends the address space used in data dependency management, potentially increasing the pressure on the respective parts of the runtime system.

With slight modifications, it is possible to turn the unmatched input dependencies into output dependencies. Although we have included this modification in our benchmarks, we do not present the results due to space constraints and since we have not observed significant differences between the input and the output version of this pattern.

3.2 Advanced Patterns

P_3: **The Stencil Pattern** resembles a stencil with different numbers of neighboring cells needed to compute the current cell. Thus, for this pattern N denotes the number of neighboring cells. In order to maintain the general structure of the pattern, a task also defines the current cell as input from the previous and output for the next iteration, employing a double buffering scheme to ensure independence of tasks in one iteration. Consequently, each task in this pattern has $N + 2$ dependencies defined, $N + 1$ input and one output dependency.

Commonly, a 1D domain decomposition resembles a stencil pattern with $N = 2$, as depicted in Fig. 1c. Likewise, a cell in a 2D domain decomposition has either five $(4 + 1)$ or nine $(4 + 1)$ input dependencies, depending on whether the corner cells are required as input or not. In a 3D domain decomposition, up to 27 $(26 + 1)$ input dependencies can be required for each cell.

In this pattern, a significant number of dependencies may remain unmatched depending on the arrangement of the tasks. Naturally, in the first iteration the input dependencies are not matched as there have not been previous tasks with matching output dependencies. Likewise, tasks on the boundaries and in the last iteration will always have unmatched dependencies. We decided to choose $W = 1000$ as the number of tasks per iteration (width of the task graph) and use the number of iterations to control the overall number of tasks. The fraction of unmatched dependencies can be approximated as $\frac{3}{4}N * (\frac{1}{W} - \frac{1}{T}) + \frac{W}{T}$, ranging from 1 for $T = 1000$ tasks to 0.216 for $T = 5000$ with 32 dependencies.

Abandoned: The N-ary tree pattern would have been an obvious choice but was eventually abandoned, considering that in a perfect N-ary tree of height h the majority of nodes exhibits unmatched dependencies for large N, i.e., N^h with $h = \lceil log_N(N - 1) + log_N(T) - 1 \rceil$. Given $N = 32$ output dependencies and a tree height $h = 4$, approximately 97% of all nodes are leaf nodes, which do not have any matched output dependencies. We decided to avoid this inconsistency.

3.3 Implementation

As mentioned in Sect. 2, we have implemented our benchmarks as an extension of the EPCC OpenMP benchmark suite. The task dependencies have been

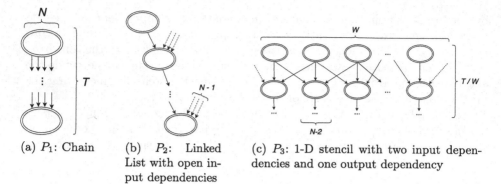

(a) P_1: Chain

(b) P_2: Linked List with open input dependencies

(c) P_3: 1-D stencil with two input dependencies and one output dependency

Fig. 1. Patterns used to measure the performance of OpenMP tasks with dependencies (N: Variable number of dependencies; T: Number of tasks; W: Width of the task graph or number of tasks per iteration). Matched dependencies are depicted as bold arrows, unmatched as dashed arrows.

```
1  char *depbuf = (char *)0xDEADBEEF;
2  #pragma omp parallel
3  {
4  #pragma omp barrier
5  #pragma omp master
6    {
7        start_time = timer();
8        for (int i = 0; i < num_tasks; ++i) {
9  #pragma omp task depend(out: depbuf[0], depbuf[1]) \
10                   depend(out: depbuf[2], depbuf[3])
11         { delay(delayLength); }
12      }
13  #pragma omp taskwait
14        end_time = timer();
15    } // omp master
16  } // omp parallel
```

Listing 1.1. Simplified example of the Chain pattern implementation with 4 dependencies.

implemented as a separate module, which makes use of the shared infrastructure of the benchmark suite.[1]

An example of the Chain pattern (P_1) is depicted in Listing 1.1 and shows the basic control flow of the benchmarks. Inside a parallel region, the master thread takes care of the timing (lines 7 and 14), with threads being synchronized by barriers. The master thread then further creates the specified number of tasks with the given number of dependencies before waiting for the tasks to be executed by all threads in the `taskwait` statement (line 14). In our implementation, the number of tasks is configurable at runtime while the number of dependencies is provided as a C++ template parameter to allow the compiler to optimize the selection of the code path creating the desired number of dependencies. Since OpenMP task

---

[1] The code and result files are available at https://github.com/devreal/omp-tdb.

creation and dependency specification are both static, we have to provide individual statements for each dependency configuration.

The tasks themselves only perform a small amount of work in the `delay` function (line 11) to ensure correct time measurement. This functionality is taken from the EPCC benchmark suite, where `delayLength` describes the number of instructions to be executed, which is determined dynamically based on information provided by the user, e.g., the minimum delay time ($0.1\,\mu s$ by default).

4 Measurement Methodology

All experiments have been repeated 20 times and the arithmetic mean has been used as average for the plots in Sect. 5. To improve readability in these plots, error bars have been omitted. However, the relative error has been consistently below 8% throughout our measurements. Given the scale of the differences between the compilers presented below, we are confident that this error does not harm the significance of our conclusions.

Unless specified otherwise, the default task granularity has been $0.1\,\mu s$.

4.1 Runtime Libraries

The GNU compiler collection (GCC) as well as the Intel and Clang compilers all support tasking with data dependencies. The set of considered compiler versions include GCC versions 6.3.0, Intel 16.0.3 and 17.0.1, as well as Clang 3.9.1. Initially, we also considered GCC version 5.3.0 but have not observed significant performance differences.

In contrast to them, the manual for the Cray compiler (as of version 8.5.7) states that *"the task 'depend' clause is supported, but tasks with dependences are serialized"* [6, p. 70]. Our measurements have reflected this behavior. Cray kindly provided us with access to a pre-release of the next Cray Compiler Environment (8.6), which will come with full support for OpenMP 4.5. While we can confirm that dependencies are handled correctly in the upcoming release, we decided not to publish performance measurements of a pre-release version.

The PGI compiler (as of version 17) does not support the OpenMP 4.0 standard [13, Chap. 5]. We thus omitted both compilers from our measurements presented below. At the time of this writing, the authors do not have access to any other compiler suite.

In addition to the production-level compiler mentioned above, we also included the OmpSs [9,12] compiler in version 16.06.3 in our measurements. This compiler has a long-standing tradition of being used as a research vehicle for the implementation of upcoming OpenMP features, most notably the tasking concepts. The OmpSs compiler can be used in two modes: in the **openmp** mode, the compiler links a standard compliant runtime library while **ompss** mode the OpenMP pragmas are mapped to the OmpSs runtime implementation, which diverges from the OpenMP standard with regards to certain semantics. We were able to successfully build and run our benchmarks in both modes.

4.2 Parameter Space

In our measurements, we have considered different parameters that might influence the performance of the different OpenMP runtime implementations, as described below.

The Number of Dependencies N is central to our measurements and has been motivated in Sect. 3.2 already. Our initial approach was to determine the influence of the number of dependencies on the overhead induced by the runtime. We decided to include 1, 2, 4, 8, 12, 16, 24, and 32 dependencies per task in our measurements, providing a smaller step size for lower counts while also covering the higher counts.

The Number of Tasks T might have an impact on the performance since a higher number of tasks may require more resources for scheduling. Moreover, in the case of the Stencil pattern P_3, the number of tasks also control the percentage of matched output dependencies in the dependency graph. We ran our benchmarks with 1000 and 5000 tasks and provide numbers for both if significant differences were observable.

The Number of Threads used to execute the benchmark may have a significant impact on the overhead with some runtime libraries, including GCC, Intel, and Clang. The runtime may skip processing of dependencies in single-threaded environments, in which tasks can be executed immediately without queuing. In fact, the open source Clang runtime library (which is also used by the Intel compiler) avoids any scheduling overhead by immediately executing tasks created in a serial execution context. The GNU compiler does not seem to employ this optimization. In our measurement setup, further increasing the number of threads may lead to artificial contention because the master thread cannot create tasks fast enough to keep all other threads busy. We have thus only included benchmark results for runs using 1 and 2 threads. The times presented in Sect. 5 are CPU times, i.e., we have multiplied the measured time by two for runs with two threads.

4.3 Measurement Environment

All experiments were conducted on the Cray XC40 "Hazelhen" installed at HLRS. The system is comprised of dual-socket Haswell nodes with 128 GB main memory. Correct pinning of all threads to a single socket was ensured through the PBS scheduler (using `aprun -cc numa_node`). The default Cray Programming Environment (PE) version 5.2.82 has been used for the pre-installed compilers. It should be noted that the GCC 6.3.0 and Intel 16.3.0 serve as the current default for the respective PE modules. We have built both the Clang and OmpSs compiler from vanilla sources using the GCC 6.3.0 compiler.

5   Results

5.1 P_1: Chain Pattern

The mean times required to create and execute a single task of length $0.1\,\mu s$ with N dependencies in the output Chain pattern P_1 are depicted in Fig. 2. We have not found significant differences in overhead when increasing the number of tasks from 1000 to 5000.

However, we have found significant differences between runs with one and two threads, as depicted in Fig. 2. For single-threaded runs, Fig. 2a shows that the Intel and Clang compiler exhibit almost no overhead while there is a slightly increasing overhead visible for the GNU Compiler. This is in-line with the expectaions expressed in Sect. 4.2.

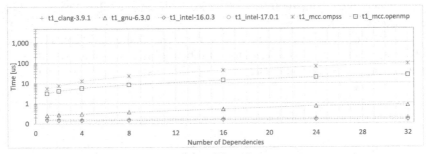

(a) 1 Thread

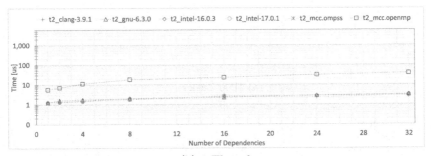

(b) 2 Threads

Fig. 2. Mean time per task for 1000 tasks in pattern P_1 (output chain) with 2 threads and increasing number of dependencies.

Using two threads, the GNU runtime as well as the Intel and Clang runtimes exhibit similar overheads depicted in Fig. 2b, which are higher than for single-threaded execution. No significant performance difference can be observed between these compilers with the runtimes ranging from $1.28\,\mu s$ for $N = 1$ to $2.58\,\mu s$ for $N = 32$ for a single task of length $0.1\,\mu s$.

Above that, the OmpSs research compiler in `openmp` mode can be found. Unfortunately, we were unable to produce meaningful results in `ompss` mode at the time of this writing.

5.2 P_2: Linked List Pattern

The results for 1000 tasks in the second task pattern P_2 are presented in Fig. 3a.

Both the Intel 17 and Clang runtimes exhibit a steeper slope for rising numbers of dependencies such that the GNU runtime outperforms both starting at 16 dependencies, the former reaching 10 μs per task for 32 dependencies. Most surprisingly, though, is the performance of the Intel 16 compiler running with 2 threads (red dashed line): we can observe a significantly overhead, which is even higher than the OmpSs compiler in `openmp` mode, reaching up to 220 μs for 32 dependencies. Figure 3b shows that the slope for both Intel 17 and Clang increases when going from 1000 to 5000 tasks. Still, this overhead remains below 100 μs for both.

An interesting effect can be observed in both the Clang and Intel 17 runtime: for 1000 tasks, the impact of increasing numbers of dependencies is only visible above 8 dependencies. For 500 tasks, this threshold is above 4 dependencies. Our

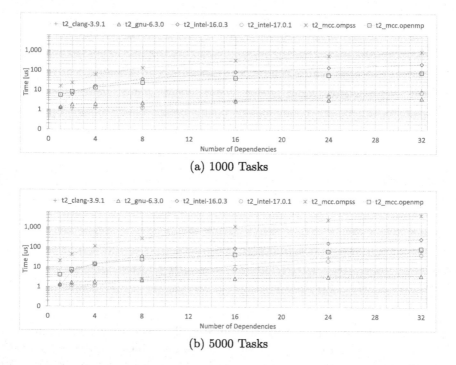

(a) 1000 Tasks

(b) 5000 Tasks

Fig. 3. Mean time per task for pattern P_2 (input linked list) with 2 threads and increasing number of dependencies. (Color figure online)

initial guess is that this effect is related to the hashmap implementation used to track dependencies but have not investigated this any further.

The performance of the GNU compiler seems not to be affected by the number of tasks. However, for lower numbers of dependencies (1 to 4) the GNU compiler is outperformed by both Intel and Clang.

We have also performed measurements using the output version of this pattern but have not observed significant performance differences.

5.3   Stencil Pattern

Figure 4 shows the measurements for the Stencil pattern P_3. The previously mentioned performance patterns repeat here as well, although less pronounced. The difference between 1000 and 5000 tasks is marginal with only the Intel 16 compiler being significantly impacted, indicating that the higher number of tasks does not impact the other compilers. It is interesting to note that the Intel 16 compiler exhibits a significantly higher overhead for 1000 tasks, presumable due to some constant overhead whose per-task impact becomes smaller with smaller numbers of tasks.

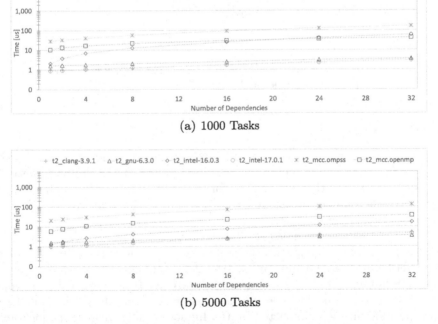

(a) 1000 Tasks

(b) 5000 Tasks

Fig. 4. Mean time per task creation with different compilers for pattern P_3 (stencil) with 2 threads and increasing number of dependencies.

As described in Sect. 3.2, none of the output dependencies are actually matched for $T = W = 1000$ while with 5000 tasks and the same width of the task graph almost 80% of the output dependencies are matched.

5.4   Relative Overhead

Figure 5 presents the relative overhead for the Stencil pattern (P_3) using $N = 8$ of the different OpenMP runtime libraries for increasing task workloads, ranging from 0.1 µs to 12.8 µs. For short running tasks smaller than 0.8 µs, the overhead remains above 50% for all tested implementations. It is only for tasks larger than 10 µs that the overhead drops below 10%. Again, we were unable to fully benchmark the OmpSs compiler but the data we have gathered suggests that significantly longer tasks are required to reach the 10% overhead goal. Due to space constraints we omitted overhead measurements for other task graph configurations.

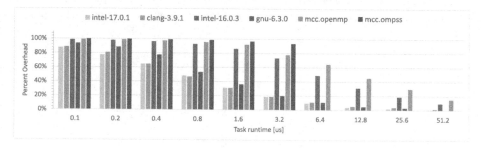

Fig. 5. Percentage of overhead with increasing task runtimes for 1000 tasks in the Stencil pattern with 8 dependencies and 2 threads.

5.5   Discussion

The different runtime libraries under test exhibit different performance characteristics when executing the patterns described in Sect. 3. All production-ready compilers exhibit a rather uniform performance for the simple Chain pattern (P_1), where the number of dependencies has only a slight impact on a task's creation and execution time (factor 2).

This picture changes significantly for the Linked List pattern (P_2) where the spread between the different implementations is more significant. In particular, this pattern creates a large amount of dependencies pointing to distinct memory location, totalling to $(N - 1) * T$ memory locations. Thus, the change in slope between 1000 and 5000 tasks leaves us to conclude that the Clang and Intel 17 compilers seem to be impacted by the higher number of memory locations while the GNU compiler exhibits rather stable performance. This pattern also demonstrated that the impact of the dependency type is negligible.

As a more realistic example, the Stencil pattern (P_3) shows only a small advantage of Clang and Intel 17 over the GNU compiler for small numbers of dependencies but no major difference when scaling the number of dependencies. Given the ratio of unmatched dependencies in our setup (100% for 1000 tasks, ≈20% for 5000 tasks) we conclude that this ratio does yield any substantial impact on the overhead.

It should be noted however, that the Intel 16 compiler has significant performance issues. Given that this compiler might still be the default on many HPC systems, users should be encouraged to use the latest release of the Intel compiler.

6   Conclusion

This work presents a set of micro-benchmarks to evaluate the performance characteristics of OpenMP compilers with regards to the handling of task data dependencies, which had been introduced with the OpenMP 4.0 standard. The benchmarks can be used to assess the impact of the number of tasks, the number and type of dependencies between them, the ratio of matched and unmatched dependencies, as well as the number of threads used to execute the tasks. Based on the data presented in Sect. 5.4, we can conclude that in production-level compilers, tasks with the specified configuration should not be shorter than 10 µs or 2500 cycles (on a 2.5 GHz CPU) in order to keep the overhead below 10%. However, this threshold likely depends on several additional factors, including the system configuration, the overall size of the task-graph, and the load on the system.

An initial attempt to derive a model of the performance characteristics from the performance data we gathered was not conclusive. We thus plan to further refine the benchmarks and collect additional information on the overhead characteristics, including PAPI counter values, to better understand the behavior of the different runtime libraries. We also plan to investigate the impact of a higher number of threads, which requires adjustments to the runtime of individual tasks to provide sufficient work for all threads. Extending the benchmark suite to measure the performance implications of multiple threads creating tasks should be considered as future work as well.

Acknowledgements. Part of this work has been supported by the European Community through the project Mont Blanc 3 (H2020 programme under grant agreement number 671697). We gratefully acknowledge funding by the German Research Foundation (DFG) through the project SmartDASH under the German Priority Programme 1648 Software for Exascale Computing (SPPEXA). The authors would like to thank Christoph Niethammer for his initial input.

References

1. OpenMP Application Programming Interface, Version 4.5, November 2015. http://www.openmp.org/wp-content/uploads/openmp-4.5.pdf. Accessed 2 June 2017
2. Aslot, V., Domeika, M., Eigenmann, R., Gaertner, G., Jones, W.B., Parady, B.: SPEComp: A New Benchmark Suite for Measuring Parallel Computer Performance. Springer, Heidelberg (2001)

3. Bull, J.M., Reid, F., McDonnell, N.: A microbenchmark suite for OpenMP tasks. In: Chapman, B.M., Massaioli, F., Müller, M.S., Rorro, M. (eds.) IWOMP 2012. LNCS, vol. 7312, pp. 271–274. Springer, Heidelberg (2012). doi:10.1007/978-3-642-30961-8_24
4. Chasapis, D., Casas, M., Moretó, M., Vidal, R., Ayguadé, E., Labarta, J., Valero, M.: PARSECSs: evaluating the impact of task parallelism in the PARSEC benchmark suite. ACM Trans. Archit. Code Optim. **12**(4) (2015). Article No. 41
5. Contreras, G., Martonosi, M.: Characterizing and improving the performance of intel threading building blocks. In: IEEE International Symposium on Workload Characterization, September 2008
6. Cray Inc.: Cray C and C++ Reference Manual (8.5), June 2016. http://docs.cray.com/PDF/Cray_C_and_Cplusplus_Reference_Manual_85.pdf. Accessed 2 Mar 2017
7. Dallou, T., Engelhardt, N., Elhossini, A., Juurlink, B.H.H.: Nexus#: a distributed hardware task manager for task-based programming models. In: IEEE International Parallel and Distributed Processing Symposium, IPDPS (2015)
8. Duran, A., Teruel, X., Ferrer, R., Martorell, X., Ayguade, E.: Barcelona OpenMP tasks suite: a set of benchmarks targeting the exploitation of task parallelism in OpenMP. In: International Conference on Parallel Processing, September 2009
9. Duran, A., Ayguadé, E., Badia, R.M., Labarta, J., Martinell, L., Martorell, X., Planas, J.: OmpSs: a proposal for programming heterogeneous multi-core architectures. Parallel Process. Lett. **21**(02), 173–193 (2011)
10. Lagrone, J., Aribuki, A., Chapman, B.: A set of microbenchmarks for measuring OpenMP task overheads. In: International Conference on Parallel and Distributed Processing Techniques and Applications (2011)
11. Müller, M.S., Baron, J., Brantley, W.C., Feng, H., Hackenberg, D., Henschel, R., Jost, G., Molka, D., Parrott, C., Robichaux, J., Shelepugin, P., van Waveren, M., Whitney, B., Kumaran, K.: SPEC OMP2012 – An Application Benchmark Suite for Parallel Systems Using OpenMP. Springer, Heidelberg (2012)
12. Perez, J., Badia, R., Labarta, J.: A dependency-aware task-based programming environment for multi-core architectures. In: IEEE International Conference on Cluster Computing, September 2008
13. PGI Compilers and Tools: PGI Compiler User's Guide for Intel 64 and AMD64CPUs. http://www.pgroup.com/doc/pgiug-x64.pdf. Accessed 2 Mar 2017
14. Virouleau, P., Brunet, P., Broquedis, F., Furmento, N., Thibault, S., Aumage, O., Gautier, T.: Evaluation of OpenMP dependent tasks with the KASTORS benchmark suite. In: DeRose, L., Supinski, B.R., Olivier, S.L., Chapman, B.M., Müller, M.S. (eds.) IWOMP 2014. LNCS, vol. 8766, pp. 16–29. Springer, Cham (2014). doi:10.1007/978-3-319-11454-5_2
15. Yazdanpanah, F., Álvarez, C., Jiménez-González, D., Badia, R.M., Valero, M.: Picos: a hardware runtime architecture support for OmpSs. Future Gener. Comput. Syst. **53**, 130–139 (2015)

Adaptive and Architecture-Independent Task Granularity for Recursive Applications

Antoni Navarro[1]([⊠]), Sergi Mateo[1]([⊠]), Josep Maria Perez[1]([⊠]),
Vicenç Beltran[1]([⊠]), and Eduard Ayguadé[1,2]([⊠])

[1] Barcelona Supercomputing Center, Barcelona, Spain
{antoni.navarro,sergi.mateo,josep.m.perez,vbeltran,eduard.ayguade}@bsc.es
[2] Universitat Politècnica de Catalunya, Barcelona, Spain

Abstract. In the last few decades, modern applications have become larger and more complex. Among the users of these applications, the need to simplify the process of identifying units of work increased as well. With the approach of tasking models, this want has been satisfied. These models make scheduling units of work much more user-friendly. However, with the arrival of tasking models, came granularity management. Discovering an application's optimal granularity is a frequent and sometimes challenging task for a wide range of recursive algorithms. Often, finding the optimal granularity will cause a substantial increase in performance.

With that in mind, the quest for optimality is no easy task. Many aspects have to be considered that are directly related to lack or excess of parallelism in applications. There is no general solution as the optimal granularity depends on both algorithm and system characteristics. One commonly used method to find an optimal granularity consists in experimentally tuning an application with different granularities until an optimal is found. This paper proposes several heuristics which, combined with the appropriate monitoring techniques, allow a runtime system to automatically tune the granularity of recursive applications. The solution is independent of the architecture, execution environment or application being tested. A reference implementation in OmpSs—a task-parallel programming model—shows the programmability, ease of use and competitive performance of the proposed solution. Results show that the proposed solution is able to achieve, for any scenario, at least 75% of the performance of optimally tuned applications.

Keywords: OmpSs · Cost · Autotuning · Threshold · Granularity · Cutoff

1 Introduction

The optimal unit of work in a parallel code depends on many factors. To name a few; input data, resources allocated or the current load of a machine are some of the most important ones to take into account. Statically setting a certain granularity for an application in a specific environment, machine and/or input

© Springer International Publishing AG 2017
B.R. de Supinski et al. (Eds.): IWOMP 2017, LNCS 10468, pp. 169–182, 2017.
DOI: 10.1007/978-3-319-65578-9_12

may cause a dramatic decrease of performance when that same application runs with other parameters or on different machines. Once the granularity is set, often, it will be immutable for the entire execution. Static granularities then, are too rigid and cause applications to suffer a decrease in performance when executed with different configurations.

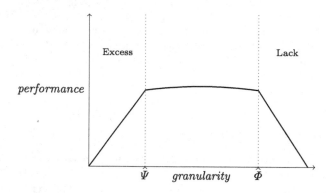

Fig. 1. Effects of different granularities in performance

Figure 1 generically illustrates the consequences of choosing incorrect granularities. When a certain limit Ψ of granularity is not met, fine-grained tasks are generated and that leads to an excess of parallelism. This is worsened by stressing runtime libraries with the management of an excessive amount of tasks. On the other hand, once a certain threshold Φ on granularities is surpassed, tasks are too coarse, which leads to a lack of parallelism and load imbalance. These granularity thresholds are highly dependent on a large number of factors. Some are linked to the hardware architecture, and some others are related to the dynamic behavior of the application and the system on which it runs.

Offline tuning is an extensively used technique when searching for good granularities. It is based on executing applications with different input parameters and granularity cutoffs until an optimal performance is reached. Negative impacts on performance caused by choosing inadequate granularities can be softened by limiting the number of tasks from a runtime's point of view. This is done in order not to stress the runtime with the creation and handling of fine-grained tasks that would not payoff in computation. The latter approach behaves as expected when tasks are fine grained and thus the creation of too many of these would expose too much parallelism. However, for coarse-grained tasks this technique prevents a level of parallelism which is needed.

Visible flaws from the aforementioned techniques and the difficulty of writing architecture-independent code raise interest for a way to auto-tune applications and to detect optimal granularities, taking into account factors such as input sizes or resources. These techniques could improve if precise information about the computation being performed by the tasks is known. Simultaneously, this interest creates a demand for task-based programming models [1] that are able to manage themselves through monitoring. By monitoring, these would have access to certain metrics, which could be used to take scheduling decisions.

This paper presents the OmpSs Autofinal Module. Its purpose is to enable the automatic detection of the optimal granularity of recursive applications, regardless of the architecture, input size or execution environment being used. It consists of a monitoring infrastructure, several heuristics and language support through clauses. The monitoring infrastructure provides precise execution metrics that combined with the heuristics and usage of language constructs, provide information to the runtime to decide when it is worth to instantiate tasks. In addition, this paper shows what kind of language support is recommended to provide useful information to the monitoring infrastructure. Results show that the usage of this technique achieves performance that is competitive in comparison to manually tuned applications on several architectures and diverse applications.

The rest of the paper is structured as follows. Section 2 overviews the related work and introduces the most frequent techniques on granularity management. Section 3 introduces the idea of the *cost* clause from a programming model's point of view. Section 4 thoroughly explains an implementation of Autofinal on OmpSs. Section 5 presents a case study and evaluates its performance and lastly, Sect. 6 concludes this work.

2   Related Work

In most task-based recursive codes, the overhead of task creation and management causes the overall performance of the code to decrease at a certain recursion depth. Because of this, runtime libraries provide techniques to ensure limits on these depths. Managing and limiting granularities have previously been considered in task-based programming models. For instance, OpenMP [2] provides several clauses to tune the task granularity. Below are some of the clauses that are most related to this paper.

– *final:* For recursive problems it may be beneficial for performance to stop task creation at certain depths to expose enough parallelism and reduce overhead. That is, the task will not instantiate children. Instead the code is executed on a single unit of work. Its syntax is

$$final \ (expression)$$

where *expression* evaluates into a boolean value that determines whether the task is *final*.
– *if:* Its syntax is the following:

$$if \ (expression)$$

Before instantiating the task, the *expression* is evaluated. If its value is false, the task is not instantiated and instead its code runs as part of the current task.

– *mergeable:* In certain scenarios, if this clause is present, the task's parent will share its data environment with the task.

Autotuning is often described as a general technique to automatically adapt the execution of a program to a given parallel computer. This adaptation is done in order to optimize one or more runtime performance metrics such as execution time [3]. Other works, such as the one conducted by Ray S. Chen [4] or the one conducted by Chung and Hollingsworth [5], researched ways to autotune applications. Their works rely on running applications several times by differing parameters until an optimal configuration or granularity is found. This paper focuses on dynamically autotuning applications without a previous training phase. The tuning determines the granularity to apply to the *final* clause.

Other works such as the one conducted by Alejandro Duran [6] discussed a similar way of autotuning granularity, however without the usage of the *final* clause nor the *cost* clause. It made use of bare execution times in order to determine when a granularity is fine enough, regardless of the type of the task. This approach might work as expected with some specific architectures, applications and input sizes, however introducing variability in any of these three factors might trigger wrong cutoff decisions, resulting in decreases of performance. This paper however, focuses on precisely determining the computational weight of the tasks and make accurate predictions of execution times, regardless of the architecture, input size or application.

3   Language Support

To make the most of the OmpSs Autofinal module, application developers have to provide additional hints to the runtime. First, the developer must express the intention to use Autofinal. This is necessary in order for task monitoring to happen. Therefore, one could extend the *final* clause to accept keywords like the following:

$$final\,(auto)$$

where *auto* is the keyword that expresses the desire to automatically establish *final* cutoffs.

Furthermore, the accuracy of the data obtained by monitoring can be improved by normalizing it. This is done through information about the computational weight of tasks. For this purpose, the *cost* clause is introduced with the following syntax:

$$cost\,(expression)$$

where *expression* corresponds to a single or a combination of algebraic functions that evaluate into a positive real number.

4   Implementation

The OmpSs Autofinal implementation consists of the following parts: a monitoring infrastructure, several heuristics and a collection of constructs used by the runtime and provided by the programming model. Each of these parts is explained in the next sections.

The following work was implemented in the OmpSs [7] programming model. OmpSs—OpenMP Superscalar—is a task-based, data-flow aware parallel programming model developed at the Barcelona Supercomputing Center. Its proximity to OpenMP makes it relevant to runtime developers working on similar implementations.

4.1   Task Monitoring

A monitoring infrastructure was added to give the runtime the ability to decide when a task's granularity is fine enough. The infrastructure is capable of providing a histogram of task execution times. Once a task has been executed, its metrics are aggregated per task type. However, this information is not used as-is, the metrics are first normalized. This is explained in the next subsection. Some of the metrics provided are execution time, runtime execution time, number of leaf tasks and number of tasks that have at least created one task.

4.2   Final Clause

This sections explains the implementation of the *final* clause in OmpSs. The compiler first makes use of closures and duplicates every function of the user application which creates tasks. Once those functions are executed and if the *final* clause evaluates to true, the task enters in *final* mode. This mode prevents the task from generating any other task.

4.3   Cost Clause

Predictions on execution times could be done by simply using the metrics obtained by the monitoring infrastructure. This approach is exactly the one taken if no other information is available. Nonetheless, the information provided by the *cost* clause can be used to normalize the predicted execution time of a task. The normalization and the contents of the *cost* clause are important because the execution time of a task does not depend only on the type of the task. The contents of the *cost* clause allow comparing the expected execution time with other tasks of the same type. When a task does not rely on any algorithmic function, and thus does not contain the *cost* clause, the normalized *cost* will simply be the average execution time and thus the clause will not have any negative impact on the decision. However if the task's computation follows an algorithmic function, the normalized average will provide much more veracious information towards the runtime's decision. For the OmpSs implementation of Autofinal, this normalization consists on dividing the expected execution time by the contents of the *cost* clause. Figure 2 shows the normalization under the assumption that *cost* is available for the task.

This clause however is not bound to be the computational weight of a task, as it could evaluate other kinds of expressions. As an example, an I/O intensive

Function *normalize_ cost(task)*:

> expected_time = get_prediction(task->get_type());
> normalized_cost = expected_time / task->get_cost();
> return normalized_cost;

end

Fig. 2. Normalization of *cost* for a task.

task could use the *cost* clause by giving hints about the I/O operations it is going to perform. Other tasks such as memory bound tasks, could make use of the *cost* clause by specifying the number of load/stores it is going to perform.

The usefulness of the clause then, relies on acting as a hint given to the runtime library. This hint is mostly used as information about the relative computational weight of a task—In other words, the algorithmic cost. However, it may be used for other purposes such as the ones discussed previously and in Sect. 6. Figure 3 shows the usage of this clause applied to a few well known algorithms.

```
1 #pragma  oss  task  cost (N*N)
2 void  InsertionSort (int * src, int * dst, size_t N);
3
4 #pragma  oss  task  cost (N*N*N)
5 void  MatMul (int  N, double * A, double * B, double * C);
6
7 #pragma  oss  task  cost (N*log (N))
8 void  MergeSort (int * src, int * dst, size_t N);
```

Fig. 3. A few algorithms showcased using the *cost* clause.

In order to achieve an adaptive strategy, OmpSs' implementation of Autofinal has an average normalized *cost*. This *cost*, also referred in this document as *unitary cost*, is seen by the runtime as the expected execution time for a unit of *cost* extracted from the clause. That is, taking into account that the *cost* evaluates into a positive real number, as explained in Sect. 3. The average unitary cost is obtainable by having a window of measurements of unitary cost. By using this strategy, normalized costs are adapted throughout the execution of the application and its changes of behavior. In other words, the average is obtained using the 'N' latest measurements.

OpenMP's *final* clause, as shown previously in Sect. 2, allows users to manually set a threshold on task granularities. To use it, the developer must have knowledge of application behaviors and the computation being done by the affected tasks. All of this forces the developer to study said applications and to execute them with different thresholds and figure out their behavior on the given hardware and software setup.

Hence why it is interesting for the runtime to monitor the behavior of tasks and automatically activate the *final* clause when desired. It is from this idea that Autofinal was created. Autofinal uses task monitoring in order to estimate the execution time of future tasks and determine whether they should be *final* or not. Figure 4 shows a pseudo code with the heuristics that have been chosen to be taken into account in the decisions of automatic *final* appliance. These are thoroughly explained immediately after.

```
Function is_automatically_final(task):
    arity = children_tasks / parent_tasks;
    if no_cost_available(task) then
        current_tasks = pow(arity, recursive_depth);
        maximum_tasks = total_cpus × TASKS_PER_CPU;
        return current_tasks > maximum_tasks;
    end
    else
        expected_time = cost × unitary_cost;
        return expected_time < THRESHOLD;
    end
end
```

Fig. 4. Pseudo code of heuristics used to determine if a task should be *final*.

The decision has two well-differentiated heuristics. When executing a certain task, if the runtime does not have timing information of its type it can be due to two reasons. The first occurs when a task is the first of its type to be executed. The second occurs when all previous tasks from the same type have not finalized their execution and therefore have not contributed to task monitoring yet. For better understanding of the second scenario, one could think of recursive algorithms like mergesort or fibonacci in which non-leaf tasks contain a taskwait, which waits for its children to finish. In these, there is no complete timing information available until one of the recursive branches of the algorithm reaches a leaf task.

When either of the previous scenarios is met and therefore no timing information is available, it is still useful to limit the number of instantiated and not finalized tasks. Otherwise, tasks with very fine granularity end up being created. The best way to do this is limiting the maximum number of tasks of a certain type at a certain moment and, in order to do this, some metrics are needed. In OmpSs, these metrics are the recursive depth of tasks from the same type— recursive_depth—and the average number of tasks created by a certain type or, as referred in the pseudocode, the arity of a task. The arity is computed taking into account the number of tasks from a certain type which have at least a children task (parent_tasks) and the number of leaf tasks (children_tasks). If at a task's creation point the average (current_tasks) surpasses a limit, the task is created as a *final* task. This limit is calculated using a configurable number of tasks per CPU and the total number of CPUs.

In the event that the runtime has timing information for a certain type of task, it can estimate the execution time for future tasks of that type. This estimation can be more precise if the developer provides computational information about the task through the *cost* clause. If the execution time estimation does not meet a certain configurable threshold, the task is generated as a *final* task.

5   Results

To test Autofinal's effectiveness, four very different recursive benchmarks were used.

- **The Fibonacci sequence:** Fibonacci was chosen because it is a benchmark with very fine granularity. The computation of tasks at the end of recursivity is as simple as returning an integer. The sequence of the first 35 Fibonacci numbers was chosen as the size for this benchmark.
- **Mergesort:** The mergesort algorithm was chosen to test a wide range of granularities. The computation of a task can be as simple as a comparison between two numbers or as coarse as sorting and merging two big chunks of an array. An array of 10^8 `doubles` was used as this benchmark's input.
- **NQueens problem:** In the NQueens benchmark, granularities grow exponentially. Testing this attribute challenges effectiveness and accuracy of predictions. The board size used for this benchmark is 15 rows by 15 columns.
- **Strassen Matrix Multiply:** The Strassen matrix multiplication algorithm was chosen to evaluate a data intensive compute-bound benchmark. The size of the matrixes was 2^{13}.

5.1   Autofinal Heuristics

- **Cost:** For this heuristic, a warmup iteration was executed for every benchmark. That is, a whole execution of the benchmark was performed to fill histograms with timing information. By doing this, in the second iteration, even the first tasks to be executed will be compared against a prediction. This heuristic covers the scenario of having previous timing information of tasks.
- **Hybrid:** This heuristic cuts recursive depth early to avoid fine-grained tasks. Once the histograms are filled with timing information, this heuristic abandons the first technique and continues by using the cost heuristic. Hence why this heuristic is named hybrid. This heuristic covers the scenario of not having previous timing information of tasks.

5.2   System Configuration

Benchmark results were obtained on four different architectures in order to test variability of performance in different architectures and configurations. Results were always obtained in a single node using all the available CPUs in the node. Next is a list of all the machines used and the number of cores used in each.

- **MinoTauro:** Contains a cluster with 39 R421-E4 Servers, each with 2 Intel Xeon E5-2630v3 (Haswell) 8-core processors, each @ 2.4 GHz. 16 cores were used.

- **ThunderX:** Contains 4 Nodes each equipped with 2 Cavium ThunderX sockets, each of them with 48 ARMv8-A cores, each @ 1.8 GHz. 96 cores were used.
- **KNL:** Each KNL machine contains an Intel Xeon Phi socket @ 1.40 GHz, with 68 cores in each socket and 4 threads per core. 68 cores were used with 1 thread per core.
- **Power8:** Contains 2 Machines with 2 sockets Power8 10C @ 3.49 GHz, 8 threads each core. 20 cores were used.

5.3   Performance Results

The obtained measurements demonstrate how a statically chosen granularity for one architecture does not perform well on others and how Autofinal improves this situation. For each benchmark, the best granularity was manually found on four different architectures. After that, the benchmarks were ran in every machine with the best granularities of all four machines and with autofinal with two different heuristics.

Figure 5 shows the results. It contains four plots, from top to bottom: Fibonacci, Mergesort, NQueens & Strassen. The horizontal axis corresponds to the execution of a host, and each host has six measurements. The first 4 correspond to the best granularity of the benchmark in each host, and the last two correspond to autofinal executions with two different heuristics. These are explained in Sect. 5.1.

The first plot then, contains the comparison of the Fibonacci benchmark. In the horizontal axis are the hosts where the benchmark is ran. That means that the very first six bars in the plot correspond, from left to right to:

1. Executing Fibonacci on MinoTauro with MinoTauro's optimal granularity. Hence why the speedup is 1.
2. Executing Fibonacci on MinoTauro with ThunderX's optimal granularity.
3. Executing Fibonacci on MinoTauro with KNL's optimal granularity.
4. Executing Fibonacci on MinoTauro with Power8's optimal granularity.
5. Executing Fibonacci on MinoTauro with Autofinal's cost heuristic.
6. Executing Fibonacci on MinoTauro with Autofinal's hybrid heuristic.

Sometimes, statically choosing a granularity for a certain architecture causes a dramatic decrease on performance on every other. This is highly visible when executing Fibonacci in the ThunderX system with KNL's optimal granularity. In this scenario, it barely achieves 20% of the performance of the optimal granularity. Autofinal however, achieves at least 90% of ThunderX's optimal performance. Another scenario, but not the last, is when executing Strassen in the KNL system with Power8's optimal granularity. The performance obtained is around 68% of the performance of the optimal granularity, while Autofinal achieves more than 90%.

The cost heuristic is used with a previous warmup iteration of the application and therefore can make timing predictions from the start of the execution. These plots also exposed that the cost heuristic behaves better than the hybrid

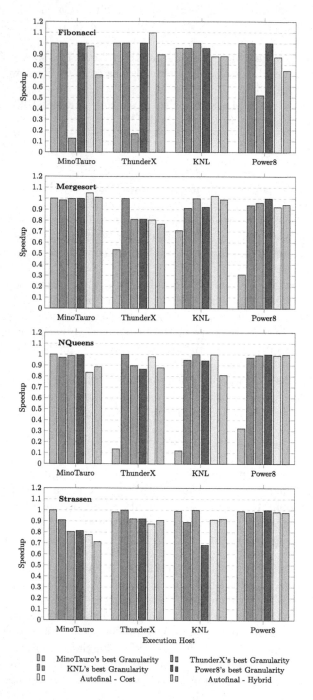

Fig. 5. Performance comparison of heuristics vs. optimal granularities.

heuristic because the cost heuristic is fed on a warmed up environment. It relies on previous timing information. The loss of performance of the hybrid heuristic due to not having previous timing information is at most 20%, while the penalty for using a granularity from another architecture can be as high as 90%.

Autofinal then, achieves competitive performance regardless of the architecture and benchmark where it is tested. Results show that it achieves at least 75% of the optimal performance in every scenario and that using granularities from other architectures can lead to only obtaining around 20% of the optimal performance.

Results also show that in some cases, Autofinal is able to find an even better granularity than the apparently optimal one. This is possible because it does not just set a fixed granularity. Instead, it decides at execution time whether a task should be *final*. Hence, in some cases it chooses a mix of granularities. This is visible when executing Mergesort on the KNL system or the MinoTauro system, with any Autofinal heuristic. The results indicate that the optimal granularity is a mixture of tasks with *final* granularity 10^7 and 10^6.

Figure 6 shows the performance of Autofinal against manually tuning the granularity of tasks for the NQueens Benchmark with the *final* clause. This comparison is done by executing NQueens with different input sizes in order to test Autofinal's adaptiveness to an application's settings. As shown, the optimal granularity often comes linked to the input size of the application and Autofinal is able to adapt to these settings. For completeness, this section includes Figs. 7 and 8. These show the speedup obtained by executing the previous benchmarks with Autofinal versus executing them with a wide range of manual cut-off

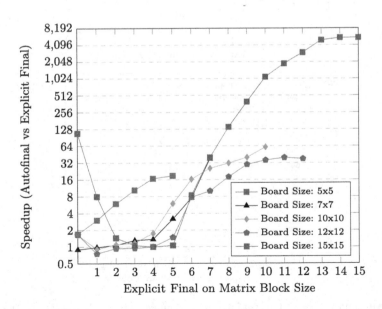

Fig. 6. Autofinal vs. manual tuning for the NQueens benchmark with different input sizes

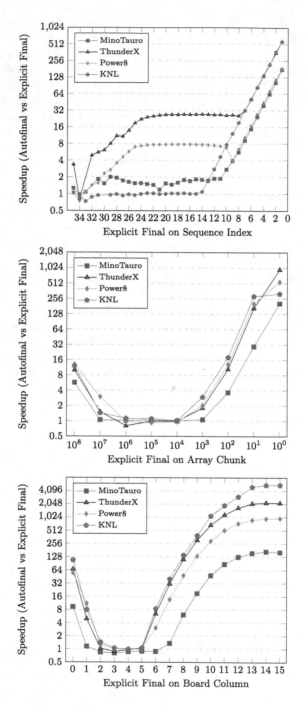

Fig. 7. Autofinal vs. manual tuning for Fibonacci (Top), Mergesort (Middle) & NQueens (Bottom)

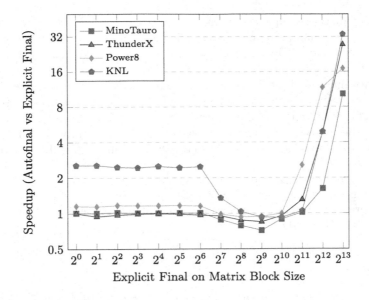

Fig. 8. Autofinal vs. manual tuning for the Strassen benchmark

depths. Each series corresponds to an architecture and the speedup is computed comparing Autofinal's cost heuristic's performance against each cutoff step's performance. These plots show which are the appropriate granularities for each benchmark in each architecture as well, and how Autofinal performs against these. The best granularity for each benchmark then was chosen to plot the performances seen in Fig. 5.

For the Fibonacci plot, each cutoff corresponds to the index number of the sequence at which recursive depth is cut with the *final* clause. The Mergesort plot's cutoffs correspond to the array chunk size at which recursive depth is cut. For the NQueens benchmark, the cutoff corresponds to the board's column index. Lastly, for the Strassen benchmark, the cutoff chosen is the matrix block size at which recursive depth is cut.

6   Conclusion and Future Work

This paper presented how automatically detecting optimal granularity cutoffs can be integrated into a task parallel programming model. Furthermore, it showed which runtime features, as well as language support, are needed to allow using Autofinal. Having specific information about the computation of tasks allows making precise predictions as well as offering a general solution to automatically find well performing granularities for applications. The evaluations show that making the runtime aware of the computational weight of tasks and monitoring them allows to predict with precision task execution times and hence to find granularities that adapt to the architecture and the runtime environment.

The Autofinal technique raised interest in exploring its behavior with processors that allow dynamic frequencies. With that in mind, it would also be interesting to compare static granularities against the usage of Autofinal in the aforementioned processors.

The introduction of the *cost* clause in the language also provides specific metrics to create new capabilities on the runtime library, like *cost* based scheduling policies. This raised interest in using the *cost* clause with the taskloop construct. The idea relies on having extra information about the computational weight of iterations from a taskloop in order to better balance and schedule the workload.

Acknowledgments. This work has been supported by the Spanish Ministry of Science and Innovation (contract TIN2015-65316), the grant SEV-2015-0493 of Severo Ochoa Program awarded by the Spanish Government, and by Generalitat de Catalunya (contract 2014-SGR-1051).

References

1. Ayguadé, E., Copty, N., Duran, A., Hoeflinger, J., Lin, Y., Massaioli, F., Teruel, X., Unnikrishnan, P., Zhang, G.: The design of OpenMP tasks. IEEE Trans. Parallel Distrib. Syst. **20**(3), 404–418 (2009)
2. OpenMP Architecture Review Board: OpenMP Application Program Interface Version 4.5, November 2015
3. Rajaraman, V., Murthy, C.S.R.: Parallel Computers: Architecture and Programming, pp. 378–380. Prentice-Hall, New Delhi (2004)
4. Chen, R.S.: Finding Chapel's Peak: Introducing Auto-Tuning to the Chapel Parallel Programming Language, November 2012
5. Chung, I-H., Hollingsworth, J.K.: Using Information from Prior Runs to Improve Automated Tuning Systems, November 2004
6. Duran, A., Corbalán, J., Ayguadé, E.: An adaptive cut-off for task parallelism. In: Proceedings of the 2008 ACM/IEEE Conference on Supercomputing, November 2008
7. Barcelona Supercomputing Center: OmpSs Specification, 30 March 2017

OpenMP 4 Application Evaluation

The Productivity, Portability and Performance of OpenMP 4.5 for Scientific Applications Targeting Intel CPUs, IBM CPUs, and NVIDIA GPUs

Matt Martineau[✉] and Simon McIntosh-Smith

HPC Group, University of Bristol, Merchant Venturers Building,
Woodland Road, Bristol BS81UB, UK
{m.martineau,cssnmis}@bristol.ac.uk

Abstract. This research considers the productivity, portability, and performance offered by the OpenMP parallel programming model, from the perspective of scientific applications. We discuss important considerations for scientific application developers tackling large software projects with OpenMP, including straightforward code mechanisms to improve productivity and portability. Performance results are presented across multiple modern HPC devices, including Intel Xeon, and Xeon Phi CPUs, POWER8 CPUs, and NVIDIA GPUs. The results are collected for three exemplar applications: hydrodynamics, heat conduction and neutral particle transport, using modern compilers with OpenMP support. The results show that while current OpenMP implementations are able to achieve good performance on the breadth of modern hardware for memory bandwidth bound applications, our memory latency bound application performs less consistently.

Keywords: OpenMP-4 · High-performance-computing · Mini-apps

1 Introduction

The diversification of modern architecture has lead to increasing demand for parallel programming models that improve the productivity and future portability of large scientific applications. An implicit expectation is that parallel programming models will provide the features that are necessary to achieve near optimal performance, with some understanding that there is a trade-off between improved productivity and portability, and absolute performance.

OpenMP provides an extensive feature set that allows application developers to tune their applications for performance, while providing an intuitive interface that enables relatively un-intrusive parallelisation of applications. The performance achieved in practice is dependent not only on the features provided by the specification, and the developer's use of those features, but by the implementation provided by the compiler vendors.

© Springer International Publishing AG 2017
B.R. de Supinski et al. (Eds.): IWOMP 2017, LNCS 10468, pp. 185–200, 2017.
DOI: 10.1007/978-3-319-65578-9_13

It is essential that both computer scientists and domain scientists are able to effectively explore the potential programming environments without the constraints of porting large scientific applications. Mini-apps are widely accepted as a powerful tool for evaluating the performance of parallel programming models, but it is essential that a broad range of performance profiles are assessed to observe the edge cases of performance exposed by production applications [1].

In this research we will be using a suite of mini-apps that fall under the arch project[1], developed at the University of Bristol. Each of the mini-apps has been developed to provide research tools for computer scientists to support applications scientists in porting real codes. Although an understanding of the core Physics of each package is not required in this paper, we will discuss the performance profile of each application as we present results.

2   Contributions

It is expected that the results of this research will be of use to domain scientists and application architects looking to determine if OpenMP is a good fit for their project, and may offer support to developers already using OpenMP for their software projects. Through evaluating a range of proxy applications on cutting edge hardware, we provide insights into the differences between available OpenMP implementations that can feed into future optimisation.

This research specifically contributes the following:

- Specific code suggestions for improving productivity and portability of large scientific applications, based on real porting experience.
- A discussion of limitations of the specification, and important differences between OpenMP implementations.
- An extensive performance analysis of OpenMP 4 ports of three distinct application classes: explicit hydrodynamics, sparse linear algebra, and Monte Carlo neutral particle transport, on modern HPC hardware: Intel Xeon and Xeon Phi CPUs, IBM POWER8 CPUs, and NVIDIA K20X and P100 GPUs.

3   Productivity

The authors have encountered issues with productivity that we expect will be encountered by developers using OpenMP 4 for non-trivial applications.

3.1   Structured and Unstructured Data Regions

Maintaining data resident on a device is generally one of the most important considerations for offloading to accelerators. We previously discussed the difficulties that are encountered when attempting to copy data to and from the device using the structured target enter data directive [2].

---

[1] https://github.com/uob-hpc/arch.

Listing 1.1. OpenMP 4.0 approach to copying data for an application.

```
double* density0 = (double*)malloc(sizeof(double)*nx);

#pragma omp target enter data map(to: density0[:nx])
{
  for(int tt = 0; tt < ntimesteps; ++tt) {
    // Do work
  }
}
```

With OpenMP 4.0, the initial copying of resident data into the device data environment would be approached as shown in Listing 1.1. When the number of arrays increases, this approach becomes less readable and maintainable. As the structured data regions only operate upon a structured block, the application structure will be limited if developers want to avoid redundant data movement.

Listing 1.2. OpenMP 4.5 approach to copying data for an application.

```
void allocate_data(double** array, size_t len) {
  (*array) = (double*)malloc(sizeof(double)*len);

  double* local_arr = *array;
  #pragma omp target enter data map(to: local_arr[:len])
}

allocate_data(&density, nx);

for(int tt = 0; tt < ntimesteps; ++tt) {
  // Do work
}
```

The unstructured data mapping introduced in OpenMP 4.5 allowed us to combine the allocation and mapping into a method, as seen in Listing 1.2. This significantly reduced the code duplication, and improved the productivity of our porting efforts by abstracting OpenMP data allocations from the core of the codes. Another benefit is that when arrays were resized during development it was only necessary to propagate the change to a single location.

3.2 Copying Members of Structures

The OpenMP specification does not handle the copying of pointer members of a structure into the device data environment. In many codes, pointer data is exclusively passed around in structures, and developers generally want to be able to access that data in the manner demonstrated in Listing 1.3. Unfortunately, the specification does not state how the pointer members of the structure should be copied onto the device. The Cray compiler implementation of OpenMP 4 currently emits a compile-time error, whereas the Clang compiler supports the form of Listing 1.3, in spite of the limitation in the specification.

Listing 1.3. Mapping an array section that is a member of a structure.

```
#pragma omp target teams distribute parallel for \
    map(some_struct.a[:len])
for(int ii = 0; ii < n; ++ii) {
  some_struct.a[ii] = 0.0;
}
```

The consequence of this missing functionality is that codes currently attempting to achieve portability between compilers with OpenMP 4.5 will have to deserialise the pointer members of structures before they are mapped, and change all kernel accesses to reference the private variables, as seen in Listing 1.4. This significantly limits productivity for large applications, especially where Structure of Arrays style data structures have been adopted.

Listing 1.4. Privatising an array section that is a member of a structure and then mapping it.

```
double* a = some_struct.a;
#pragma omp target teams distribute parallel for map(a[:len])
for(int ii = 0; ii < n; ++ii) {
  a[ii] = 0.0;
}
```

All of the applications we have ported, including the mini-apps investigated in this research, pass their pointer variables through the kernel interfaces, rather than copying them into private variables before each kernel invocation. This approach still requires a significant refactoring when porting codes, but minimises the resulting overhead in terms of new lines of code.

3.3 Tools

Access to high quality tooling is one of the most significant influences on productivity. While porting the suite of mini-apps presented in this research, the process was supported by the compiler vendors' tool suite. For the CPU, tools such as VTune and CrayPat are all compatible with OpenMP, and provide detailed OpenMP-specific insights. The NVIDIA CUDA toolkit, which includes nvprof, also works with the OpenMP 4 implementations discussed in this paper. Application developers can expect this tool support to improve even further with future releases of the OpenMP specification as a new tools interface is set to be included in version 5.0 of the specification [3].

4   Portability

OpenMP 4.5 is becoming increasingly accepted within the community, and the implementations that can target heterogeneous architectures are constantly improving. Intel, Cray Inc., IBM, and GNU, are all actively developing OpenMP support for the newest features of OpenMP. The thread parallelism features of OpenMP 3.0 are mature and well supported, whereas the offloading features were added more recently, and introduced new challenges to implement in a compiler.

4.1   OpenMP Compilers

There are many OpenMP compilers available, and we discuss and evaluate a cross section of the most popular.

The Intel Compilers provided the first vendor-supported OpenMP 4 implementation, targeting the Intel Xeon Phi Knights Corner architecture, but Intel has since moved away from the offloading models for their future architectures. In spite of this, Intel's OpenMP 4.5 compliant compiler (version 17.0+) can be used to target the Intel Xeon and Intel Xeon Phi processors.

The Cray Compilers provided the first vendor-supported implementation of OpenMP 4 that allowed developers to target NVIDIA GPUs. Cray subsequently ceased development of their OpenACC implementation, suggesting that they see OpenMP as the future parallel programming model for targeting their heterogeneous supercomputers. The Cray compiler (version 8.5.7) is not yet OpenMP 4.5 compliant, although it is fully OpenMP 4.0 compliant and supports a number of OpenMP 4.5 features.

The Clang/LLVM Compiler Infrastructure was recently forked to develop OpenMP 4.5 support for targeting NVIDIA GPUs by IBM Research. The fork of the compiler[2] is now OpenMP 4.5 compliant, and the support is being actively patched into the main trunk of the Clang front-end [4]. Although the implementation was developed from the perspective of running on the POWER8/POWER9 and NVIDIA GPU nodes, such as those being installed in Sierra and Summit [5], the compiler will also allow users to compile for NVIDIA GPUs hosted on X86 platforms. One limitation for scientific application developers is that Clang is a C/C++ front-end for LLVM. A team at the Portland Group are currently implementing an open source Fortran front-end, codenamed Flang, which will eventually support OpenMP 4.5.

The PGI Compilers do not yet support any OpenMP 4.0 features, but provide full support for OpenMP 3.0. The compilers support an alternative to OpenMP, OpenACC, which is similar except for some additional features and limitations, but allows users to offload to both CPUs and GPUs.

The XL Compilers are a closed-source compiler suite developed by IBM, and deployed with the POWER architecture, that will support OpenMP 4.5 in time for the installation of the Summit and Sierra supercomputers. The Clang effort for targeting NVIDIA GPUs is more advanced at this stage, and the research is being fed directly into XL. A subset of OpenMP 4.5 features are supported in the version 13.1.5, which we had access to, however support was not available for the `reduction` clause on `target` regions, or `atomic` operations, making it impossible to collect results for XL targeting NVIDIA GPUs in this research.

---

[2] https://github.com/clang-ykt.

The GNU Compiler Collection has officially supported OpenMP 4 offloading since version 5.0, but feature-rich implementations that target specific architecture such as GPUs are still not available. Offloading support exists for AMD GPUs via HSA, but the support is limited to a single combined construct with no clauses. The compiler is capable of targeting Intel Xeon Phi KNLs with OpenMP 4.5, and GNU are currently working on an OpenMP 4.5 implementation that can target NVIDIA GPUs, as mentioned in the *in progress* documentation for GCC 7.1.

4.2   Homogeneous Directives

We have previously shown that it is not yet possible to write a single homogeneous line of directives to achieve performance portability with OpenMP [2,6]. Standardisation of the compiler implementations is important for future performance portability, for instance, the newest Clang implementation automatically chooses optimal team and thread counts, so that the developer does not have to list architecture-specific values. This is one of many issues with standardisation:

- The impact of the simd directive will vary significantly between architectures. For instance, on CPUs it will generally command the compiler to generate SIMD instructions, whereas on the GPU it might tell the compiler to spread the iterations of a loop across the threads in a team.
- Setting a thread_limit and num_teams for one architecture means you cannot choose the default compiler behaviour for other architectures.
- As seen with the porting exercises, there can be significant performance implications when using the collapse statement on different architecture.

Achieving performance portability with a single codebase requires the preprocessor, or abstractions above OpenMP. We are hopeful that future versions of the specification will introduce conditional capabilities to make it possible for developers to write a homogeneous set of directives at the loop-level.

4.3   OpenMP 4.0 to OpenMP 4.5

The authors of this paper strongly believe that OpenMP implementations need to support some key features of version 4.5 to avoid future portability issues. Having ported scientific codes to use OpenMP 4.0 and OpenMP 4.5, we have come across some compatibility issues between the versions. Developers who are using compilers that target OpenMP 4.0 compliant implementations should be aware that these pitfalls can lead to subtle bugs caused by implicit behaviour.

In OpenMP 4.0, the default copying behaviour of scalar variables was to copy them to and from the device, when entering and leaving a target region. This implicit behaviour was as if the map(tofrom: *scalar-variable*) clause had been included on the target region. In OpenMP 4.5 the default behaviour is that variables are declared firstprivate, and so the scalar variable will not be copied back from the device. Developers who have written their applications to rely upon the scalar variables being returned at the end of the target region will encounter potentially difficult to diagnose application bugs.

5   Mini-app Studies

No algorithmic changes are present between versions of the mini-apps, which ensures that they resolve to within tolerance of a single result having executed the same computational workload, regardless of the OpenMP implementation or target device. The purpose of this section is not to compare the different architectures or the algorithms, for which discussions can be found in other literature [2]. This section is instead intended to consider the differences in performance achieved by the different OpenMP compilers targeting the same architecture. Developers familiar with OpenMP may expect there to be minor variations between compiler implementations, but we aim to expose some cases where more significant variance can be observed.

5.1   HPC Devices

The performance evaluation in this paper considers five modern HPC devices, which feature, or will feature, in some of the largest supercomputers in the world.

Where possible, we compare OpenMP to optimised MPI and CUDA ports of the mini-apps, allowing an objective assessment of the performance of the OpenMP implementations compared to the best performance achievable. Subsequent performance evaluation is conducted with the compilers in Table 1.

5.2   Hot and Flow

The flow mini-app[3] is a 2d structured Lagrangian-Eulerian hydrodynamics code, that explicitly solves the Euler equations using a chain of threaded kernels executed across the computational mesh. The application contains little branching, and a minor load imbalance with the artificial viscous terms, but this does

Table 1. The HPC devices used in this performance evaluation, where Intel Xeon Broadwell means dual socketed 22 core CPUs, POWER8 means dual socketed 10 core CPUs, and *Mem BW* is the maximum benchmarked memory bandwidth [7]. The clang-ykt compiler was built with all commits up to date 30th May 2017.

Device name	Mem BW	Compiler
Intel Xeon Broadwell E5-2699 v4	120 GB/s	ICC 17.0.2, GCC 6.1.0, PGI 17.3.0, CCE 8.5.7
NVIDIA K20X	180 GB/s	CUDA 8.0 + GCC 4.9.3, CCE 8.5.7, clang-ykt
IBM POWER8	298 GB/s	XL 13.1.5, GCC 6.1.0, PGI 17.3.0
Intel Xeon Phi Knights Landing 7210	440 GB/s	ICC 17.0.2, GCC 6.1.0
NVIDIA P100	500 GB/s	CUDA 8.0 + GCC 4.9.3, CCE 8.5.7, clang-ykt

---

[3] https://github.com/uob-hpc/flow.

not generally affect performance. Due to the low computational intensity and regular mesh access, flow is memory bandwidth bound.

The hot mini-app[4] is a 2d heat diffusion code, that uses the Conjugate Gradient method to implicitly solve the sparse linear system. The application is memory bandwidth bound, and comprised of short linear algebra kernels, including a sparse matrix-vector multiplication and several reductions. The kernels are highly data parallel, with low register usage and no branching.

Both applications are optimised to achieve roughly 70–80% of achievable memory bandwidth in the best case on the target architecture.

Porting: Both applications are comprised of multiple simple kernels, and parallelisation of those kernels was achieved with #pragma omp parallel for, or #pragma omp target teams distribute parallel for for offloading. Data allocations are handled by the arch project's data allocation wrappers, so a simple overload of the wrappers for OpenMP 4 meant data could be mapped into the device data environment at allocation, as described in Sect. 3.1. The reduction clause was required in both applications, and, due to the specification implicitly mapping the scalar reduction variable as firstprivate, it was necessary to explicitly map the reduction variable as tofrom to copy the results back from the device. Also, vectorisation was forced on the CPUs and KNL using the #pragma omp simd clause on the inner loops.

A major limitation with the current specification is that it was not yet possible to express CPU and GPU parallelism at the same time for our mini-apps, meaning that multiple instances of the directives were required, as discussed in Sect. 4.2. For the GPU ports, we noted that using collapse on the outer loops of the applications' kernels resulted in significantly reduced performance when compiling with CCE, for instance hot's runtime worsened from 44 s to 49 s on the P100. This is due to the way that CCE maps the iteration space to the GPU's threads, but serves as a case where the collapse clause can have unexpected negative influences on performance. The effort to port both applications was minimal, and amounted to roughly two additional lines of code per kernel.

Problem Specification: The mesh size for both applications is 4000^2, a large but realistic mesh size, and each application starts with a timestep of 1.0×10^{-2}s for the two test cases. The hot test case sets up a high density, high temperature region next to a low density, low temperature region. The flow test case sets up a two-dimensional interpretation of the sod shock problem, where an immobile square of high density, high energy fluid is surrounded by low density material.

Intel CPU and KNL Results: The Intel Xeon Broadwell (BW) results in Figs. 1 and 2 were highly consistent between compilers. Intel and flat MPI performed the best, and the largest performance difference was seen with GCC, which required 1.03x the runtime compared to the Intel compiler.

---

[4] https://github.com/uob-hpc/hot.

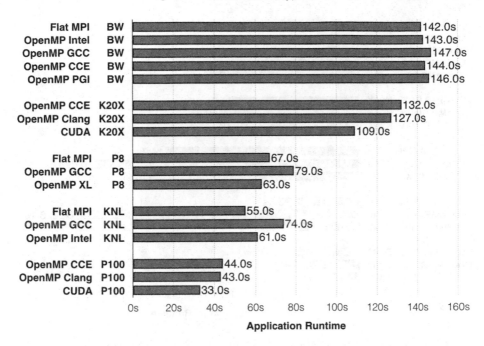

Fig. 1. The results of running hot on the target HPC devices. Devices are ordered from least to greatest achievable memory bandwidth.

On the KNL, application data was placed in MCDRAM, improving the runtime by roughly 5.0x compared to DRAM, as both applications are memory bandwidth bound. The MPI results are shown for running 128 ranks, whereas the OpenMP implementations performed better when using all four hyperthreads for 256 threads total. OpenMP hot experienced a 1.11x performance penalty compared to flat MPI, due to improved decomposition of the problem into cache seen with the MPI implementation. For flow, the difference was not significant. OpenMP hot compiled with GCC suffered a 1.21x performance penalty compared to Intel, while OpenMP flow compiled with GCC suffered a penalty of 4.28x. Disabling vectorisation with the Intel compiler resulted in a runtime equivalent to GCC, suggesting that a lack of vectorisation accounts for the performance difference, in spite of the use of the simd directive.

POWER8 Results: On the POWER8 CPU we found 160 threads, or 8 Simultaneous Multi-Threads (SMT) per core, was optimal, and OpenMP compiled with XL was fastest for hot, while flat MPI was fastest for flow. GCC experiences a significant performance penalty of roughly 1.25x compared to XL for both hot and flow, which is significantly more than seen with the Intel CPU.

NVIDIA GPU Results: The CUDA results included for the NVIDIA GPUs represent an upper bound on performance for each mini-app. On the K20X, CCE

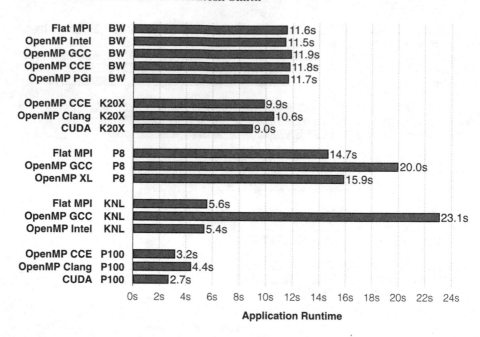

Fig. 2. The results of running flow on the target HPC devices. Devices are ordered from least to greatest achievable memory bandwidth.

achieved impressive performance for flow, requiring only 1.10x the runtime of CUDA, while hot was slightly less efficient at 1.20x compared to CUDA. When compiled with Clang, flow and hot both required 1.17x the runtime of CUDA. The performance penalty for OpenMP compared to CUDA was at worst 1.20x, which is an impressive result and would be tolerable for the improvements to portability and productivity offered by the programming model.

We observed a larger performance difference on the newer P100 GPUs, with the worst case being flow at 1.63x, but we feel that this is likely a performance bug given the results with other combinations, and continue to investigate the root cause. Apart from this result, the performance difference increased to around 1.25x to 1.30x, a significantly higher variation than seen on the CPU.

5.3   Neutral

The neutral mini-app[5] is a new Monte Carlo Neutral Particle Transport application that tracks particle histories across a 2d structured mesh [8,9]. The application has high register utilisation, and inherently suffers from load imbalance at the intra and inter node level. The algorithm parallelises over the list of particle histories, each of which is in principal independent. Particle histories exhibit a dependency on the computational mesh, to store tallies of the energy deposited

---

[5] https://github.com/uob-hpc/neutral.

throughout the space, which means the application suffers from random memory access and sensitivity to memory latency. At this stage in the mini-app's development, there is not an optimal MPI implementation, and so results for MPI are excluded.

Porting: Given that there is a single computational kernel, the porting process was straightforward and fast for all target architectures, following the same approach as for `flow` and `hot`. The only challenge when porting the application was that it depends upon a library, Random123 [10], for random number generation (RNG), which meant it was necessary to persuade the implementations to compile that code correctly. A load imbalance between threads is caused by the varying amounts of work for each history, and so we used `schedule(guided)` to optimise this, generally achieving a 5–10% improvement.

When targeting NVIDIA GPUs, adding `simd` to the combined construct, as `#pragma omp target teams distribute parallel for simd`, was essential to achieve good performance with CCE, improving the result from 211 s to 11 s on the P100. The reason that this directive is required is that CCE relies upon the kernel being vectorisable, and this particular kernel was so complex it needed the `simd` directive as a guarantee that there were no dependencies.

Problem Specification: The test case chosen for the `neutral` mini-app is the *center square problem*, where there is a region of high density material in the center of a low density space. A square neutron source is placed in the bottom left of the space, with all particles having a starting energy of 1 MeV, considering particle histories for 10 timesteps of length 1.0×10^{-7}s.

Intel CPU and KNL Results: The results shown in Fig. 3 are significantly less consistent between the compiler vendors than seen with either `flow` or `hot`. CCE required 1.18x the runtime of Intel and GCC required 1.98x the runtime, on the Intel Xeon Broadwell, which is significantly less optimal than we would have expected. The PGI compiler achieved worse than serial performance and, through the use of the *Minfo* flag, we determined it was transforming the `atomic` operations into `critical` regions. The application invokes billions of `atomic` operations, and so this serialisation is highly inefficient. We tested the issue further by removing the `atomic` operation, and the PGI result improved.

On the KNL we observed a 1.43x performance penalty for using GCC compared to the Intel compilers. We know that vectorisation is not the cause in this instance, and hypothesise that this is due to the way that registers are allocated by the compilers, which we know the application is sensitive too.

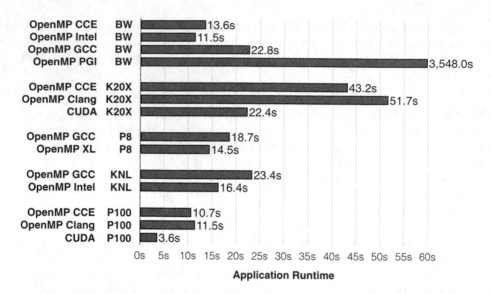

Fig. 3. The results of running `neutral` on the target HPC devices. Devices are ordered from least to greatest achievable memory bandwidth.

POWER8 Results: As with the other mini-apps, we observed a significant performance penalty for compiling with GCC on the POWER8, of 1.29x compared to the XL compiler. Interestingly, the compiler has achieved a better relative result on the POWER8 than it did on the Intel hardware when compared to the Intel compiler. It will be important future work to understand the root cause of this difference, and determine whether it can be easily optimised.

NVIDIA GPU Results: On the K20X, CCE suffered a 1.92x performance penalty compared to CUDA, while Clang suffered a 2.30x performance penalty, which is significantly less efficient than for the other mini-apps. As previously discussed, the `neutral` mini-app uses a single large computational kernel that requires many registers. When compiling CUDA for the P100, ptxas recognised 79 registers for CUDA, and when executing the OpenMP 4 code compiled with Clang, nvprof showed that 224 registers were used during the execution of the main computational kernel. This means that CUDA was 2.9x more efficient allocating registers, which is a considerable difference that we expect would be even worse for production applications with extensive Physics capabilities.

We could see that the occupancy achieved by CUDA was on average 37%, which is an acceptable level when targeting the P100 with this application. When compiled with Clang, the occupancy drops to 12%, demonstrating that CUDA is achieving 3.08x the occupancy on the P100, which likely explains the majority of the 3.19x difference in overall runtime. The best performance that we achieved with Clang was with the number of registers restricted to 128 for both GPUs, which was the default behaviour for CCE.

5.4   Performance Discussion

The productivity and portability of OpenMP were highly consistent between the mini-apps, however, the performance was not. By far the most consistent was hot, which is intuitive as it is the simplest application, and hides many implementation inefficiencies behind long streaming data accesses. The flow mini-app exposed increased complexity, which meant that there was greater variation in the performance between the implementations. Also, it demonstrated that if you are not able to achieve vectorisation on the KNL, you may encounter significant performance issues, and the standard techniques failed for GCC in this case. The CCE and Clang compilers achieved impressive consistency for both applications on the NVIDIA GPUs, and we expect maturity to improve this even further in the future.

Although neutral has fewer kernels than the other two mini-apps, that kernel is long and complex, and the implementations performed significantly less consistently as a consequence. All architectures suffered from high variations in performance, and some did not emit hardware atomics correctly. On the GPU the primary issue was register pressure, which is actually quite a positive outcome, as we feel that this issue should be resolvable in the long term, and we expect that the implementations will be able to deliver significantly better performance relative to CUDA in the near future.

6   Future Work

It will be important to continue this research in the future to include new OpenMP 4 compilers, as well as tracking improvements to the existing implementations. As the *arch* project expands it will be insightful to extend the research to consider diverse applications, for instance stressing the task parallel features of the specification.

7   Related Work

An annual hackathon event for the improvement of OpenMP is hosted by IBM, where a live porting exercise is performed involving multiple US labs [11]. As an outcome of the 2015 hackathon, Karlin et al. [12] ported the applications Kripke, Cardioid, and LULESH to OpenMP, demonstrating some issues with the interoperability with some features of C++, and achieving performance with LULESH within 10% of an equivalent CUDA port.

There are many examples of studies that have looked at performance, portability and productivity of OpenMP with one or more applications [2,13–16], generally demonstrating that OpenMP is capable of highly productive application porting and high performance tuning. Other important studies have looked at the differences between OpenMP and other parallel programming models [6,17]. Lopez et al. [18], for instance, explored the ability for OpenMP 4.5 *and* OpenACC to achieve performance portability, and demonstrated success with multiple test cases, showing only minor performance differences between the two directive-based models.

8   Conclusion

The OpenMP specification has been designed to provide performance and portability, with some productivity enhancements compared to other models. Through this research we have discovered that performance and portability are certainly possible to an extent, but some aspects are limited by the specification and differences between compiler implementations. For instance, there have been few improvements to the standardisation of compiler implementations, which continues to preclude the writing of a single homogeneous directive to target multiple heterogeneous devices.

While porting a number of applications, we found that coupling data allocation with moving data onto the device reduces the amount of duplicate code, and ensures that data sizes are kept consistent, reducing bugs and increasing productivity. Also, relying on the implicit behaviour of OpenMP 4.0 for mapping scalar variables into a `target` region, as `map(tofrom: scalar-variable)`, can result in bugs when moving to OpenMP 4.5 compliant compilers.

Application developers who are used to the consistent performance delivered by the mature OpenMP implementations targeting CPU need to be aware that the implementations targeting other architectures are less mature. We even demonstrated that performance on the IBM POWER8 CPU is not necessarily consistent between implementations, likely due to maturity as well. This does not mean that the specification is not capable of enabling high performance on those architectures, but that the compiler implementations need time to improve.

The performance results we observed on modern HPC devices showed that, for applications with memory bandwidth bound kernels, OpenMP could generally achieve within 20–30% of the best possible performance. For the latency-bound application, the overheads introduced by the OpenMP implementations had a significant impact when offloading, and more variance was seen between compilers. Register pressure posed a significant issue for the `neutral` mini-app, which is something we expected from previous research efforts. It is not yet clear how to resolve the register issues, but it will be an important step towards achieving optimal OpenMP implementations.

Acknowledgements. The authors would like to thank the EPSRC for funding this research. We would also like to thank the Intel Parallel Computing Center (IPCC) at the University of Bristol for access to Intel hardware, and the EPSRC GW4 Tier 2 Isambard service for access to phase 1 of the Isambard supercomputer.

References

1. Heroux, M., Doerfler. D., et al.: Improving performance via mini-applications, Sandia National Laboratories, Technical report SAND2009-5574 (2009)
2. Martineau, M., McIntosh-Smith, S., Gaudin, W.: Evaluating OpenMP 4.0's effectiveness as a heterogeneous parallel programming model. In: Proceedings of 21st International Workship on High-Level Parallel Programming Models and Supportive Environments, HIPS 2016 (2016)
3. Eichenberger, A.E., et al.: OMPT: An OpenMP tools application programming interface for performance analysis. In: Rendell, A.P., Chapman, B.M., Müller, M.S. (eds.) IWOMP 2013. LNCS, vol. 8122, pp. 171–185. Springer, Heidelberg (2013). doi:10.1007/978-3-642-40698-0_13
4. Antao, S.F., Bataev, A., Jacob, A.C., Bercea, G.T., Eichenberger, A.E., Rokos, G., Martineau, M., Jin, T., Ozen, G., Sura, Z., Chen, T., Sung, H., Bertolli, C., O'Brien, K.: Offloading support for OpenMP in Clang and LLVM. In: Proceedings of the Third Workshop on LLVM Compiler Infrastructure in HPC, LLVM-HPC 2016, Piscataway, NJ, USA, pp. 1–11. IEEE Press (2016). https://doi.org/10.1109/LLVM-HPC.2016.6
5. Mellor-Crummey, J., Missing pieces in the OpenMP ecosystem. In: Keynote at International Workshop on OpenMP (2015)
6. Martineau, M., McIntosh-Smith, S., Boulton, M., Gaudin, W.: An evaluation of emerging many-core parallel programming models. In: Proceedings of the 7th International Workshop on Programming Models and Applications for Multicores and Manycores, PMAM 2016 (2016)
7. Deakin, T., Price, J., et al.: BabelStream (UoB HPC Group) (2017). https://github.com/UoB-HPC/BabelStream
8. Lewis, E., Miller, W.: Computational Methods of Neutron Transport. Wiley, New York (1984)
9. Gentile, N.: Monte Carlo Particle Transport: Algorithm and Performance Overview. Lawrence Livermore, Livermore (2005)
10. Salmon, J.K., Moraes, M.A., Dror, R.O., Shaw, D.E.: Parallel randomnumbers: as easy as 1, 2, 3. In: 2011 International Conference for High Performance Computing, Networking, Storageand Analysis (SC), pp. 1–12. IEEE (2011)
11. Draeger, E.W., Karlin, I., Scogland, T., Richards, D., Glosli, J., Jones, H., Poliakoff, D., Kunen, A.: OpenMP 4.5 IBM November 2015 Hackathon: current status and lessons learned, Technical report LLNL-TR-680824, Lawrence Livermore National Laboratory, Technical report (2016)
12. Karlin, I., et al.: Early experiences porting three applications to OpenMP 4.5. In: Maruyama, N., Supinski, B.R., Wahib, M. (eds.) IWOMP 2016. LNCS, vol. 9903, pp. 281–292. Springer, Cham (2016). doi:10.1007/978-3-319-45550-1_20
13. Bercea, G., Bertolli, C., Antao, S., Jacob, A., et al.: Performance analysis of OpenMP on a GPU using a coral proxy application. In: Proceedings of the 6th International Workshop on Performance Modeling, Benchmarking, and Simulation of High Performance Computing Systems, p. 2. ACM (2015)

14. Lin, P.-H., Liao, C., Quinlan, D.J., Guzik, S.: Experiences of using the OpenMP accelerator model to Port DOE stencil applications. In: Terboven, C., Supinski, B.R., Reble, P., Chapman, B.M., Müller, M.S. (eds.) IWOMP 2015. LNCS, vol. 9342, pp. 45–59. Springer, Cham (2015). doi:10.1007/978-3-319-24595-9_4
15. Bertolli, C., Antao, S., Bercea, G.-T., et al.: Integrating GPU support for OpenMP offloading Directives into Clang. In: Proceedings of the Second Workshop on the LLVM Compiler Infrastructure in HPC, LLVM 2015 (2015)
16. Hart, A.: First experiences porting a parallel application to a hybrid supercomputer with OpenMP4.0 device constructs. In: Terboven, C., Supinski, B.R., Reble, P., Chapman, B.M., Müller, M.S. (eds.) IWOMP 2015. LNCS, vol. 9342, pp. 73–85. Springer, Cham (2015). doi:10.1007/978-3-319-24595-9_6
17. Wienke, S., Terboven, C., Beyer, J.C., Müller, M.S.: A pattern-based comparison of OpenACC and OpenMP for accelerator computing. In: Silva, F., Dutra, I., Santos Costa, V. (eds.) Euro-Par 2014. LNCS, vol. 8632, pp. 812–823. Springer, Cham (2014). doi:10.1007/978-3-319-09873-9_68
18. Lopez, M.G., Larrea, V.V., Joubert, W., Hernandez, O., Haidar, A., Tomov, S., Dongarra, J.: Towards achieving performance portability using directives for accelerators. In: Proceedings of the Third International Workshop on Accelerator Programming Using Directives, WACCPD, 162016 (2016)

Extended Parallelism Models

User Co-scheduling for MPI+OpenMP Applications Using OpenMP Semantics

Antoine Capra[1]([⊠]), Patrick Carribault[3], Jean-Baptiste Besnard[1],
Allen D. Malony[2], Marc Pérache[3], and Julien Jaeger[3]

[1] ParaTools SAS, Bruyeres-le-Chatel, France
{capra,jbbesnard}@paratools.com
[2] ParaTools Inc., Eugene, USA
malony@paratools.com
[3] CEA, DAM, DIF, 91297 Arpajon, France
{patrick.carribault,marc.perache,julien.jaeger}@cea.fr

Abstract. The evolution of parallel architectures towards machines with many-core processors and high node-level concurrency is putting an end to the pure-MPI programming model. Simulations codes must expose multiple levels of parallelisms inside and between nodes, combining different programming models (e.g., MPI+X), to productively use current and future supercomputers. MPI+OpenMP is a common hybridization approach. However, recent evolutions in the OpenMP standard presents options for how OpenMP tasking constructs might be used when mixing fine-grained computation and communications. Various approaches are discussed and compared in this context. Advantages and limitations of the approaches are detailed, including potential improvements to OpenMP in order ease both the integration and progress of MPI calls. These methods are applied to a representative stencil code and demonstrate improvements on the overall execution time as a result of more efficient mixing of MPI and OpenMP.

1 Introduction

Parallel scientific applications are designed to take advantage of the resources they are provided for execution. When considering current architectures, the optimization spectrum is wide, ranging from vectorization at a core level to distributed operations involving millions of cores. The present rise of many-core processors is shaping the spectrum further with greater node-level concurrency, resulting in less memory per thread of execution. Whereas a pure MPI model [5] has been adequate before, memory replication within a node and communication overhead across many threads is becoming problematic. Hybrid programming methods that combine a shared-memory model with a distributed-memory one are has now a compulsory avenue when it comes to writing efficient parallel code. When considering MPI+X hybridization, X = OpenMP has become the de-facto standard. In hybridizing legacy codes, it is most often the case that OpenMP is applied at loop level for intra-node parallelism [6], with MPI for

© Springer International Publishing AG 2017
B.R. de Supinski et al. (Eds.): IWOMP 2017, LNCS 10468, pp. 203–216, 2017.
DOI: 10.1007/978-3-319-65578-9_14

inter-node communication. However, by separating MPI and OpenMP phases, parallelism is essentially bulk-synchronous, alternating between communication and computation phases. In such a model, communications are done by a single thread, creating a loss of parallelism combined with extra fork-join overheads. Thus, despite being a practical approach, secluding MPI and OpenMP from each other will expose performance factors that eventually prevent the program from scaling.

We propose to rethink MPI+X hybridization with respect to their runtime requirements and flexibility for closer mixing of models. In particular, we are interested in how a program written with MPI+X in mind can express fine-grained parallelism and communication through OpenMP. Given the new features introduced in the OpenMP standard for programs to invoke MPI functions inside parallel regions, the opportunity is there for mitigating the bulk-synchronous nature of most MPI+OpenMP applications. Our work focuses on OpenMP tasks and presents an approach for hybrid tasking patterns that can be more performant. In this process, we observe some limitations in existing OpenMP runtimes and propose extensions to OpenMP oriented towards runtime stacking.

By considering a task-based model, the expression of both MPI and computation phases is more natural. Iterations are seen as a directed graph mixing MPI and compute tasks. Tasks are vertexes in the graphs and edges represent dependencies between tasks. This leads to the expression of an MPI+OpenMP program as a Directed Acyclic Graph (DAG). One benefit of a DAG representation is that finer-grained parallelism is more exposed, as are the dependencies and critical paths that constrain performance.

To demonstrate our approach, we focus on the critical path arising in DAGs representing stencil-based computations, including spatial dependencies. In particular, our goal is to reduce the coupling arising from communications between distributed memory regions, by identifying as soon as possible those parts of the computation where dependencies were satisfied. In this formalism, MPI tasks are the one leading to the highest parallel overhead, possibly delaying computation. From this starting point, it is shown how tasking patterns can mitigate communication impact, giving a higher priority to MPI tasks and splitting computational border into multiple regions – eventually moving communications inside the parallel region.

In the rest of the paper, we first describe task support in the context of OpenMP runtimes and discuss how it is beneficial to the expression of hybrid computation. After exploring various alternatives, we present an approach leveraging OpenMP tasks with dependencies to mix MPI and computation. The approach is validated using the stencil benchmark, demonstrating the impact of communication progress on the overlaps. We then present potentials improvements to the OpenMP standard for model mixing when applying the tasking model. Other research have contributed to our ideas and we give an overview of this related work. The paper concludes with future prospects to pursue.

2   OpenMP Tasking

OpenMP's origins began with loop-level parallelization, but over time an increasing variety of parallel constructs have been proposed for adoption in the OpenMP standard. One of the main drawbacks of parallel execution only in loops is that it breaks the program (within a node) into sequential and parallel regions. There is also the fact that not all loops are easily parallelized. Some may have complex dependencies and others may rely on external sequential (not thread-safe) libraries. Or it might simply be that time has not be taken to rewrite the loop code properly to enable parallel execution. In any case, limiting parallelism to just loop regions can constrain the performance gain in an OpenMP program. The well-known Amdahl Law states that the sequential part of a parallel code will bound its strong scaling speedup. For example, if 20% of the time an OpenMP program executes in a sequential region, maximum speedup is 5, even under the assumption of 100% efficiency in parallel loop execution. Thus, it is crucial to consider how OpenMP can express parallelism beyond loops.

To this end, the concept of tasks is being considered by parallel programmers to improve the scalability of their applications. OpenMP did not provide task until Version 3. At this point, `task` and `taskwait` are defined and the `barrier` is a scheduling point for tied tasks. OpenMP v4 introduced `taskgroups` to allows more abstraction and hierarchy, with `depend` being used to express dependencies and explicit scheduling points for untied tasks removed. The latest version of the OpenMP standard (v4.5) adopted `taskloop` and priorities. With these tasks constructs and their functional and runtime support, OpenMP now provides a way of defining parallel execution at a fine-grained level.

OpenMP tasking will notably enhance the opportunities for shared-memory parallelism and efficiency. Consequently, tasking capabilities also afford us a path to develop hybrid (MPI+OpenMP) codes with better performance than previously obtained.

3   Hybrid Alternatives

When mixing MPI and OpenMP one crucial aspect is how runtimes are going to interoperate. Because the MPI runtime is managing communications, it is by definition not performing computational work. While MPI asynchronous communication allows for the overlap of communication and computation, a main interest of hybridization is to enable node-level parallelism in a manner whereby the OpenMP runtime more efficiently interfaces with communication operations. To better describe our approach, we present three different MPI scenarios and reason about the performance costs involved.

In this Section we consider the `MPI_Irecv` and `MPI_Isend` calls. These functions allow for the posting of an asynchronous message. Both functions create an `MPI_Request` which can be used to either wait for the communication completion with `MPI_Wait` or test for its completion with `MPI_Test`. Using these calls, it is therefore possible to recover communications with computation, reducing the overall communication cost. This mechanism is similar to task usage in OpenMP. Tasks can be delayed and the user can use synchronization (taskgroup/taskwait) to ensure their completion.

The first scenario (*IW*) is where an MPI process does an asynchronous receive (`MPI_Irecv`) and immediately waits (using `MPI_Wait`) for it to be satisfied. The second scenario (*ITCW*) is where an MPI process does an `MPI_Irecv` immediately followed by the execution of an OpenMP parallel region. One thread of the parallel region checks for the receive to be satisfied (using `MPI_Test`), while the others do some minor computation followed by a wait at the end. The third scenario (*ICW*) is the same as the first except `MPI_Irecv` is immediately followed by 500 µs computation before waiting. In this last case, we made sure that the overall computing had the same duration than in the second case – to allow direct comparison.

Figure 1 shows results from measuring the time spent in MPI_Wait in the three different MPI scenarios. The communication duration is the time from when `MPI_Irecv` is called to when `MPI_Wait` returns (or `MPI_Test` returns true). In our case, we focus on `MPI_Wait` time in order to measure the time needed to complete an MPI call relatively to the associated asynchronism construction. If we consider the scenarios run on a single node where MPI is using shared memory, it is clear that if `MPI_Test` is not called, the MPI runtime is less efficient for some reason. Not directly waiting is worse for small messages, due likely to

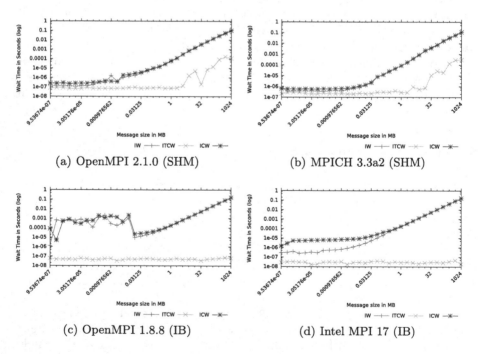

(a) OpenMPI 2.1.0 (SHM)   (b) MPICH 3.3a2 (SHM)

(c) OpenMPI 1.8.8 (IB)   (d) Intel MPI 17 (IB)

Fig. 1. Comparing our progress scenarios on the receiver side when running over both a shared memory segment and an Infiniband network (averaged 1000 times).

the extra 500 μs processing, and comparable for larger ones. Of course, these results are highly dependent on the underlying network. Maybe the results are an anomaly of running in MPI shared memory. However, if we repeated the experiments using InfiniBand in an dual-node configuration, the same pattern appears in Fig. 1(c).

MPI runtimes have to make a decision about how to implement waiting for asynchronous communication. The tradeoff has to do with how much overhead is spent in checking for communication completion, versus latency between when the communication actually completed and when it was detected by the MPI runtime. In other words, it is a decision about how to implement *progress* in the MPI runtime. What is seen in the graphs is the result of progress latency for the IW and ICW cases. In the case of ITCW, the `MPI_Test` acts like an immediate progress step. It should be able to take advantage of the overlap and that is what is observed.

The ramifications of these experiments is that progress is needed to achieve good performance in a heterogeneous computation context. More specifically, testing MPI requests is important for communication progress, but it pushes the responsibility for progress to the computational runtime (i.e., OpenMP), which must fill up the asynchronous periods as much as possible with work to get high performance.

How can we do this with OpenMP? Suppose we progressively insert MPI calls inside the parallel region, this while accounting for the requirement of progressing the MPI runtime. Our idea is to do this with our tasking patterns, iteratively increasing the functionality they offer. The extension of the OpenMP standard will then allow us to submit an increasingly complete DAG of execution and thus to prioritize more effectively the tasks carrying out MPI actions. For a working parallel example, we consider a 1D model (say a $10e6$ double array) evenly split between MPI ranks, where each rank has a core computation and ghost cells for communication to neighbor cells. In this case, each ghost cell might consists of 4096 doubles for each side with a periodic condition on the borders.

```
while (! finished && mpi_comm_complete != MPI_COMM_NUM ) {
  for ( i = 0; i < MPI_COMM_NUM; i++ )
    if ( ! Atomic_load_int ( tab_flags[i] ) ) {
      MPI_Test ( &(tab_reqs[i]) , &mpiflag , ↩
      MPI_STATUS_IGNORE ) ;
      if (mpiflag && !Atomic_cas_int ( &(tab_flag[i]) , 0, 1 ↩
      )) {
        Atomic_incr_int (mpi_comm_complete ) ;
        compute_ghost_associated_part (i) ;
      }
    }
  finished = compute_core_part () ; // yield
}
```

Listing 1.1. MPI AWARE Select (loop splitting)

Suppose we had to using OpenMP 2.0 and we wanted to mix MPI calls in an OpenMP parallel region. We could do something similar to what is illustrated in Listing 1.1. In this case, the loop computing the core computations would be separated. Then border communications would be progressed using MPI_Test, and associated border computation triggered on completion. Then if communications have not competed yet, the core calculation can be used to recover communications. In order to extend this MPI query polling in the MPI_THREAD_MULTIPLE case, we have based our selection on the basis of an atomic value table. The calculation phase ends when all the MPI communications and the associated actions are realized (i.e., computation of the border and MPI_Isend, but also the core part). The execution path is constrained according to MPI dependencies. However, two computing functions are effectively parallelized internally at the price of a critical section choosing the next action based on communication completion. This reduces the potential overhead of MPI communications by constraining OpenMP behavior. Indeed, to be able to improve granularity, the core compute function would have to be chunked, in order to regularly progress and check communication dependencies. This code is, in fact, doing different kinds of tasks, encouraging us to rely on OpenMP tasks.

```
#pragma omp parallel
{
  #pragma omp for nowait
    for (i = 0; i < CORE_PART_NUM; i++)
      #pragma omp task
      compute_core_part(i);

  #pragma omp single
  {
    while(mpi_comm_complete != MPI_COMM_NUM)
    {
      for( i = 0; i < MPI_COMM_NUM; i++ )
        if( ! Atomic_load_int( tab_flags[i] ) )
          #pragma omp task
          __progress_mpi_comm( i );
      #pragma omp taskyield
    }
  }
}
```

Listing 1.2. MPI AWARE Select (standard task)

Now, consider the use of OpenMP v3. Listing 1.2 shows multiple OpenMP tasks being created to handle a certain number of computing cores and multiple OpenMP tasks are dedicated to the progress of MPI communications. Moreover, thanks to the taskyield, MPI-related tasks are at most the number of MPI requests not completed. Dedicating a actual hardware core communications progression does not necessarily induce a penalty for the user code, especially when considering architectures with a large number of cores such as the Intel KNL with 68 cores (272 hyper-threads). A hyper-thread, corresponds to 0.4% of a KNL – a totally acceptable overhead.

As we can not modify the task scheduler, MPI progress will not be multi-threaded or prioritized. In most OpenMP implementations, an OpenMP thread performs its own tasks before stealing from other threads. In our scenario, stealing of communication tasks will only occur when a thread will have completed its own tasks – actually yielding the desired behavior. In this configuration without priority, only the stealing mechanism can give us a form of priority. For instance, when running this code, the GOMP runtime did not allow the `taskyield` construct. As far as Intel OpenMP is concerned, it was not providing expected performance gains. When waiting for communication we expected to schedule computing-related tasks. These runtime limitations required us to explore another task approach presented below in order to correctly progress communications.

```
#pragma omp for nowait
for (i = 0; i < CORE_PART_NUM; i++)
  #pragma omp task priority(1)
  compute_core_part(i);


#pragma omp single nowait
{
  for( i = 0; i < MPI_COMM_NUM; i++ ){
#pragma omp task depend(inout: req_mpi ...) priority(100)
    {
      while( __mpi_request_not_match() )
      #pragma omp taskyield
    }
    if( i > MPI_COMM_SEND_NUM ){ // RECV REQUEST
#pragma omp task depend(inout:req_mpi ...) priority(100)
      {
        __compute_associated_border( i )
      }
#pragma omp task depend(inout: req_mpi ...) priority(100)
      {
        __send_ghost_associate( i );
      }
    }
  }
}
```

Listing 1.3. MPI AWARE Select (standard task)

Our initial idea was to rely on priorities and dependencies to pre-post MPI actions. To do so, valid and computable dependencies are required at compilation time. This leads to a problem when considering communications, a given MPI process may have a varying neighboring (mesh corners) while these dependencies have to be known at compilation time (no dynamic dependencies). In our example, MPI_Requests are static variables. Aware of `taskyield` limitations, we proposed in Listing 1.3 with OpenMP 4.x in mind. This is a version based on `single`, allowing us to force a thread to poll MPI Request. We can use the `taskgroup` ensures that all threads participate in the execution of the sets of tasks, including the one testing for MPI communications. Eventually, the send task has two dependencies, ensuring that the previous send is complete before issuing the next.

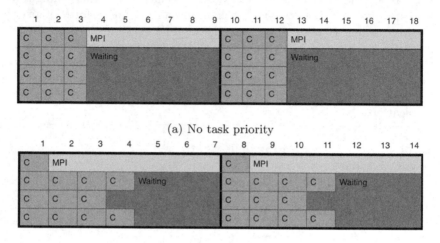

(a) No task priority

(b) With high priority on MPI task

Fig. 2. Interest of task priority with heterogeneous task

If we consider an abstract time unit with a computing task that is worth 1 unit and an MPI task worth 6, then looking at Fig. 2 observe that the choice of scheduling can have an impact on the total execution time. We have illustrated the execution time of four threads with 12 computational tasks and 1 MPI task per time step. It is recognized that a greedy algorithm favoring the task taking the most time generally allows to reach a relevant local minimum. The developer can not make assumption about the behavior of the OpenMP support. For this reason, OpenMP priorities are of interest to handle such heterogeneous tasks.

4   Evaluation

With the introduction of OpenMP tasks, it begs the question of how tasks would compete with the traditional parallel loop approach. In one respect, by avoiding successive fork-join, tasks are able to improve the overall scheduling. Returning to our reference benchmark, in a loop-based version, Isend/Irecv are posted, the core part is computed, communications waited on, and then borders processed. In the task-based version, the tasks are pushed immediately when the progress thread completes a test. Thus, only a single parallel region with a computation split in tasks is required.

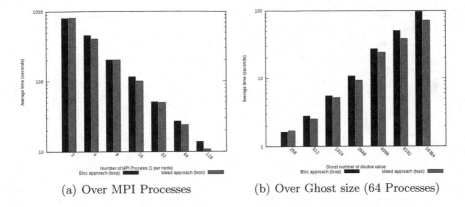

(a) Over MPI Processes   (b) Over Ghost size (64 Processes)

Fig. 3. Comparison of our bulk-synchronous (loop parallelism) and our proposed task-based approach over both process count and message size (fixed at 64 MPI processes).

We compared these two versions on an Intel Sandy-bridge machine up to 2048 cores. Each dual-socket node gathers 16 cores on which we ran 16 OpenMP threads. In order to generate the results presented in Fig. 3, we ran the code for 1000 timesteps, conducted 10 experiments, and averaged the execution times. We observe that in this first case the task approach is better than the loop one when the number of nodes is higher than 16, this despite one core is used to progress communications. We believe this performance difference is due to the increasing noise in MPI messages, creating irregularities in the communication scheme. Moreover, as the number of cores increases, the overall computation decreases (strong scaling), due likely to increase communication jitter.

To get a sense of effective MPI overlap, we increased the ghost cell size to increase the size of communication. We observed that MPI overlaps is almost null with the runtime that we used on the target machine (OpenMPI 1.8.8), justifying our efforts to integrate progress inside our parallel OpenMP constructs. Figure 3(b) shows the effects as we see performance gains with greater communications sizes, demonstrating the importance of progressing MPI messages.

5   Progress and OpenMP

MPI communication progress is a key factor in hybrid parallelism. Consequently, in order to take advantage of asynchronous messages within an MPI+OpenMP program, communications must be explicitly progressed through MPI runtime calls (`MPI_Test`, `MPI_Probe`). Not doing so shifts most of the message completion responsibility to the actual `MPI_Wait` operation (at least in the configurations we measured). This can all but eliminate any benefits in overlapped communication and communication. Our proposed remedy to overcoming this problem is to utilize task-based constructions. However, additional constructs in OpenMP may help solving this progress issue and more generally support better runtime stacking.

```
1  void idle( void *prequest ) {
     if(__mpi_request_match(prequest)){
3      omp_trigger("ghost_done");
       return  0;
5    }
     return  1;
7  }

9  #pragma omp parallel progress(idle , &request)
   {
11     #pragma omp noprogess
       {
13        MPI_Wait(request , MPI_STATUS_IGNORE);
          omp_trigger("ghost_done");
15     }
       #pragma omp task depends(inout:"ghost_done")
17     {/* BORDER */}
       #pragma omp task
19     {/* CENTER */}
   }
```

Listing 1.4. Proposed implementation for a progress enabled OpenMP

In general, as presented in Listing 1.4, OpenMP could gain from a notion of progress. Indeed, one could define what processing has to be done to satisfy task dependencies, letting the runtime invoke the **progress** function to trigger dependencies. In order to realize this idea, two things are needed. First, a progress parameter would be included for parallel regions to define which function should be called when the runtime is idle or switching between tasks. This should be a function as it contains code which may not be executed if not compiled with OpenMP support; if this function returns "0" it is not called further, if it is "1" it continues to be called as there is work remaining. In this case, the otherwise ignored **noprogress** code section is executed, replacing the non-blocking progress calls with blocking ones.

Second, we need *named dependencies* between tasks. This is because we want another runtime to satisfy a dependency which cannot be known at compilation time as an address, for example, *"ghost_done"*. To do so, we define **omp_trigger** which satisfies a named dependency. Using this simple construct, we are then able to express in a compact manner, a communication dependency with a direct fallback to a blocking version if OpenMP is not present. This abstraction seems reasonable based on our experiments, and we are in the process of implementing this feature to validate it further.

6   Related Work

Scalable, heterogeneous architectures are putting increasing pressure on the pure MPI model [5]. Hybrid parallel programming is necessary to expose multiple levels of parallelism, inside and between nodes. However, in order to leverage and mix our existing models, their runtime systems must interoperate more efficiently.

Hybridization appeared with accelerators and programming languages such as Cuda or OpenCL [18]. Here the host node retains its own cores and memory for program execution, but off-loads computation and data to the accelerator device. Accelerators such as GPUs are generally energy efficient and expose a high level of stream oriented parallelism. One issue with their use is the need for explicit transfers to and from the device, requiring important programming efforts to manage data. Moreover, CPU resources might be underutilized if only used to move data. This argues for another hybrid parallelism level. Pragma-based models such as OpenMP target [3,4], OpenACC [20], Xkaapi [11] and StarPU [2] proposed abstractions combining GPUs and CPUs in an efficient manner, abstracting data-movements.

For the most part, MPI has not been integrated in shared-memory computations. Rather, an MPI process is primarily seen as a container for the shared computation, and most programs evolved from MPI to handle new parallelism models [6]. For these practical reasons, there were fewer efforts to embed MPI in another model (e.g., X+MPI), versus expressing parallelism inside MPI processes (MPI+X). The advent of many-core architectures, such as the Intel MIC [9] and the Intel KNL enforced the use of larger shared-memory contexts, requiring some form of hybridization. MPI+OPenMP is nowadays accounting for a large number of applications, nonetheless, neither MPI or OpenMP have collaborative behaviors. Both of them are distinct runtimes with their respective ABI/API. However, there are several programming models aimed at providing an unified view of heterogeneous or distributed architectures: Coarray Fortran [17], Charm++ [13], HPF [15], Chapel [7], Fortress [1] and X10 [8]. Several of them rage various communication models, including message passing (MPI) and (partitioned) global address space ((P)GAS).

A complementary approach is based on Domain Specific Languages [10] which is aimed at abstracting parallelism expression [12] in order to "free" codes from programming model constraints, for example by targeting multiple models [19]. There is a wide range of such specialized languages with clear advantages, however, they transpose the dependency from a model to a dedicated language with its own constraints [14].

Our work is close to the idea developed by Marjanovic et al. [16], they proposed a set of pragma to improve the processing of non-blocking MPI communications in a multithreaded context. The use of new pragmas requires a specific compiler and results in a loss of portability. Our initial solutions based on tasks differs in the sense that they are only based on the use of standard OpenMP pragmas without any hypothesis of specific executive support mechanisms.

Model mixing and unified models, in general, is a very active research area with a wide variety of approaches. In this paper, we focused on two common building blocks, MPI and OpenMP, trying to see how MPI could be embedded inside OpenMP constructs in an efficient manner. In a way, this takes a reverse approach when most efforts tend to embed OpenMP inside MPI.

7   Conclusion

In this paper, we first introduced the need for hybridization in parallel applications. Indeed, when scaling multiple nodes gathering hundreds of cores, the MPI+X paradigm becomes compulsory to limit both memory and communication overhead. Unfortunately, most MPI+OpenMP codes rely on alternating phases between communication and compute. This can constrain parallel performance due to the fork-join nature of OpenMPI parallelism and the sequentiality of MPI phases outside of a parallel region. Instead, we explored an alternative approach relying on tasks and how they could help to maintain MPI progress during OpenMP parallel computation. With the latest OpenMP version, multiple approaches are possible to mix MPI with OpenMP.

Our hybridization ideas essentially advocate that the program become a Directed Acyclic Graph (DAG) to be scheduled by the OpenMP runtime. The DAG is made of tasks that combine processing from both OpenMP (computation) and MPI (communication). However, such combination is not natural in OpenMP, particularly when considering `MPI_Request` handles which are generated dynamically during the execution. Indeed, OpenMP does not allow tasks dependencies to be expressed on the fly, instead, they have to be resolvable at compilation time. Consequently, in this paper, we propose three different approaches to mixing OpenMP tasks and MPI despite this static dependency resolution. Each approach is described and evaluated with a simple benchmark. The measurements show that a task-based approach was beneficial to the overall execution, in particular, by allowing greater computation overlap. However, a key issue is MPI progress. Efficient hybrid execution (MPI+OpenMP) can only be achieved if MPI calls are regularly invoked during parallel OpenMP computation, as our task-based examples demonstrate.

8   Future Work

In general, effective runtime inter-operation and stacking for hybrid parallel programming requires interactions to coordinate progress. It is important to consider then the integration of this support in programming standards. For instance, in our study of MPI+OpenMP, if the `taskyield` call could be defined as an arbitrary function, it would be possible for the OpenMP runtime to notify the MPI runtime that it may progress communications. With this progress issue solved, dynamic (on request addresses) or label-based dependencies would be an alternative to the jump-table we relied on in this paper. There can be side effects when combining two runtimes that need some additional support to resolve.

References

1. Allen, E., Chase, D., Hallett, J., Luchangco, V., Maessen, J.W., Ryu, S., Steele, G.L., Tobin-Hochstadt, S.: The Fortress language specification. Tech. report, Sun Microsystems, Inc., version 1.0, March 2008

2. Augonnet, C., Thibault, S., Namyst, R., Wacrenier, P.-A.: STARPU: a unified platform for task scheduling on heterogeneous multicore architectures. In: Sips, H., Epema, D., Lin, H.-X. (eds.) Euro-Par 2009. LNCS, vol. 5704, pp. 863–874. Springer, Heidelberg (2009). doi:10.1007/978-3-642-03869-3_80

3. Ayguade, E., et al.: A proposal to extend the OpenMP tasking model for heterogeneous architectures. In: Müller, M.S., Supinski, B.R., Chapman, B.M. (eds.) IWOMP 2009. LNCS, vol. 5568, pp. 154–167. Springer, Heidelberg (2009). doi:10.1007/978-3-642-02303-3_13

4. Bertolli, C., Antao, S.F., Eichenberger, A.E., O'Brien, K., Sura, Z., Jacob, A.C., Chen, T., Sallenave, O.: Coordinating GPU threads for OpenMP 4.0 in LLVM. In: Proceedings of the 2014 LLVM Compiler Infrastructure in HPC, LLVM-HPC 2014, pp. 12–21. IEEE Press, Piscataway (2014). http://dx.doi.org/10.1109/LLVM-HPC.2014.10

5. Besnard, J.B., Malony, A., Shende, S., Pérache, M., Carribault, P., Jaeger, J.: An MPI halo-cell implementation for zero-copy abstraction. In: Proceedings of the 22nd European MPI Users' Group Meeting, EuroMPI 2015, NY, USA, pp. 3:1–3:9 (2015). http://doi.acm.org/10.1145/2802658.2802669

6. Brunst, H., Mohr, B.: Performance analysis of large-scale OpenMP and hybrid MPI/OpenMP applications with Vampir NG. In: Mueller, M.S., Chapman, B.M., Supinski, B.R., Malony, A.D., Voss, M. (eds.) IWOMP 2005. LNCS, vol. 4315, pp. 5–14. Springer, Heidelberg (2008). doi:10.1007/978-3-540-68555-5_1

7. Chamberlain, B., Callahan, D., Zima, H.: Parallel programmability and the Chapel language. Int. J. High Perform. Comput. Appl. 21(3), 291–312 (2007). http://dx.doi.org/10.1177/1094342007078442

8. Charles, P., Grothoff, C., Saraswat, V., Donawa, C., Kielstra, A., Ebcioglu, K., von Praun, C., Sarkar, V.: X10: an object-oriented approach to non-uniform cluster computing. SIGPLAN Not. 40(10), 519–538 (2015). http://doi.acm.org/10.1145/1103845.1094852

9. Duran, A., Klemm, M.: The intel many integrated core architecture. In: 2012 International Conference on High Performance Computing Simulation (HPCS), pp. 365–366, July 2012

10. Fowler, M.: Domain-Specific Languages. Pearson Education, Boston (2010)

11. Gautier, T., Lima, J.V.F., Maillard, N., Raffin, B.: XKaapi: a runtime system for data-flow task programming on heterogeneous architectures. In: 2013 IEEE 27th International Symposium on Parallel and Distributed Processing, pp. 1299–1308, May 2013

12. Hamidouche, K., Falcou, J., Etiemble, D.: Hybrid bulk synchronous parallelism library for clustered SMP architectures. In: Proceedings of the Fourth International Workshop on High-level Parallel Programming and Applications, HLPP 2010, NY, USA, pp. 55–62 (2010). http://doi.acm.org/10.1145/1863482.1863494

13. Kale, L.V., Krishnan, S.: Charm++: a portable concurrent object oriented system based on c++. SIGPLAN Not. 28(10), 91–108 (1993). http://doi.acm.org/10.1145/167962.165874

14. Karlin, I., Bhatele, A., Keasler, J., Chamberlain, B.L., Cohen, J., Devito, Z., Haque, R., Laney, D., Luke, E., Wang, F., Richards, D., Schulz, M., Still, C.H.: Exploring traditional and emerging parallel programming models using a proxy application. In: 2013 IEEE 27th International Symposium on Parallel and Distributed Processing, pp. 919–932, May 2013
15. Loveman, D.B.: High performance Fortran. IEEE Parallel Distrib. Technol. Syst. Appl. **1**(1), 25–42 (1993)
16. Marjanović, V., Labarta, J., Ayguadé, E., Valero, M.: Overlapping communication and computation by using a hybrid MPI/SMPSS approach. In: Proceedings of the 24th ACM International Conference on Supercomputing, ICS 2010, NY, USA, pp. 5–16 (2010). http://doi.acm.org/10.1145/1810085.1810091
17. Numrich, R.W., Reid, J.: Co-array Fortran for parallel programming. SIGPLAN Fortran Forum **17**(2), 1–31 (1998). http://doi.acm.org/10.1145/289918.289920
18. Stone, J.E., Gohara, D., Shi, G.: OpenCL: a parallel programming standard for heterogeneous computing systems. Comput. Sci. Eng. **12**(3), 66–73 (2010)
19. Sujeeth, A.K., et al.: Composition and reuse with compiled domain-specific languages. In: Castagna, G. (ed.) ECOOP 2013. LNCS, vol. 7920, pp. 52–78. Springer, Heidelberg (2013). doi:10.1007/978-3-642-39038-8_3
20. Wienke, S., Springer, P., Terboven, C., Mey, D.: OpenACC — first experiences with real-world applications. In: Kaklamanis, C., Papatheodorou, T., Spirakis, P.G. (eds.) Euro-Par 2012. LNCS, vol. 7484, pp. 859–870. Springer, Heidelberg (2012). doi:10.1007/978-3-642-32820-6_85

Asynchronous OpenMP Tasking with Easy Thread Context Switching and Pool Control

Xing Fan$^{(\boxtimes)}$, Oliver Sinnen, and Nasser Giacaman

Parallel and Reconfigurable Computing Lab, Department of Electrical
and Computer Engineering, The University of Auckland, Auckland, New Zealand
fxin927@aucklanduni.ac.nz, {o.sinnen,n.giacaman}@auckland.ac.nz

Abstract. OpenMP tasking is a very effective approach for many parallelization problems. In order to introduce this advanced parallelism tool to Java community, this paper presents an implementation of Java OpenMP tasking. In addition, by emphasizing on concurrency for event-driven programming framework, a new virtual target concept is proposed. By comparing the concepts between OpenMP tasking and virtual target, it shows how virtual target is more suitable for event-driven parallelization. To analyze event-driven parallelization performance, a performance model is presented, and it sheds light on the performance issues in an event-driven system. The experiment shows the effectiveness of the new proposed virtual target tasking approach, and it enables a more flexible performance tuning with task pool control.

1 Introduction

Task parallelism has been an important part of OpenMP programming model, since its initial release of version 3.0 [1]. OpenMP tasking enables programmers to handle irregular and unsymmetrical parallelism problems that the traditional worksharing constructs could not solve. The evolution of the OpenMP specification has provided increased flexibility and expressiveness with tasks, such as dependency handling [6] and task-generating loops [14].

Java is consistently rated as the most popular programming language [15], yet very few Java OpenMP implementations exist [4,5,10,16]. To further depress the Java community, it is rare to see these Java OpenMP implementations support the powerful aforementioned OpenMP tasking constructs. It is worthwhile exploring the potential benefits that Java can gain from a more advanced OpenMP version with tasking.

As an object-oriented language, Java is widely used for many application developments. Many of the applications are based on the event-driven model, ranging from mobile apps, desktop applications to web services. In general, these types of programs have an interactive nature, where the execution of the program is determined by the events or requests generated at runtime. To ensure that these applications do not freeze and remain responsive, the Event Dispatching Thread (EDT) is expected to offload heavy computations to a background thread. Such an asynchronous execution is necessary to achieve concurrency such

© Springer International Publishing AG 2017
B.R. de Supinski et al. (Eds.): IWOMP 2017, LNCS 10468, pp. 217–230, 2017.
DOI: 10.1007/978-3-319-65578-9_15

that the EDT remains active to respond to other events. Some efforts of using OpenMP for web services have been tried. The experiences show that using traditional OpenMP directives to parallelize web service calls is possible, but it requires non-trivial programming efforts to achieve high level performance [2,13].

In our earlier work, we proposed a virtual target model [7] as a complementary part for OpenMP tasks to facilitate event-driven parallel programming. Here, we verify our model through our Java implementation of OpenMP, known as Pyjama [16]. With the OpenMP-like directives, a single-threaded Java program is easily converted to a multi-threaded version, making the application both parallel and asynchronous in nature. By adapting the queue theory model, we model the parallel event-driven programming problem. By doing the experiments, we discover some interesting facts about the parallelization of event-driven programs. The contributions of this paper are as follows:

1. This work, to the best of our knowledge, is one of the two Java implementations of the OpenMP tasking concept (Another implementation is the newest version of JaMP [10]). Furthermore, a special virtual target tasking concept is proposed and implemented for event-driven parallelization.
2. A performance model for event-driven parallelization is proposed. In this model, factors that influence the event-driven performance are profiled. It gives a theoretical reference and baseline for the benchmarks.
3. The experiment demonstrates the effectiveness of using the virtual target concept for event-driven framework. It offers more usability and flexibility compared to the traditional OpenMP tasking concept. Its design also enables categorizing different tasks, to be submitted to different thread pools according to their sizes or run time, which thereby minimizes the mean event handling flow time.

The structure of the paper follows: Sect. 2 gives a brief overview how our Java version of the OpenMP tasking is implemented. Section 3 introduces the concept of virtual targets, distinguishing it with OpenMP tasks. Section 4 describes the theoretical background of parallelizing event-driven programs and a mathematical model is presented to quantify the performance. Section 5 presents the experiment performed and the results obtained. Finally, in Sect. 6 we conclude.

2   OpenMP Task for Java

This section briefly introduces our implementation of OpenMP tasking in Java.

2.1   Directive Syntax

The syntax remains faithful to the C/C++ OpenMP specification, except Java does not support #pragma so a comment-like identifier //#omp is used instead. The current implementation conforms to OpenMP Specification 3.0. The task

```
//#omp task [clause[[,]clause]...]
   structured-block
```

clause:
    data-handling-clause
    if-clause
where *data-handling-clause* is one of the following:
    firstprivate(*list*) **shared**(*list*)
and *if-clause* is:
    if(*scalar-expression*)

Fig. 1. The task directive for Java.

construct defines an explicit task, and it is only active when this construct block is within a parallel region. One noticeable remark is the clause **untied** is not implemented, because the Java Virtual Machine (JVM) thread scheduling is delegated to the operating system, and from Java's perspective a task will always been executed by one specific thread (Fig. 1).

2.2 Implementation

The implementation is composed of two parts. First is the source-to-source compiler that transforms the sequential Java source code into parallel code. Second is the runtime support, providing the underlining thread-pool management, scheduling, and OpenMP runtime functions.

Auxiliary Class Generation. An auxiliary class (which is an inner class of the current compilation unit) is generated to represent the specific OpenMP construct block. In general, when the compiler processes the sequential code, each task code block is refactored into an inner class, and this inner class inherits an abstract class called OmpTask. The abstract interface call() is implemented to include the user code. Meanwhile, all the variables which are used in the target block are also required as field variables in the auxiliary class, and they should be passed in and initialized by the auxiliary class constructor.

Task Block Invocation. In the generated code, the invocation of every task block is converted to the invocation of its paired auxiliary class. First, an instance of its auxiliary class is initialized, with proper arguments. Second, by checking the current Internal Control Variable (ICV), the runtime detects if the current thread is a member of the OpenMP parallel thread group. If yes, this task will be submitted to the corresponding thread pool. Otherwise, the task block executes sequentially.

2.3 Compared to C/C++ Version of OpenMP Task

The implementation overhead of the Java version is clearly more than that of a C/C++ version. For example, an implementation based on light-weight execution units called nano-threads [12] has been proposed [1]. The nano-thread layer is implemented with POSIX's pthreads and this layer has a slight impact on efficiency. In contrast, because of the nature of Java, it cannot directly involve any system calls and all operating system level calls have to be delegated to the JVM runtime. In the meantime, the code transformation from sequential version to parallel version inevitably introduces new classes and their invocations cause more overhead in the runtime. It is foreseeable that the Java version of OpenMP tasking has a higher threshold than C/C++ to see the real benefit of task parallelization. In another words, the purpose of using Java tasking should mainly target coarse-grained tasks rather than fine-grained tasks.

3   Virtual Target: An Event-Driven Parallelization Solution

OpenMP tasking does not address concurrency[1]. In order to offload computation from the current executing thread, the proposed syntax in Fig. 2 is inspired by the **target** directive introduced in the OpenMP 4.0 specification. The initial purpose of the **target** directive is to utilize available accelerators in addition to multicore processors in the system. The **target** directive offloads the computation of its code block to a specified accelerator, if a **device** clause is followed.

3.1   Directive Syntax Extensions

Virtual Target. In line with the existing **target** directive, this work proposed an extension of the target syntax by introducing the concept of *virtual target*. A *virtual target* means the computation is not offloaded to a real physical device. Instead, it is a software-level executor capable of offloading the target block from the thread which encounters this **target** directive. Conventionally, a *device target* has its own memory and data environment, therefore the data mapping and synchronization are necessary between the host and the target. That is why

```
//#omp target virtual(name-tag) [clause[[,]clause]...]
   structured-block
```
clause:
    data-handling-clause
    asynchronous-property-clause
where *data-handling-clause* is one of the following:
    firstprivate(*list*) **shared**(*list*)
where *asynchronous-property-clause* is one of the following:
    nowait name_as(*name-tag*) **await**

Fig. 2. Extended target directive.

---

[1] In the context of an event-driven application, "concurrency" refers to the computation being offloaded to a background thread allowing the EDT to progress.

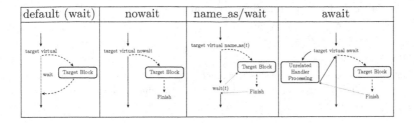

Fig. 3. Different asynchronous modes, by using different *asynchronous-property-clause*s.

normally some auxiliary constructs or directives such as `target data` and `target update` are used when using `target` directives. In contrast, a *virtual target* still actually shares the same memory that the host holds, so the data context remains the same when entering the target code block. Generally, a *virtual target* is a syntax-level abstraction of a thread pool executor, such that the `target` block is executed by the executor specified by the *target-name*. Therefore, the newly introduced directives are compatible with existing OpenMP directives. With the combination of different directives, programmers are able to express different forms of parallelization and concurrency logic.

Target Block Scheduling. By default, an encountering thread may not proceed past the target code block until it is finished by either the device target or virtual target. However, a more flexible and expressive control flow of the encountering thread can be achieved by adopting the *asynchronous-property-clause*. Therefore, a target block can also be regarded as a task with an asynchronous nature. Figure 3 lists all the asynchronous property a target code block can have in the program. A more detailed explanation of *asynchronous-property-clause* can be found in [7].

Runtime Support. A virtual target is essentially a thread pool executor, or can be an event dispatching thread. Its lifecycle lasts throughout the program. Conceptually, a virtual target represents a type of execution environment defining its thread affiliation (to ensure operations not thread-safe are only executed by a specified thread), and scale (confine the number of threads of a thread pool). This design enables programmers to flexibly submit different code snippets to different execution environments. Table 1 describes the additional OpenMP APIs supported by Pyjama, which are used for managing virtual targets at runtime.

3.2   The Distinctions Between omp Task and omp Target Virtual

The virtual target concept allows programmers to easily change the thread context, and submit the code blocks to a different thread pool, without knowing any underlying implementation details. The salient advantage of using virtual

Table 1. Runtime functions to create virtual targets in Pyjama.

Name	virtual_target_register()	virtual_target_create()
Parameters	tname:String	tname:String, n:Integer
Description	The thread which invokes this function will be registered as a virtual target named tname	Creating a worker virtual target with maximum of n threads, and its name is tname

Table 2. Comparisons between omp task and omp target virtual.

Distinction	omp task	omp virtual target
Objective	Task parallelization	Concurrency
Scenario used	Task decomposition and parallelization	Event-driven offloading and context switching
Effectiveness region	Only in parallel region	Everywhere
Dependency handling	Data dependency	Control flow dependency

```
void server(){
  #pragma omp parallel
  {                                 void event_handler1(){
    #pragma omp single                #pragma omp target virtual(worker) await
    while(1) {                          compute_half1();
      #pragma omp task                #pragma omp target virtual(edt) nowait
      event_handler1();                 notify("Task_half_finished");
      #pragma omp task                #pragma omp target virtual(worker) await
      event_handler2();                 compute_half2();
    }                                 #pragma omp target virtual(edt) nowait
  }                                     notify("Task_finished");
}                                   }
        (a)                                       (b)
```

Fig. 4. Two simple examples: (a) The example of using OpenMP tasks; (b) The example of using virtual targets.

targets is its compatibility with an event-driven framework. For most event-driven frameworks, only event handlers are exposed to the programmers, and programmers cannot directly modify the dispatching mechanism. Under this circumstance, using OpenMP task directives shows its disadvantage because a task is only active when it is within a parallel region, but the programmers cannot use the parallel directive to parallelize the dispatching framework. These differences are summarized in Table 2.

Figure 4a and b show the simple examples of using the two directive types. The example of using omp tasks forces the code change onto the event loop, then asynchronization of the event handlers becomes possible. In contrast, for virtual targets, programmers can directly use the target virtual directive inside event handlers to offload computations away from event handling thread. Another big distinction of these two concepts is in OpenMP tasking, the master thread is a part of the thread group. As a comparison, in virtual targets, the master thread and task threads are explicitly distinguished. If the current thread is not a member thread of the target virtual's thread pool, the target code block will not be executed by the current thread.

4 Performance Measurement of the Event Handling Execution

In an event-driven system, we cannot simply measure speedup and execution time to evaluate the performance of a parallelism and concurrency framework, as events become available/are released at different times. Hence we need some other measure to handle events in a system. For this reason we establish here a performance model based on queue theory, before the experimental evaluation in the next section.

4.1 The Flow Time of an Event Handling

The flow time t_F measures the time span from the triggering of the event to the finish of its related event handling. We assume only the EDT is able to dispatch the events, and an event request queue is maintained by the EDT. The notation t_R measures the residual service time current event handler that is under processing. The queuing time t_Q indicates the handling function cannot process until all previous queued handling functions are complete. Afterwards, the service time t_S is conducted for the processing of this event handling.

Considering for an event binding $e \rightarrow \mathcal{F}$, the event e happens. At that time, there are potentially unprocessed event handlers in event queue, and $\mathbf{F}$ indicates the set of all queued handling functions at the event triggering point. Then the flow time of the event handling is the sum of three parts: The residual time of the current event handling; Its queuing time and the its handling function execution time, shown as below:

$$t_F = t_R + t_Q + t_S = t_R + \sum_{f \in \mathbf{F}} t_S(f) + t_S$$

Processing Events in a Multi-threaded Environment. For an application in a multi-threaded system, two approaches to reduce the flow time t_F of each event handling are possible. The first approach is enabling the system to have more asynchronous workers to process the queued requests, then t_Q is reduced. The second approach is to parallelize the event handlers, which makes the service time faster than the sequential execution time, decreasing the t_S and in turn the t_Q.

Denote N_a as the asynchronization scale, and N_p as the parallelization scale. Ideally, assume the asynchronous workers do not suffer from any performance degradation and increasing the number of asynchronous works always gets N_a speedup, in other words the execution load of all tasks to be executed concurrently is ideally balanced across the N_a workers. As a comparison, because of the nature of the handling function, it is not always true to get ideal speedup when adopting parallelization. We define parallelization efficiency function as $\epsilon(N_p) = \eta N_p$, in which the handling function gains $\epsilon(N_p)$ speedup when using N_p threads to parallelize this event handler. η is the parallelization efficiency factor.

$$t_F(\mathbf{F}) = \frac{t_R}{\epsilon'(N_p)} + \left(\sum_{f \in \mathbf{F}} \frac{t_Q(f)}{\epsilon_f(N_p)} \right) N_a^{-1} + \frac{t_S(\mathcal{F})}{\epsilon(N_p)}$$

4.2   Modeling of the Parallel Event-Driven System

There is no widely-used performance model relating to the parallelization of event-driven programs. As a consequence, it is not very clear how parallelization influences the performance of event-driven executions. An interesting question arises if the event handlers have the potential to be parallelized. Since computational resource is usually limited, to what extend to use parallelization is the best way to boost the event-driven performance with limited maximum core number, along with the use of asynchronous offloading.

To model the parallel event-driven system, we use the Kendall Notation to describe the system. D.G. Kendall proposed describing queuing models using three factors written A/S/c in 1953 [9] where A denotes the time between arrivals to the queue, S is the size of jobs and c is the number of servers at the node. As a default, we assume that this model has unlimited capacity of the queue, and the queuing principle is First In First Out (FIFO).

- A: The arrival process
- S: The service time distribution
- c: The number of servers

Queue Model with Parallel Property. Now we extend the $A/S/c$ model with parallel execution property. Define N_a as the asynchronization scale of the multi-core machine, and N_p as the parallelization scale of a multi-core machine. The maximum threads in this system is $N_a N_p$. Then the $A/S/c$ model is extended as $A/S/N_a/N_p$.

Suppose the arrivals of the event requests are governed by a Poisson Distribution [8], and the sequential handling times for the handlers are Exponentially Distributed. In this parallel queue system, there are N_a multiple asynchronous workers that can process the requests at the same time, and there are N_p parallel threads in a paralleled handling function. This model is described as $M/M/N_a/N_p$.

In order to better analyze the performance of this model, the factors related to this model are listed as below:

- λ is the mean arrival rate of the requests/events.
- μ is the mean **sequential** service rate; if the mean sequential service time of the handlers is T_{seq}, then $\mu = \frac{1}{T_{seq}}$.
- N_a is the asynchronization scale, which is the number of asynchronous workers in the queue system.
- N_p is the parallelization scale, which is the number of parallel threads in event handler's parallel region.
- W is the mean flow time spent at the queue both of waiting and being serviced.

Utilization. Define the service utility as ρ, which presents the utilization of each processor. Then:

$$\rho = \frac{\lambda}{\mu N_a \epsilon(N_p)} \tag{1}$$

The utilization measures the occupation of the processors. If this value is too low, it means the incoming tasks do not create a high usage of the computation resources. A good use of a parallel system is keeping the utilization of the processors under a relative high usage.

Mean Flow Time. The average flow time W is one of the key factor to evaluate the performance of the system. The theoretical calculation of the mean flow time of each event handling can be calculated as follows, based on the traditional $M/M/c$ queue model. Define Π_W to be the probability that an event request has to wait. So Π_W is the sum of the probabilities this system contains i requests, where $i \geqslant c$:

$$\Pi_W = p_c + p_{c+1} + p_{c+2} + \dots$$

$$= \frac{p_c}{1-\rho} = \frac{(c\rho)^c}{c!} \left((1-\rho) \sum_{n=0}^{c-1} \frac{(c\rho)^n}{n!} + \frac{(c\rho)^c}{c!} \right)^{-1}$$

Then the mean waiting queue length L_q is:

$$L_q = \sum_{n=0}^{\infty} n p_{N_a+n} = \Pi_W \cdot \frac{\rho}{1-\rho}$$

According to Little's Law [11], The average waiting time W_q is:

$$W_q = L_q \cdot \rho = \Pi_W \cdot \frac{1}{1-\rho} \cdot \frac{1}{\mu N_a \epsilon(N_p)}$$

Then the average flow time W is [3]:

$$W = W_q + \frac{1}{\mu \epsilon(N_p)} = \Pi_W \cdot \frac{1}{1-\rho} \cdot \frac{1}{\mu N_a \epsilon(N_p)} + \frac{1}{\mu \epsilon(N_p)} \tag{2}$$

4.3   Remarks

Relationship Between Flow Time and Processor Utility. According to the Eq. 2, Fig. 5 shows a plot of the relationship between W and ρ in the $M/M/N_a/N_p$ model. If N_a and N_p are fixed value, it is easily found that the average flow time W increases rapidly when utilization ρ is above 80%. This leads to a dilemma that the system cannot reach both very high utilization and high performance. If the computation requests arrival rate is known and fixed, even though increasing N_a and N_p can reduce the mean request flow time W, it is unwise to distribute very large number of N_a and N_p since it causes a low processor utilization. In practice, keeping the utilization ρ from 70% to 80% is considered a good operational level, without degrading much performance.

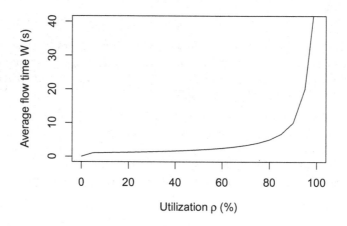

Fig. 5. The theoretical relationship between processor utilization ρ and the mean event-handling flow time W in an event-driven system.

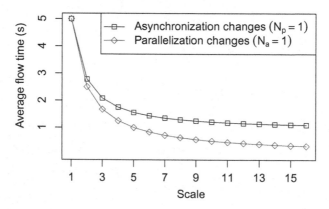

Fig. 6. The performance comparison between merely increasing asynchronous scale or parallel scale.

Distribution of Asynchronization and Parallelization. When arrival rate λ and sequential service rate μ are fixed and if the computational resources are limited and the event handlers are parallelizable, increasing the parallelization scale is a better choice to decrease the average flow time W. Figure 6 shows the results when the total number of processors is fixed as 16, how merely increasing N_a or N_p effects the average flow time (assume $\lambda = 1, \mu = 1$ and parallel with idea speedup $\epsilon(N_p) = N_p$).

5   Experiment

This section discusses how the experiment is conducted. The system environment consisted of a 64-core AMD Opteron Processor 6272 SMP machine with 256 GB memory, and Java 1.8.0_101 HotSpot 64-Bit Server VM. We simulate a computational server, in which several web services are provided. Respectively, they are Crypt, Monte Carlo, Series and Ray Tracer. Every time a client requests a computation, they send the request data via web socket. When the server receives a computation request, it queues its related handler function and until the handler function is executed, then the related data is sent back to the client. For simplicity, when an event handler is queued, it cannot be canceled from the queue.

The sequential running times of all computational kernels are initially measured. It is assumed all requests are subjected to a Poisson Progress and with specific arrival rates. The information of each computation is listed in Table 3. For this experiment, the notation PxAy defined as x threads are used to parallelize every handler kernel (P1 means the kernel runs in the sequential way), and y threads are used for asynchronous workers. If y is a list $(y_1, y_2, y_3, ...)$, it means the total asynchronous workers are separated into groups with specific number of workers that are distributed to different kernel handlers.

5.1   Adopt Asynchronization to Decrease Queue Time

If the handlers are not parallelized, and only asynchronization is used, adopting asynchronization enables the system to reduce the queue times. We implement the parallel version in two different ways. First, we use traditional OpenMP task directive to offload event handler executions to the parallel region thread pool.

Table 3. Computational kernels and their arrival rates and sequential service rates.

Computational kernel	T_{seq}	λ	μ
Crypt	260 ms	10	3.85
MonteCarlo	570 ms	4	1.75
Series	780 ms	10	1.28
RayTracer	1255 ms	4	0.80

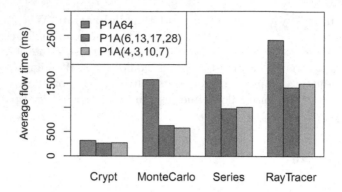

Fig. 7. The mean flow times (ms) of four kernels implemented by three different asynchronization scale distributions.

Second, we use virtual targets to offload different handlers to different virtual targets, and the thread pool sizes are distributed according to the handling times.

Figure 7 compares the performance of three approaches. More specifically, they are:

P1A64: In this approach, all 64 processors are assigned as asynchronous workers, but all handlers share a single 64-thread task pool. This approach can be implemented by traditional OpenMP tasking concept. However, the performance is not as good as expected. For three out of four kernels, The mean flow times are drastically longer than the kernel sequential running times (The mean flow time of every kernel takes 122%, 276%, 215%, 191% of its sequential running time respectively), which means each handler takes very long time on queuing.

P1A(6, 12, 18, 28): This approach is implemented according to the virtual target concept. Four virtual targets are used with different thread-pool sizes. The total 64 asynchronous workers are distributed to four kernel handlers according to their sizes of sequential running times. Therefore, every kernel handler gains the proportion of 9%, 20%, 27%, 44% of the total asynchronous workers. Under this distribution, the results show a better performance than P1A64, although the total number of used threads does not change.

P1A(4, 3, 10, 7): In this approach, in order to ensure a high utilization, the number of asynchronous works for each kernel handler is calculated by $N_a = \lceil \frac{\lambda}{\mu\rho} \rceil$ (according to Eq. 1 where $\rho = 0.8$). Therefore, a total number of 24 asynchronous workers are distributed to four kernel handlers as A(4, 3, 10, 7). The results show a very close performance comparing to P1A(6, 12, 18, 28) but only 24 processors are used.

From this experiment, it can be discovered that offloading event handling tasks based on their run times can effectively decrease the mean flow times for handlers. Moreover, according to the performance model developed in Sect. 4, a succinct use of processors can be achieved without degrading the performance.

Table 4. 64-processor distribution and its mean flow time (ms), categorized by different kernel handlers.

Distribution	Crypt	MonteCarlo	Series	RayTracer
P1A64	248	590	966	1405
P2A32	148	365	573	805
P4A16	98	335	305	729
P6A14	96	309	309	752
P8A8	89	192	193	478
P14A6	125	190	195	360
P16A4	138	193	188	312
P32A2	337	413	376	405
P64A1	1750	1731	1746	1785

5.2   Adopt Both Asynchronization and Parallelization to Decrease Flow Time

Here, both parallelization and asynchronization are applied together. The mean flow time of each type of event handler can be further reduced, therefore increasing the throughput of the server. Table 4 reveals that the different distributions between N_a and N_p can drastically influence the performance. The performance tuning of the parallel event-driven system is subjected to many factors. The design requires the trade off between computational budget, latency and special requirements for particular event handlers. Comparing with the OpenMP tasking concept, virtual target enables programmers to have a more flexible processor distribution among a group of handlers, and its fine-grained thread pool control has the potential to gain a better performance.

6   Conclusion

This paper shows an implementation of task concept for Java OpenMP. In order to parallelize an event-driven program, a new OpenMP directive and its model are proposed. We compare the differences between the proposed virtual target model and traditional OpenMP tasking model, and prove this proposal is more compatible for event-driven programmings. We have discussed the concerns of building up a parallelization event-driven system. The experiments show the effectiveness of adopting this approach to an event handling system. Virtual target concept shows its advantage because this model enables programmers to tune the performance according to the properties of event handlers. The future work involves a further study of the relationship between parallelization scale and asynchronization scale, and exploring the solution to maximize the event-driven performance in a parallel system.

References

1. Ayguade, E., Copty, N., Duran, A., Hoeflinger, J., Lin, Y., Massaioli, F., Teruel, X., Unnikrishnan, P., Zhang, G.: The design of OpenMP tasks. IEEE Trans. Parallel Distrib. Syst. **20**(3), 404–418 (2009)
2. Balart, J., Duran, A., Gonzàlez, M., Martorell, X., Ayguadé, E., Labarta, J.: Experiences parallelizing a web server with OpenMP. In: Mueller, M.S., Chapman, B.M., Supinski, B.R., Malony, A.D., Voss, M. (eds.) IWOMP -2005. LNCS, vol. 4315, pp. 191–202. Springer, Heidelberg (2008). doi:10.1007/978-3-540-68555-5_16
3. Braband, J.: Waiting time distributions for M/M/N processor sharing queues. Stoch. Models **10**(3), 533–548 (1994)
4. Bull, J.M., Kambites, M.E.: JOMP–an OpenMP-like interface for Java. In: Proceedings of the ACM 2000 Conference on Java Grande, JAVA 2000, pp. 44–53. ACM, New York (2000)
5. Cook, R.P.: An OpenMP library for Java. In: 2013 Proceedings of IEEE on SoutheastCon, pp. 1–6. IEEE (2013)
6. Duran, A., Perez, J.M., Ayguadé, E., Badia, R.M., Labarta, J.: Extending the OpenMP tasking model to allow dependent tasks. In: Eigenmann, R., Supinski, B.R. (eds.) IWOMP 2008. LNCS, vol. 5004, pp. 111–122. Springer, Heidelberg (2008). doi:10.1007/978-3-540-79561-2_10
7. Fan, X., Sinnen, O., Giacaman, N.: Towards an event-driven programming model for OpenMP. In: 2016 45th International Conference on Parallel Processing Workshops (ICPPW), pp. 240–249, August 2016
8. Haight, F.A.: Handbook of the Poisson Distribution. Wiley, New York (1967)
9. Kendall, D.G.: Stochastic processes occurring in the theory of queues and their analysis by the method of the imbedded Markov chain. Ann. Math. Stat. **24**, 338–354 (1953)
10. Klemm, M., Bezold, M., Veldema, R., Philippsen, M.: JaMP: an implementation of OpenMP for a Java DSM. Concurrency Comput. Pract. Exp. **19**(18), 2333–2352 (2007)
11. Little, J.D.C.: A proof for the queuing formula: L = λw. Oper. Res. **9**(3), 383–387 (1961)
12. Polychronopoulos, C.D.: Nano-threads: compiler driven multithreading. In: 4th International Workshop on Compilers for Parallel Computing (1993)
13. Salva, S., Delamare, C., Bastoul, C.: Web service call parallelization using OpenMP. In: Chapman, B., Zheng, W., Gao, G.R., Sato, M., Ayguadé, E., Wang, D. (eds.) IWOMP 2007. LNCS, vol. 4935, pp. 185–194. Springer, Heidelberg (2008). doi:10. 1007/978-3-540-69303-1_21
14. Teruel, X., Klemm, M., Li, K., Martorell, X., Olivier, S.L., Terboven, C.: A proposal for task-generating loops in OpenMP*. In: Rendell, A.P., Chapman, B.M., Müller, M.S. (eds.) IWOMP 2013. LNCS, vol. 8122, pp. 1–14. Springer, Heidelberg (2013). doi:10.1007/978-3-642-40698-0_1
15. TIOBE Software BV: TIOBE programming community index (2017)
16. Vikas, N.G., Sinnen, O.: Multiprocessing with GUI-awareness using OpenMP-like directives in Java. Parallel Comput. **40**, 69–89 (2013)

A Functional Safety OpenMP* for Critical Real-Time Embedded Systems

Sara Royuela[1]($\boxtimes$), Alejandro Duran[2]($\boxtimes$), Maria A. Serrano[1]($\boxtimes$),
Eduardo Quiñones[1]($\boxtimes$), and Xavier Martorell[1]($\boxtimes$)

[1] Barcelona Supercomputing Center, Barcelona, Spain
{sara.royuela,maria.serrano,eduardo.quinones,xavier.martorell}@bsc.es
[2] Intel Corporation Iberia, Madrid, Spain
alejandro.duran@intel.com

Abstract. OpenMP* has recently gained attention in the embedded domain by virtue of the augmentations implemented in the last specification. Yet, the language has a minimal impact in the embedded real-time domain mostly due to the lack of reliability and resiliency mechanisms. As a result, functional safety properties cannot be guaranteed. This paper analyses in detail the latest specification to determine whether and how the compliant OpenMP implementations can guarantee functional safety. Given the conclusions drawn from the analysis, the paper describes a set of modifications to the specification, and a set of requirements for compiler and runtime systems to qualify for safety critical environments. Through the proposed solution, OpenMP can be used in critical real-time embedded systems without compromising functional safety.

1 Introduction

There is a visible trend in the critical real-time embedded industry to adopt parallel processor architectures, with the objective of providing the performance requirements needed to support advanced functionalities, e.g. autonomous driving and unmanned aerial vehicles. These recent advances on parallel embedded architectures are driving an interesting convergence between the high-performance and the embedded domain [1]. In this context, the use of parallel programming models is of paramount importance. To begin with, to efficiently exploit the performance opportunities of these architectures. Besides, to provide programmability and portability. All crucial to meet productivity.

OpenMP* has recently gained much attention in the real-time embedded domain owing to the augmentations of the latest specification. These address the key issues in parallel heterogeneous embedded architectures: (a) the coupling of a main host processor to one or more accelerators, where highly-parallel code kernels can be offloaded for improved performance/watt; and (b) the capability of expressing fine-grained, both structured and unstructured, and highly-dynamic task parallelism. As a result, OpenMP is already supported by several chip and compiler vendors targeting embedded systems such as Kalray, Texas Instruments and ARM. A fact that relaxes portability issues.

B.R. de Supinski et al. (Eds.): IWOMP 2017, LNCS 10468, pp. 231–245, 2017.
DOI: 10.1007/978-3-319-65578-9_16

Furthermore, recent studies demonstrate that the structure and syntax of the OpenMP tasking model resembles the Directed Acyclic Graph (DAG) scheduling real-time model [32]. This enables the analysis of the timing properties for such a model. However, the analysis of the OpenMP thread-centric model in terms of timing and progress guarantees is still an open issue. Last but not least, the use of OpenMP to enable fine-grained parallelism in critical real-time suitable languages like Ada has already been proposed [28].

Overall, critical real-time embedded systems can benefit from the flexibility delivered by OpenMP. Yet, the impact of the language in such a domain is very limited. The reason is that critical real-time systems require *functional safety* guarantees, imposing the system to operate correctly in response to its inputs from both functional and timing perspectives. This paper focuses on the former. Functional safety is verified by means of safety standards as the ISO26262 [13] for automotive, the DO178C [5] for avionics or the IEC61508 [12] for industry. The use of reliability and resiliency mechanisms allow guaranteeing the correct operation of the (parallel) execution. Moreover, the complete system stack must be guaranteed, from the processor architectural perspective to the operating system. In this respect, OpenMP lacks the required reliability and resiliency mechanisms at both compiler and runtime levels.

Section 2 analyses in detail the latest specification of OpenMP [2] to identify the features that may entail a hazard regarding functional safety on critical real-time embedded systems. Along with the analysis, Sect. 3 proposes changes in the specification as well as a series of implementation considerations to take into account in both compilers and runtimes. This proposal aims to eliminate non-determinism, increase efficiency and simplify the kernel of high-integrity applications, covering most issues that can prevent OpenMP from being used in a safety-critical environment.

2   OpenMP Hazards for Critical Real-Time Embedded Systems

The current section discusses the OpenMP specification with the aim of: (a) detecting those features that can be a hazard for functional safety when used in a critical real-time embedded system, and (b) proposing solutions to avoid the hazard at design, compile or run time, depending on the case.

2.1   Unspecified Behavior

OpenMP defines the situations that result in an unspecified behavior as: non-conforming programs, implementation defined features and issues documented to have an unspecified behavior. The impact of each situation to the safety-critical domain, as well as the solutions we propose, are exposed below.

Non-conforming Programs

The OpenMP specification defines several requirements to applications that are parallelized with OpenMP. Programs that do not follow these rules are called *non-conforming*. According to the specification, OpenMP compliant implementations are not required to verify conformity. Despite this, safety-critical environments compel frameworks to do this validation to certify functional safety.

OpenMP restrictions affect directives, clauses and the associated user code. Checking some restrictions just requires the verification of OpenMP constructions (e.g. which clauses and how many times a clause can be associated with a specific directive, for example, *at most one if clause can appear on the task directive*). However, checking some restrictions requires visibility of different parts of the application (e.g. some regions cannot be nested and/or closely nested in other regions, for example, *atomic regions must not contain OpenMP constructs*).

Compilers must implement inter-procedural analysis to have access to the whole application. This capability has been successfully implemented in many vendors following different approaches, such as the Intel®C/C++ compiler IPO [11] or the GCC LTO [9]. Nevertheless, access to the whole code is possible only for monolithic applications. This is not very common in the critical domain, where systems consist of multiple components developed by different teams, and rely on third-party libraries. In these cases, additional information may be needed. We discuss this situation and propose a solution to it in Sect. 3. This solution is based on new directives that provide the required information. Henceforward, we assume that the information needed to perform whole program analysis is always accessible.

Implementation Defined Behavior

Some aspects of the implementation of an OpenMP compliant system are not fixed in the specification. These aspects are said to have an *implementation defined* behavior, and they may indeed vary between different compliant implementations. The different aspects can be grouped as follows:

1. Aspects that are naturally implementation defined, so the specification can be used in multiple architectures: definitions for *processor*, *device*, *device address* and *memory model* features.
2. Aspects that are implementation defined to allow flexibility: internal control variables (e.g.: *nthreads-var* and *def-sched-var* among others); selection, amount and distribution of threads (e.g. `single` construct); dynamic adjustment of threads; etc.
3. Aspects caused by bad information specified by the user: values out of range passed to runtime routines or environment variables (e.g. the argument passed to `omp_set_num_threads` is not a positive integer).

Aspects in groups 1 and 2 may not lead to an execution error or prevent the program from validating. This is not the case for aspects in group 3, where an implementation may decide to finish the execution if a value is not in the range it was expected to be. Besides, cases in group 2 may result in different outcomes depending on the platform used for the execution. For example, when the `runtime` or the `auto` kinds are used in the `schedule` clause, the decision of how the iterations of a loop will be scheduled is deferred until runtime.

In the light of all that, some aspects in groups 2 and 3 are not suitable in a safety-critical environment because they are non-deterministic and may cause an undesired result. Situations such as the application aborting due to an unexpected value passed to either an environment variable or a runtime routine can be solved by defining a default value which will not cause the application to end (note that this value can be different across implementations without affecting functional safety). Situations such as an `auto` or `runtime` value in the `schedule` clause can be solved by taking a conservative approach at compile time (i.e. if a deadlock may occur for any possible scheduling option, then the compiler will act as if that scheduling always happens). Situations such as runtimes defining different default values for ICVs like *nthreads-var* do not need to be addressed, because they do not bring on any hazard regarding functional safety.

Other Unspecified Behavior

The rest of situations resulting in an undefined behavior are errors and need to be addressed to guarantee functional safety. These situations can be classified in three groups, depending on the moment at which they can be detected:

1. Situations that can be detected at compile time. In this case we can distinguish those that can be solved by the compiler (e.g. data-race conditions could be solved by automatically protecting accesses with a `critical` construct or synchronizing the accesses - Sect. 2.3 shows more details about data race management), and those that need user intervention (e.g. compilers should abort compilation and report to the user situations such as the use of non-invariant expressions in a linear clause).
2. Situations that can be detected at run time. In this case, safety relies on programmers because the results deriving from these situations cannot be handled automatically. Thus, users are compelled to handle errors such as reduction clauses that contain accesses out of the range of an array section, or using the `omp_target_associate_ptr` routine to associate pointers that share underlying storage (Sect. 2.5 explores error handling techniques).
3. Situations that cannot be detected. These involve the semantics of the program, for example, a program that relies on the task execution order being determined by a priority-value. This case is further discussed in Sect. 2.5.

2.2   Deadlocks

OpenMP offers two ways to synchronize threads: via directives (`master` and synchronization constructs such as `critical` and `barrier`), and via runtime routines (lock routines such as `omp_set_lock` and `omp_unset_lock`). Although both mechanisms may introduce deadlocks, the latter is much more error-prone because these routines work in pairs. Furthermore, OpenMP introduces the concept of nestable locks, which differ from the regular locks in that they can be locked repeatedly by the same task without blocking.

Synchronization directives may cause deadlocks if various `critical` constructs with the same name are nested. Synchronization directives can introduce other problems as well, like enclosing a `barrier` construct in a condition that is special to a thread. Since barriers must always be encountered by all threads of a team, the previous situation will be non-conforming. Such errors can be easily caught by a compiler implementing whole program analysis.

Locking routines may cause errors in the following situations: attempt to access an *uninitialized* lock, attempt to unset a lock owned by another thread or attempt to set a simple lock that is in the *locked* state and is owned by the same task. There exist numerous techniques for deadlock detection, such as Chord [23] and Sherlock [7], that apply to different programming models. Most of the approaches pursue scalability without losing accuracy, thus effectiveness. However, safety-critical environments require soundness. In this regard, the only sound approach, to the best of our knowledge, for detecting deadlocks in C/Pthreads programs is the one developed by Kroening et al. [15]. OpenMP simple locks are comparable to Pthreads mutex, so the previous technique can be extended to OpenMP. Nestable locks have other peculiarities and it may not be possible to detect deadlocks at compile time. In such a case, they should not be permitted.

The use of untied tasks may cause deadlocks that may not exist when using tied tasks. This is because task scheduling constraints (particularly constraint #2) prevent from certain situations involving tied tasks to cause a deadlock by restricting the tasks that can be scheduled at a certain point. Based on that, using tied tasks may seem more suitable for critical real-time embedded systems. It has been, however, demonstrated that timing analysis for untied tasks is much more accurate than for tied tasks [30]. There is thus a trade-off between functional safety and predictability. For the sake of correctness, untied tasks may be disabled at compile time only when the static analysis detects that a deadlock caused by untied tasks may occur.

2.3   Race Conditions

Race conditions appear in a concurrent execution when two or more threads simultaneously access the same resource and at least one of them is a write. This situation is not acceptable for a safety-critical environment since the results of the algorithm are non-deterministic. The problem of detecting data races in a program is NP-hard [24]. On account of this, a large variety of static, dynamic and hybrid data race detection techniques have been developed over the years.

On the one hand, dynamic tools extract information from the memory accesses of specific executions. Despite this, there exist algorithms capable of finding at least one race when races are present, as well as not reporting false positives [3]. On the other hand, static tools still seek a technique with no false negatives and minimal false positives. Current static tools have been proved to work properly on specific subsets of OpenMP such as having a fixed number of threads [19] or using only affine constructs [4]. A more general approach can be used to determine the regions of code that are definitely non-concurrent [18]. Although it is not an accurate solution, it does not produce false negatives, which is paramount in the safety-critical domain. Therefore, the previously mentioned techniques can be combined to deliver conservative and fairly accurate results.

2.4   Cancellation

Until version 4.0, all OpenMP constructs based their execution model in the *Single Entry Single Exit (SESE)* principle. This means that no thread encountering an OpenMP region can jump out of the region skipping a part of it. This is no longer true after the incorporation of the cancellation constructs (i.e. `cancel` and `cancellation point`), which allow exiting parallel computation at a certain point that may not be the end of the region.

Unlike other models such as the Pthreads asynchronous cancellation, OpenMP only accepts synchronous cancellations at cancellation points. Although this eliminates resource leak risks, the technique introduces non-determinism, which is not desirable in a safety-critical environment. Due to the use of cancellation constructs, non-determinism appears in the following situations:

1. The order of execution between one thread that activates cancellation and another thread that encounters a cancellation point.
2. The final value of a reduction or lastprivate variable in a canceled construct.
3. The behavior of nested regions suitable of being canceled.

If a code is well written, case 1 may only affect performance, but the code will deliver a valid result whether cancellation occurs or not. Case 2, instead, may lead to errors if some threads have not finished their computation. Nonetheless, static analysis can verify that reduction and lastprivate variables are not used within a construct that may be subject to cancellation, or that the variables are used only when no cancellation occurs. Finally, case 3 can be solved by statically verifying that regions subject to cancellation are not nested.

Another issue arises when locks are used in regions subject to cancellation, because users are responsible for releasing those locks. Current deadlock detection techniques do not take into account the semantics of the cancellation constructs. Nonetheless, these techniques can easily be extended because the effect of a cancellation is similar to the existence of a jump out of the region.

2.5   Other Features to Consider

Although they do not necessarily involve a hazard, there are other issues that are worth to mention in the context of this paper. These are explained next.

Error Handling

Resiliency is a crucial feature in the safety-critical domain. However, OpenMP does not prescribe how implementations must react to situations such as the runtime not being able to supply the number of threads requested, or the user passing an unexpected value to a routine. While the former is a problem caused by the runtime environment, the latter is an error produced by the user. Both eventually become an unspecified behavior according to the specification, but they can be addressed differently. On the one hand, if the error is produced by the environment, users may want to define what recovery method needs to be executed. On the other hand, errors produced by the user are better caught at compile time or handled by the runtime (we discuss the latter in Sect. 2.1).

Several approaches have been proposed with the aim of adding resiliency mechanisms to OpenMP. There are four different strategies for error handling [33]: exceptions, error codes, call-backs and directives. Each technique can be applied according to its features to different languages and situations. Exception based mechanisms fit well in programs exploiting the characteristics of exception-aware languages (e.g. C++, Ada) [8]. Error code based techniques are a good candidate when using a language unaware of exceptions (e.g. C, Fortran). Call-back methods have the advantage of isolating the code that is to be executed when an exception occurs, and thus enhance readability and maintainability [6]. Finally, the use of specific OpenMP directives has the advantage of being simple, although they cannot cover all situations and users cannot define an exact behavior. The latter is the only approach already adopted in the specification with the cancellation constructs (see more details in Sect. 2.4).

A safety-critical framework supporting OpenMP will require the implementation of error-handling methodologies in order to ensure functional safety.

Nested Parallelism

OpenMP allows nesting parallel regions to get better performance in cases where parallelism is not exploited at the same level. A distributed shared-memory machine with an appropriate memory hierarchy is necessary to exploit the benefits of this feature (the major HPC architectures).

The nature of critical real-time embedded systems is quite different, where both memory size and processor speed are usually constrained. Furthermore, the use of nested parallelism can be costly due to the overhead of creating multiple parallel regions, possible issues with data locality, and the risk of oversubscribing system resources. For the sake of simplicity, and considering that current embedded architectures will not leverage the use of nested parallelism, this feature could be deactivated by default.

Semantics of OpenMP

For an analysis tool, it is possible to address correctness based on how the program is written. However, addressing whether the program behaves as the user wants is another matter altogether. This said, some features of OpenMP may be considered as hazardous because their use may derive in errors involving the semantics of the program. We discuss some of them as follows:

- A program that relies on an specific order of execution of the tasks based on their priorities is non-conforming.
- When and how some expressions are to be executed is not defined in OpenMP. Some examples are: whether, in what order, or how many times any side effects of the evaluation of the `num_threads` or `if` clause expressions of a

parallel construct occur; and the order in which the values of a reduction are combined is unspecified. Thus, an application that relies on any ordering of the evaluation of the expressions mentioned before is non-conforming.
- The storage location specified in task dependencies must be identical or disjoint. Thus, runtimes are not forced to check whether two task instances have partially overlapping storage (which eases the runtime considerably).
- The use of flushes is highly error-prone, and makes it extremely hard to test whether the code is correct. However, the use of the **flush** operation is necessary for some cases such as the implementation of the producer-consumer pattern.

Frameworks cannot prevent users from writing senseless code. However, some of the features mentioned before could be deactivated if the level of criticality demands it. It is a matter of balance between functionality and safety. Thus, if necessary, support for task priorities and flushes could be deactivated. The case regarding side-effects could be simplified to using associative and commutative operations in reductions, and expressions without side-effects in the rest of clauses. Finally, the case regarding task dependency clauses could be solved at runtime by resuming parallel execution when a task contains non-conforming expressions in its dependency clauses (although this solution causes a serious impact in the performance of the application).

3   OpenMP Support for Critical Real-Time Systems

Based on the discussion in Sect. 2, this section exposes our proposal to enable the use of OpenMP in safety-critical environments without compromising functional safety. The proposal can be divided in two facets: different changes to the specification, and a series of compiler and runtime implementation considerations.

3.1   Changes to the Specification

As we introduce in Sect. 2.1, whole program analysis may not be enough if the system includes multiple components developed by different teams or make use of third-party libraries implemented with OpenMP. In such a case, we propose that these components or libraries augment their API with information about the OpenMP features used in each method. As a result, compilers will be able to detect, on the one hand, illegal nesting of directives and data accessing clauses (i.e. data-sharing attributes, data mapping, data copying and reductions) and, on the other hand, data-races.

To tackle illegal nesting, we propose to add a new directive called **usage**. This directive is added to a function declaration and followed by a series of clauses. The clauses determine the features of OpenMP that are used within the function and any function in its call graph, and can cause an illegal nesting. Note that the use of this directive is a promise that a construct might be used in a possible path within the function. Overall, the clauses that can follow the directive **usage** are one of the following:

- Directive related: `parallel`, `worksharing` (which epitomizes `single`, `for/do`, `sections` and `workshare`), `master`, `barrier`, `critical`, `ordered`, `cancel`, `distribute_construct` (which epitomizes `distribute`, `distribute simd`, distribute parallel loop and distribute parallel loop SIMD), `target_construct` (which epitomizes `target`, `target update`, `target data`, `target enter data` and `target exit data`), `teams`, `any` (which epitomizes any directive not included in the previous items).
- Clause related: `firstprivate`, `lastprivate`, `reduction`, `map`, `copyin` and `copyprivate`.

Based on the restrictions that apply to the nesting of regions (Sect. 2.17 of the specification [2]) and the restrictions that apply to the mentioned data accessing clauses, we extract the set of rules that define how the previous clauses are to be used. These rules are the following:

- Clauses `parallel`, `worksharing`, `master`, `barrier` and `ordered` are required when the corresponding construct is the outermost construct.
- Clauses `critical` and `target_construct` are required if there is any occurrence of the corresponding construct.
- Clause `teams` is required if the corresponding construct is orphaned.
- Clauses `cancel` and `cancellation point` are required if the corresponding constructs are not nested in their corresponding binding regions.
- Clause `any` must be specified if OpenMP is used and no previous case applies.
- Data accessing clauses are required when they apply to data that is accessible outside the application and particular constraints apply to them:
  - Clause `firstprivate` if used in a worksharing, `distribute`, `task` or `taskloop` construct not enclosed in a `parallel` or `teams` construct.
  - Clauses `lastprivate` and `reduction` if used in a worksharing not enclosed in a `parallel` construct.
  - Clauses `copyin`, `copyprivate` and `map` in any case.

To avoid data races, we propose to add a new directive called `globals`. This directive, added to a function declaration, defines which data is used within the function while it can be accessed concurrently from outside the function, thus producing a data-race. Different clauses accompany this directive: `read`, `write`, `protected_read` and `protected_write`, all accepting a list of items. While `read` and `protected_read` must be used when global data is only read, `write` and `protected_write` are required when global data is written, independently of it being read as well. The *protected* versions of these clauses must be used when the access is within an `atomic` or a `critical` construct.

Listings 1.1 and 1.2 illustrate the use of the two mentioned directives within the context of a system component that can be used without accessing its source code. The former listing contains the definition of function *foo*, which uses one of the most determining features for OpenMP to be used in parallel heterogeneous embedded architectures: the `target` construct. This function defines an asynchronous task that offloads some parallel computation to a device. The parallel computation within the device is synchronized using the **critical** construct, and is cancelled if the **cancel** directive is reached. The latter listing contains the declaration of function *foo*, augmented with the **usage** and **globals** directives. Clauses **target_construct** and **critical** associated to directive **usage** indicate that the function executes one or more **target** and **critical** constructs. A programmer and/or compiler can avoid calling function *foo* from within a **target** and a **critical** constructs, thus avoiding an illegal nesting. Note that directive **cancel** is not included because it is nested in its binding region, clauses **task** and **parallel for** are not included because no rule applies to them, and the **firstprivate** data-sharing clause is not included because it does not concern to data that is visible from outside the function. Additionally, clauses **write** and **protected_write** associated to directive **globals** indicate that variables *arr[0:N-1]* and *sum* are both written, being *sum* written within a **critical** construct. A programmer and/or compiler can determine whether these variables are in a race condition without knowing the code of the function, and therefore synchronize the accesses to the variables appropriately.

Listing 1.1. Example of OpenMP function definition

```
1  void foo(float* arr, unsigned N, unsigned M,
2              float &sum, float MAX_SUM)
3  {
4    #pragma omp task shared(arr, sum) \
5                    firstprivate(N, M, MAX_SUM)
6    #pragma omp target map(tofrom: arr[0:N-1])
7    #pragma omp parallel for
8    for (int i=0; i<N; ++i) {
9      arr[i] = bar(i);
10     if (i % M == 0) {
11       #pragma omp critical
12         sum +=arr[i];
13     }
14     if (sum > MAX_SUM) {
15       #pragma omp cancel for
16     }
17   }
18 }
```

Listing 1.2. Function declaration for method in Listing 1.1 using the extensions for safety-critical OpenMP

```
1  #pragma omp usage target_construct critical \
2                    map(tofrom: arr[0:N-1])
3  #pragma omp globals write(arr[0:N-1]) protected_write(sum)
4  void foo(float* arr, unsigned N, unsigned M,
5              float &sum, float MAX_SUM);
```

Listings 1.3 and 1.4 show another example of the proposed directives. In this case, the function definition in the former listing performs the *factorial* computation parallelized using the **for** worksharing; and the function declaration in the latter listing shows the clauses required for the method to be used in a functional safe environment. Clause **any** is specified because no rule applies to directive **for**, and clause **reduction** is specified because the reduction is used in a worksharing not enclosed in a parallel region. With this information a programmer and/or compiler can check whether the variable being reduced is shared in the parallel regions to which any of the worksharing regions bind. Analysis may also verify whether the *factorial* function is called from within an atomic region, thus causing the program to be non-conforming. Finally, race analysis can detect whether the variable *factorial* is in a race condition by means of the clause `write`.

Listing 1.3. Factorial computation parallelized with OpenMP

```
1  void factorial(int N, int &fact)
2  {
3      fact = 1;
4      #pragma omp for reduction(*:fact)
5      for(int i=2; i <= N; ++i)
6          fact *= i;
7  }
```

Listing 1.4. Function declaration for method in Listing 1.3 using the extensions for safety-critical OpenMP

```
1  #pragma omp usage any \
2                      reduction(factorial)
3  #pragma omp globals write(factorial)
4  void factorial(int N, int &factorial);
```

3.2   Implementation Considerations

Both compilers and runtime systems used within a critical real-time system must be qualified against the corresponding functional safety standard, e.g. ISO26262 for automotive or DO178C for avionics, to preserve functional safety. The following paragraphs introduce which constraints apply in our case.

Compiler Contract

The development tools used for critical real-time systems need to qualify to the same integrity level[1] as the application they are helping to develop. Nonetheless, current guidelines make the qualification of development tools very difficult [14]. As an example, the standard for Software Considerations in Airborne Systems and Equipment Certification (DO-178C) [5] reads: *"Upon successful completion of verification of the software product, the compiler is considered acceptable for that product"*. As a result, sometimes compilers do not need to be qualified. Nonetheless, to gain assurance, some characteristics must be incorporated, such as being fully tested for complete coverage analysis[2], and being used in the same configuration, options, and environment as the one used to compile any other objects related to the application.

---

[1] The *integrity level*, also called *criticality level*, refers to the consequences of the incorrect behavior of a system. These levels are defined in different scales such as the *Safety Integrity Level* (SIL) for automotive and the *Development Assurance Level* (DAL) for avionics.

[2] *Code coverage* is a measure used to describe the amount of the source code of a program being executed when a particular test suite runs.

However, for an OpenMP compiler to be valid in a critical real-time environment, it must ensure the source code is compliant with the OpenMP specification. For that reason, the compiler must implement the necessary analysis techniques to allow whole program analysis. Additionally, the compiler must also include specific and sound techniques for data-race and deadlock detection, as well as the correctness analysis that allows statically detecting and fixing the unspecified behaviors commented in Sect. 2.1.

Runtime Contract

As a result of the analysis presented in Sect. 2, we conclude that runtime libraries used in safety-critical environments shall follow some requirements to avoid unexpected aborts and fix some programmer errors. The following list is an starting point for these systems to address such undesired results:

- Runtimes should define a default value for all environment variables. This value shall be used when the value specified in the application is out of range, e.g. OMP_NUM_THREADS could be 1 by default, and OMP_NESTED could be false.
- Some clauses, such as num_threads and device, take a number as a parameter that must evaluate to a positive integer. Runtimes should define the value to be used if the expression is out of range, for example, 1.
- Other errors can be caught and fixed at runtime, e.g. different instances of the same task or sibling tasks expressing dependency clauses on list items which storage location is neither identical nor disjoint may be executed sequentially.

4   Related Work

Parallel heterogeneous embedded architectures certainly require the use of parallel programming models to provide high throughput, low latency and energy-efficient solutions. Efforts to introduce OpenMP in such environments [20] reveal that OpenMP runtimes can efficiently be aware of the heterogeneity and the memory hierarchy to deliver good performance. However, all works that intend to introduce OpenMP in the embedded domain conclude that, although the language is very useful in such environments, some extensions with real-time processing and power-awareness functionalities [10] are needed.

Critical real-time embedded systems, add additional, more restrictive, constraints to those of the embedded domain. Concretely, timing guarantees and functional safety. Regarding the former, significant attempts to analyze the time predictability properties of OpenMP [30], as well as deriving response time analysis for both work-conserving dynamic and purely static schedulers [16,21,29], confirm the OpenMP tasking model as a perfectly suitable parallel pattern for safety-critical environments. In this sense, the suitability of the thread-centric model still remains unproved. Furthermore, situations such as starvation when a barrier construct is found shall be addressed.

With regard to functional safety, different works have tried to study, classify and solve mistakes commonly appearing in OpenMP applications [22,31]. These works are very useful mostly for unexperienced programmers in order to avoid errors. Beyond the theoretical approaches, many articles propose different techniques tackling correctness in general, and OpenMP correctness in particular. Section 2 introduces several techniques for detecting specific errors in concurrent programs (i.e. race conditions and dead-locks). Additionally, some techniques have been developed specifically for OpenMP to compute and verify data scoping, task dependencies and locks among others [17, 25–27].

Finally, there exist works towards the adoption of OpenMP in Ada [28], a language commonly used in safety-critical and high-security domains such as avionics and railroad systems. In Ada, concepts as safety and reliability are crucial. However, there are still some caveats about the integration of the Ada and OpenMP runtimes, because both will be mapped to the underlying threads of the operating system.

5   Conclusions and Future Work

OpenMP is increasingly being considered a suitable candidate to be used in critical real-time embedded systems considering its benefits: programmability, portability and efficiency, among others. However, such systems impose strict constraints to ensure functional safety in terms of functional correctness and timing predictability. This paper has focused on the former aiming to shorten the distance between OpenMP and the critical real-time domain.

In this scope, we prove that most features specified in OpenMP can be used without compromising safety, as long as compilers implement a series of analyses that can prevent errors such as dead-locks and race conditions. Indeed, analysis must involve the entire program which can be a challenging scenario. To ease this, we propose some new directives that allow whole program analysis even when third-party libraries are used. The majority of the unspecified behaviors defined in the specification can be solved at compile time either automatically by the compiler (e.g. synchronizing variables that otherwise could be accessed after their life-time has ended), or by the programmer (e.g., the use of non-invariant expressions in a linear clause). Other issues can be successfully addressed at runtime (e.g. unexpected values passed to environment variables and runtime libraries can be solved by defining default values to be used in such cases). In some cases, supporting the required level of criticality might incur more overhead than a traditional OpenMP implementation (e.g., tracking task dependencies' overlap). Last but not least, there are a series of features that can be used erroneously if their semantics are not properly exploited (e.g. tasks priorities or flushes). We conclude that support for these features can be deactivated if the level of criticality requires so.

The small modifications that this paper proposes back up OpenMP's safety. Nonetheless, we note some lacks in the current specification, e.g. error handling techniques to improve resiliency. Hence, despite the functional safety aspect is deeply addressed in this paper, the same analysis concerning time predictability, including starvation, remains as future work. In that regard, we plan to analyze the latest specification to find out how timing analyses could be affected by the use of OpenMP.

Acknowledgments. This work was funded by the EU project P-SOCRATES (FP7-ICT-2013- 10) and the Spanish Ministry of Science and Innovation under contract TIN2015-65316-P.

Disclaimers

Intel is a trademark or registered trademark of Intel Corporation or its subsidiaries in the United States and/or other countries.

*Other brands and names are the property of their respective owners.

References

1. P-SOCRATES European Project: Parallel Software Framework for Time-Critical Many-core Systems. http://p-socrates.eu
2. OpenMP Application Programming Interface (2015). http://www.openmp.org/wp-content/uploads/openmp-4.5.pdf
3. Banerjee, U., Bliss, B., Ma, Z., Petersen, P.: A theory of data race detection. In: Parallel and Distributed Systems: Testing and Debugging (2006)
4. Basupalli, V., Yuki, T., Rajopadhye, S., Morvan, A., Derrien, S., Quinton, P., Wonnacott, D.: ompVerify: polyhedral analysis for the OpenMP programmer. In: Chapman, B.M., Gropp, W.D., Kumaran, K., Müller, M.S. (eds.) IWOMP 2011. LNCS, vol. 6665, pp. 37–53. Springer, Heidelberg (2011). doi:10.1007/978-3-642-21487-5_4
5. DO-178C: Software considerations in airborne systems and equipment certification (2011)
6. Duran, A., Ferrer, R., Costa, J.J., Gonzàlez, M., Martorell, X., Ayguadé, E., Labarta, J.: A proposal for error handling in OpenMP. IJPP **35**(4), 393–416 (2007)
7. Eslamimehr, M., Palsberg, J.: Sherlock: scalable deadlock detection for concurrent programs. In: SIGSOFT (2014)
8. Fan, X., Mehrabi, M., Sinnen, O., Giacaman, N.: Exception handling with OpenMP in object-oriented languages. In: Terboven, C., Supinski, B.R., Reble, P., Chapman, B.M., Müller, M.S. (eds.) IWOMP 2015. LNCS, vol. 9342, pp. 115–129. Springer, Cham (2015). doi:10.1007/978-3-319-24595-9_9
9. GNU: Link Time Optimization (2017). https://gcc.gnu.org/onlinedocs/gccint/LTO.html
10. Hanawa, T., Sato, M., Lee, J., Imada, T., Kimura, H., Boku, T.: Evaluation of multicore processors for embedded systems by parallel benchmark program using OpenMP. In: Müller, M.S., Supinski, B.R., Chapman, B.M. (eds.) IWOMP 2009. LNCS, vol. 5568, pp. 15–27. Springer, Heidelberg (2009). doi:10.1007/978-3-642-02303-3_2
11. Intel® Corporation: Interprocedural Optimization (2017). https://software.intel.com/en-us/node/522666
12. International Electrotechnical Commission: IEC 61508, Functional Safety of Electrical/Electronic/Programmable Electronic Safety-Related Systems, 2.0nd edn. (2009)
13. International Organization for Standardization: ISO/DIS 26262. Road Vehicles - Functional Safety (2009)
14. Kornecki, A.J.: Software Development Tools for Safety-Critical. Real-Time Systems Handbook. Office of Aviation Research and Development, FAA (2007)
15. Kroening, D., Poetzl, D., Schrammel, P., Wachter, B.: Sound static deadlock analysis for C/Pthreads. In: ASE (2016)

16. Lakshmanan, K., Kato, S., Rajkumar, R.: Scheduling parallel real-time tasks on multi-core processors. In: RTSS (2010)
17. Liao, C., Quinlan, D.J., Panas, T., Supinski, B.R.: A ROSE-based OpenMP 3.0 research compiler supporting multiple runtime libraries. In: Sato, M., Hanawa, T., Müller, M.S., Chapman, B.M., Supinski, B.R. (eds.) IWOMP 2010. LNCS, vol. 6132, pp. 15–28. Springer, Heidelberg (2010). doi:10.1007/978-3-642-13217-9_2
18. Lin, Y.: Static nonconcurrency analysis of OpenMP programs. In: Mueller, M.S., Chapman, B.M., Supinski, B.R., Malony, A.D., Voss, M. (eds.) IWOMP-2005. LNCS, vol. 4315, pp. 36–50. Springer, Heidelberg (2008). doi:10.1007/978-3-540-68555-5_4
19. Ma, H., Diersen, S.R., Wang, L., Liao, C., Quinlan, D., Yang, Z.: Symbolic analysis of concurrency errors in OpenMP programs. In: ICPP (2013)
20. Marongiu, A., Burgio, P., Benini, L.: Supporting OpenMP on a multi-cluster embedded MPSoC. Microprocess. Microsyst. 35(8), 668–682 (2011)
21. Melani, A., Serrano, M.A., Bertogna, M., Cerutti, I., Quinones, E., Buttazzo, G.: A static scheduling approach to enable safety-critical OpenMP applications. In: ASP-DAC (2017)
22. Münchhalfen, J.F., Hilbrich, T., Protze, J., Terboven, C., Müller, M.S.: Classification of common errors in OpenMP applications. In: DeRose, L., Supinski, B.R., Olivier, S.L., Chapman, B.M., Müller, M.S. (eds.) IWOMP 2014. LNCS, vol. 8766, pp. 58–72. Springer, Cham (2014). doi:10.1007/978-3-319-11454-5_5
23. Naik, M., Park, C.S., Sen, K., Gay, D.: Effective static deadlock detection. In: ICSE (2009)
24. Netzer, R.H., Miller, B.P.: What are race conditions? Some issues and formalizations. LOPLAS 1(1), 74–88 (1992)
25. Royuela, S., Duran, A., Liao, C., Quinlan, D.J.: Auto-scoping for OpenMP tasks. In: Chapman, B.M., Massaioli, F., Müller, M.S., Rorro, M. (eds.) IWOMP 2012. LNCS, vol. 7312, pp. 29–43. Springer, Heidelberg (2012). doi:10.1007/978-3-642-30961-8_3
26. Royuela, S., Duran, A., Martorell, X.: Compiler automatic discovery of OmpSs task dependencies. In: Kasahara, H., Kimura, K. (eds.) LCPC 2012. LNCS, vol. 7760, pp. 234–248. Springer, Heidelberg (2013). doi:10.1007/978-3-642-37658-0_16
27. Royuela, S., Ferrer, R., Caballero, D., Martorell, X.: Compiler analysis for OpenMP tasks correctness. In: International Conference on Computing Frontiers (2015)
28. Royuela, S., Martorell, X., Quinones, E., Pinho, L.M.: OpenMP tasking model for ADA: safety and correctness. In: AE (2017)
29. Serrano, M.A., Melani, A., Bertogna, M., Quinones, E.: Response-time analysis of DAG tasks under fixed priority scheduling with limited preemptions. In: DATE (2016)
30. Serrano, M.A., Melani, A., Vargas, R., Marongiu, A., Bertogna, M., Quinones, E.: Timing characterization of OpenMP4 tasking model. In: CASES (2015)
31. Süß, M., Leopold, C.: Common mistakes in OpenMP and how to avoid them. In: OpenMP Shared Memory Parallel Programming (2008)
32. Vargas, R., Quinones, E., Marongiu, A.: OpenMP and timing predictability: a possible union? In: DATE (2015)
33. Wong, M., Klemm, M., Duran, A., Mattson, T., Haab, G., Supinski, B.R., Churbanov, A.: Towards an error model for OpenMP. In: Sato, M., Hanawa, T., Müller, M.S., Chapman, B.M., Supinski, B.R. (eds.) IWOMP 2010. LNCS, vol. 6132, pp. 70–82. Springer, Heidelberg (2010). doi:10.1007/978-3-642-13217-9_6

Performance Analysis and Tools

OpenMP Tools Interface: Synchronization Information for Data Race Detection

Joachim Protze[1,2], Jonas Hahnfeld[1,2], Dong H. Ahn[3(✉)], Martin Schulz[3], and Matthias S. Müller[1,2]

[1] RWTH Aachen University, 52056 Aachen, Germany
{protze,hahnfeld,mueller}@itc.rwth-aachen.de
[2] JARA – High-Performance Computing, 52062 Aachen, Germany
[3] Lawrence Livermore National Laboratory, Livermore, CA 94550, USA
{ahn1,schulzm}@llnl.gov

Abstract. When it comes to data race detection, complete information about synchronization, concurrency and memory accesses is needed. This information might be gathered at various levels of abstraction. For best results regarding accuracy this information should be collected at the abstraction level of the parallel programming paradigm. With the latest preview of the OpenMP specification, a tools interface (OMPT) was added to OpenMP. In this paper we discuss whether the synchronization information provided by OMPT is sufficient to apply accurate data race analysis for OpenMP applications. We further present some implementation details and results for our data race detection tool called ARCHER which derives the synchronization information from OMPT.

1 Introduction

OpenMP is the de facto standard for parallel programming on shared memory machines. It is also becoming increasingly popular on extreme-scale systems as it offers a portable way to harness the growing degree of parallelism available on each node. However, porting large HPC applications to OpenMP often introduces subtle errors. Of these, data races are particularly egregious, as well as challenging to identify. Data races may remain undetected during testing, but nevertheless manifest during production runs by often resulting in confusing (and/or non-reproducible) executions that the programmer wastes considerable amounts of time debugging. In extreme situations, data races may simply end up silently corrupting user data. For all these reasons, data race detection remains one of the central concerns in parallel programming, in particular for shared memory programming models.

In previous papers [2,7], we presented the tool ARCHER [1], based on Thread-Sanitizer (TSan) [8,9], which is able to find data races in OpenMP applications, that are run with the LLVM/OpenMP runtime on x86 machines. The fact which makes this tool unique from other approaches of available data race detection tools for OpenMP applications is that we cover almost all host-side OpenMP directives as provided in the OpenMP 4.5 specification. To make the tool portable

B.R. de Supinski et al. (Eds.): IWOMP 2017, LNCS 10468, pp. 249–265, 2017.
DOI: 10.1007/978-3-319-65578-9_17

across OpenMP runtime implementations and hardware platforms, we want to base the annotation of OpenMP synchronization on OMPT events.

In this paper we investigate whether the information provided by OMPT is sufficient to derive all OpenMP synchronization semantics. We will describe OMPT based annotations of OpenMP synchronization. The annotations are provided as happened-before arcs, which can be understood by ThreadSanitizer, but also by the Valgrind based data race detection tool Helgrind. This approach is portable across OpenMP runtime implementations, as long as these implement and provide the necessary OMPT callback function invocations.

In Sect. 2 we look at OpenMP directives with synchronization semantics from a happened-before point of view. In Sect. 3 we describe the OMPT events, that we use to annotate the synchronization and how we specify the happened-before arcs. In Sect. 4 we discuss challenges we encountered on the way, implementing the tool and discuss information missing in the OpenMP tools interface.

2   Synchronization in OpenMP

According to the OpenMP specification [3]: "... if at least one thread reads from a memory unit and at least one thread writes without synchronization to that same memory unit [...], then a data race occurs. If a data race occurs then the result of the program is unspecified."

To enable a data race detection tool to identify a data race, complete understanding of synchronization is needed. In this section we provide a summary of the synchronization concepts in OpenMP, as they need to be understood by an analysis tool, to identify synchronized memory accesses. In this paper we focus on data races that happen between threads on a host device. Thus, we do not consider constructs for offloading to an accelerator device.

2.1   The `parallel` Construct

When a thread encounters a parallel construct, the thread creates a team of threads to execute the parallel region. Each thread of the team executes the structured block of the parallel region within an implicit task.

Encountering the parallel construct *happens before* the execution of all implicit tasks of the team.

There is an implicit barrier at the end of the parallel region, which *happens before* the master thread continues execution.

2.2   The `barrier` Construct

The barrier in OpenMP applies for the innermost parallel team. On encountering a barrier construct, a thread cannot continue executing the implicit task until all threads in the team reached the barrier.

For all threads in the team, encountering the barrier construct *happens before* they continue execution of the implicit task.

2.3   The **reduction** Clause

The reduction clause provides a mechanism to reduce results at the end of a work-sharing region into a single value. The clause takes a reduction identifier to specify the reduction operation, the synchronization of the reduction is provided by the OpenMP implementation.

If no **nowait** clause is used on the same construct, the reduction *happens before* the end of the region. Otherwise the reduction *happens before* the next barrier.

2.4   The **critical** Construct

The critical construct provides mutual exclusion for the critical region. The critical construct can have a name, that provides mutual exclusion only for critical regions with the same name. The critical region is equivalent to getting a lock at the begin of the region and releasing the lock at the end, with different locks for different names and an extra lock for all unnamed critical regions. Thus, the synchronization semantics are the same as for Locking routines.

2.5   Locking Routines

OpenMP provides routines to init, destroy, acquire and release locks and nested locks. Locks provide mutual exclusion for code between acquiring and releasing a lock.

As a strict measure, a lock-set algorithm can be used to express the synchronization of critical region and locking routines. But lock-set is in general too strict and can lead to false positives The reason is that an application might implement *happens before* semantics in the locked sections. The alternative is to express locks with a happens before relation: Releasing a lock *happens before* acquiring the same lock.

This might over-estimate the synchronization semantics of the application and lead to omission of actual data races. This is a point, where large numbers of repetition and concurrency helps to stochastically execute the right interleaving of locked regions, so that the race can still be observed.

2.6   The **ordered** Construct

The ordered construct provides mutual exclusion for the ordered region. Additionally, the ordered construct also provides an ordering for the execution.

Thus, when observing the execution of an OpenMP program, the end of an ordered region *happens before* the begin of the next iteration of the same ordered region.

2.7 The `task` Construct

When a thread encounters a task construct, the thread generates a task from the associated structured block. The thread might execute the thread immediately, or defer the task for later execution.

Encountering the task construct *happens before* the execution of the task. The end of a task region *happens before* the next barrier of the team finished synchronization. Without further clauses or constructs, there is no more synchronization at the end of a task.

2.8 The `taskwait` Construct

The taskwait construct lets the encountering task wait for completion of all direct child tasks that this task created before encountering the taskwait.

Finishing all child tasks *happens before* the taskwait regions ends and the task can continue execution.

2.9 The `taskgroup` Construct

The taskgroup construct lets the encountering task wait at the end of the task group region for completion of all child tasks this task created in the taskgroup region and their descendants.

Finishing all child and descendant tasks *happens before* the taskgroup regions ends and the task can continue execution.

2.10 The `depend` Clause

The depend clause provides synchronization for task as the provided *in, out,* and *inout* dependencies define constraints for the scheduling of tasks. A depend clause can have a list of storage locations, which describe *in* or *out* dependencies. The end of a task with an *in* dependency on a storage location **x** *happens before* the start of any task with an *out* or *inout* dependency on the same storage location **x**. The end of a task with an *out* or *inout* dependency on a storage location **x** *happens before* the start of any task with an *in, out,* or *inout* dependency on the same storage location **x**.

To summarize, only *in* dependencies with the same storage location **x** do not synchronize. All other dependencies with the same storage location **x** synchronize.

2.11 Untied Tasks

Deferring a task *happens before* scheduling the same task again. This is especially important for untied tasks, that can migrate from one thread to another thread after being deferred during execution.

2.12   The flush Construct

The flush construct makes a thread's temporal view of memory consistent with memory and enforces a specific ordering of memory operations. The flush construct takes an optional list of variables, the *flush-set*. With the right combination of loads, stores and flushes, an application programmer can achieve fine-grain synchronization. Modeling the semantics of flushes with plain happened-before relation introduces synchronization which possibly hides any data race. A better approach for handling flushes is discussed by Lidbury and Donaldson [5]. They extend ThreadSanitizer to understand and handle C++11 flush semantics.

3   OMPT Events for Synchronization

In this section we explain the synchronization events provided by the OpenMP tools interface as it is integrated into the preview of the OpenMP specification 5.0 [4]. Since we implemented our prototype along with the LLVM/OpenMP runtime implementation, we used the version of OMPT, that is implemented there. The latest specification of OMPT describes events as points of interest in the execution of a thread. Tool callback functions are implemented in a tool and invoked by the runtime when a matching event happens. Multiple events might trigger the same callback; the tool can differ the events by some *kind* and *endpoint* arguments provided with the callback invocation. On tool initialization the OpenMP runtime implementation provides information to the tool, whether requested callback invocations are provided or not. For some groups of events invocation is mandatory, for some it is optional.

3.1   Team Related OMPT Events

The following events mark the synchronization points for a team from the creation of the team to the end:

- *parallel-begin*
- *implicit-task-begin*
- *barrier-begin*
- *barrier-end*
- *implicit-task-end*
- *parallel-end*

On a *parallel-begin* event, we generate a new team information object and start a happened-before arc for the team.

On an *implicit-task-begin* event, we generate a new task information object and end the happened-before arc for the team. This synchronizes the team creation.

On a *barrier-begin* event, we start a happened-before arc on an address from the team's information object. This event is specified to happen before the actual synchronization of the barrier.

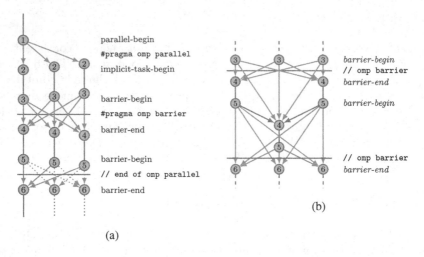

Fig. 1. (a) Happened-before arcs in a parallel region with explicit barrier and implied barrier at the end. (b) If a thread returns late from the barrier code (red *barrier-end* (4)), others might be already in the next barrier. In this case, we would add wrong happened-before arcs, if all barriers use the same token for the happened-before annotation (Color figure online)

On the *barrier-end* event, we end the happened-before arc on the same address from the team's information object. Since there is no synchronization between the barrier end event and the next barrier begin event, it is possible as depicted in Fig. 1b, that a thread of the team reaches the next barrier before another thread finished the previous barrier. Therefore, consecutive barriers should use distinct synchronization tokens. The OpenMP specification states that all threads in a team need to participate on each barrier, so we use two addresses for barriers in the team information object and each implicit task toggles between the two addresses.

The parallel region ends with an *implicit-task-end* event and a *parallel-end* event where we free the task and team information objects. The synchronization at the end of the region happens solely in the implied barrier at the end of the region. This is the second barrier in Fig. 1a.

As a missing piece in OMPT we will discuss the OpenMP reduction clause in Sect. 4.

3.2   Task Related OMPT Events

The following events mark the synchronization points for a task from the creation of a task to the end:

- *task-create*
- *task-dependences*
- *task-schedule*

- *taskwait-end*
- *taskgroup-begin*
- *taskgroup-end*

On a *task-create* event, we generate a new task information object and start a happened-before arc for the generated task. This synchronizes the task creation with the execution of the task. If this event is invoked before all data are copied to the task data structures, there might be some false data race alerts. Especially the copying of first-private data, which is then accessed by the task, might be a problem. See Fig. 2 for an illustration of the task-related events and happened-before synchronization.

On a *task-dependences* event we save all dependences information into the task information object for later use.

On the first *task-schedule* event for a new task, we end the happened-before arc from the generation of the task. Further, we iterate over all task dependences and end happened-before arcs for all dependences. If the dependency is an *in* dependency, we only end happened-before arcs from *out* or *inout* dependencies on this storage location. If the dependency is an *out* or *inout* dependency, we

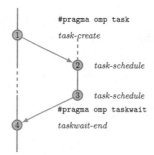

Fig. 2. Execution of a task happens after the task was generated from the parent; in case the parent task does a taskwait, the taskwait finishes after the generated task finished; end of taskgroup is similar

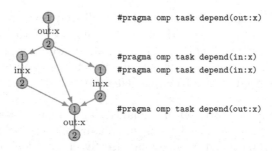

Fig. 3. This is the dependency graph for a set of tasks which were created with *out, in, in,* and *out* dependency on x; the end of a task with *out* dependency happens before all *task-begin* of tasks with a dependency on the same address. Tasks with the same *in* dependency run concurrently.

end happened-before arcs from all dependencies on this storage location. See Fig. 3 for an illustration of the dependencies-related events and happened-before synchronization. This also highlights the necessity to store the dependency information from task creation until task completion.

If the **prior_task_status** signals completion of the previous task, we start happened-before arcs for the completed task:

- towards a potential **taskwait** of the parent task
- if the task is in a **taskgroup** towards the end of the taskgroup
- if the task has dependencies, an arc per dependency.

On a *taskwait-end* event, we end the happened-before arc from all child tasks. We use a common token for all child tasks, so this is a single operation.

On a *taskgroup-begin* event, we push a taskgroup information object on the taskgroup stack of the encountering task. The stack is necessary because multiple taskgroup regions might be closely nested within a task. All child tasks inherit the taskgroup stack on task generation, so they know about their enclosing taskgroup.

On a *taskgroup-end* event, we end the happened-before arcs of all child tasks, targeting to the taskgroup end. Then we pop the taskgroup from the stack of taskgroups.

3.3 Locking Related OMPT Events

The following events mark the begin and end of mutual exclusion:

- *acquired-lock*
- *acquired-nest-lock-first*
- *acquired-critical*
- *acquired-atomic*
- *acquired-ordered*
- *released-lock*
- *released-nest-lock-last*
- *released-critical*
- *released-atomic*
- *released-ordered*

The latest OMPT specification consolidates all above events into a single callback for acquired and released with a **kind** argument for the kind of synchronization. For the happened-before synchronization, we only use the **wait-id** argument, so the handling of events is symmetric for all kind of mutex events.

On an *acquired* event, we end a happened-before arc, that starts on a previous *released* event.

To represent the synchronization semantics of locks in a data race analysis, it is important to start and end the happened-before arc inside of the locked region. Otherwise, another thread might already enter a locked region, before the released information is available. To reduce the potential overhead of an OMPT tool, the *released* event is invoked after the lock was released and there is no *releasing* event in OMPT. We discuss in Sect. 4.1 how we worked around this issue.

3.4 OMPT Flush Event

The flush event doesn't fit into the semantics of the previously discussed event groups. As touched in Sect. 2.12, happened-before semantics are too strict. But omitting the handling of flush, we experience false reports on data races in applications that use flush for synchronization. Implementing the right semantics for flush in our tool is subject of future work. But for now, we found that the information provided by the flush event is not sufficient for data race analysis as we will discuss in Sect. 4.6.

3.5 Team and Task Information Structures

We create an information object for each team and each task, which we store in the runtime scope of this team or task using the **parallel_data** and **task_data** fields provided by OMPT. In this section we detail on the necessary members of these objects. Both kinds of objects contain tokens, that we use to annotate different synchronization points.

A team object contains:

– two tokens for **barriers**, the tasks of the team use them alternating; we also use one of the tokens for the fork of the team.

A task object contains:

– a token for the **task**, that is used for the annotation, task-create before task-execution and task-deferring before rescheduling,
– a token for **taskwait**, which is used to annotate synchronization between the end of all child tasks and the taskwait,
– a **barrier index**, that toggles between odd and even barrier count,
– a **reference count** for direct child tasks, the object is only freed when the task and all child tasks finished execution,
– a reference to the **parent** task object,
– a reference to the **implicit** task object in the stack next to this task,
– a reference to the currently active **taskgroup** object,
– a copy of the *list of dependencies* and a *dependency count*.

A taskgroup object contains:

– a token for the *taskgroup*,
– a reference to the enclosing taskgroup.

4 Implementation Challenges and OMPT Shortcomings

In this section we discuss challenges, potential pitfalls and open issues which we encountered implementing the synchronization annotations in an OMPT-based tool.

4.1 Annotation of Locking

For TSan a happened-before annotation consists of writing memory at the start of the happened-before arc and reading the memory at the end of the arc. If the memory access is not synchronized, expressing the happened-before arc fails, since the read possibly happens before the write. For the annotation of locking this means, that the annotation needs to take place, while the thread owns a lock, that prevents the other thread from entering the locked region.

OMPT only provides the events *acquiring* (i.e. asking for the lock), *acquired* (when the lock is acquired) and *released* (after the lock was released) of a lock. OMPT does not provide a *releasing* event to safe the potential overhead in the critical path of execution. As depicted in Fig. 4a we would need to describe a happened-before arc from a *releasing* event to the next *acquired* event. And an arc from a *released* event to the *acquired* event goes potentially backwards in time.

As work-around for this issue we set an own mutex in each *acquired* event, before we end the happened-before arc and release the mutex in the matching *released* event after we started the happened-before arc. This approach is depicted in Fig. 4. This way we can guarantee that we annotate the end of a happened-before arc only after we annotated the begin of the happened-before arc. Since the OpenMP runtime already acquired a lock, we don't expect lock contention. It just might be the case, that the previous locked region still holds the mutex to finish the *released* event.

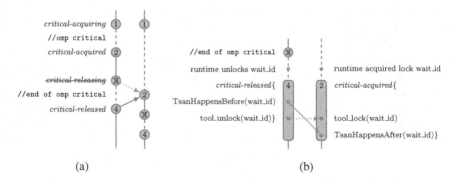

Fig. 4. (a) OMPT doesn't provide a *releasing* event. Using the *released* event to start the happened-before arc potentially results in a happened-before arc backwards in time. (b) We use an additional lock in the tool, to extend the exclusive region into the *released* callback. This way we can express the proper happened-before semantics.

4.2 Annotation of Task Dependencies

As discussed in Sect. 3.2, the synchronization behavior is different for *in* and *out* dependencies. The end of a task with an *in* dependency happens before a task begins with the same *out* dependency. The end of a task with an *out* dependency happens before a task begins with the same *in* or *out* dependency. That means, at the task begin with an *in* dependency, we need to differ the happened-before arcs that come from *in* or *out* dependencies.

So, we need two different tokens for starting the happened-before arc of *in* dependencies and *out* dependencies. This token need to be common knowledge of all task using the dependency and for TSan the requirement for a token is that it needs to be a valid memory address of the process. For this reason, it is natural to use the address of the dependency as the token to annotate the happened-before arc. Since we need two tokens, we use the address provided as dependency and the address next to this address, assuming that applications will not use byte-sized variables as dependencies.

4.3   Ordered Construct with Depend Clause

For the online analysis that we apply in our data race detection tool, we rely on the scheduling decision provided by the runtime. We simply annotate any acquire of an ordered construct to happen after any release of the same ordered construct. This might be an overestimation and potentially hide data races. Since the depend clause allows the runtime to schedule multiple ordered regions at the same time, our tool might detect races in these concurrently executed regions. A tool which performs post-mortem analysis might not be able to observe this runtime decision and would assume mutual exclusive execution of all ordered regions in a loop. To improve precision of the analysis, we suggest to extend the notion of OMPT dependences to cover also the ordered construct.

4.4   Taskwait Construct with Depend Clause

Similar as with the ordered construct, we currently overestimate the synchronization effect of a taskwait construct with depend clause. In the analysis we assume that all tasks that finished before the taskwait region ends are synchronized by this taskwait region. With the additional information about the depend clause, the analysis would be more precise.

4.5   OMPT Events of Reductions

The current specification of OMPT provides no events for a reduction. The OpenMP specification does not require a specific point in the application execution, where the reduction needs to take place. Also an OpenMP implementation has a lot of freedom to implement the reduction algorithm, which results in various scenarios of memory access patterns. Threads might accumulate the own value to another thread's reduction value, threads might fetch other thread's reduction value and accumulate at the own reduction value, a master thread might collect all reduction values. The reduction might also be implemented solely with atomic operations.

We propose the following events for the implementation of reductions:

- *release-reduction:* thread will not touch reduction variable after this event
- *reduction-begin:* begin of reduction operations
- *reduction-end:* end of reduction operations

We think, that *release-reduction* and *reduction-end* can share the same callback function. The callback function needs to provide information about the local copy of the reduction variable.

The LLVM/OpenMP runtime implements most reductions inside the synchronization of the barrier. So as a temporary workaround, we ignore memory accesses inside of OpenMP barriers. If a task is scheduled in the barrier, we turn of ignoring memory accesses and turn it back on, when the barrier gets active again. This works in most cases for this specific runtime, but we don't expect this to be a portable workaround.

4.6 Information on Flush-Set

The current specification of the flush event as of TR4 only provides information on the source code of the flush (*codeptr_ra*) and the current thread, but no information on the provided *list* argument, which describes the flush-set of the flush operation. To derive the right flush semantics for data race detection, this information would be necessary.

We propose to extend the definition of **ompt_callback_flush_t** by an array of pointers, an array of length and a size argument:

```
1  typedef void (*ompt_callback_flush_t) (
2    ompt_data_t * thread_data,
3    const void * list_item,
4    size_t * list_item_length,
5    int list_length,
6    const void * codeptr_ra);
```

5 Implementation Results

To evaluate the overhead introduced by the TLC-aware data race analysis, we run SPEC OMP 2012 [6,11] on a machine with Intel Xeon E5-2650 v4 CPUs with 12 cores. We bind all threads to the same socket using **OMP_BIND=close** and **OMP_PLACES=cores**. Since the tool introduces a runtime overhead of about 2–20x – in some cases up to 125x – we only use the train dataset, which is the medium size for this SPEC benchmark.

ThreadSanitizer is optimized to run fast for race-free programs. If TSan detects data races, handling the report introduces significant runtime overhead. Printing the report happens under mutual exclusion to guarantee readable output without interleaving from multiple threads printing at the same time. Furthermore, TSan filters the output, so the report function also compares the latest finding with previous reports. Because of the filtering, TSan typically prints reports only in the first few iterations; later races would mainly be duplicates. For actual debugging a user would typically interrupt the execution after some reports were printed, fix the issue and restart execution.

For better comparison we measure the overhead for the plain analysis without generating reports. Also ThreadSanitizer suggests this mode for benchmarking. In this mode, TSan intercepts all memory accesses, logs the memory access, analyses the memory access for potential data races. Also synchronization information is processed. The only difference from the normal mode is that in case of a detected data race TSan returns like there was no race instead of processing the report.

We use the LLVM/clang compiler 4.0 for the C/C++ codes and gfortran 6.2.0 for the Fortran codes. Both compilers provide the flag **-fsanitize=thread** to activate the compile time instrumentation for ThreadSanitizer. For the OpenMP runtime we use the LLVM/OpenMP runtime of the OpenMP tools subcommittee that implements the TR4 interface of OMPT.

5.1   Overhead Results

In Fig. 5 we plot the slowdown of the tool, which is runtime with tool divided by runtime without tool. We set the x-axis to 1, which is the normalized runtime of the application, i.e., the bar represents the tool overhead. As depicted, the overall measured slowdown is in the 2–20x range as claimed in the ThreadSanitizer documentation ("5–15x"[10]). But there are a some exceptions. Looking into the specific applications, this increased overhead mainly comes from fine-grain synchronization. In Table 1 we list some statistics important for the analysis tool. The two benchmarks where the tool shows overall high runtime overhead are 359.botsspar and 370.mgrid331. Both applications run for less than a second.

In this short time 359.botsspar already creates a large number of tasks. The synchronization for tasks happens from task to task. Hence, most of the time only one OS thread is involved. Another reason for a higher overhead is the use of untied tasks in this application. Since the tasks have no further task scheduling point, the tasks can only execute straight to the end. The code that the compiler

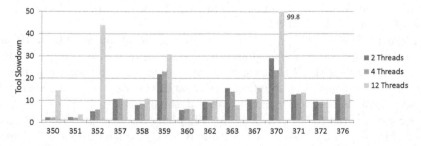

Fig. 5. Runtime overhead for executing SPEC OMP 2012 with ThreadSanitizer and synchronization annotations based on OMPT events

Table 1. OMPT synchronization events during the execution of SPEC OMP 2012, size train on 12 threads

application	runtime (s)	lang	parallel	barrier	task implicit	create	switch	other
350.md	181	F	47	564	564	1		
351.bwaves	34.8	F	610	7320	7320	1		atomic: 384
352.nab	23.26	C	12428	350376	105048	2		
357.bt331	27.13	F	1011	21912	12132	1		
358.botsalgn	1.47	C	1	24	12	4951	9900	
359.botsspar	.14	C	1	12	12	88351	353400	taskwait: 200
360.ilbdc	72.93	F	1004	12048	12048	1		
362.fma3d	11.3	F	4367	52416	52404	1		atomic: 17292
363.swim	4.84	F	5601	86412	67212	1		atomic: 9600
367.imagick	11.17	C	13	138	138	1		
370.mgrid331	.35	F	6383	104784	76596	1		atomic: 48 ordered: 240
371.applu331	3.85	F	517	21432	6204	1		
372.smithwa	3.18	C	4	60	48	1		flush: 32369
376.kdtree	15.6	C++	4	72	48	1.53×10^9	3.06×10^9	taskwait: 1.53×10^9

generates for the untied task leads to a total of 4 task switches per task. This creates double the synchronization cost as for tied tasks.

370.mgrid331 creates more than 6000 parallel regions in just 0.3 s. Each parallel region ends with an implicit barrier, according to the data, about every third parallel region contains an additional barrier. For the happened-before analysis a barrier means a store to the same synchronization clock from every participating thread and a load afterwards. The writes to the synchronization clock need to be locked, so the synchronization cost for the barrier grows linearly with the number of threads, additionally we can expect increasing lock contention for a bigger number of threads. With less threads, chances are higher that a thread already finished the store when another thread arrives at the barrier. This results in the big increase of overhead for 12 threads.

For 352.nab we see another spike for 12 threads. This application also has a lot of barriers, which lead to the same issue as discussed for 370.mgrid331. For both applications the strong scaling contributes to the issue; with increasing number of threads, the work per thread decreases. This means the frequency of barriers also increases with number of threads. These two linear effects multiply and lead to quadratic overhead.

376.kdtree is the only application in the benchmark that uses OpenMP tasks in a recursive algorithm. This results in 1.5 billion of task in the train size. In an average execution with 12 threads, this application has a maximum number of about 550 concurrent tasks, counting tasks that are created, but not finished. For recursive algorithms with OpenMP tasks, at some point task creation gets too expensive compared to the workload; at this point, applications can use a serial cut-off. The remaining recursion is executed in a serialized fashion. 376.kdtree implements the cut-off by using **#pragma omp task if** with a dynamic condition. This means the task cannot be deferred and executes immediately. Taking this information into account, there are only 1.5 million tasks that are not undeferred. By handling the undeferred tasks in a special way, we were able to reduce the runtime for 376.kdtree with 12 threads and ThreadSanitizer from about 450 s to 200 s. This reduced the overhead from 30x to 13x.

Finally, there is another spike for 350.md. This application is compute-bound on this machine since the problem size fits into cache and hence even 12 threads are not sufficient to exhaust the memory bandwidth. For smaller number of threads, this leads to the low runtime overhead with the tool. The code balance changes with the additional memory accesses coming from ThreadSanitizer, which adds about 4 times the memory foot print.

5.2   Data Race Results

Running the analysis, we were able to detect a data race in 367.imagick, which is caused by a concurrent write to a shared variable inside of a parallel region in magick_decorate.c:492. Making this variable private for the parallel region would resolve the data race.

Further, we could detect data races in 371.applu331. For this application we had the problem, that it uses custom synchronization on the base of conditional variables and flushes (in syncs.f90). The tool reports data races for the accesses of the conditional variable. By annotating these parts of the code, we were able to feed ThreadSanitizer with the synchronization information. With this annotations in the code, ThreadSanitizer only reports actual data races:

- blts.f90:76 read after write in blts.f90:66, caused by the do nowait and the access to v(1, i, j-1, k).
- buts.f90:77 read after write in buts.f90:243-247, caused by the access to v(1, i, j+1, k), v(2, i, j+1, k), ...

372.smithwa is the other application that uses flushes to implement synchronization with conditional variables. For this application we don't see reported data races after the annotation of the synchronization in the application. We reported the identified data races to the SPEC group.

For some of the Fortran applications we see warnings about lock-order inversion coming from libgfortran. Because the file accesses in the application only happen in the serial part, the lock-order inversion is a benign issue. It is a known issue with ThreadSanitizer, that it reports lock-order inversion, although only a single thread accesses the lock.

6   Conclusions

In this paper we discussed whether OMPT provides sufficient information to derive all synchronization semantics needed for data race detection. We based the analysis on a happened-before based model. But we think, the observations would also apply for a different analysis model, based on lock-set or plain analysis of OpenMP flush semantics. We implemented a data race detection tool based on OMPT. With OMPT based annotations, the tool passes most of the tests in our test suite. We pointed out three missing pieces of information in the OMPT interface, that is information about reduction, information about depend clause on taskwait and ordered constructs, and information on flush-set for flushes. We provided guidance on how to apply on-the-fly analysis for OpenMP mutual exclusion with the missing *releasing* event.

Further, we discussed the necessary OMPT events, to derive the synchronization information for data race analysis. To enable data race analysis based on these events, an OpenMP implementation needs to implement and provide callback invocation for these events. The issue here is that some of these callback invocations are optional according to current specification. This affects especially the events for taskwait, taskgroup, barrier and locks. If a data race detection tool cannot rely on these events, the advantage of portability across OpenMP implementations is gone. Therefore we suggest to make these callback invocations mandatory in the OpenMP specification.

Acknowledgments. The authors would like to thank the anonymous reviewers for their valuable comments and suggestions to improve the paper.

Part of this work was performed under the auspices of the U.S. Department of Energy by Lawrence Livermore National Laboratory under Contract DE-AC52-07NA27344. (LLNL-PROC-730143). Part of this work was possible under funding by the German Research Foundation (DFG) through the German Priority Programme 1648 Software for Exascale Computing (SPPEXA).

References

1. Archer project and source code. https://github.com/PRUNERS/archer
2. Atzeni, S., Gopalakrishnan, G., Rakamaric, Z., Ahn, D.H., Laguna, I., Schulz, M., Lee, G.L., Protze, J., Müller, M.S.: ARCHER: effectively spotting data races in large openmp applications. In: 2016 IEEE International Parallel and Distributed Processing Symposium, IPDPS 2016, Chicago, IL, USA, 23–27 May 2016, pp. 53–62 (2016)
3. OpenMP Architecture Review Board: OpenMP Application Program Interface. http://www.openmp.org/wp-content/uploads/openmp-4.5.pdf
4. OpenMP Architecture Review Board: TR4: OpenMP Version 5.0 Preview 1. http://www.openmp.org/wp-content/uploads/openmp-tr4.pdf
5. Lidbury, C., Donaldson, A.F.: Dynamic race detection for C++11. In: Proceedings of the 44th ACM SIGPLAN Symposium on Principles of Programming Languages, POPL 2017, Paris, France, 18–20 January 2017, pp. 443–457 (2017)
6. Müller, M.S., et al.: SPEC OMP2012 — an application benchmark suite for parallel systems using openMP. In: Chapman, B.M., Massaioli, F., Müller, M.S., Rorro, M. (eds.) IWOMP 2012. LNCS, vol. 7312, pp. 223–236. Springer, Heidelberg (2012). doi:10.1007/978-3-642-30961-8_17
7. Protze, J., Atzeni, S., Ahn, D.H., Schulz, M., Gopalakrishnan, G., Müller, M.S., Laguna, I., Rakamaric, Z., Lee, G.L.: Towards providing low-overhead data race detection for large openMP applications. In: Proceedings of the 2014 LLVM Compiler Infrastructure in HPC, LLVM 2014, New Orleans, LA, USA, 17 November 2014, pp. 40–47 (2014)

8. Serebryany, K., Iskhodzhanov, T.: Threadsanitizer: data race detection in practice. In: Proceedings of the Workshop on Binary Instrumentation and Applications, WBIA 2009, pp. 62–71. ACM, New York (2009)
9. Serebryany, K., Potapenko, A., Iskhodzhanov, T., Vyukov, D.: Dynamic race detection with LLVM compiler. In: Khurshid, S., Sen, K. (eds.) RV 2011. LNCS, vol. 7186, pp. 110–114. Springer, Heidelberg (2012). doi:10.1007/978-3-642-29860-8_9
10. The Clang Team: Clang 5 documentation: Threadsanitizer. https://clang.llvm.org/docs/ThreadSanitizer.html
11. Brian Whitney: SPEC OMP2012 documentation. https://www.spec.org/omp2012/Docs/

Accurate and Complete Hardware Profiling for OpenMP

Multiplexing Hardware Events Across Executions

Richard Neill[✉], Andi Drebes, and Antoniu Pop

School of Computer Science, The University of Manchester, Manchester, UK
{richard.neill,andi.drebes,antoniu.pop}@manchester.ac.uk

Abstract. Analyzing the behavior of OpenMP programs and their interaction with the hardware is essential for locating performance bottlenecks and identifying performance optimization opportunities. However, current architectures only provide a small number of dedicated registers to quantify hardware events, which strongly limits the scope of performance analyses. Hardware event multiplexing can help cover more events, but incurs a significant loss of accuracy and introduces overheads that change the behavior of program execution significantly. In this paper, we present an implementation of our technique for building a unique, coherent profile that contains all available hardware events from multiple executions of the same OpenMP program, each monitoring only a subset of the available hardware events. Reconciliation of the execution profiles relies on a new labeling scheme for OpenMP that uniquely identifies each dynamic unit of work across executions under dynamic scheduling across processing units. We show that our approach yields significantly better accuracy and lower monitoring overhead per execution than hardware event multiplexing.

Keywords: Performance analysis · Hardware events · Performance monitoring counters · OpenMP profiling

1 Introduction

Monitoring hardware behavior during the execution of an OpenMP program can reveal performance bottlenecks arising from the parallel structure of the software, characteristics of the hardware, and the complex interactions over shared resources. This behavior can be investigated by counting the number of occurrences of specific hardware events during execution using *Performance Monitoring Counters* (PMCs; dedicated on-chip registers). The counts can then be related to the individual regions of an OpenMP program during post-mortem performance analysis to enable reasoning about the variation in performance and hardware behavior across the program's execution. Various tools use hardware event monitoring to enable performance analysis of parallel programs [1,2,4,19]. However, as the number of available PMCs is generally orders of magnitude lower than the number of hardware events, only a small fraction of available hardware

© Springer International Publishing AG 2017
B.R. de Supinski et al. (Eds.): IWOMP 2017, LNCS 10468, pp. 266–280, 2017.
DOI: 10.1007/978-3-319-65578-9_18

events can be monitored simultaneously, which severely limits analyses involving multiple hardware events. Furthermore, there are architecture-specific design constraints for PMCs that often result in incompatibilities between events. Certain sets of events can therefore not be monitored simultaneously with other events, even if there are enough PMCs.

Hardware Event Multiplexing (HEM) is a common technique for alleviating the limitations imposed by event incompatibility and a lack of PMC availability. It consists of time-sharing the PMCs: subsets of hardware events are regularly rotated to be monitored, intending that each event is monitored over a representative sample of the execution. The Linux kernel's *perf_event* subsystem provides a standard implementation of HEM, although other works have attempted to enhance HEM by improving its interpolation mechanism between sampled counts [8–10] or optimizing its event scheduler to achieve better coverage of events [3]. However, because HEM time-shares the events, for any particular profiled event, there are necessarily periods of execution during which the event is not monitored. In previous work [14], we investigated the accuracy of profile data acquired from OpenStream [17] programs via HEM, and found that HEM is unable to produce accurate hardware event values for dynamic fine-grained task-parallel programs. In [14] we presented a significantly more accurate profiling technique for OpenStream programs, where data acquired during multiple executions is fused into a single, coherent execution profile. A somewhat related concept, known as *trace alignment* [6,12], was studied for sequential programs, but it hinges on identifying sequentially ordered execution phases, and is therefore not applicable to OpenMP's dynamic parallel schedules. To our knowledge, there is no other work which aims to reconcile the hardware event performance data observed in distinct executions to produce a complete, consistent view of hardware behavior of OpenMP programs.

In this paper, we present a multi-execution combination approach for OpenMP programs and evaluate its accuracy in comparison to HEM. Our approach targets a model-centric analysis and therefore focuses on monitoring at the granularity of *execution units* (XUs), a term we use in this paper to refer to two *kinds* of dynamically executed work in an OpenMP program: an executed instance of an OpenMP `task` construct or an executed range of iterations from an OpenMP `for` loop instance. Accurate performance monitoring data at this granularity is important to allow for a statistical approach to performance analyses, enabling the detection of performance bottlenecks arising from program and architecture characteristics, such as in [5,11]. Furthermore, by ensuring performance data reliability at this granularity, we enable all analyses that operate at higher levels of abstraction, ensuring, for example, accurate measurements of performance metrics aggregated across sets of XUs, e.g., per core, per NUMA node or per OpenMP construct.

This paper makes the following two main contributions:

- We present a labeling scheme for OpenMP XUs, which uniquely identifies each XU irrespective of runtime scheduling, ensuring that XUs are identifiable across multiple dynamic executions.

– We present an implementation of our multi-execution combination approach for OpenMP and evaluate its accuracy against HEM. We implement three strategies for combination: *Label Graph Location*, *Behavior Clustering*, and present a new strategy called *Chronological Type Combination*.

We describe our use of the Aftermath-OpenMP [4] instrumented OpenMP runtime to generate per-XU hardware event monitoring data in Sect. 2. An overview of our multi-execution combination approach and implementation strategies are detailed in Sect. 3. Section 4 presents our new OpenMP labeling scheme. Section 5 contains our evaluation for the combination approaches and HEM.

2   Generating OpenMP Execution Profiles

Our approach operates on the set of all *XUs* executed during a program and their associated performance monitoring data. Our definition of XUs is based on the higher-level OpenMP language constructs rather than on their generated code and dynamic execution. This means that even if the runtime system reaches a scheduling point and breaks down an XU into multiple chunks, possibly executing across multiple worker threads, the XU is considered to be the sum of its parts.

```
1   int main(int argc, char** argv){
2
3     #pragma omp parallel num_threads(2)
4     {
5       #pragma omp for schedule(static)        // 2 XUs
6       for (int i = 0; i < 8; i++) {
7         #pragma omp task                      // 8 XUs
8         {...}
9       }
10
11      #pragma omp for schedule(dynamic, 2)  // 4 XUs
12      for (int i = 0; i < 8; i++) {
13        ...
14      }
15
16      #pragma omp task                        // 2 XUs
17      {...}
18    }
19
20    return 0;
21  }
```

Listing 1.1. Example OpenMP program and resulting execution units.

The example OpenMP program in Listing 1.1 creates 16 XUs as follows. On Line 5, the static schedule of the **for** construct implies that each of the two worker threads declared in the team of the **parallel** construct (Line 3) receives half of the iterations, which makes up 2 XUs. Each iteration of this same loop further creates one **task** on Line 7, resulting in 8 XUs. In the second **for** construct, in Line 11, the dynamic schedule with a chunk size of 2 results in 4 XUs, each containing 2 iterations. Finally, the last **task** construct, on Line 16, occurs within the body of the parallel region, so each of the two worker threads will create their own instance, creating the last 2 XUs.

A set of hardware events are monitored during a profiling execution of a program. Each executed XU u is therefore associated with a set of pairs composed of the event and the number of occurences during the execution of u, referred to as the *event counts*. In this paper, we define the function $count\_set(u,E)$ to return the set of counts associated to u for all events in the event set E, where for simplicity E is the complete set of hardware events associated with u if the second argument of the function is omitted. For a given execution, we refer to the entire set of XUs together with their complete set of profiled event counts as an *execution profile*, or *profile* for short. We finally define the *type* of an XU to be a syntactic identifier for its corresponding language construct within the code, with $\mathcal{T}$ being the set of all XU types defined in the program specification.

We rely on Aftermath-OpenMP [4] to trace OpenMP execution and enable generation of execution profiles. In this paper, we note $\mathcal{E}$ to be the set of available hardware events on the system. As described in the introduction, hardware event monitoring is limited by the available PMCs. Assuming for simplicity that there are no incompatibilities and any hardware event can be monitored in any PMC, event counts cannot be associated with all XUs in an Aftermath-OpenMP execution profile when the number of events to be profiled exceeds the number of available PMCs N_{PMC}. To overcome this problem, we combine the data of XUs profiled during multiple distinct executions into a single, coherent profile where all XUs are associated with event counts for each event in $\mathcal{E}$, thus achieving complete execution profiles.

3   Execution Profile Combination

To generate a complete execution profile, where each XU has hardware event values for all available hardware events, our approach is to execute a program repeatedly and to monitor a different set of hardware events for each run, instead of rotating hardware events over the duration of a single execution as in HEM. The different profiles are then combined using one of the three strategies described below. Among them, the *Chronological Type Combination* is new in this paper, while the other two have been adapted to OpenMP from our previous work [14], notably requiring the development of an XU labeling scheme.

Execution profile combination starts by generating n subsets of $\mathcal{E}$, where each subset can be monitored simultaneously on the system. The union of all subsets must cover $\mathcal{E}$, but subsets need not be exclusive and event overlaps can even be

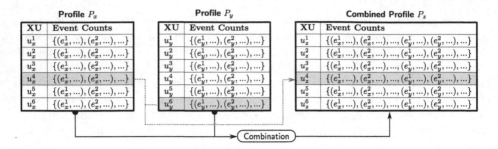

Fig. 1. Combination of two profiles. The highlights denote an example derived XU u_z^4 that is generated from two source XUs u_x^4 and u_y^6.

necessary depending on the combination strategy. The target program is then executed n times with the same input and configuration but with each execution monitoring a different event subset, to produce a set of execution profiles.

The goal of execution profile combination is to apply a *combination* to these profiles in order to produce a *combined profile*. A combined profile consists of a set of derived XUs that are each generated from a unique set of XUs $\{u_1, \ldots, u_n\}$, with each XU's subscript indicating a different source execution profile. A derived XU is therefore associated with the hardware event monitoring data from each of the associated XUs. This ensures that it has monitored hardware event counts for all events in $\mathcal{E}$, where each associated event count was observed in an execution during which the event was monitored throughout the entire duration. Figure 1 illustrates the approach in the case of a combination of two profiles P_x and P_y, where for clarity we include a superscript identifier with each XU. The highlighted XUs and the dotted line represent an example of a combination step, in which the task profiles of u_x^4 and u_y^6 are combined for u_z^4.

Selecting the set of XUs to combine across distinct executions of an OpenMP program is non-trivial. OpenMP programs can exhibit highly dynamic behavior at execution time, such that two executions of the same program with identical input may vary significantly. Such variability is unavoidable in modern systems. Firstly, because of the complexity of the hardware, possibly starting execution in different states (e.g., CPU power-modes), the complex interactions between the software and hardware (e.g., the cache hierarchy, memory prefetcher, branch predictor), or interference from the software stack (e.g., the OS scheduler). Secondly, because the execution of OpenMP constructs (e.g., `task`, `for`) can be scheduled dynamically to worker threads by the runtime system. Furthermore, as the same workers may be assigned entirely different work during different executions, particularly for OpenMP programs that specify very unbalanced work shares through the use of `single`, `master` or `section` directives, this may cause partial reordering of work between different executions. If the behavior at execution time of selected XUs significantly varied between the executions, then the combination may produce inaccurate profiles that have hardware event counts that are not representative of what occurs in any single program execution. To alleviate these issues, we have devised the following combination strategies.

Chronological Type Combination. Assuming that executions could be identical in their scheduling, system environment and behavior at execution time, then the execution times and allocation of XUs to worker threads across distinct executions of the program would be the same. Moreover, one would expect the same hardware events to occur at the same relative time across each execution of the program. Under these optimistic assumptions, a combination strategy that selects XUs of the same *type* by the chronological order of their start timestamps, called *Chronological Type Combination* (CTC), is a natural first choice.

Let $\{P_1, \ldots, P_n\}$ be the unordered set of execution profiles to be combined via CTC into a resulting combined profile P_{CTC}. Let further $\{U_1, \ldots, U_n\}$ denote the corresponding sets of XUs within each profile. Here we assume the basic case, where events monitored during an execution are not also monitored during any other execution. If the event sets of executions overlap, then the first profile containing each event contributes the event's counts to the combined profile, and subsequent monitored event values are unused and therefore redundant. The CTC combination strategy is as follows:

1	For each type $\tau \in \mathcal{T}$:
2	From each profile, get all XUs with type τ, to give $\mathbf{U}^\tau = \{U_1^\tau, \ldots, U_n^\tau\}$
3	Sort each $U \in \mathbf{U}^\tau$ chronologically by start duration
4	While all $U \in \mathbf{U}^\tau$ have remaining tasks:
5	Select the first XU from each $U \in \mathbf{U}^\tau$ to give the set $U_{\mathrm{selected}}^\tau$
6	Create a new, derived XU denoted u
7	For each $u' \in U_{\mathrm{selected}}^\tau$, add *count_set*$(u')$ to u
8	Add u and its event counts to P_{CTC}
9	Remove all $u' \in U_{\mathrm{selected}}^\tau$ from the respective sets $U \in \mathbf{U}^\tau$

Label Graph Location. The Label Graph Location (LGL) combination strategy maps the XUs from multiple profiles by uniquely identifying each dynamic instance across executions. These XUs are of the same type, have identical input data and generate identical output data, and are created following the same path of execution through OpenMP constructs in the code. In order to combine OpenMP programs with LGL, we attach to each XU a unique identifier called a *label*, that is consistent for that XU across dynamic executions. We define a function *label* that associates a label to an XU, which we present for OpenMP programs in Sect. 4. The LGL combination strategy selects those XUs with matching labels across executions.

The LGL combination, as with CTC, operates on an unordered set of profiles $\{P_1, \ldots, P_n\}$, again assuming no overlapping events between the monitored executions. The combined profile P_{LGL} is generated as follows:

1	For each *label* $\in L$:
2	Get the set of XUs with *label* from each profile, to give U_{label}
3	Create a new, derived XU denoted u
4	For each $u' \in U_{\mathrm{label}}$, add *count_set*$(u')$ to u
5	Add u and its event counts to P_{LGL}

Behavior Clustering. The Behavior Clustering (BC) combination strategy accounts for dynamic execution variation between profiles by selecting XUs of the same type that had similar hardware behavior at execution time in each profile. This means that XUs that are combined by BC may be different sets of iterations of the same parallel loop, or different instances of the same task construct, but that exhibit more similar hardware behavior (e.g., interaction with cache) than XUs with equivalent label across executions.

BC combination operates on an ordered set of profiles $\langle P_1, \ldots, P_n \rangle$ with corresponding sets of events monitored during each execution $\langle E_1, \ldots, E_n \rangle$. The BC process is recursive, combining two profiles in each recursion step to accretively build up to the final combined profile. At each step, the resulting profile of the previous combination P_{prev} is combined with the next profile in the ordered set P_{cur} to produce the profile P_{combined}, which becomes P_{prev} for the next step. The first step combines P_1 and P_2 directly, with the final profile therefore produced after $n-1$ combinations.

BC combines two profiles by selecting the XUs that behaved similarly during each execution, with respect to a subset of hardware events. To do this, in contrast to CTC or LGL, BC requires *overlapping* events between P_{prev} and P_{cur}, such that $E_{\text{prev}} \cap E_{\text{cur}} \neq \emptyset$. The process is defined as follows:

---

1   For each type $\tau \in \mathcal{T}$
2   Select XUs of type τ from P_{prev}, P_{cur} to give U^τ_{prev}, U^τ_{cur}
3   For each grid division parameter $d = d_{\text{max}}$ to 1:
4   Cluster XUs of U^τ_{prev}, U^τ_{cur} on $E_{\text{prev}} \cap E_{\text{cur}}$ according to d
5   For each XU cluster, containing XU sets $U^\tau_{\text{prev,cluster}}$, $U^\tau_{\text{cur,cluster}}$:
6   Sort $U^\tau_{\text{prev,cluster}}$ by labels
7   Sort $U^\tau_{\text{cur,cluster}}$ by labels
8   Select each pair of XUs by sorted position to give $(u_{\text{prev}}, u_{\text{cur}})$:
9   Create a new, derived XU denoted u
10   Add *count_set*$(u_{\text{prev}}, E_{\text{prev}})$ to u
11   Add *count_set*$(u_{\text{cur}}, E_{\text{cur}} \setminus E_{\text{prev}})$ to u
12   Add u and its event counts to P_{combined}
13   Remove u_{prev} and u_{cur} from U^τ_{prev} and U^τ_{cur}, respectively

---

In line 4, XUs are clustered. To do this, a grid is defined of dimension N_{dim}, where each dimension corresponds to an overlapping hardware event. The value range for each event is divided by a grid division parameter d to produce $d^{N_{\text{dim}}}$ cells, which we term *clusters*. The XUs from each profile are then allocated to clusters according to their values for each of the overlapping events, where in Line 8, XUs are selected for combination by corresponding position in the label-ordered sets. As there may not be the same number of XUs from P_{prev} and P_{cur} populated in each cluster, not all XUs may be combined after this clustering process. To ensure that all XUs can be combined, the clustering process is repeated with a decremented grid division parameter, resulting in larger clusters and a reduced constraint on the event count similarity of selected XUs. This process continues until at least one profile is exhausted of XUs.

In this paper, we also evaluate a slightly modified version of BC, where the combined XU pairs within each cluster are selected at random and not according to the label order. This was done to evaluate whether labeling is necessary for BC, and therefore BC's applicability to OpenMP runtimes which do not carry out the necessary instrumentation to enable labeling of XUs.

All three combination strategies are designed to combine execution profiles of the same program with the same inputs, differing in their handling of XU behavior variation between profiles. The three strategies may also be applied to non-deterministic programs with different numbers of XUs across the executions. In this case, the CTC and BC combined profiles consist of the maximum number of XUs that exist across all execution profiles, for each task type. The LGL combined profile consists of XUs corresponding to the subset of labels present in all profiles.

The LGL and BC combination strategies are described in further detail in [14]. To work on OpenMP programs, LGL and BC require the labeling scheme presented in the next section.

4 Labeling OpenMP Programs

Both LGL and BC rely on a labeling scheme that uniquely identifies the same XU, as statically defined in the parallel structure of the program, across a set of executions. The labeling is independent from any external influence, such as the scheduling of XUs or resource allocation. The notion of identity is similar for the identity that we defined for task-parallel languages in [14]. In such models, each task t except the *root* task, representing the initial sequential execution of the program, has a parent task t_p that is defined as the task that executed the instructions creating t. Two tasks t and t' are considered identical iff their respective parents are identical and iff the number of tasks created by their respective parents t_p and t'_p before t and t' is the same. The label of a task is defined as the concatenation of the label of its parent, a delimiter and the number of tasks created by its parent before its own creation with an artificial label '0' for the root task. Since the execution within a task is sequential, the labels are independent of the actual order of task execution by the scheduler and allows tasks to be identified reliably across executions.

We now extend this scheme to the XUs of OpenMP programs.

4.1 Labeling Scheme

An XU can only be created if the creating thread has previously encountered one or more OpenMP constructs, as an OpenMP task or iteration range must be specified within at least one **parallel** construct or **for** construct, respectively. As OpenMP supports nested parallelism, XUs may be created during the execution of others. For the remainder of this section, we define the function *par* to return the *parent* XU or OpenMP construct of another XU or OpenMP construct. To define the labeling scheme, we make a distinction between an XU and an OpenMP *construct*. A *construct* is the entity in the structure of an OpenMP program corresponding to an `omp pragma` that a worker can encounter during its execution, whereas an XU is an executable instance of a `task` construct or block of iterations from a `for` construct. For example, referring to the program given in Listing 1.1, the OpenMP runtime creates the first iteration range XU spanning four iterations after the thread encounters a `parallel` construct and a subsequent `for` construct. The labeling function *label* applies to an XU when it is initially created, or to an instance of a worker encountering a construct, and we refer to either as *uc*. A worker encountering a `task` construct and creating a task instance XU are equivalent with respect to the labeling, and are treated as the same *uc*.

The labeling function is defined as follows:

$$label(uc) = \begin{cases} \text{`0'} & \text{if } uc \text{ is root} \\ label(par(uc)) \oplus sibidx(uc) & \text{otherwise} \end{cases}$$

where $\oplus$ denotes the concatenation of two labels with a delimiter. The function *sibidx* returns a value depending on the kind of *uc*:

$$sibidx(u) = \begin{cases} start\_iteration(uc) & \text{if } uc \text{ is iteration range} \\ next\_rank(par(uc)) \oplus addr(uc) & \text{if } uc \text{ is } \mathtt{for} \\ next\_rank\_TID(uc) \oplus addr(uc) & \text{if } uc \text{ in } \mathtt{task}, \mathtt{parallel}, \mathtt{section} \end{cases}$$

In this rule set, $start\_iteration(uc)$ returns the index of first executed iteration of the iteration set *uc* as the label index, and $addr(uc)$ returns the memory address of the source location of the OpenMP construct associated to *uc*. A *rank* is a monotonically increasing integer that is initialized to 1 and represents the rank of *uc* in the creation order of it and its siblings. The function $next\_rank(par(uc))$ therefore retrieves the next sibling index from the parent. This means that the label indexes are dependent on an order existing between *uc* and its siblings. As it is legal for a `task`, `section` or `parallel` construct to be defined directly inside a parent `parallel` construct, the semantics of the program define no order that they are encountered by the threads in the parallel team. In this special case, *uc*'s rank within its parent `parallel` construct is set to 0, and a further label index is concatenated using the TID that created the instance of *uc* with respect to the number of workers in the team. This is a forced ordering that ensures unique labels for all XUs are maintained. The function $next\_rank\_TID$ carries out this special case of the labeling scheme, should it occur:

$$next\_rank\_TID(uc) =$$
$$\begin{cases} \text{`0'} \oplus TID + prev\_calls(par(uc)) \cdot workers(par(uc)) & \text{if } par(uc) \text{ is } \mathtt{parallel} \\ next\_rank(par(uc)) \oplus addr(uc) & \text{otherwise} \end{cases}$$

A `for` construct can also occur directly within a parent `parallel` construct. However, the XUs created from it will be strictly ordered by their start iteration so do not require special labeling.

In the presented labeling scheme, `single`, `master` and `critical` constructs were not included. This is because they are not necessary for the purposes of labeling XUs that are encountered within them, as they either define which worker should create the XU or enforce timing constraints on the creation, both of which the labeling scheme is insensitive to.

For the experimental evaluation, we have implemented the labeling scheme into Aftermath-OpenMP, such that profiling data from different executions can be related to the same instances of work as defined in the program code, subject to the aforementioned variability at execution time.

By labeling the XUs of an OpenMP program, the set of XUs and their creation relationships can be depicted as a *Label Graph*. Each node of this graph represents an XU or OpenMP construct and edges represent the casual relationships between their creations in the program.

4.2 Labeling Example

Figure 2 shows the label graph for the example OpenMP program in Listing 1.1 with 16 profiled XUs. The label for each of the XUs highlighted in gray can

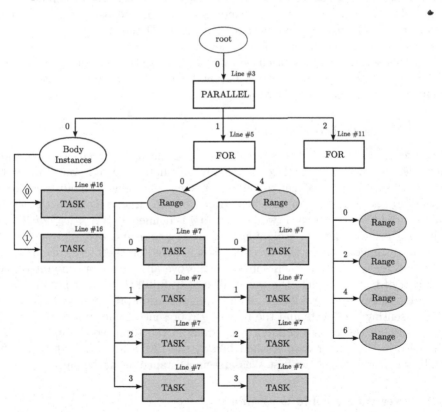

Fig. 2. OpenMP Label Graph of example program, where gray highlights the profiled XUs. Memory addresses are replaced by line numbers for purposes of illustration.

be constructed by concatenating the edge indexes and OpenMP construct line numbers, descending the graph in order from *root* to the XU. In this example, the line numbers represent the memory locations given as the result of *addr* in the above ruleset, and the oval-shaped entities are included only to aid clarity and do not represent actual OpenMP constructs. The diamond-shaped edge indexes represent forced ranking, where there is no strict ordering for these XUs with respect to their siblings in the semantics of the OpenMP program.

In the next section, we use the labels together with our combination strategies to evaluate the capability of our approach to produce full and accurate hardware event monitoring data for OpenMP programs.

5   Evaluation

We evaluate our approach with the different combination strategies using *Execution Profile Dissimilarity* (EPD), a metric derived from the Earth Mover's Distance (EMD) [18]. EPD quantifies the relative accuracy of generated performance monitoring data, where we define *accuracy* as its similarity with performance monitoring data produced in reference executions. In a reference execution, all of the hardware events are monitored simultaneously, i.e., without any form of multiplexing or combination. A lower EPD therefore represents higher accuracy and thus better reliability when used for analysis.

In this section we first briefly outline EMD before describing its usage for EPD as presented in earlier work [14]. Following this, we describe the experimental setup and present our results.

5.1   The Earth Mover's Distance

The EMD, as presented in [18], calculates the similarity between two histograms, here denoted p and q. EMD conceptually calculates the minimum amount of 'work' required to transform the bins of p such that they are equivalent to the bins of q, where the bins in each histogram contain an amount of earth specified by its *weight*. Work between two bins i and j is defined as $W_{ij} = \omega_{ij} \cdot dist(\lambda_i, \lambda_j)$ with ω_{ij} representing the weight moved from i to j and *dist* representing the ground distance between the two bins that is based on the bin locations λ_i and λ_j respectively. EMD is then solved as the overall minimum amount of work necessary to either deplete the weight of p or to fulfill the weight requirement of q, and is therefore a formulation of the transportation problem, with the bins of p representing producers and the bins of q representing consumers.

Assuming the total weight in p is equal to the total weight in q, which is the case in this paper as described below, the EMD is equivalent to the first Mallow's distance and the first Wasserstein Distance in mathematics [7].

5.2   Execution Profile Dissimilarity

We now define our usage of EMD, that we term EPD. The similarity of the complete set of hardware event monitoring data within a profile cannot be directly calculated against a single reference profile when its profiled hardware events are not simultaneously compatible on the system. Therefore we define a reference profile for each possible pair of the hardware events. EPD is then given as the geometric mean of its calculated EPDs against each reference profile, with respect to each pair of hardware events.

We denote the pair of hardware events in a given reference profile as E_{ref}. The two profiles are each represented as a two-dimensional histogram where each event $e \in E_{ref}$ forms a dimension. The histograms are created by dividing each event's range of values in the reference profile into n equally spaced intervals, to produce a two-dimensional grid. Each cell of this grid is a histogram bin to which the XUs are assigned based on their associated hardware event counts.

EPD defines a histogram bin's weight as the proportion of XUs allocated to the bin from the profile. The distance function $dist(\lambda_i, \lambda_j)$ is defined as the Euclidean distance between the two bin locations, where a bin location is specified as a two-dimensional Cartesian coordinate. The coordinate component, with respect to the dimension for one of the hardware events e, is given by the distance along that dimension from the histogram's origin to the mean event count for e calculated from the XUs populated in the bin. This distance is expressed in fractional bin-intervals, where the bin interval for an event e is equivalent to its value range in the reference divided by n.

The EPD between the two histograms is then calculated by solving the EMD algorithm following these definitions. The result is normalized according to the *Calibration EPD*. We define the Calibration EPD as the mean dissimilarity calculated between the profiles of repeated reference executions of the program, meaning it therefore quantifies the average expected variability of the event counts. The final EPD result between the target evaluation profile and a particular reference profile is then its mean EPD calculated against each of the repeat reference profiles.

5.3 Experimental Methodology

We evaluate our combination approach against HEM on a 32-core machine equipped with Intel Xeon E5-2690 processors running with Hyper-Threading enabled and an operating frequency of 2:93 GHz, with 396 GB main memory distributed over two NUMA nodes. The machine was configured with version 3.19 of the Linux kernel, using the kernel's default multiplexing implementation of the *perf_event* subsystem with the default multiplexing scheduling period of 4 ms for HEM. In our experiments, we used the FastEMD library [16].

For evaluation, the loop-based parallel benchmarks *MG* and *CG* from the C implementation of the NPB benchmark suite [13,15], and a custom task-parallel OpenMP C implementation of the branch-and-bound solution to the knapsack problem were used. Two versions of *MG* and *CG* programs were profiled, one using static loop scheduling and the other using dynamic scheduling. The dynamic scheduling was configured with chunk sizes of 10 and 100 respectively.

For each benchmark, each reference execution was repeated 3 times and the mean dissimilarity between each repeat was calculated as the Calibration EPD for the reference event-pair. The set of profiles to be combined were executed and the combination strategies were applied to produce a set of combined profiles. The EPD of each combined profile against each reference pair was calculated as the mean EPD between the profile and each repeat reference profile corresponding to the pair. The final EPD value for a profile was then the geometric mean of the EPD calculated across the full set of reference pairs. This process was repeated 3 times, with the final EPD result for a strategy calculated as the mean EPD of the repeat combined profile, and error calculated as standard deviation.

5.4   Results

Figure 3 shows the resulting EPDs for the different combination schemes when applied to the 5 combinations of benchmarks and loop schedules. HEM displays by far the highest dissimilarities compared to simultaneous profiling of the events. This major decrease in accuracy is inherent to single-profile sampling techniques like HEM: since it is impossible to monitor all hardware events throughout the entire execution, a significant part of the data is obtained through statistical interpolation. Depending on the number of events, the multiplexing period and the duration of XUs, this might result in event counts for XUs interpolated from the values of previously executed XUs with different characteristics. The large number of hardware events that can be monitored on modern systems and the short durations of XUs in OpenMP programs would require a sampling period that is significantly shorter than the default 4 ms in the experimental setup in order to obtain samples for all events for each XU. However, a significantly shorter multiplexing period would incur significant overhead and generate

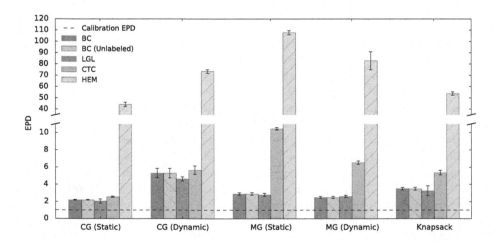

Fig. 3. EPD results for generated hardware event profiles

biased results. Therefore, HEM provides meaningful results only for a limited set of analysis scenarios.

The multi-execution profile combination strategies achieve hardware event profiles with vastly more accurate results. The EPD values for these are close to the Calibration EPD. For most of the benchmarks, CTC clearly produces less accurate combined profiles than the other combination strategies. The CTC strategy assumes that the same XUs perform the same amount of work, execute in the same order and on the same CPUs across the multiple executions of an OpenMP program. The higher EPD results for CTC indicate that this assumption is not valid for most of the benchmarks. However, the results for CTC applied to the statically scheduled *CG* benchmark are close to the Calibration EPD, meaning that, as expected, the validity of this assumption heavily depends on the nature of the benchmark. Furthermore, as no significant event-scheduling work is required when monitoring the executions necessary for our combination approach, each monitored execution does not exhibit the significant monitoring overhead produced during HEM executions with short mutiplexing periods.

Comparing the results of the LGL and BC combination strategies, there is no clear difference in accuracy, as their resulting EPDs are similarly close to the Calibration EPD across each of the benchmarks. The graph also shows that labeling in BC only has little influence on the accuracy, as indicated by the similar results for BC and BC (Unlabeled). This suggests that the additional trace processing required to apply labels to XUs is not necessary to obtain accurate hardware event profiles and that our combination approach may be used directly on OpenMP runtimes that are unable to produce the necessary instrumentation for labeling purposes.

6 Conclusion

We presented a new approach for building accurate and complete hardware profiles of OpenMP programs that consists of combining information gathered from multiple executions of the same program into a unique, coherent execution profile. We presented three combination strategies: *Chronological Type Combination* (CTC), *Label Graph Location* (LGL) and *Behavior Clustering* (BC). We introduced CTC as a novel combination strategy technique and presented the work required to adapt LGL and BC to OpenMP, mainly consisting in an appropriate labeling scheme for OpenMP execution units and constructs. Based on our EPD metric, a variant of the Earth Mover's Distance, we showed that our approach can be used to build execution profiles that contain information about all hardware event types available, while achieving significantly better accuracy than Hardware Event Multiplexing.

References

1. Adhianto, L., Banerjee, S., Fagan, M., Krentel, M., Marin, G., Mellor-Crummey, J., Tallent, N.R.: HPCTOOLKIT: tools for performance analysis of optimized parallel programs. Concurrency Comput. Pract. Exp. **22**(6), 685–701 (2010)

2. Intel Corporation: Intel VTune Amplifier (2017). https://software.intel.com/en-us/intel-vtune-amplifier-xe. Accessed 30 Apr 2017
3. Dimakopoulou, M., Eranian, S., Koziris, N., Bambos, N.: Reliable and efficient performance monitoring in Linux. In: Proceedings of the International Conference for High Performance Computing, Networking, Storage and Analysis, p. 34 (2016)
4. Drebes, A., Bréjon, J.-B., Pop, A., Heydemann, K., Cohen, A.: Language-centric performance analysis of OpenMP programs with aftermath. In: Maruyama, N., Supinski, B.R., Wahib, M. (eds.) IWOMP 2016. LNCS, vol. 9903, pp. 237–250. Springer, Cham (2016). doi:10.1007/978-3-319-45550-1_17
5. Drebes, A., Pop, A., Heydemann, K., Cohen, A., Drach-Temam, N.: Aftermath: a graphical tool for performance analysis and debugging of fine-grained task-parallel programs and run-time systems. In: 7th Workshop on Programmability Issues for Heterogeneous Multicores (MULTIPROG), Vienna, Austria (2014)
6. Hauswirth, M., Diwan, A., Sweeney, P.F., Mozer, M.C.: Automating vertical profiling. In: Proceedings of the 20th Annual ACM SIGPLAN Conference on Object-oriented Programming, Systems, Languages, and Applications, OOPSLA 2005, pp. 281–296. ACM, New York (2005)
7. Levina, E., Bickel, P.: The earth mover's distance is the Mallows distance: some insights from statistics. In: Proceedings Eighth IEEE International Conference on Computer Vision, ICCV 2001, vol. 2, pp. 251–256 (2001)
8. Lim, R.V., Carrillo-Cisneros, D., Scherson, I.D.: Computationally efficient multiplexing of events on hardware counters. In: Linux Symposium, pp. 101–110 (2014)
9. Mathur, W., Cook, J.: Towards accurate performance evaluation using hardware counters. In: ITEA Modeling and Simulation Workshop (2003)
10. Mathur, W., Cook, J.: Improved estimation for software multiplexing of performance counters. In: Proceedings - IEEE Computer Society's Annual International Symposium on Modeling, Analysis, and Simulation of Computer and Telecommunications Systems, MASCOTS, vol. 2005, pp. 23–32. IEEE (2005)
11. Muddukrishna, A., Jonsson, P.A., Brorsson, M.: Characterizing task-based OpenMP programs. PLoS ONE 10(4), e0123545 (2015)
12. Mytkowicz, T., Sweeney, P.F., Hauswirth, M., Diwan, A.: Time interpolation: so many metrics, so few registers. In: 40th Annual IEEE/ACM International Symposium on Microarchitecture, MICRO 2007, pp. 286–300. IEEE (2007)
13. NASA: NAS Parallel Benchmarks. https://www.nas.nasa.gov/publications/npb.html. Accessed 30 Apr 2017
14. Neill, R., Drebes, A., Pop, A.: Fuse: accurate multiplexing of hardware performance counters across executions (2017)
15. University of Versailles Saint Quentin en Yvelines: NAS Parallel Benchmarks 3.0 Unofficial OpenMP C Version (2014). https://github.com/benchmark-subsetting/NPB3.0-omp-C. Accessed 30 Apr 2017
16. Pele, O., Werman, M.: A linear time histogram metric for improved SIFT matching. In: Forsyth, D., Torr, P., Zisserman, A. (eds.) ECCV 2008. LNCS, vol. 5304, pp. 495–508. Springer, Heidelberg (2008). doi:10.1007/978-3-540-88690-7_37
17. Pop, A., Cohen, A.: OpenStream: expressiveness and data-flow compilation of OpenMP streaming programs. ACM Trans. Architect. Code Optim. 9(4), 5301–5325 (2013)
18. Rubner, Y., Tomasi, C., Guibas, L.J.: The earth mover's distance as a metric for image retrieval. Int. J. Comput. Vis. 40(2), 99–121 (2000)
19. Shende, S.S., Malony, A.D.: The Tau parallel performance system. Int. J. High Perform. Comput. Appl. 20(2), 287–311 (2006)

OpenMP® Runtime Instrumentation for Optimization

Taru Doodi[✉], Jonathan Peyton, Jim Cownie, Maria Garzaran,
Rubasri Kalidas, Jeongnim Kim, Amrita Mathuriya, Terry Wilmarth,
and Gengbin Zheng

Intel Corporation, Austin, USA
{taru.doodi,jonathan.l.peyton,james.h.cownie,maria.garzaran,
rubasri.kalidas,jeongnim.kim,amrita.mathuriya,terry.l.wilmarth,
gengbin.zheng}@intel.com

Abstract. The OpenMP (The OpenMP name is a registered trademark of the OpenMP Architecture Review Board.) application programming interface provides a simple way for programmers to write parallel programs that are portable between machines and vendors. Programmers parallelize their programs to obtain higher performance, but, as the number of cores per processor increases, taking advantage of parallelism efficiently becomes more difficult. To facilitate efficient parallelization and avoid poor utilization of machine resources, programmers need to know where an application is spending time and what factors hinder scalability.

In this paper, we present a Tool for Runtime Instrumentation of OpenMP programs (TRIO) that automatically collects statistics about an application's use of the OpenMP runtime. TRIO provides statistics such as the total number of times an OpenMP construct is called, the time spent in each OpenMP construct, and the total time spent within the OpenMP runtime. TRIO helps to identify the runtime calls where a program spends most of the time and which constructs are called the most at runtime.

Keywords: Runtime instrumentation · OpenMP constructs

1 Introduction

The OpenMP API is a directive-based programming model that facilitates the implementation of shared memory parallel programs that are portable between machines and vendors. Programmers parallelize their programs to reduce their execution time, but they often find that the speedups of the parallel programs are significantly lower than expected or even that there is slowdown with respect to the sequential program. In many cases the highest performance is not obtained when all the hardware threads and/or cores are used. This can sometimes be explained because synchronization operations take longer as the number of threads increases, and the benefit of running the application with extra threads

© Springer International Publishing AG 2017
B.R. de Supinski et al. (Eds.): IWOMP 2017, LNCS 10468, pp. 281–295, 2017.
DOI: 10.1007/978-3-319-65578-9_19

cannot compensate for the additional synchronization overhead. Programmers use profilers, such as TAU [1] or Intel® VTune™ Amplifier [2], to determine the overheads that limit the scalability of their applications. Profilers can give information about time spent in each function or number of cache misses, but they often lack information about where the time is spent inside the OpenMP runtime.

TRIO is implemented as instrumentation inside the OpenMP runtime. It collects statistics from unmodified OpenMP programs as they execute. These statistics provide information about the number of times a given OpenMP construct is called and the time the application spends inside each OpenMP construct. TRIO separates the time the application is doing useful computation (compute time) from the time inside the runtime (non-compute time), where threads are not performing any useful computation.

TRIO was developed to analyze whether the OpenMP runtime was a limiting factor in the scalability of the applications and to set priorities for OpenMP runtime development. The goal was to have a low-overhead mechanism to study the use of the OpenMP runtime in real applications. Evaluating the OpenMP runtime with micro-benchmarks can produce the wrong conclusions, as, since benchmarks do little or no real computation, the runtime's data structures remain in cache across invocations, which is not the case when running real applications.

After TRIO was developed, we realized that the information it produces is also useful to application programmers who need to optimize their codes. The information provided by TRIO can help the programmer to determine how to re-structure their code and reason about the possible performance improvements that could be obtained if issues are addressed. For instance, using TRIO, a programmer can find the time spent in fork-join or plain barrier. If this time is large, the programmer can use TRIO to determine whether this time is due to work imbalance in parallel loops or to a large number of fork-join and/or plain barriers. However, since the focus of TRIO is OpenMP constructs implemented in the OpenMP runtime, it does not provide all the information the programmer needs to scale the application. For instance, in parallel programs, memory bandwidth frequently becomes a bottleneck as the number of threads increases. The instrumented OpenMP runtime cannot provide that information, which can be provided by profilers, such as Intel® VTune™ Amplifier.

TRIO can be used on hybrid MPI+OpenMP applications. Currently, it gives aggregated information for all the threads in a process. Providing per-thread information is possible, but TRIO was designed to provide an overview of the OpenMP usage, not detailed information. Thus, TRIO is a complement to profilers, but not a substitute. TRIO provides high-level profiling information by setting LD_LIBRARY_PATH to point to the instrumented OpenMP runtime library.

In this paper, we show the output produced by TRIO for some CORAL benchmarks [3] and discuss how to use TRIO to pinpoint the tradeoffs of different approaches. The paper is organized as follows. Section 2 discusses Related Work. Section 3 describes how TRIO works. Section 4 presents Experimental Setup.

Section 5 discusses the data provided by TRIO with some CORAL application. Section 6 uses some examples to show the usage of TRIO. Section 7 concludes. Finally, the Appendix shows the text file produced by TRIO.

2   Related Work

A lot of work has been done on profiling tools, such as Intel® VTune™ Amplifier which provide in depth analyses to identify bottlenecks for scalability. Tools such as MAQAO [4], TAU [1], ompP [5], Kojak [6], Scalasca [7] and Vampir [8] provide thread-level information and can report some OpenMP specific information when this is available. Many of these tools, like TAU, Kojak, and Scalasca, use a source-to-source code transformation utility (Opari [9]) to parse C/C++ and Fortran source code, locate OpenMP pragmas, and insert instrumentation via the POMP interface [9]. TRIO, on the other hand, can be used without code recompilation or re-linking and does not depend on any external tool or GUI to work.

There have been earlier attempts to define a tool interface for OpenMP, such as POMP [9] and the OpenMP Runtime API (ORA) known as the Collector API [10]. Neither of these approaches has been widely adopted.

HPC Toolkit [11] is a more complex set of tools than TRIO, that instruments the binary and profiles it at runtime and that can handle hybrid MPI and OpenMP applications.

It is undoubtedly the case that the information collected by TRIO could also be derived from the more detailed information collected by other, more general, profilers. However the very generality of such tools makes it hard to provide the limited, but focused, information that we are looking for easily and at low overhead.

Since TRIO is implemented inside the OpenMP runtime, it is very easy to use. There is no need to install any profiler or device drivers that enable access to performance monitor counters. All that is required is to ensure that the appropriate version of the OpenMP runtime is used. Thus, no privileges or interaction with owners/managers of the systems on which the code is run is needed. TRIO's low overhead and ease of use mean that it is an appropriate tool for initial performance assessments of the use of the OpenMP runtime in real applications.

The TRIO code is available in the LLVM OpenMP runtime[1], and can be enabled by compiling the runtime with the -DLIBOMP_STATS=on flag to cmake.

2.1   Comparison Between TRIO and OMPT

Since OpenMP 4.0, the tools sub-committee of the OpenMP language committee has been working to create a portable interface between performance tools and OpenMP implementations, known as OMPT [12]. An initial version of OMPT was presented as a "technical report" (TR2) to OpenMP 4.5, and a revised

---

[1] http://openmp.llvm.org.

version of those interfaces is included in OpenMP TR4 which is the working draft for the OpenMP 5.0 standard. Here we explain the differences between OMPT and TRIO.

OMPT is a standard set of interface definitions that allow an external tool to interact with the OpenMP implementation at places where events happen in the conceptual execution of the user's OpenMP code. It is a general framework that, on its own, does not generate any information at all. To use it a performance tool's data collector must be loaded into the application process' address space (normally by using LD_PRELOAD) that then interacts with the OMPT interfaces in the OpenMP runtime library which will then make callbacks into the data collector at the points which were requested. The details of what data is collected and how it is processed or saved are left to the data collection library, and, ultimately, the profiling tool which is used. OMPT is therefore extremely general and intended to support multiple profiling tools.

TRIO has much lower ambition. It is not intended as a general interface standard to support multiple other profilers, nor is it trying to provide detailed analysis of user code. Instead, it is designed easily to provide detailed information about the behavior of the OpenMP runtime code itself, and information for the runtime authors about which runtime interfaces are being used. It is not intended to be portable between different runtimes, or to support general tools. It outputs text files which can be read directly, or post-processed with simple Python scripts.

Since OMPT instrumentation points are specified in terms of the abstract execution model, they are not appropriate for the simple timing of operations inside the OpenMP runtime. For instance, OMPT allows a callback to be made into the data collection library when a thread enters or leaves a worksharing construct such as an omp for/do loop. However, there are no OMPT calls that wrap the entry and exit from the runtime functions which are used to perform loop scheduling operations. TRIO, on the other hand, counts and times these operations explicitly. Similar constraints apply to other areas which we are interested in examining.

When used with a sampling based profiler, the OMPT interfaces can provide information about the internals of an OpenMP runtime. However, for simplicity, TRIO does not use sampling (which potentially requires the installation of a device driver) but simply records timestamps at specific places in the OpenMP runtime and assigns the measured elapsed time to different operations.

3   Methods

To assess the time that an application spends inside the OpenMP runtime we use multiple mechanisms. Firstly, we use the EPCC OpenMP microbenchmarks [13] to measure the overheads of each individual OpenMP construct (Sect. 3.1). Secondly, to count the number of times an application calls a given OpenMP construct and the time each thread spends inside the OpenMP runtime, we instrumented the OpenMP runtime (Sect. 3.2).

3.1   OpenMP Construct Overheads Using Benchmarks

To estimate the wall-clock time an application spends inside the runtime we need to know the number of times a given OpenMP construct is called and the overhead of the construct for a given number of threads. We used the EPCC OpenMP microbenchmarks (v3.1) to measure the overhead of various OpenMP constructs. In addition we extended EPCC to measure the overheads of `#pragma omp for nowait`, which eliminates the barrier at the end of the for loop, thus measuring only the overhead of the `for` construct. To compute the overhead of creating a task, we wrote our own benchmark. We did this to measure just the overhead of task creation, as the numbers reported by EPCC also include the cost of a fork-join barrier in a parallel region.

3.2   Instrumented OpenMP Runtime

We used our instrumented OpenMP library to collect information about the CORAL applications (this instrumented library has been open sourced and is now part of LLVM [14]). The instrumentation provides counters and timers. The counters count the number of times a given OpenMP construct is called. The timers collect information about the amount of time the OpenMP runtime spends in each construct. The timers are classified as either compute time or non-compute time. The compute times represent the time that the application spends doing useful computation, such as time inside a parallel or master region. The non-compute time represents time spent inside the runtime (such as in scheduling an `omp for` construct) or otherwise not doing useful work (such as idle time in worker threads while the master is executing serial code or time spent inside a fork-join or plain barrier). The complete list of compute and non-compute timers is shown in Table 1.

For the instrumentation we used a set of timers to partition the application's clock ticks into a series of separate events. To do this, whenever an event switch occurs, e.g., a thread enters a parallel region, the thread stops its current timer by recording the current time-stamp counter (obtained via the `RDTSC` instruction). Then it starts the next event's timer by again recording the current time-stamp counter. After a timer is stopped, that timer's statistics are updated. In between event switches, there are small gaps of time not counted in any explicit timer which count as timer overhead. When the timer overhead is a relatively large percentage of the application's execution time, this indicates that numerous OpenMP event switches occur and the application is spending too much time inside the OpenMP runtime library. The counters increment whenever a particular event occurs e.g. a parallel region is encountered. They allow the user to see the number of event occurrences during the lifetime of the application.

Overheads in Terms of Resource Units. The instrumented OpenMP runtime measures overhead in terms of resource units, not wall time. (A resource unit represents resources which could have been used, so is measured in CPU seconds, however it is not the same as CPU time measured by the kernel, since

Table 1. OpenMP counters and timers in the instrumented OpenMP runtime

Timers		Counters
Compute time	Non compute time	
OMP_parallel	OMP_plain_barrier	OMP_PARALLEL
OMP_serial	OMP_fork_join_barrier	OMP_NESTED_PARALLEL
OMP_master	FOR_static_scheduling	OMP_FOR_static
OMP_single	FOR_dynamic_scheduling	OMP_FOR_dynamic
OMP_critical	OMP_critical_wait	OMP_DISTRIBUTE
OMP_task_plain_bar	OMP_idle	OMP_BARRIER
OMP_task_immediate		OMP_CRITICAL
OMP_task_taskwait		OMP_SINGLE
OMP_task_taskgroup		OMP_MASTER
OMP_task_join_bar		OMP_TEAMS
OMP_task_taskyield		OMP_set_lock
		OMP_test_lock
		REDUCE_wait
		REDUCE_nowait
		OMP_TASKYIELD
		TASK_executed
		TASK_cancelled
		TASK_stolen

we count time even if a thread has been put to sleep in the kernel and is not executing). Thus if the application is running with 10 threads, when the master thread is running serially between parallel regions, the sequential time in the master thread will be reported as OMP_serial. However, the idle time of the other 9 threads is reported in OMP_idle, which reports the sum of the idle time in each thread. Thus, when the application runs with a large number of threads, a small percentage of serial time can result in a significant amount of idle time. For the synchronization constructs in Table 1, such as plain_barrier or fork_join_barrier, the instrumented OpenMP runtime allows us to measure the amount of time that an application spends in a barrier in terms of resource units, that is, the sum of the times that each thread spends waiting at a barrier. The problem with this metric is that it measures both the time it takes to execute the barrier itself and the imbalance of the barrier. Thus, we have tried to split the time spent executing the barrier from the time the threads are idle due to imbalance. We can do that because we know the number of times a given OpenMP construct is called. In addition, we know the overhead of a given construct (from the EPCC benchmark). Thus, we can assume that the overhead due to the execution of a given construct in the program is #OpenMP_construct * overhead_construct. Hence, we can compute the real imbalance as below. Notice that the overhead of a construct usually depends on the number of threads executing the application, so we need to use the appropriate value.

$$Real\ Imbalance = \frac{cycles\_spent\_in\_a\_construct}{freq\_processor} - (\#construct \times overhead\_\#threads)$$

Walltime Overheads of the OpenMP Runtime. We modeled the wallclock overhead of the OpenMP runtime in addition to the run time of the application. To perform this analysis, we need to compute the time the application spends inside the OpenMP runtime. This can be done by multiplying the number of times an application calls a given construct by the time it takes to execute that construct. Since the total count reported is a sum of calls per thread, we divide it by the number of threads. The overhead of each OpenMP construct can be estimated based on the data collected from the EPCC benchmarks. These times represent the minimum possible time for each construct because all data required for those constructs in EPCC will be in cache, as the benchmark does no other intervening work that might remove that data from cache.

As mentioned in the introduction, the experimental results collected with microbenchmarks do not represent faithfully the usage pattern of the construct in the real application, but we have used them to provide an estimate of the walltime the application spends inside the runtime or the imbalance of the application.

4   Experimental Setup

We performed experiments on an Intel® Xeon Phi™ CPU 7210 (formerly known as "Knights Landing", and referred to here as KNL). Our KNL has 64 cores, 4 threads/core and a frequency of 1.30 GHz. It has 96 GB of RAM (DDR4 2400 MHz, 6 * 16 GB DIMMS), 32 KB of L1 data and instruction cache and 1 MB of L2 cache. The L2 cache is shared by two cores, which comprise a single tile. The KNL also has 16 GB (8 * 2 GB) of MCDRAM. The KNL is configured to be in flat memory mode and quadrant cluster mode. Flat memory mode presents us with the options to use only DDR, both MCDRAM and DDR, or only MCDRAM. The application can be run with our instrumented OpenMP runtime.

We ran experiments for several of the CORAL benchmarks (HACC, Nekbone, QMCPACK, QBOX, CAMSE, UMT and AMG) with varying combinations of MPI ranks and OpenMP threads to find the best performing configuration for a single node run. The runs for overhead analysis were done with the maximum number of OpenMP threads and small data sets, to limit data parallelism and stress the OpenMP runtime. For space reasons we show only selected results.

5   Results

In this Section we show the data collected by TRIO (Sect. 5.1) and the Walltime Overheads of the OpenMP runtime (Sect. 5.2).

5.1   Data from Instrumented OpenMP

In this Section, we report the experimental data. Figure 1 shows the results for HACC. We use radar plots to show the counters for the OpenMP constructs that the application uses. To be able to compare counters across applications, the counters are normalized with respect to the execution time, giving a rate at which the counted event is occurring. Thus, for a given construct, the plots show the $log(\frac{OMPCount \times 10e^9}{TotalTime})$. However, when the quotient becomes smaller than 1, the log becomes a negative value. Thus, for values smaller than 1, we use a linear representation and do not compute the logarithm; for values larger than 1, we compute the logarithm. To visualize this in a single plot, the linear values are represented with a red line, while the logarithmic values are represented with a blue line. This normalization enables us to compare these radar charts across applications.

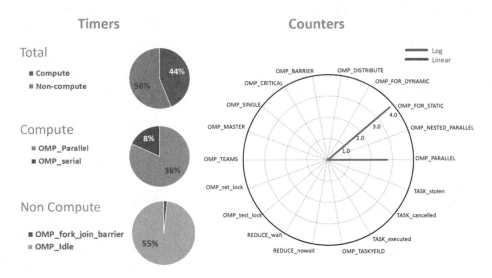

Fig. 1. Timers and counters for HACC. Geometry $= 2 \times 2 \times 2$, NP $= 128$, 8 MPI Rank and 8 OpenMP threads

Pie plots are used to represent the OpenMP timers. First, the total time of the application is decomposed in compute and non-compute time. Then, the compute and non-compute times are further decomposed in separate pie plots. Remember that these times are measured in terms of resource units, not wall times, as explained in Sect. 3.2. In Fig. 1, the pie-charts show the distribution of total time in terms of compute and non-compute time. With a configuration of 8 MPI Ranks and 8 OpenMP threads we see 44% compute time and 56% non-compute time. The major share of non-compute here is due to OMP_idle which appears as a result of the 8% OMP_serial time in the compute region, which means that 7 threads have no work to do, so they are idle. Therefore $7 \times 8\% \approx 56\%$ of the resources are idle

Table 2. HACC real imbalance. Geometry $= 2 \times 2 \times 2$, NP $= 128$, 8 MPI ranks and 8 OpenMP threads, Runtime $= 29.51$ s

Construct	Application imbalance (%)	Runtime overhead (%)
OMP_fork_join_barrier	0.05	0.64

for this period, which is close to 55% time reported by TRIO. The counters are represented using radar charts. For this application, the non-zero values were high and the linear representation was not needed. Table 2 splits the barrier time into imbalance and barrier overhead using the method explained in Sect. 3.2. Imbalance is a property of the application, but barrier time might be improved with a better barrier implementation or improved hardware. Overall we see that the main problem with this application is that a significant portion of time is spent in a serial region and as the number of cores increases, this causes a lot of inefficiency. Notice that the overhead of TRIO is very low. In fact, in our experiments, we barely see any difference between the runtimes of the application running with TRIO versus the runtimes of the application running with the un-instrumented OpenMP library.

The radar and pie plots used here are not part of TRIO itself. TRIO generates a text file (shown in the Appendix at the end) that contains all the information needed to assess the impact of the OpenMP runtime on the application running times. We have written separate Python scripts that process the information in that text file to obtain these plots.

5.2   Walltime Overheads of the OpenMP Runtime

In this Section, we analyze the wallclock overhead of the OpenMP runtime. For that, we have used the overheads of the different OpenMP constructs on KNL for the different number of threads using the EPCC benchmarks, as shown in Table 3. Since our KNL machine has 64 cores, for number of threads ≤ 64, we placed one Thread per Core (1T/C). For larger number of threads, we placed more than one thread per core (2-4T/C). As explained in Sect. 3.1, the overheads of `task creation` and `for nowait` (in the last two columns in Table 3), were measured using our own benchmarks. As the table shows, these overheads increase with the number of threads. The increase rate is different for each construct, but in all the cases it is significantly less than linear.

Table 5 shows the walltime overheads of the OpenMP runtime for the different CORAL applications. We performed this study with 1 MPI rank and 256 OpenMP threads running on KNL (notice that this point is rarely the one that delivers the best speedups; actually, for some applications it gives significant slowdowns, but this ensures the maximum OpenMP overhead). For each application, the walltime is shown in Table 4. Table 5 also shows the number of times a construct is called and the overhead of each construct for 256 threads. Based on these times, the table shows the percentage of time each application spends in the OpenMP runtime; this is $\leq 1\%$ of the time in most cases.

Table 3. OpenMP construct overheads for different number of threads. Experimental data were collected using the EPCC benchmark on KNL. (T/C = threads/core)

OpenMP threads	Overhead times (µs)								
	BARRIER	FOR	PARALLEL	PARALLEL FOR	REDUCTION	SINGLE	CRITICAL	Task-creation	FOR-nowait
1 (1T/C)	0.08	0.20	0.81	0.93	1.00	0.19	0.24	0.44	0.13
2 (1T/C)	0.46	0.63	1.51	1.75	1.73	0.53	0.23	0.77	0.16
4 (1T/C)	0.93	1.13	2.12	2.34	2.34	1.12	0.57	0.77	0.16
8 (1T/C)	1.72	1.90	3.00	2.96	3.12	2.03	0.60	0.77	0.16
16 (1T/C)	2.21	2.42	3.29	3.52	6.83	2.70	0.64	0.78	0.16
32 (1T/C)	3.12	3.29	4.38	4.61	8.71	3.89	0.79	0.8	0.16
64 (1T/C)	4.33	5.23	6.03	6.29	11.66	5.91	0.90	0.8	0.17
128 (2T/C)	5.74	6.25	8.38	8.71	15.68	6.78	1.01	1.57	0.24
192 (3T/C)	7.21	7.74	10.49	11.09	20.26	7.94	1.21	2.60	0.33
256 (4T/C)	8.77	9.96	12.45	13.60	24.73	9.45	1.52	4.38	0.40

Table 4. Runtime of application with 1 MPI rank and 256 OpenMP threads (KNL)

Application	MPI ranks	OpenMP threads	Input size	Time (s)
Nekbone	1	256	NELM:4096	10.46
QMCPACK	1	256	DMCSAMPLES = 1280	1881.7
HACC	1	256	NG = 64	36.83
QBOX	1	256	mgo.N64.i	116.6
UMT	1	256	numzones(5, 5, 5)	33.27
AMG	8	32	-r 36 36 36	12.05

Table 5. Overheads due to OpenMP constructs w.r.t. wall clock time (KNL)

OpenMP Constructs	Counters/thread						EPCC Overheads (µs)	Overhead(%)					
	Nekbone	QMCPACK	HACC	UMT	QBOX	AMG		Nekbone	QMCPACK	HACC	UMT	QBOX	AMG
OMP_PARALLEL	2	-	30830	1210	974480	9520	12.45	0.00	-	1.04	0.05	10.41	0.98
OMP_FOR_STATIC	0	7344	30781	1206	972109	9514	0.39	0.00	0.00	0.03	0.00	0.33	0.03
OMP_BARRIER	3606	-	-	-	-	-	8.77	0.30	-	-	-	-	-
OMP_CRITICAL	0	35	-	-	-	-	1.52	0.00	0.00	-	-	-	-
OMP_SINGLE	1	-	-	-	-	-	25.96	0.00	-	-	-	-	-
OMP_MASTER	5	-	-	-	-	-	-	0.00	-	-	-	-	-
REDUCE_nowait	-	80	-	-	-	3167	24.73	-	0.00	-	-	-	0.65

For HACC, the application spends 1% of time inside `#pragma omp parallel`, but this application has 30830 calls to `#pragma omp parallel`, for a walltime of 36 s (an average of about 850 fork-join operations per second, or one every 1.2 ms). Nekbone spends 0.3% of time inside the OpenMP barrier, but this application executes 3606 barrier in walltime of 10 s (one every 2.8 ms). AMG spends around 1.66% of time inside the OpenMP runtime due to fork-join constructs and reduce constructs when running with 8 MPI ranks and 32 threads.

QBOX is the only application that spends a non-negligible amount of time (10.74%) inside the OpenMP runtime. This is due to the large number of fork-join constructs when running with a single MPI rank and 256 threads, when it executes an average of 8400 fork-join constructs per second (one every 119 μs). In fact, it seems there is a linear relationship between the frequency of fork-join constructs and the overhead of the OpenMP runtime. In HACC, with a frequency of about 850 fork-join constructs per second, we have 1% overhead, whereas for QBOX, with a frequency 10 times greater (8400 fork-join constructs per second), we have 10% overhead. Remember that these are worst case scenario numbers, because a fork-join construct for 256 threads has a cost of 13.60 μs while for 64 threads it has a cost of 6.29 μs and the application is not scaling, so we are paying a higher overhead in the runtime, while the application is not running faster with the added threads. We notice that for QBOX the best configuration is 16 MPI ranks and 4 threads per rank with walltime of 11.15 s and 1.70% overhead due to fork-join constructs. In this case, there are a total of 89860 `#pragma omp parallel` calls i.e., 8060 calls per second. Even though the frequency of call is approximately the same, the cost of fork-join construct is 6 times greater for 256 threads than for 4 threads (2.34 μs versus 13.6 μs).

To assess the overheads of TRIO we ran the CLOMP benchmark, only for static scheduling, 10 times with and without TRIO. It was observed that at times, runs using TRIO completed faster than non-TRIO runs. CLOMP was run as `./clomp 64 -1 512000 400 32 1 100` and reported runtime of about 30–31 s for all the runs. The difference between the fastest and slowest runs with the two configurations varied from −4.71% to 4.66%. This can be attributed to the variability in runtime across executions of the same configuration. For example, the difference between the best and worst runtimes of the 10 executions of CLOMP without TRIO show a difference of 4.49%. The raw TRIO output for a single run is included in the Appendix.

6   Examples of How to Use TRIO

In this Section, we discuss some examples of how to use TRIO. In the first example we discuss how TRIO can be used to analyze the time spent inside the OpenMP runtime. For example, if an application calls `#pragma omp parallel for` inside an outer serial loop, the application will incur the overhead of the fork-join once for each outer iteration. Sometimes this can be avoided by placing `#pragma omp parallel` outside the loop so that the fork-join only happens once. Here we show such a scenario in QMCPACK.

We have evaluated three different versions of the QMCPACK microbenchmark, "baseline", "nested" and "parallel-for", as shown in Figs. 2(a), (b) and (c), respectively. "Baseline" represents the best implementation. This version divides the OpenMP threads into application teams[2], the number of application teams

---

[2] These are application teams and crews and do not refer to OpenMP constructs.

```
1   #pragma omp parallel      #pragma omp parallel      #pragma omp parallel
2   {                         {                         {
3   int var=0;                int var=0;                int var=0;
4   int ip=tid();
5   int kI=L/crews*ip;
6   int kF=L/crews*(ip+1);    #pragma omp parallel
7                             {                         for(i=0;i<N;i++){
8   for(i=0;i<N;i++){         for(i=0;i<N;i++){          for(j=0;j<M;j++){
9    for(j=0;j<M;j++){         for(j=0;j<M;j++){
10
11   //explicit               #pragma omp for nowait    #pragma omp parallel for
12   for(k=kI; k<kF;k++)        for(k=0; k<L;k++)          for(k=0; k<L;k++)
13   {                         {                         {
14    ...                      ...                       ...
15   }                         }                         }
16
17                            #pragma omp master        //NxM fork-join constructs
18   var++;                    var++;                    var++;
19   }                         }                         }
20                            //N plain barriers
21                            #pragma omp barrier
22  }}                        }}}                       }}
23    (a) baseline                (b) nested               (c) parallel-for
```

Fig. 2. QMCPACK pseudo-code. For simplicity, $L\%crews == 0$.

depends on the number of crews, i.e. for 256 threads with 4 crews, there are 64 teams. The work of an individual team is divided among its 4 crew members. This code exploits parallelism in a similar way to that obtained by nesting, but without using nesting, and it is the programmer who takes care of data mapping. The dimension of the work is NxMxL. We use var++ to represent a big code section for synchronization and reduction among the crews in a team.

Both "nested" and "parallel-for" exploit nested OpenMP parallelism. The major difference is the placement of nested parallel. In the "nested" version the nested parallel is placed outside a series of for loops and the main kernel calls #pragma omp for for parallelism. This approach makes threads perform redundant, replicated, computation but reduces the number of fork-joins. The "parallel for" version calls the level 2 parallelism from within a series of for loops. This leads to multiple fork-joins, hence greatly increasing the running times.

Figure 3 show the counters and execution times for the three different code versions in Fig. 2 running on KNL. The configurations compared are for the same amount of work. The splines for input were set to 2k, the tile size was chosen to be 64, and experiments were run for 100 iterations.

The implementation of the "parallel-for" code has about 1M more fork and join barriers due to the placement of the nested parallel region. As a result, the "parallel-for" code is significantly slower than the "nested" version (3750 s versus 1554 s). In the "nested" version threads perform some redundant work and use a plain barrier and master constructs, but this version significantly reduces the number of fork-join constructs This example shows how to reduce OpenMP overheads by considering the overheads of different runtime constructs and removing costly ones. Notice that the difference in execution times between

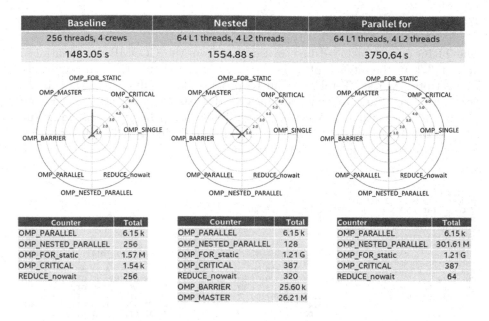

Baseline	Nested	Parallel for
256 threads, 4 crews	64 L1 threads, 4 L2 threads	64 L1 threads, 4 L2 threads
1483.05 s	1554.88 s	3750.64 s

Counter	Total
OMP_PARALLEL	6.15 k
OMP_NESTED_PARALLEL	256
OMP_FOR_static	1.57 M
OMP_CRITICAL	1.54 k
REDUCE_nowait	256

Counter	Total
OMP_PARALLEL	6.15 k
OMP_NESTED_PARALLEL	128
OMP_FOR_static	1.21 G
OMP_CRITICAL	387
REDUCE_nowait	320
OMP_BARRIER	25.60 k
OMP_MASTER	26.21 M

Counter	Total
OMP_PARALLEL	6.15 k
OMP_NESTED_PARALLEL	301.61 M
OMP_FOR_static	1.21 G
OMP_CRITICAL	387
REDUCE_nowait	64

Fig. 3. Counters for baseline, nested and parallel-for QMCPACK versions

"baseline" and "nested" is small (1483 vs. 1554 s). A similar problem to the one in "parallel-for" version is observed in the QBOX(1M fork-joins) and AMG codes.

TRIO also helps to identify cases where frequent calls do not represent an issue with small number of threads, but as the number of threads increases, the construct overhead becomes a significant contributor to total non-compute time. One such example is seen with the QBOX benchmark code, as shown in Table 5.

7   Conclusion

In this paper, we have discussed TRIO, a simple and easy to use tool that collects information about an application's use of the OpenMP runtime. TRIO is useful for an initial performance evaluation, specially in complex codes, where OpenMP directives are nested inside MPI, but not to fine tune applications. TRIO is also useful to optimize the OpenMP runtime itself. TRIO does not require any change in the application (not even relinking), has negligible overhead, and does not need a GUI. Counters and timers in TRIO provide feedback to the user about the OpenMP runtime overheads. According to our observations, well written codes should normally spend a small amount of time inside the OpenMP runtime.

Acknowledgement. This material is based upon work supported by Subcontract No. B609815 with Argonne National Laboratory and Intel Federal LLC. We thank professor John Mellor-Crummey for his feedback on OMPT and its comparison with TRIO.

Appendix

The TRIO output included here in Fig. 4 is from the CLOMP run mentioned in Sect. 3.2. In the interest of space, we have included only the non-zero fields. The scripts use the "Total" column to process the results. Even though the fork and join barrier times are measured separately, we sum them up for plots. The raw output provides a clearer relationship between OMP_idle and OMP_serial, i.e. Total_OMP_idle can be computed using Total_OMP_serial as, $((num\_threads) - 1) \times Total\_OMP\_serial$.

```
# Time of run: Wed Jun 7 16:31:00 2017
# Hostname: node002.default
# CPU:  Intel(R) Xeon Phi(TM) CPU 7210 @ 1.30GHz
# Family: 6, Model: 87, Stepping: 1
# Nominal frequency:   1.30 GHz
Statistics on exit
Aggregate for all threads
Timer,                        ,Sample Count,    Min,       Mean,        Max,       Total,          SD
OMP_worker_thread_life        ,   64.00  ,   37.77 GT,   37.79 GT,   37.86 GT,    2.42 TT,   12.59 MT
FOR_static_scheduling         ,   1.41 k ,  520.00  T,    3.00 kT,   44.42 kT,    4.22 MT,    2.26 kT
OMP_idle                      ,   1.39 k ,   20.01 kT,  594.15 MT,   10.19 GT,  823.50 GT,    2.18 GT
OMP_fork_barrier              ,   1.47 k ,    3.21 kT,   12.57 MT,   87.70 MT,   18.49 GT,   15.96 MT
OMP_join_barrier              ,   1.41 k ,  767.00  T,    3.37 MT,    3.33 GT,    4.74 GT,   88.70 MT
OMP_parallel                  ,   1.41 k ,  183.71 MT,    1.11 GT,   19.71 GT,    1.56 TT,    4.05 GT
OMP_serial                    ,   1.00   ,   13.17 GT,   13.17 GT,   13.17 GT,   13.17 GT,    0.00  T
OMP_set_numthreads            ,   2.00   ,   64.00  ,   64.00  ,   64.00  ,  128.00  ,    0.00
OMP_PARALLEL_args             ,  22.00   ,    0.00  ,  909.09 m ,    1.00  ,   20.00  ,  287.48 m
FOR_static_iterations         ,   1.41 k ,  512.00 k ,  512.00 k ,  512.00 k ,  720.90 M ,    0.00
Total_OMP_worker_thread_life, 64.00  ,   37.77 GT,   37.79 GT,   37.86 GT,    2.42 TT,   12.59 MT
Total_FOR_static_scheduling ,  64.00  ,   23.47 kT,   65.94 MT,   91.43 kT,    4.22 MT,   15.21 kT
Total_OMP_idle              ,  64.00  ,    0.00  T,   12.87 GT,   13.07 GT,  823.50 GT,    1.62 GT
Total_OMP_fork_barrier      ,  64.00  ,  592.33 kT,  288.97 MT,  414.86 MT,   18.49 GT,   64.66 MT
Total_OMP_join_barrier      ,  64.00  ,   44.71 kT,   74.05 MT,    3.67 GT,    4.74 GT,  455.33 MT
Total_OMP_parallel          ,  64.00  ,   21.02 GT,   24.34 GT,   24.49 GT,    1.56 TT,  421.89 MT
Total_OMP_serial            ,  64.00  ,    0.00  T,  205.77 MT,   13.17 GT,   13.17 GT,    1.63 GT

Counter,                      ThreadCount,    Min,       Mean,        Max,       Total,        SD
OMP_PARALLEL                  ,   1.00  ,   22.00  ,   22.00  ,   22.00  ,   22.00  ,   0.00
OMP_NESTED_PARALLEL           ,  64.00  ,    0.00  ,    0.00  ,    0.00  ,    0.00  ,   0.00
OMP_FOR_static                ,  64.00  ,   22.00  ,   22.00  ,   22.00  ,   1.41 k ,   0.00
```

Fig. 4. Raw output from TRIO

References

1. Shende, S.S., Malony, A.D.: The Tau parallel performance system. Int. J. High Perform. Comput. Appl. **20**(2), 287–311 (2006)
2. Intel Vtune Amplifier. https://software.intel.com/en-us/intel-vtune-amplifier-xe
3. CORAL Benchmarks. https://asc.llnl.gov/CORAL-benchmarks/

4. Barthou, D., Charif Rubial, A., Jalby, W., Koliai, S., Valensi, C.: Performance tuning of x86 OpenMP codes with MAQAO. In: Müller, M., Resch, M., Schulz, A., Nagel, W. (eds.) Tools for High Performance Computing, pp. 95–113. Springer, Heidelberg (2010)

5. Fürlinger, K., Gerndt, M.: ompP: a profiling tool for OpenMP. In: Mueller, M.S., Chapman, B.M., Supinski, B.R., Malony, A.D., Voss, M. (eds.) IWOMP 2005. LNCS, vol. 4315, pp. 15–23. Springer, Heidelberg (2008). doi:10.1007/978-3-540-68555-5_2

6. Mohr, B., Wolf, F.: KOJAK – a tool set for automatic performance analysis of parallel programs. In: Kosch, H., Böszörményi, L., Hellwagner, H. (eds.) Euro-Par 2003. LNCS, vol. 2790, pp. 1301–1304. Springer, Heidelberg (2003). doi:10.1007/978-3-540-45209-6_177

7. Geimer, M., Wolf, F., Wylie, B., Abraham, E., Becker, D., Mohr, B.: The Scalasca performance toolset architecture. Concurr. Comput. Pract. Exper. 22(6), 702–719 (2010)

8. Knupfer, A., Brunst, H., Doleschal, J., Jurenz, M., Lieber, M., Mickler, H., Muller, M., Nagel, W.: The Vampir Performance analysis tool set. In: Resch, M., Keller, R., Himmler, V., Krammer, B., Schulz, A. (eds.) Tools for High Performance Computing, pp. 139–155. Springer, Berlin, Heidelberg (2008)

9. Mohr, B., Malony, A., Shende, S., Wolf, F.: Design and prototype of a performance tool interface for OpenMP. J. Supercomput. 23(1), 105–128 (2002)

10. Itzkowitz, M., Mazurov, O., Copay, N., Lin, Y.: An OpenMP runtime API for profiling, OpenMP official ARB White Paper 314, pp. 181–190 (2007)

11. HPC Toolkit. http://hpctoolkit.org/manual/HPCToolkit-users-manual.pdf

12. Eichenberger, A.E., et al.: OMPT: an OpenMP tools application programming interface for performance analysis. In: Rendell, A.P., Chapman, B.M., Müller, M.S. (eds.) IWOMP 2013. LNCS, vol. 8122, pp. 171–185. Springer, Heidelberg (2013). doi:10.1007/978-3-642-40698-0_13

13. Bull, J.M., O'Neill, D.: A microbenchmark suite for OpenMP 2.0. SIGARCH Comput. Archit. News 29(5), 41–48 (2001)

14. LLVM OpenMP. openmp.llvm.org

Assessing the Performance of OpenMP Programs on the Knights Landing Architecture

Dirk Schmidl[✉], Bo Wang, and Matthias S. Müller

Chair for High Performance Computing, IT Center, RWTH Aachen University,
Aachen, Germany
{schmidl,wang,mueller}@itc.rwth-aachen.de

Abstract. Intel's Knights Landing processor (KNL) is the latest product in the Xeon Phi product line. As a self-hosted system it is the first commercially available many-core architecture which can run unmodified applications. This makes KNL a very interesting option for HPC centers which have to support many different applications including community and ISV codes, where code changes are hard or impossible. Of course running any application and running any application efficiently is not the same, so it remains to investigate how efficient KNL is in executing unmodified codes from x86 servers.

In this work we will investigate the Knights Landing architecture with a focus on its ability to run OpenMP applications efficiently. Kernel benchmarks are used to investigate basic characteristics like memory latency and bandwidth. Furthermore, application-like benchmarks like the NAS parallel benchmarks or SPEC OpenMP benchmarks are used as well as real applications from RWTH Aachen University. The performance is compared to a 2-socket Broadwell system. We consider this a fair comparison as both architectures are state-of-the-art today and both roughly cost the same amount of money and consume the same amount of energy.

1 Introduction

The latest generation of the Intel Xeon Phi family, the Knights Landing (KNL), is delivered as a stand-alone server. Compared to the predecessor, Knights Corner, and other accelerators, this eliminates the need to use a host server and transfer data over a relatively slow PCIe bus. From a total-cost-of-ownership (TCO) perspective this is very attractive, since the host server is also a significant cost factor in accelerator based clusters and using host and accelerator simultaneously in an application has proven to be extremely difficult.

Many operators of high-performance computing centers with a large and diverse user community hesitate to use accelerators as the main working horse, because they require code changes from all users. For such centers the KNL architecture offers an attractive alternative as it offers theoretical peak performance comparable to accelerator based systems without the need for code changes. However, the fact that code written for host systems can be executed on a KNL system does not necessarily mean that the application performs as desired.

© Springer International Publishing AG 2017
B.R. de Supinski et al. (Eds.): IWOMP 2017, LNCS 10468, pp. 296–308, 2017.
DOI: 10.1007/978-3-319-65578-9_20

In this work we want to answer the question if the Intel KNL architecture is able to replace a two socket host system for shared memory applications. Therefore, we compare a two-socket Intel Broadwell based system with KNL. The purchase price we got for both systems differs by 3%, furthermore the energy consumption is nearly identical (215 W for KNL and 2x 105 W for Broadwell). As the purchase price and operation costs of both systems are nearly identical, the system performance determines the most attractive architecture. As many developers of community codes or ISVs as well as in-house application developers do not optimize their code for every new architecture, we want to investigate the performance without manual architecture specific optimization in this work (Only recompilation for KNL is done). We focus on applications parallelized with OpenMP in this paper as the most widely used paradigm for shared-memory parallelization in HPC.

The paper is structured as follows: We present related work in Sect. 2 and describe the platforms used in Sect. 3. Then kernel benchmark results to investigate machine characteristics are presented in Sect. 4, before we present results for more application like benchmarks (i.e. NAS parallel benchmarks and SPEC OMP benchmarks) in Sect. 5. Finally, we present results for real application codes developed at RWTH Aachen in Sect. 6 and conclude in Sect. 7.

2   Related Work

Previous studies show that throughput-oriented processors like GPUs are one way to fulfill the requirement for more and more compute capabilities. This is not only valid for dense linear algebra kernels [17], but also for memory-bound kernels like sparse matrix vector multiplication [2] (depending on the matrix storage format). The Intel Xeon Phi coprocessor Knights Corner (KNC) has also proven to deliver high throughput performance under some circumstances [5]. In order to benefit from the compute capabilities of GPUs or KNC, programming offload kernels either direct through CUDA [12] or OpenCL [8] or through higher-level directive based abstractions like OpenMP [13] is required. In contrast, the Intel Xeon Phi processor Knights Landing investigated throughout this work is not operated as a PCIe accelerator card which makes this offloading step unnecessary. The KNL is a throughput-optimized host processor rather than an accelerator. The KNL platform is brand new as well as Intel's published optimization guidelines [15]. Intel also provided several performance results for KNL, but an independent performance evaluation of the architecture was not present at the time of writing this article.

Benchmarks to investigate the performance of different aspects of an architecture have been developed in many different studies. Standard benchmarks to investigate the memory performance of a system are the Stream benchmark [9] and the LMBench benchmark suite [10]. For OpenMP programs the EPCC microbenchmarks [3,4] can be used to measure the overhead of OpenMP constructs. Furthermore, benchmark suites exist which can be used to compare the performance of architectures and OpenMP implementations for application-like kernels, e.g. the SPEC OMP benchmark suite [11] or the NAS parallel benchmarks [1]. For OpenMP programs using the new tasking paradigm the Barcelona OpenMP Task Suite (BOTS) [6] can be used. All of these benchmarks come with published performance results on different architectures, but only a very few results for KNL are present so far. Furthermore, this article focuses on different characteristics of the machine and compares it to a state-of-the-art 2-socket host system. The insights gained hereby cannot be obtained by a single benchmark suite as the goal is to give an overall evaluation for OpenMP programs instead of focusing on a single aspect. We performed a similar study for the predecessor architecture KNC [16], where we compared the KNC to a SandyBridge host system which was the current Xeon host at that time.

3   Architecture Comparison

In this section we compare the architectural differences between both investigated systems, the Intel Knights Landing and the 2-socket Broadwell server.

3.1   Intel Knights Landing

The core used in KNL is based on the Silvermont microarchitecture with changes for HPC. The probably most important change is the addition of two 512-bit wide vector units to each core. Two cores together with a shared L2 cache of 1 MB and a Tag Directory (TD) form a tile which is the building block of this architecture. Up to 36 tiles are placed on a chip connected cache-coherently through a 2D-mesh topology, as sketched in Fig. 1(a). 16 GB of MCDRAM which is high-bandwidth memory is also located on-package. Furthermore, up to 384 GB of DDR4 memory can be attached to the KNL.

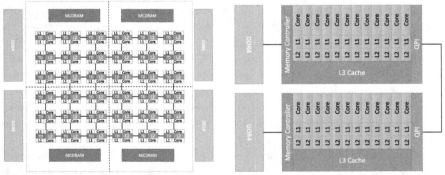

(a) Sketch of the Intel Knights Landing architecture

(b) High-level view of the Broadwell system

Fig. 1. Comparison of both test systems

The version of KNL investigated throughout this work is an Intel Xeon Phi Processor 7210 with 64 cores, a base frequency of 1.30 GHz and 96 GB of DDR4 memory.

The Knights Landing has different modes of operation which can be configured through BIOS options. Two of them which are investigated further in this work are:

Memory Modes: The high-bandwidth memory (HBM), i.e. the MCDRAM, can be operated in three different modes.

Cache Mode: If booted in cache mode, the HBM is used as a 16 GB cache. The memory is not visible to the user and used data is automatically cached into HBM. This mode is the most convenient usage mode, as no changes to software or environment are needed.

Flat Mode: The HBM is visible to Linux and the user as a NUMA node in the system without any core associated to it. As a result all cores allocate memory in DRAM first, according to the first-touch policy applied by Linux. The user explicitly has to make use of the HBM by allocating on the corresponding NUMA node using Linux mechanisms for NUMA aware memory placement, e.g. `libnuma` API calls or the command line tool `numactl`.

Hybrid Mode: The hybrid mode is a combination of both other modes. A part of the memory is used as cache and the other part is provided to the user as a separate NUMA node. Possible splittings are 8 GB/8 GB or 4 GB/12 GB.

Cluster Modes: Different cluster modes allow to control the memory usage of the cores further. The three most important modes are:

All-to-all: In this mode, all cores use all memory addresses without any preference. So there is no mapping between tile, tag directory and memory location.

Quadrant: As depicted in Fig. 1(a) the chip can be virtually divided in four quadrants. In this mode, addresses are hashed to a tag directory (TD) in the same quadrant of the chip as the memory. This results in short distances between TD and memory reducing the overall traffic on the 2D-mesh interconnect. The core accessing the memory can still be in any quadrant of the KNL.

Sub-NUMA-clustering: When sub-NUMA-clustering (SNC-4) is used, each quadrant is used as an individual NUMA node. When the application is programmed in a NUMA aware manner this allows to have the accessing core, the tag directory and the memory located in the same quadrant in many cases, reducing the traffic over the 2D-mesh interconnect even further.

3.2   Broadwell System

The Broadwell based server used in this comparison is a 2-socket system equipped with Intel Xeon E5-2650v4 processors clocked at 2.20 GHz. As illustrated from a high-level perspective in Fig. 1(b), each chip contains 12 cores where each core has a private L1 and L2 cache and all cores on a chip share a 30 MB L3 cache. Each socket is connected to 64 GB of main memory and the two sockets are coupled cache-coherently through the Quick-Path Interconnect (QPI). This leads to a Non Uniform Memory Access (NUMA) architecture with 24 cores and 128 GB of memory.

4   Kernel Benchmarks

This section contains results of basic kernel benchmarks on the KNL and Broadwell test systems. Kernel tests are used to investigate single machine characteristics. Understanding the behavior of kernels is therefore a prerequisite to understand the performance of complex application codes. All tests throughout this work were compiled using the Intel Compiler v.16.0.

4.1   Memory Performance

First, the performance of the memory subsystem is investigated. Many applications in HPC are bound by memory accesses and since the KNL is the first x86 architecture with HBM on-chip, these tests give a first indication of the system performance.

Latency: A benchmark to measure the latency to access memory with a random access pattern was used. The benchmark is similar to the pointer-chasing benchmark in the LMbench benchmark suite [10], but it uses a pre-computed random offset for every access to prevent prefetching. The benchmark runs single threaded and with an increasing memory footprint.

Figure 2 shows the memory access latency per data element on Broadwell and for different scenarios on KNL. `KNL-ram` and `KNL-hbm` are measured with the HBM in flat mode, where `numactl` is used to let the benchmark use the DDR (`KNL-ram`) or HBM (`KNL-hbm`). For `KNL-cache` measurements the HBM was running in cache mode.

For a small memory footprint typical cache behavior can be observed on both systems. The latency increases with every cache level and levels out after the

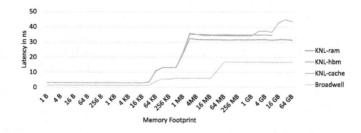

Fig. 2. Memory latency for different memory footprints on the KNL and Broadwell system

capacity of the last level cache is reached, 1 MB L2 on the KNL and 30 MB L3 on the Broadwell system. On the Broadwell system the latency to main memory, observed for all larger memory footprints is then about 17 ns and on the KNL a performance between 30 and 35 ns is reached for both, DDR and HBM. For latency bound applications there seems to be no difference in the performance of the on-chip and off-chip memory. If the KNL is running in cache mode, the latency is the same as long as the memory footprint does not exceed the capacity of the HBM (i.e. 16 GB). For larger arrays the latency increases as the KNL first needs to check in the cache (HBM) before the data is loaded from DDR. The frequency of the KNL is lower than the frequency of the Broadwell system, a memory load takes about 37 cycles on Broadwell and 38 cycles on the KNL, so the difference in performance is negligible.

Bandwidth: Bandwidth is another important characteristic of an architecture, as more HPC applications are bound by bandwidth constraints and not latency constraints. We used the STREAM benchmark [9] to investigate the memory bandwidth. STREAM performs simple vector operations on large vectors and calculates the bandwidth. Results presented in Fig. 3 are for the `Triad` operation and for different memory footprints. The benchmark was run with 256 threads on the KNL and 24 threads on the Broadwell system. OpenMP affinity support was used to achieve a `close` thread binding.

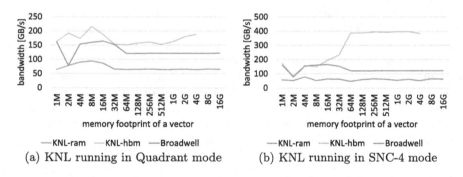

(a) KNL running in Quadrant mode   (b) KNL running in SNC-4 mode

Fig. 3. Memory bandwidth reached on the Broadwell and KNL system measured with STREAM for different memory footprints

In Fig. 3(a) the maximum memory bandwidth achieved is shown for the Broadwell system and the KNL system running in Quadrant clustering mode. Quadrant mode is the default mode. Figure 3(b) shows the same with the KNL running in SNC-4 mode. On the Broadwell system it can be observed that for smaller memory sizes a performance of up to 150 GB/s is reached within the L3 cache, but for larger arrays the bandwidth levels out at about 120 GB/s. Accessing the DDR memory the KNL shows a similar behavior with overall lower performance, the bandwidth levels out at about 65 GB/s. The HBM achieves a better performance and reaches between 150 and 200 GB/s for larger memory footprints in quadrant and up-to 400 GB/s in SNC4 mode.

We assume the reason for the worse performance in Quadrant mode is a lot of traffic on the 2D-mesh interconnect and as a result a lot of contention. For memory bound applications it seems to be a good set-up to run the KNL in SNC-4 mode.

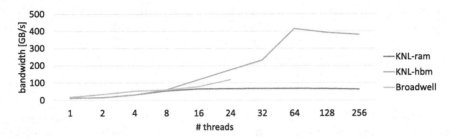

Fig. 4. Bandwidth reached for an increasing number of threads on the Broadwell and the KNL system

The speedup of memory bound application is often limited by the scaling of the memory bandwidth with the number of threads. Figure 4 shows the achieved bandwidth for an increasing number of threads on both systems. A `close` OpenMP thread placement is used. On the Broadwell system the typical behavior of a 2-socket Xeon based machine is observed, the memory bandwidth of one socket is saturated with roughly half of the cores of a socket and a boost in performance can be observed once the second socket is also used. This is because the second socket has its own memory channels which increase the overall bandwidth reached. On the KNL the bandwidth of the DDR memory can be saturated with only 8 threads whereas the bandwidth increases for the HBM up to 64 threads. This indicates, that the scaling of bandwidth bound applications depends a lot on the ability to use the HBM.

4.2 Synchronization Overhead

Another important performance aspect of OpenMP programs is the overhead introduced by OpenMP constructs. In general the overhead rises with the number of threads and since the KNL requires to use a lot of threads to utilize the whole system, the OpenMP runtime overhead will be more important on such a system. On the other hand, the system resides on a single chip in contrast to the 2-socket Broadwell system, and thus the physical distances between cores is shorter which might lower the synchronization overhead. We present performance results obtained with the OpenMP EPCC microbenchmarks (see [3,4]).

Table 1 shows the overhead of synchronization constructs and for task creation measured on both target systems. The overhead of a `parallel for` construct with a static scheduling, a `barrier` construct and of a reduction operation

Table 1. Overhead in microseconds of OpenMP constructs measured with the EPCC microbenchmarks on KNL and Broadwell

KNL						Broadwell				
#thr	Parallel for	Barrier	Reduction	Parallel tasks	Master tasks	#thr	Parallel for	Barrier	Reduction	Parallel tasks	Master tasks
1	0.80	0.08	1.33	0.32	0.32	1	0.14	0.01	0.15	0.05	0.05
4	5.93	1.54	5.93	1.28	3.39	4	0.74	0.40	0.89	0.08	2.56
8	6.75	2.35	6.84	2.37	7.91	8	1.02	0.70	2.00	0.37	7.92
32	8.74	4.05	14.13	3.24	66.80	12	1.26	0.80	2.28	0.39	14.30
64	9.32	4.66	15.74	5.91	157.03	24	2.49	1.51	4.60	3.56	79.03
256	26.77	8.17	22.52	34.01	815.58	48	3.27	2.10	6.63	11.14	146.88

is shown. For task creation the overhead to create tasks with all threads in parallel (**parallel task**) and when only the master thread creates tasks (**master tasks**) is presented. Note that in the latter case all threads will start executing tasks out of the master's task queue which involves locking.

For all constructs it can be observed, that the overhead is higher on the KNL system compared to Broadwell. Creating a team of threads and distributing a loop takes 26.77 µs compared to 3.27 µs on the Broadwell system. Of course on the KNL many more threads need to be created or picked out of the thread pool, but since the architecture requires such a large amount of threads to utilize all cores efficiently this needs to be taken into account. The barrier, reduction and both task creation operations are still slower on the KNL, but only by a factor of about 4 to 5. This might still be a problem for scaling of an application, but in most cases reduction operations and barriers are not used that frequently.

Kernel tests in this chapter have shown, that there are no large differences in the memory latency on both systems relative to the clock rate of the system. On the KNL also no difference between both types of memory (DDR and HBM) could be observed regarding latency. The bandwidth however differed a lot, while the DDR on KNL delivered roughly half the bandwidth of the Broadwell system (65 GB/s vs. 120 GB/s), the HBM was able to deliver 400 GB/s if the SNC-4 mode was used. For memory bound applications using the HBM seems to be key to reaching good performance on the KNL. Synchronization in OpenMP constructs was slower in all cases on the KNL but only by a factor of 4–5. This can be a performance blocker for applications frequently synchronizing or creating many small tasks but for many applications this performance should be acceptable.

5   Benchmarks

The kernel benchmarks presented so far help understand single machine characteristics like the reached memory bandwidth. The performance of real applications of course is influenced by many of these characteristics. Therefore, in this section performance results are presented for application-like benchmarks.

5.1 NAS Parallel Benchmarks

The NAS Parallel Benchmarks [1] are a set of benchmarks designed by NASA Ames to evaluate the performance of parallel supercomputers. We ran the OpenMP parallel reference implementation of version 3.3 and used the input size C for all tests.

Table 2 presents performance results on both investigated architectures. Again the numactl tool was used to run in DDR (KNL-ram) or HBM (KNL-hbm). All tests were done with different numbers of threads and only the best result is shown.

Looking at the serial performance it can be observed that the performance difference is marginal on the KNL between DDR and HBM. The runtime on Broadwell in comparison is lower for all tests in the serial case. As the clockrate of the KNL core is about 60% of the Broadwell core this is not surprising.

The performance running in DRAM is worse than for HBM as expected. The benefit of using the HBM varies from 12% improvement for CG up to 396% for FT. Overall, the speedup reached on the KNL is between 32 and 145, where most of the tests reach a speedup of 50 or higher.

KNL outperforms the Broadwell system for all but two benchmarks (BT and UA). Here the performance drop is 3% and 5% whereas the gain for other benchmarks is 94% in average with 258% being the top value.

Overall, if an application can run in the HBM the NPBs show that KNL is advantageous compared to the Broadwell system.

Table 2. Runtime in seconds measured for the NAS Parallel Benchmarks on the KNL and Broadwell system. Best is the best result from tests with 64/128/192/256 threads on KNL and 8/12/24/48 threads on Broadwell. Relative for Broadwell means the relative runtime compared to KNL

	KNL-ram			KNL-hbm			Broadwell			
	1 thr	Best	Speedup	1 thr	Best	Speedup	1 thr	Best	Speedup	Relative
BT	2497.7	66.7	37.4	2553.3	46.18	55.3	682.5	**44.6**	15.3	−3%
CG	584.1	12.8	45.5	721.1	**11.48**	62.8	341.5	16.7	20.4	+46%
EP	179.9	3.0	59.8	180.2	**1.25**	144.2	81.0	4.5	18.1	+258%
FT	300.4	45.9	6.6	302.1	**9.25**	32.7	201.1	11.6	17.3	+25%
IS	27.1	0.6	49.2	27.4	**0.47**	58.2	13.8	0.9	16.2	+81%
LU	2044.1	48.8	41.9	2097.9	**32.84**	63.9	537.0	35.9	15.0	+9%
MG	66.8	7.6	8.8	67.2	**1.7**	39.6	44.4	4.2	10.5	+148%
SP	1774.9	139.5	12.7	1848.8	**34.43**	53.7	462.7	67.2	6.9	+95%
UA	3955.0	91.4	43.3	4058.0	64.43	63.0	660.2	**61.1**	10.8	−5%

5.2   SPEC OMP2012

SPEC OMP2012 [11] is the latest version of the SPEC benchmark suite for OpenMP and the version we used for the comparison in this work.

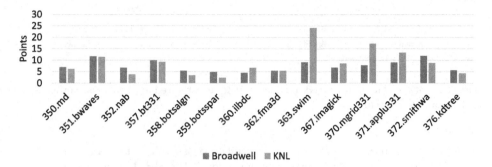

Fig. 5. Performance points obtained for SPEC OMP benchmarks on both target systems

The performance results reached are shown in Fig. 5. SPEC reports points for each benchmark, where a higher value represents better performance. On both systems we ran with different numbers of threads and on KNL in the DRAM, HBM and also in the cache mode.

The most points reached on both target platforms are presented in Fig. 5. The picture here is not as clear as with NPB, on more than half of the benchmarks the Broadwell system achieves more points than KNL. However, when an application profits from the KNL the performance gain is larger (e.g. 2.5x improvement for swim) than the penalty for other applications. In total on KNL 125 points are reached and 105 on Broadwell.

6   Applications

Finally, real application codes are used to compare the KNL and the Broadwell system. The applications used here are:

- **NestedCP:** NestedCP [7] was developed at the Virtual Reality Group of the RWTH Aachen University and is used to extract critical points in unsteady flow field datasets.
- **TrajSearch:** TrajSearch is a code to investigate turbulences which occur during combustion. It is a post-processing code for dissipation element analysis developed by Peters and Wang [14] from the Institute for Combustion Technology at the RWTH Aachen University.

Figure 6 shows the performance results obtained on both systems for both applications. The bar charts show runtime and the line charts the corresponding speedup. The scaling on KNL is good (speedup close to 100) in both cases, but

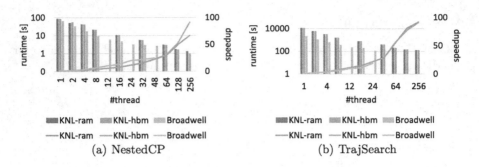

Fig. 6. Runtime (bars) and speedup (lines) of the investigated applications on the KNL and Broadwell system

the serial performance is worse compared to the Broadwell system. For NestedCP KNL is faster than the Broadwell system, even if the HBM is not used. When the HBM is used the best result is reached which is 173% faster. For TrajSearch the Broadwell system is about 10% faster than KNL with no difference if the DDR or HBM is used.

7   Conclusion

We compared the performance of OpenMP programs on the KNL architecture to a 2-socket Broadwell system. With kernel benchmarks the memory performance was investigated where we found that the latency for DRAM and HBM on the KNL is nearly the same and also close to the latency on the Broadwell system with respect to clock cycles of the machine. The Bandwidth of the HBM was much higher than the DRAM on KNL (65 vs. 400 GB/s) if the KNL was virtually devised into 4 NUMA quadrants by using the sub-NUMA-clustering (SNC-4) BIOS option. In the default configuration which was the Quadrant mode roughly half the performance was reached. Tests with the EPCC microbenchmarks revealed that synchronization in OpenMP and task creation in OpenMP are more expensive on the KNL system but only by a factor of up to 5 for synchronization and 8 for the creation of teams. Reasons might be the 2D-mesh interconnect or the fact that the runtime is not yet optimized well enough for KNL.

With the NAS parallel benchmarks and SPEC we have seen, that it is key to use the HBM to have a chance to reach comparable performance on the KNL in many cases. When the HBM was used, the KNL outperformed the Broadwell system in 7 out of 9 tests with NPB. When the Broadwell system was faster it was by up to 5% whereas the KNL was 258% faster in other cases. With SPEC OMP the KNL reached overall more points than the Broadwell, but the difference was smaller than for the NPBs. Although with the two tested applications KNL was faster (+173%) for one and slower (−10%) for the other test.

In summary, if the HBM can be used on the KNL, the system outperformed the Broadwell in most cases. When the KNL was faster it was often by a much higher percentage than in cases where the Broadwell system was faster. This shows that in average there is more to win for same applications than the penalty to pay for applications which do not fit too well on the KNL architecture. Overall, this makes the KNL the winner in our comparison if the HBM can be used by the applications.

Future work is to investigate different kinds of applications, in particular MPI parallel applications are the next logical class to investigate. As the KNL architecture will be available with on chip Omni-path interconnect, the scaling across nodes is very interesting.

References

1. Bailey, D.H., Barszcz, E., Barton, J.T., Browning, D.S., Carter, R.L., Fatoohi, R.A., Frederickson, P.O., Lasinski, T.A., Simon, H.D., Venkatakrishnan, V., Weeratunga, S.K.: The NAS parallel benchmarks. Technical report. NASA Ames Research Center (1991)
2. Bell, N., Garland, M.: Implementing sparse matrix-vector multiplication on throughput-oriented processors. In: Proceedings of the Conference on High Performance Computing Networking, Storage and Analysis, SC 2009, pp. 18:1–18:11, New York. ACM (2009)
3. Bull, J.M., O'Neill, D.: A microbenchmark suite for OpenMP 2.0. SIGARCH Comput. Archit. News **29**(5), 41–48 (2001)
4. Bull, J.M., Reid, F., McDonnell, N.: A microbenchmark suite for OpenMP tasks. In: Chapman, B.M., Massaioli, F., Müller, M.S., Rorro, M. (eds.) IWOMP 2012. LNCS, vol. 7312, pp. 271–274. Springer, Heidelberg (2012). doi:10.1007/978-3-642-30961-8_24
5. Cramer, T., Schmidl, D., Klemm, M., an Mey, D.: OpenMP programming on intel xeon phi coprocessors: an early performance comparison. In: Proceedings of the Many-core Applications Research Community Symposium, pp. 38–44, November 2012
6. Duran, A., Teruel, X., Ferrer, R., Martorell, X., Ayguade, E.: Barcelona OpenMP tasks suite: a set of benchmarks targeting the exploitation of task parallelism in OpenMP. In: International Conference on Parallel Processing, 2009, ICPP 2009, pp. 124–131 (2009)
7. Gerndt, A., Sarholz, S., Wolter, M., Mey, D.A., Bischof, C., Kuhlen, T.: Nested OpenMP for efficient computation of 3D critical points in multi-block CFD datasets. In: Proceedings of the ACM/IEEESC 2006 Conference, p. 46, November 2006
8. Khronos OpenCL Working Group: The OpenCL Specification, v2.2 (2016)
9. McCalpin, J.D.: STREAM: Sustainable Memory Bandwidth in High Performance Computers (1995). Accessed 24 Mar 2016
10. McVoy, L., Staelin, C.: lmbench: portable tools for performance analysis. In: Proceedings of the 1996 Annual Conference on USENIX Annual Technical Conference, ATEC 1996, pp. 23–23, Berkeley, CA, USA. USENIX Association (1996)

11. Müller, M.S., et al.: SPEC OMP2012 — an application benchmark suite for parallel systems using OpenMP. In: Chapman, B.M., Massaioli, F., Müller, M.S., Rorro, M. (eds.) IWOMP 2012. LNCS, vol. 7312, pp. 223–236. Springer, Heidelberg (2012). doi:10.1007/978-3-642-30961-8_17
12. NVIDIA: CUDA C Programming Guide, v8.0 (2016)
13. OpenMP ARB: OpenMP Application Program Interface, v. 4.5. http://www.open mp.org
14. Peters, N., Wang, L.: Dissipation element analysis of scalar fields in turbulence. C. R. Mech. **334**, 493–506 (2006)
15. Reinders, J., Jeffers, J., Sodani, A.: Intel Xeon Phi Processor High Performance Programming Knights Landing Edititon. Morgan Kaufmann Publishers Inc., Boston (2016)
16. Schmidl, D., Cramer, T., Wienke, S., Terboven, C., Müller, M.S.: Assessing the performance of OpenMP programs on the intel xeon phi. In: Wolf, F., Mohr, B., Mey, D. (eds.) Euro-Par 2013. LNCS, vol. 8097, pp. 547–558. Springer, Heidelberg (2013). doi:10.1007/978-3-642-40047-6_56
17. Volkov, V., Demmel, J.W.: Benchmarking GPUs to tune dense linear algebra. In: Proceedings of the 2008 ACM/IEEE Conference on Supercomputing, SC 2008 (2008)

Advanced Data Management with OpenMP

Double Buffering for MCDRAM on Second Generation Intel® Xeon Phi™ Processors with OpenMP

Stephen L. Olivier[1(✉)], Simon D. Hammond[1], and Alejandro Duran[2]

[1] Center for Computing Research, Sandia National Laboratories,
Albuquerque, USA
{slolivi,sdhammo}@sandia.gov
[2] Intel Corporation Iberia, Madrid, Spain
alejandro.duran@intel.com

Abstract. Emerging novel architectures for shared memory parallel computing are incorporating increasingly creative innovations to deliver higher memory performance. A notable exemplar of this phenomenon is the Multi-Channel DRAM (MCDRAM) that is included in the Intel® XeonPhi™ processors. In this paper, we examine techniques to use OpenMP to exploit the high bandwidth of MCDRAM by staging data. In particular, we implement double buffering using OpenMP sections and tasks to explicitly manage movement of data into MCDRAM. We compare our double-buffered approach to a non-buffered implementation and to Intel's cache mode, in which the system manages the MCDRAM as a transparent cache. We also demonstrate the sensitivity of performance to parameters such as dataset size and the distribution of threads between compute and copy operations.

1 Introduction

Modern high-performance scientific applications typically place a significant burden on the memory subsystem of compute nodes. Many algorithms routinely used in modern codes date back to a period where floating-point operations were the most expensive part of calculation, and as such, many algorithms are optimized to reduce *computation* sometimes at the cost of increased memory bandwidth. As processor designs from leading industry vendors have become more aggressively tuned with respect to the availability of floating-point arithmetic units, codes which make frequent use of memory-resident data structures have failed to achieve expected performance gains. Leading high-performance computing centers have therefore pushed processor designs to incorporate higher bandwidth memories in order to address the lack of balance between compute and memory subsystem performance. However, in the case of general-purpose graphics

© Springer International Publishing AG 2017
B.R. de Supinski et al. (Eds.): IWOMP 2017, LNCS 10468, pp. 311–324, 2017.
DOI: 10.1007/978-3-319-65578-9_21

processing units (GP-GPUs) and, more recently, the Intel® XeonPhi™ processor, only a limited amount of high-bandwidth memory (HBM) has been made available due to cost and engineering constraints. The limited capacity of the available HBM has pushed supercomputer designs to utilize two memories – one composed of a small but very fast on-package memory technology, and the other, a slower, capacity memory based around traditional DDR3 or 4. By splitting the available on-node memory into two domains, or multiple 'levels' of memory, the node designs have become increasingly complex with respect to the placement and movement of individual data structures.

The application developer is therefore faced with a challenge – where best to place data structures for performance. For sufficiently large data structures (*e.g.* *large arrays*), even the entire HBM may not have the capacity to hold the entire allocation. In these scenarios one must therefore either accept slower performance, or, alternatively, look for a method to split data structures into individual pieces and buffer these into/out of the faster memory resource. Completing such designs has been historically, and remains, a significant programming challenge. In this paper we explore the potential design of such an approach using OpenMP directives. The design vehicle is a simple benchmark which requires a reduction to be performed over a large array that is sized to exceed the high bandwidth memory resources and, instead, must be buffered into them. Our study explores several potential programming designs and the performance that each can achieve on a state-of-the-art Intel Xeon Phi 7250 processor.

The remainder of this paper is organized as follows: Sect. 2 explains the motivation for this work. Section 3 describes the implementation of our reduction benchmark and the use of OpenMP directives for double buffering. Section 4 provides benchmarked performance results from the Intel Xeon Phi 7250 processor. We discuss related work in Sect. 5 and conclude in Sect. 6 with some thoughts on managing complex memory hierarchies.

2   Motivation

The second generation Intel Xeon Phi architecture is a multi-core architecture with up to 72 cores. Each core appears as four logical CPUs through hyper-threading. The cores are capable of issuing two instructions per cycle out-of-order, including vector and memory instructions. Instruction sets up to and including AVX2 supported by the Intel Xeon Phi processors are compatible with those supported by Intel® XeonPhi® processors. The Intel Xeon Phi architecture implements a 512-bit SIMD instruction set known as AVX-512. Each SIMD register may contain eight double-precision (DP) or sixteen single-precision (SP) floating-point values as well as a variety of integer data sizes. The AVX-512 instruction set also supports low-overhead unaligned loads, fused-multiply and add, vector masking, shuffle and permutation instructions, advanced vector gather and scatter, histogram support, and hardware-accelerated transcendentals.

To provide the cores with enough data to feed the computing capabilities, cores are connected through a 2D mesh and to an integrated on-package Multi-Channel DRAM (MCDRAM) memory of up to 16 GiB, which can deliver up to

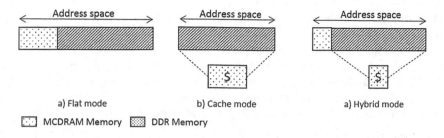

Fig. 1. Available multi-channel DRAM configuration modes.

Table 1. Benchmarked bandwidths of reduction operation on Intel Xeon Phi 7250.

Memory mode	Reduction bandwidth (GB/s)
DDR4-only	77.20
MCDRAM(flat)/DDR4 interleaved on 1:1 ratio	105.64
Cache-only	145.06 GB/s
MCDRAM(flat)-only	149.75 GB/s

490 GB/s of bandwidth [1]. The main DDR4 memory on the same platform can deliver about 90 GB/s [1]. This memory can be configured at boot time in one of three different modes shown in Fig. 1: flat, cache, or hybrid. In flat mode, the integrated memory is visible to the programmer in the same memory space as regular system memory but as different NUMA domains (which allows programmers to select which kind of memory to allocate). In cache mode, the MCDRAM cannot be accessed directly by the programmer, but it acts as additional level of cache in between the L2 caches and the DDR memory. This cache is a direct-mapped cache and is inclusive of the L2 caches. Access hits in the cache will be served directly by the MCDRAM, while misses are redirected to the DDR controllers which serve the data back to both the MCDRAM cache and the L2 that made the request. The hybrid mode allows one to configure a portion of MCDRAM as flat Mode and another in cache mode each with the same characteristics just described.

For this work, we have used a Intel Xeon Phi processor 7250 with 68 cores running at 1.4 GHz, 16 GiB of MCDRAM and 96 GiB of DDR4 memory configured in quadrant mode.

We used a simple reduction kernel, which accumulates all the values from a large array into a single value. The kernel has no blocking or buffering and it allows to obtain bandwidth values, shown it Table 1 that bound our expectations when working from the different memories and memory modes of the Intel Xeon Phi processor assuming that no code modifications are done. Using arrays that fit in the MCDRAM we can expect a good performance. But the Interleaved experiment, where data is allocated in a 1:1 ratio between the two memories, shows that using both MCDRAM and DDR4 for larger arrays will significantly impact performance. As the size of the array increases and, therefore, the amount of DDR used increases the performance will asymptomatically approach the bandwidth that can be obtained from the DDR4 memory.

Eventually, we hope to have computer architectures which permit *all* data structures to be located entirely in MCDRAM-like memory but constraints on cost, power and reliability may make this particularly challenging. In the event that high-bandwidth memories remain smaller than we would like, we might fall back to Cache mode which achieves performance close to that of Flat mode provided that there is sufficient room to hold all the allocated data.

Based on these observation in this paper we seek to answer two questions:

- How well does Cache mode perform compared to explicit use of MCDRAM?
- Can double buffering techniques, commonly used in other architectures, be successfully applied to alleviate the impact of transfers from DDR to MCDRAM? If so, has OpenMP* the appropriate language elements to implement these techniques?

For complex scientific workflows, memories such as MCDRAM are appealing because the very nature of the codes being developed typically demands large meshes over which physical simulations are performed. If caches become unavailable due to increasing hardware complexity or energy costs associated with their management then the relevance of the second question increases as application programmers will have to adopt such techniques, or, alternatively, to accept slower performance (as shown here by the DDR-only bandwidths).

3   Implementations

OpenMP offers a variety of constructs to express parallel programming patterns. In this section, we show example programs written to accomplish the task of double buffering data to exploit the MCDRAM of an Intel Xeon Phi processor.

We begin with some simple code that performs calculations over blocks of an array. The particular calculation is to multiply each element's value by its position in the block a number of times, as shown in Listing 1.1. This code constitutes a microbenchmark with parameterization of the size of the array, the block size, and the number of times the calculation is repeated.

Listing 1.1. Code to perform simple calculations over blocks of an array.

```
double dblArray = (double*)
  malloc( sizeof(double) * totalDoubles );
/* Initialization */
#pragma omp parallel for
for(size_t i = 0; i <
totalDoubles; ++i) {
  dblArray[i] = (double) i;
}

/* Blocked sums */ for(size_t blck = 0; blck < nBlcks; ++blck) {
  for(size_t repeat = 0; repeat < nRepeats; ++repeat) {
    #pragma omp parallel for reduction(+:sum)
    for(size_t i = 0; i < blckSize; ++i) {
      sum += ((double) i) * dblArray[(blck * blckSize) + i];
    }
  }
  const double sum_scaled = sum /
    ((  (double) nRepeats ) * ( (double) blckSize ));
  printf("Block
}
```

To take advantage of MCDRAM, we could use cache mode and have the system move data into the MCDRAM automatically. However, suppose that instead we would like to control the use of MCDRAM and that each block is small enough to fit into the MCDRAM. Since OpenMP does not currently support the use of multi-level memory such as MCDRAM in the specification, assume the availability of a third-party library, e.g., memkind [3], to allocate and to transfer data into MCDRAM. A modified version of our example in Listing 1.2 shows how the blocks can be moved into MCDRAM one-by-one. For brevity, allocation and initialization of the array of doubles in DDR is omitted in this listing.

Listing 1.2. Version of previous example code with blocks copied into MCDRAM.

```
double fastArray = (double*)
  mcdram_malloc( sizeof(double) * totalDoubles );

for(size_t blck = 0; blck < nBlcks; ++blck) {

  /* Copy current block */
  #pragma omp parallel for
  for(size_t i = 0; i < blckSize; ++i) {
    fastArray[i] = dblArray[(blck * blckSize) + i];
  }

  /* Blocked sum for current block */
  for(size_t repeat = 0; repeat < nRepeats; ++repeat) {
    #pragma omp parallel for reduction(+:sum)
    for(size_t i = 0; i < blckSize; ++i) {
      sum += ((double) i) * fastArray[i];
    }
  }
  const double sum_scaled = sum /
    (( (double) nRepeats ) * ( (double) blckSize ));
  printf("Block
}
```

To further optimize the program, it may be desirable to stage data into the MCDRAM using the double buffering technique. This approach involves calculating on the current block and transferring the next block concurrently. Two possible OpenMP features to leverage for this purpose are *sections* and *tasks*. First consider an implementation using sections, as shown in Listing 1.3.

This implementation allocates twice the amount of MCDRAM space to accommodate two data buffers, and a flag variable manages the use of the buffers. Only the first block is copied initially, into one of the buffers (half of the allocated MCDRAM array). The implementation then uses nested parallel regions within the loop over the blocks. The top-level parallel region creates two sections. Within the first section, data for the next block is copied into one buffer using an adjustable number of threads. Concurrently, the other section performs calculations on the current block (residing in the other buffer), also using an

Listing 1.3. Code using OpenMP sections to perform double buffering.

```
double fastArray = (double*)
  mcdram_malloc( sizeof(double) * totalDoubles * 2);

int whichBuf = 0; omp_set_nested(1);

/* Copy first block */
#pragma omp parallel for num_threads(nCopy)
for(size_t i = 0; i < blckSize; ++i) {
  fastArray[i] = dblArray[i];
}

for(size_t blck = 0; blck < nBlcks; ++blck) {
  #pragma omp parallel num_threads(2)
  #pragma omp sections
  {

    #pragma omp section
    {
      /* Copy next block */
      size_t nextBlck = blck + 1;
      #pragma omp parallel for num_threads(nCopy)
      for(size_t i = 0; i < blckSize; ++i) {
        fastArray[((!whichBuf) * scratchDoubles) + i] =
        dblArray[(nextBlck * blckSize) + i];
      }
    }

    #pragma omp section
    {
      /* Blocked sum for current block */
      for(size_t repeat = 0; repeat < nRepeats; ++repeat) {
        #pragma omp parallel for reduction(+:sum) \
          num_threads(nCompute)
        for(size_t i = 0; i < blckSize; ++i) {
      sum += ((double) i) *
        fastArray[(whichBuf * blckSize) + i];
        }
      }
      const double sum_scaled = sum /
        (( (double) nRepeats ) * ( (double) blckSize ));
      printf("Block_%llu:_sum_=_%f\n", blck, sum_scaled);
    }

  }

  whichBuf = !whichBuf;
}
```

adjustable number of threads. The flag is toggled at the end of each iteration. The implementation using OpenMP tasks is similar to the sections implementation, so we present it in abbreviated form in Listing 1.4. As before, the copy and blocked sum operations use an adjustable number of threads for each operation.

Listing 1.4. Code using OpenMP tasks to perform double buffering.

```
int whichBuf = 0; omp_set_nested(1);

/* Copy first block */
#pragma omp parallel for num_threads(nCopy)
for(size_t i = 0; i < blckSize; ++i) {
  fastArray[i] = dblArray[i];
}

for(size_t blck = 0; blck < nBlcks; ++blck) {
  #pragma omp parallel num_threads(2)
  #pragma omp single
  {

    #pragma omp task
    {
      /* Copy next block */
    }

    #pragma omp task
    {
      /* Blocked sum for current block */
    }

  }

  whichBuf = !whichBuf;
}
```

Other implementations of double buffering into MCDRAM are possible, e.g., with OpenMP task dependences or with the nowait clause on the first loop and careful scheduling of the second loop. The two methods presented above seem to be the most straightforward and expose the needed parallelism, and we leave the others for future work.

4   Evaluation

In this section we present comparisons and scaling results from the implementations described above. For the reader's reference we use the following versions:

- **Sections:** Uses OpenMP sections-based double buffering where some subset of threads is used to perform copy operations into fast memory and the remainder of the active threads perform reduction work;
- **Tasks:** Uses OpenMP task-based execution to perform a copy in of memory to fast memory prior to a work task being dispatched to perform a reduction;
- **Cache:** Performs the reduction without copy buffering but relies on hardware-based cache mechanisms to use MCDRAM;
- **No Overlap:** Performs a copy in operation using a parallel-region, followed by a separate parallel region performing the reduction;
- **DDR:** Performs each reduction without any copy buffering but uses only the DDR4 memory of the system.

All experiments ran on a cluster of Intel Xeon Phi 7250 processors and we used the Intel® 17.0.2 C/C++ compiler with code compiled for OpenMP and

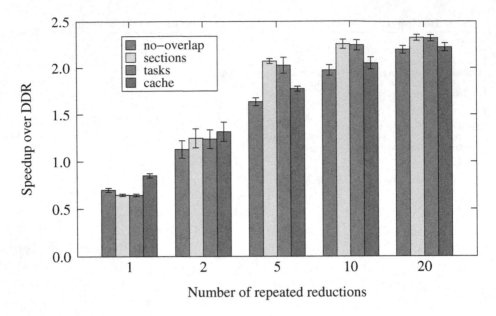

Fig. 2. Repeated reductions over 48 GB by each implementation. Speedup is shown relative to the DDR-only version.

Table 2. Execution time in seconds for repeated reductions using DDR only. Baseline for speedup results shown in Fig. 2.

Number of repeats	1	2	5	10	20
Mean execution time	0.654	1.36	3.27	6.59	13.1
Standard deviation	0.0125	0.104	0.0357	0.124	0.167

the AVX512 instruction set along with -O3 optimization. We report 5 trials per configuration on each of 7 Xeon Phi nodes, for a total of 35 individual trials per configuration. Where speedup data is shown in bar charts, each bar represents the mean speedup for that configuration relative to the DDR-only configuration and the error bars represent speedup standard deviation relative to the standard deviation of the DDR-only configuration. Tables showing the raw execution times and standard deviations for the DDR-only configuration are presented along with the corresponding speedup graphs.

For the tasks and sections implementations, we let the OpenMP runtime select the thread placement, while for the other implementations we specify OMP_PLACES=threads and OMP_PROC_BIND=close, which we find to be the best performing affinity settings. A block size of 4 GB is used for the versions in which data is explicitly copied into MCDRAM. A total of 272 threads are used for each execution, and unless otherwise specified 16 of the 272 are used for copying data in the tasks and sections implementations.

4.1   Implementation Performance Varied by Data Reuse

In Fig. 2 we benchmark each implementation of our reduction kernel, showing speedup relative to the DDR-only execution times in Table 2. Repeatedly applying the reduction once the data is copied into the fast memory to emulates the effect of more compute and therefore greater data reuse. This has the effect of reducing the overhead associated with the buffering copies. When the reduction is performed only once, DDR and cache are the strongest performers as expected: Note the speedups less than one in the first cluster of the graph. Each operand is used only once but is moved multiple times when data buffering is used. At even a small number of repeats (but larger than 1), the DDR4-only implementation becomes the most expensive method since data is repeatedly accessed from the slower memory. The implementations with buffering as well as the hardware-based caching executions now perform better than the DDR4 only runs. With increasing numbers of repeats, the performance of the implementations begins to spread, with the methods that can provide buffer-copying and reduction-execution overlap (the OpenMP Sections and Tasks implementations) outperforming hardware-based caching. The nonoverlapping implementation still outperforms DDR4-only as data is located in the MCDRAM, but the inability to overlap thread execution limits performance due to poorer simultaneous use of the available memory subsystem.

The observations of this study are that at even modest amounts of data reuse, data staging into the high bandwidth memory can be advantageous. Although hardware-based caching performs extremely well (as might be expected when data reuse is present), future hardware designs may elect to dispense with this feature to reduce implementation complexity; reduce higher energy costs associated with running caches, or, may provide greater performance disparity between cache mode and the raw high-bandwidth memory performance when used as a flat address space. These results show a software-based staging mechanism can provide similar performance gains without requiring hardware support.

4.2   Performance Variation by Size of Copying Thread Pool

In the previous section we demonstrated that the Sections and Tasks-based implementation of the staged-reduction operations can provide performance close to, or equivalent to, hardware-based caching schemes when the data reuse is greater than 1 for the data being staged into the faster memory resource. In Fig. 3 we show the effect on performance of varying the size of the copier pool, noting that for each thread we provide to perform copying, we are removing threads from our worker pool which utilize the staged data to perform reduction operations. The figure shows that for 10 repetitions, the best performance can be achieved by using 16 threads, which correlates with anecdotal results of the number of threads needed to saturate the DDR4 memory resources. Intuitively, performance of a data intensive kernel is still heavily governed by the slowest memory resource on the processor. By using a data staging pipeline, we are able to perform operations over a data set which is larger than the MCDRAM, use

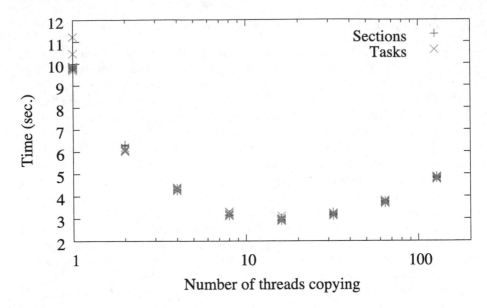

Fig. 3. Execution time for 10 repeats over the 48 GB array when varying the number of threads in the data copy pool. Scatter plot of 35 data points for each configuration.

a subset of threads to perform copying into the high bandwidth memory, while another set of threads perform the actual computations. In the presence of at least one additional reuse of the copied data, the higher bandwidth memory resource provides greater performance meaning our computations are no longer bottlenecked on the slower DDR4 directly but are instead bottlenecked on the performance of the data copying threads. Since we can now overlap the copying in and the reduction computations performance is improved. Maximizing the use of the DDR4 bandwidth makes the ideal point at which to set the size of the data copying thread pool since no additional performance can be gained, and may, instead, reduce the performance of the computation thread pool as more of these threads are required to saturate the high-bandwidth memory resources. We expect that there will be different performance curves (similar to Fig. 3) depending on the expense of the computation being performed, with extremely expensive computations driving toward a smaller thread copy pool, and cheaper computations driving closer to the 16 thread count range as shown here.

4.3   Performance Variation by Total Problem Size

The size of the overall dataset of the computation can be an important factor. Figure 4 presents the performance of the different implementations with 10 repetitions for total array sizes of 8 GB, 16 GB, 32 GB, and 48 GB, whereas the previous results were only for a 48 GB array. Speedup in the graph is relative to the DDR-only execution times in Table 3. DDR is slowest in all cases. Cache mode performs particularly well for 8 GB and 16 GB problems, which is unsurprising

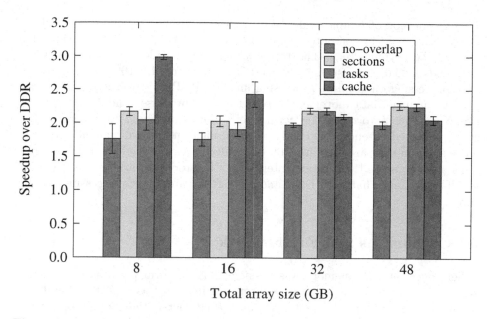

Fig. 4. Speedup for 10 repeats by each implementation relative to the DDR-only version, varying array size.

Table 3. Execution time in seconds for repeated reductions using DDR only, varying array size. Baseline for speedup results shown in Fig. 4.

Total array size (GB)	8	16	32	48
Execution time	1.35	2.44	4.36	6.59
Deviation	0.0146	0.0249	0.0586	0.124

given the 16 GB MCDRAM capacity (though less than that amount is typically available for use). Explicitly moving data into MCDRAM without overlapping computation and data movement does deliver some speedup over DDR, but not as much as cache mode or the overlapping methods. The overlapping methods demonstrate more benefit as the problem size increases, and they outperform the cache mode slightly at 32 GB and more so at 48 GB.

5   Related Work

Although the OpenMP API specification as of this writing (Version 4.5 [7]) does not provide directives or run time routines for explicit use of multi-level memory systems like the MCDRAM and DDR combination on the Intel Xeon Phi processors, such support has been proposed in a technical report from the OpenMP affinity subcommittee [8] and a previous paper [11]. Although we use the memkind library [3] in the work we have presented in this paper, our techniques should be able to leverage such future OpenMP features.

The concept of double buffering is well established, having been used for many years, e.g., in computer graphics to construct the next scene while displaying the current scene. The technique has been widely applied to devices with DMA capabilities, such as the IBM Cell processor [4,9,10] and general purpose processing on graphics processing units (GPGPU) [2,13]. It has also been used to manage data movement between a host processor and a first generation Xeon Phi coprocessor, e.g., with Intel® Threading Building Blocks [5]. Liu et al. proposed extending OpenMP with explicit support for double buffering on System-on-chip architectures [6]. Key differences between these earlier systems and the second generation Intel Xeon Phi processor used here are that it is self-hosted and that both DDR and MCDRAM are directly accessible by the cores [12].

6   Conclusions and Future Work

Where once on-node memory was a single, flat, uniform performance address space, today it is becoming less uniform and in some cases, features multiple levels of memory with different performance characteristics. Some application developers will simply scale out their applications until the working sets on each node fit into high bandwidth memory resources. Other developers, who have larger data sets or data sets which cannot scale as easily, will seek alternative solutions to manage their complex data sets. Contemporary hardware features hardware-based cache mechanisms to support such activities, at the cost of greater hardware complexity and energy consumption. Future designs may not have this luxury if the energy budget or implementation complexities required for Exascale-class computing are to be achieved.

We motivate the study of data staging or buffering for complex memory hierarchies with a simple reduction benchmark operating over data sets that exceed the capacity of the fastest memory resource. A single-level OpenMP parallel for provides a simple implementation without any ability to overlap copying and computation. OpenMP sections and tasks can be used to perform data copying and computation on independent pools of threads. The independence of the threads allows us to scale the size of these pools up and down as required to effectively consume the slower memory resources of the compute node. By permitting overlapping of the copying and computation, performance can be improved to approximately the same levels that a hardware-based cache mechanism can provide assuming moderate data reuse of the operands being staged from slow memory. In the absence of hardware caching in future systems, or the provision of faster self-management of the copy operations, this software design provides a relatively easy addition of data staging for OpenMP-based applications.

Moreover, the provision of data staging/buffering capabilities seems to be an area of interest for the growing OpenMP community, particularly given the recent adoption of offload directives to high performance compute devices and the availability of multi-level memories on systems such as the Intel Xeon Phi processors. This raises the question of whether a simpler set of directives or mechanisms are needed or whether the approaches shown in this paper are sufficient for developers' needs. Although our benchmark study is simple, by design, it acts as a demonstrator for the potential use of OpenMP to address such concerns as well as the potential performance available from OpenMP-based implementations.

Acknowledgments. Sandia National Laboratories is a multimission laboratory managed and operated by National Technology and Engineering Solutions of Sandia, LLC., a wholly owned subsidiary of Honeywell International, Inc., for the U.S. Department of Energy's National Nuclear Security Administration under contract DE-NA0003525. We wish to acknowledge our appreciation for the use of the Advanced Architecture Test Bed, Bowman, at Sandia National Laboratories. The test beds are provided by NNSA's Advanced Simulation and Computing (ASC) program for research and development of advanced architectures for exascale computing.

Disclaimers: Intel, Xeon, and Xeon Phi are trademarks or registered trademarks of Intel Corporation or its subsidiaries in the United States and other countries.
* Other brands and names are the property of their respective owners.

References

1. Optimizing Memory Bandwidth in Knights Landing on Stream Triad. https://software.intel.com/en-us/articles/optimizing-memory-bandwidth-in-knights-landing-on-stream-triad

2. Bauer, M., Cook, H., Khailany, B.: CudaDMA: Optimizing GPU memory bandwidth via warp specialization. In: 2011 International Conference for High Performance Computing, Networking, Storage and Analysis (SC11), pp. 12:1–12:11. ACM (2011)

3. Cantalupo, C., Venkatesan, V., Hammond, J., Czurylo, K., Hammond, S.: Memkind: an extensible heap memory manager for heterogeneous memory platforms and mixed memory policies. http://memkind.github.io/memkind/memkind_arch_20150318.pdf

4. Chen, T., Sura, Z., O'Brien, K., O'Brien, J.K.: Optimizing the use of static buffers for DMA on a CELL chip. In: Almási, G., Cascaval, C., Wu, P. (eds.) LCPC 2006. LNCS, vol. 4382, pp. 314–329. Springer, Heidelberg (2007). doi:10.1007/978-3-540-72521-3_23

5. Dokulil, J., Bajrovic, E., Benkner, S., Sandrieser, M., Bachmayer, B.: HyPHI - task based hybrid execution C++ library for the intel xeon phi coprocessor. In: 2013 International Conference on Parallel Processing, pp. 280–289 (2013)

6. Liu, F., Chaudhary, V.: Extending OpenMP for heterogeneous chip multiprocessors. In: 2003 International Conference on Parallel Processing, pp. 161–168, October 2003

7. OpenMP Architecture Review Board: OpenMP application programming interface, version 4.5. http://www.openmp.org/wp-content/uploads/openmp-4.5.pdf

8. OpenMP Architecture Review Board: OpenMP technical report 5: memory management support for OpenMP 5.0. http://www.openmp.org/wp-content/uploads/openmp-TR5-final.pdf

9. Perez, J.M., Bellens, P., Badia, R.M., Labarta, J.: CellSs: making it easier to program the cell broadband engine processor. IBM J. Res. Dev. **51**(5), 593–604 (2007)

10. Sancho, J.C., Kerbyson, D.J.: Analysis of double buffering on two different multi-core architectures: quad-core opteron and the Cell-BE. In: 2008 IEEE International Symposium on Parallel and Distributed Processing, pp. 1–12, April 2008

11. Sewall, J., Pennycook, S., Duran, A., Tian, X., Narayanaswamy, R.: A modern memory management system for OpenMP. In: Third International Workshop on Accelerator Programming Using Directives, pp. 25–35. IEEE Press (2016)

12. Sodani, A., Gramunt, R., Corbal, J., Kim, H.S., Vinod, K., Chinthamani, S., Hutsell, S., Agarwal, R., Liu, Y.C.: Knights landing: second-generation intel xeon phi product. IEEE Micro **36**(2), 34–46 (2016)

13. Spafford, K., Meredith, J., Vetter, J.: Maestro: data orchestration and tuning for OpenCL devices. In: DÁmbra, P., Guarracino, M., Talia, D. (eds.) Euro-Par 2010. LNCS, vol. 6272, pp. 275–286. Springer, Heidelberg (2010). doi:10.1007/978-3-642-15291-7_26

A Pattern for Overlapping Communication and Computation with OpenMP* Target Directives

Jonas Hahnfeld[1]($\boxtimes$), Tim Cramer[1], Michael Klemm[2], Christian Terboven[1], and Matthias S. Müller[1]

[1] Chair for High Performance Computing & IT Center, JARA–HPC,
RWTH Aachen University, 52074 Aachen, Germany
`{hahnfeld,cramer,terboven,mueller}@itc.rwth-aachen.de`
[2] Intel Deutschland GmbH, 85622 Feldkirchen, Germany
`michael.klemm@intel.com`

Abstract. OpenMP* 4.0 introduced initial support for heterogeneous devices. OpenMP 4.5 improved programmability and added capabilities for asynchronous device kernel offload and data transfer management. However, the programmers are still burdened to optimize data transfer for improved performance and to deal with the limited amount of memory on the target device. This work presents a pipelining concept to efficiently overlap communication and computation using the OpenMP 4.5 `target` directives. Our evaluation of two key HPC kernels shows performance improvements of up to 24% and the ability to process data larger than device memory.

1 Introduction

Accelerators and coprocessors of different kinds continue to impact the HPC landscape: From the current Top500 list, a total of 97 systems are equipped with GPU devices from NVIDIA and AMD or the Intel® Xeon Phi™ coprocessor.

OpenMP* other strives to ease the burden for the programmer by providing a rich set of compiler directives complemented by API routines to control runtime behavior. OpenMP 4.0 introduced support for heterogeneous programming with the `target` construct family. It allows to transfer the control flow from a host thread to a thread on the target device and also provides means to direct the data flow between host and device. Being vendor-neutral, a target device in OpenMP may be a GPU, a coprocessor, or other heterogeneous devices like a DSP engine or an FPGA. OpenMP 4.5 addresses some shortcomings and added support for asynchronous offloading from the host to devices.

Nevertheless, achieving good application performance on heterogeneous clusters still puts a burden on the programmer, who, for instance, has to lay out data structures and compute kernels in appropriate ways. Today's predominant configuration is a host that is equipped with DDR memory and (multiple) devices equipped with memory of much smaller capacity yet much higher memory bandwidth. Effective slicing and management of the working set that is present on

© Springer International Publishing AG 2017
B.R. de Supinski et al. (Eds.): IWOMP 2017, LNCS 10468, pp. 325–337, 2017.
DOI: 10.1007/978-3-319-65578-9_22

the device is crucial for achieving high application performance. Well-explored optimization techniques include the extension of device regions to enable data to reside on the device memory for reuse.

In this work, we emphasize on the technique of overlapping communication and computation to overcome bandwidth and latency bottlenecks in transfers between host and devices, for instance with the PCIe bus. We describe the realization of a pipeline concept based on features recently introduced with OpenMP 4.5 and present a performance evaluation with two devices per host. Applying our pattern may not only ease the implementation of complex applications exploiting accelerator devices, we will also show that it can improve performance via the overlapping and better use of the memory and bus capabilities. It can also enable the use of devices for problems that are larger than the device memory.

2   Related Work

The concept of overlapping communication and computation for parallel applications is widely spread. It is considered a key technique to obtain performance for architectures that rely on some form of message passing to transfer data to the computational units of the executing system. To best of our knowledge, we present a corresponding pipelining pattern to overlap communication with the offload target with computation for the first time. Another study [11] applies the concept to an Intel Xeon Phi coprocessor using the MPI programming model.

Several studies have shown that performance can be significantly increased by overlapping communication and computation (e.g., [3,8]). LibNBC by Hoefler et al. [8] is a portable library that provides support for non-blocking collective operations. It laid the foundation for similar concepts that have been introduced in the Message Passing Interface (MPI) version 3.0. Furthermore, their work references to further studies dealing with the overlapping of communication and computation in general. Extensions of MPI, such as the work of Aji et al. [1], address the problem of accessing GPU memory during MPI communication. In contrast to our work, these studies focus on applying non-blocking MPI primitives.

Beltran et al. [2] start multiple threads on each accelerator and achieve an overlap by efficiently scheduling them. Liu et al. [9] present double buffering for matrix multiplications and implement it with extensions to OpenMP. In contrast, we will use standard-compliant features from OpenMP 4.5 which will result in a reusable pattern across different accelerators and, thus, more portable code.

Miki et al. [10] propose language extensions for OpenACC* other that overlap communication and computation for stencil-type kernels. Cui et al. [6] propose pipelining directives to extend OpenMP. Our work uses the existing directives of OpenMP 4.5 instead and does not restrict the pattern to stencil computations that require the presence and exchange of halo cells. It is generally applicable to any type of applications that allows for splitting computations into sub-computation to overlap communication and computation.

Some OpenACC compilers employ double-buffering strategies to speed-up the data transfer itself [4]. It works by pre-allocating buffers before starting a transfer to the target device and thus physical allocation of buffers and the corresponding data transfers can be overlapped. Chen et al. [5] discuss different buffering schemes for DMA and their latencies. However, they do not investigate the overall improvement in runtime when overlapping DMA transfers and computation. Our approach is orthogonal to this, as we employ OpenMP pragmas to pipeline data transfers and computation at the application level. If an OpenMP implementation would offer such an underlying mechanism to improve low-level communication, our approach could transparently make use of it and automatically apply the low-level double buffering to further speed-up communication with the offload device.

3   OpenMP for Accelerators and Coprocessors

OpenMP's accelerator model is based on structured blocks with **target** directives to tag them for offload execution. A target region may be executed by OpenMP threads on a different device in a distinct data environment. By using **map** clauses a programmer can express which (non-scalar) variables have to be made available on a device. In OpenMP terms, this is called *mapped* from the host to the device, because the host may or may not share the memory with the device. In the case of devices with separate memory this typically involves copy operations. The **map** clause accepts, among others, the motion attributes **to**, **from**, and **tofrom** determining the point in time and the direction of copy operations.

The usage of **target data** regions allows to reduce data transfer in the case of multiple consecutive **target** regions using the same variables, as the data environment on a device is persistent for the whole duration of the **target data** region.

It is important to know that the **map** clause creates a fixed association between the host and the target device. In consequence, a re-mapping of a memory region on a device with an address on the host is not possible, if it was mapped before. In order to make the device data environment consistent between two **target** regions encountered in the same **target data** region, the **target update** construct can be used. The specified motion clause determines if the values from the host or from the target device have to be updated.

Listing 1.1. Dependencies with stand-alone directives for managing the device data environment.

```
 1  double A[100];
 2  #pragma omp target enter data nowait \
 3      ①    map(to: A[0:100]) depend(out: A[0:100])      ②
 4
 5  #pragma omp target map(to: A[0:100]) \
 6          nowait depend(inout: A[0:100])
 7  {
 8    ③// Computation that uses A[0:100]
 9  }                                                       ④
10
11  #pragma omp target exit data nowait \
12      ⑤    map(release: A[0:100]) depend(in: A[0:100])
```

Optimizing the data transfers was hard to realize in OpenMP 4.0. With all data transfers defined as being synchronous, it was impossible to overlap the computation and communication. OpenMP 4.5 defined the **target** region to be an implicit task, meaning it is executed as if it was surrounded by a `task` construct. The execution of a target task may be deferred if the `nowait` clause is added to the `target` construct to make the execution of the target code and the corresponding data transfers asynchronous.

In order to have an asynchronous data transfer without executing user code on the device, the stand-alone directive `target enter data` can be used to map data to a device. Correspondingly, the `target exit data` will unmap the specified variables from the device data environment and might copy back the values from the target device to the host. Both of these directives also generate a target task which might be deferred.

Finally, the `depend` clause can be added to all device directives to associate dependencies with the generated target task. It supports the same dependency types `in`, `out`, or `inout` introduced with the OpenMP tasking model. For the use case of asynchronous data transfer and kernel execution, this feature allows to defer the execution of a `target` region until the required data is transferred to or from a device and thus bring the data transfers and compute regions into a specific order as shown in Listing 1.1. After the `target enter data` directive ① has executed, the dependency ② is resolved and the computation ③ can start. As the mapping is already present on the device, this will not result in additional data transfer. The dependency ④ is satisfied when the kernel has finished and the `target exit data` operation ⑤ finally executes.

4   Pipelining Concept for Overlapping Communication

Depending on the available hardware, the mapping and/or the data transfer to or from a target device might be relatively slow compared to the available memory bandwidth on the host or the target device. Thus, the communication time of an application using a large amount of data might become a significant overhead factor and limit scalability and performance. To reduce this communication overhead we present a pipelining concept.

The main idea of the pipelining concept is to divide a single operation into smaller sub tasks. By interleaving these smaller sub tasks we can increase the throughput of a system, because different kinds of sub tasks can use different parts of the available hardware resources at the same time. In our case, a sub task belongs to one of the two kinds: computation or communication.

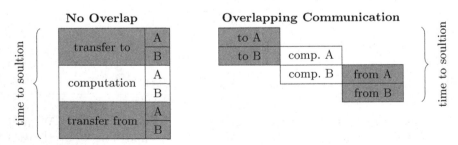

Fig. 1. Pipelining concept for overlapping computation and communication.

Figure 1 exemplifies the concept. The white boxes represent the computation and the gray boxes depict transfers. The example assumes that the computation can be split into two parts. The data required for each computation is transferred to a device and the result is transferred back to the host afterwards.

On the left hand side of Fig. 1, communication and computation are not overlapped, but are executed in order. On the right hand side, each of the two sub tasks are put into the pipeline stages. Thus, the computation on a target device does not have to wait until the complete data block is transferred to the device. As can be seen, this leads to an improved utilization of both the host and the offload device.

We refer to the first *transfer to* at the beginning as *wind-up phase* and to the last *transfer from* as the *wind-down phase*. In both of these phases, no computation can happen as the pipeline has to be filled with data transfers or the system has to wait until all in-flight data transfers have been completed. It can be seen that the time to solution using the pipelining concept decreases significantly in this case.

4.1   Performance Projection of Pipelining Pattern

To estimate the potential gain of overlapping communication and computation using the pipelining pattern, we conduct a very simple, yet effective performance projection. We will also use this simple performance model in Sect. 5 to assess the measured performance.

The total runtime t_{exec} of an offloaded kernel consists of

$$t_{exec} = t_{comp} + t_{comm}, \tag{1}$$

where t_{comp} is the time for the computation on the device and t_{comm} the communication time to transfer control and data. The latter can be predicted for a given amount of data d by

$$t_{comm} = \frac{d}{B} + t_{overhead}. \tag{2}$$

This assumes that d is sufficiently large so that the transfer of d saturates the maximum bandwidth B available. $t_{overhead}$ is the time that the runtime needs for preparational tasks. Depending on the data size d or the runtime implementation this overhead time may be significant for the overall communication time t_{comm}, as will be discussed below. In some cases, $t_{overhead}$ may also depend on data size d.

Based on these characteristics, the maximum optimization o_{max} is given as

$$o_{max} = \frac{min(t_{comp}, t_{comm})}{t_{exec}}. \tag{3}$$

Thus, pipelining transfers and computation works best in cases where the communication and computation time are equally balanced. The optimization potential approximates to a performance increase of up to $o_{max} = 0.5$, not taking the wind-up and wind-down phases into account.

Typically, the available memory of target devices like the Intel Xeon Phi coprocessor or GPUs is significantly smaller than the memory on the host. With the pipelining concept, a device kernel can use more memory than available on the device by transferring the necessary data chunk-wise and free any memory chunk as soon as the partial result was transferred back to the host. This forms a second promising application scenario for the concept in addition to the first one, namely the speedup.

4.2 Implementation with OpenMP

The `map` clause in OpenMP creates fixed associations between device and host. It is not possible to map a specific memory region from the host to a buffer on the device which was previously associated with a different address on the host.

There are multiple possibilities to overcome this limitation: First one could copy the needed data to a temporary buffer which is then transferred to the device using a `target update`. As a second option, we can allocate a single buffer for the whole array in a `target data` region. In a `target update`, we can then specify the corresponding start index to transfer the needed part of the array. Lastly, we can create a new buffer for each block of the array that has to be transferred. Here, OpenMP 4.5 offers the above mentioned stand-alone directives for mapping: `target enter data` and `target exit data`.

While the first solution would surely work, it doesn't promise to give the best performance due to the extra copy on the host. The second alternative fails to allocate the buffer if it exceeds the device memory. Creating a new buffer for each block solves this problem as memory can be freed on `target exit data` after the computation has finished. This allows to process more memory than available on the device at one moment.

Figure 2 shows the dependencies that have to be specified when working with the stand-alone directives. The first of these dependencies are based on the data usage: First, a specific block of data has to be allocated and transferred to the device. Second, the computation on the device can be done. Finally, the used data can be freed again.

Moreover, it has to be ensured that there are at most two buffers allocated at the same time. Hence, we need an explicit dependency between, for example, *exit #0* and *enter #2*. If this connection was omitted, there would be no limitation on how many *enter* tasks can start. This would be problematic because all *enter* tasks could run before *exit #0* frees the first part of the data, possibly exceeding the device memory. There are also dependencies between each *enter* and each *compute*. That is to avoid oversubscription which would negatively impact performance.

Listing 1.2 shows the code snippet with the OpenMP directives and their required dependencies. Each block of data is allocated on and transferred to the device with a `target enter data`. The computation is afterwards done in a `target` construct. After the computation has finished, `target exit data` will free the data on the device.

We specify the dependencies for data usage with the corresponding array section also given in the `map` clause. For mutual exclusion of the *enter* and

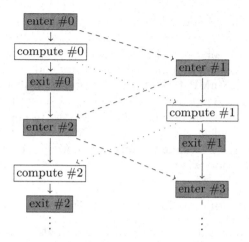

Fig. 2. Graph of the dependencies between target tasks. Continuous lines visualize dependencies based on the data usage, while dashed and dotted ones stand for the mutual exclusion of *enter* and *compute* tasks, respectively.

compute tasks one can use two `int` variables. These dummy variables are used to make the OpenMP implementation aware of the dependencies, but are not used in the code apart from their presence in the `depend` clause.

For simplicity, the code snippet only shows the default case in the middle of the loop iteration space, but not the wind-up and wind-down phase. In the first iteration of the loop with `block = 0`, we do not depend on the previous block having exited by omitting the dependence on `A[(block - 1) * LEN:LEN]`. Additionally, when the end of the iteration space is reached, there is no next block to transfer and therefore no *enter* task.

Listing 1.2. Declaring task dependencies with OpenMP for pipelining concept of multiple blocks with length *LEN* each. Special cases for `target enter data` are omitted for better readability.

```
 1  double A[BLOCKS * LEN];
 2  int enter, compute;
 3
 4  #pragma omp target enter data nowait map(to: A[0:LEN]) \
 5          depend(out: enter) depend(out: A[0:LEN])
 6  for (int block = 0; block < BLOCKS; block++) {
 7      #pragma omp target enter data nowait depend(inout: enter) \
 8              map(to: A[(block + 1) * LEN:LEN]) \
 9              depend(out: A[(block + 1) * LEN:LEN]) \
10              depend(in: A[(block - 1) * LEN:LEN])
11      #pragma omp target nowait depend(inout: compute) \
12              map(to: A[block * LEN:LEN]) \
13              depend(inout: A[block * LEN:LEN])
14      {
15          // do computation here
16      }
17      #pragma omp target exit data nowait map(release: A[block*LEN:LEN]) \
18              depend(inout: A[block * LEN:LEN])
19  }
```

Instead of creating a new buffer for each memory transfer, it would also be possible to use the *device memory routines* introduced with OpenMP 4.5. However, these routines are not available for Fortran and are only defined for C and C++. In addition, they do not support task dependencies and would thus have to be wrapped in regular OpenMP tasks to model proper synchronization between the different stages of the pipeline. They also require a developer to manage the buffers explicitly and free them manually. Thus, the usage of the stand-alone directives is more convenient and more productive compared to the usage of the *device memory routines*. For these reasons, we concentrate on the investigation of the directives in the following.

4.3 Applying the Concept for Multiple Target Devices

A natural desire is to extend the above approach to also cover multiple devices and to extend the pipelining concept such that it can overlap communication and computation across these devices. The `target` constructs support the `device` clause to specify the device a `target` construct shall use at runtime. Thus, a simple mechanism to start multiple concurrent `target` regions, e.g., by iterating over all available devices is sufficient. Managing the corresponding device data environment works in a similar way by using the stand-alone directives or `target update` as discussed above. To ensure that all of operations have finished, the `taskwait` construct is suitable.

Based on this scheme, we can apply our concept and specify dependencies between tasks as described above. That way, we can for example allow unrelated tasks to execute in parallel and overlap computation with a data transfer or exchange that is only needed in the next step of the algorithm.

5 Evaluation

To show the applicability of our approach, we evaluated the concept with the `dgemm` kernel. Therefore, we used the implementation given in the Intel® Math Kernel Library which delivers a good performance on Intel architectures. For the evaluation of the presented pipelining concept for multiple target devices, we use a sparse Conjugate Gradients (CG) [7] method as a representative real-world compute kernel.

All presented kernels were measured on a 2-socket Intel® Xeon® E5-2650 system (codename "SandyBridge"), which is clocked at 2.00 GHz and has 16 physical cores in sum. The system includes two Intel Xeon Phi 5110p coprocessors with 8 GB of main memory and 60 cores (clocked at 1.053 GHz) each, connected via PCIe Gen2 with 16 lanes. In our setup, we measured approximately 6.7 GB/s with `target update` constructs between device and host. For all kernels, we used version 17.0 of the Intel compiler that already implements all required OpenMP 4.5 features. We present the minimum runtime of 10 repetitions as this will indicate the best performance that the system can deliver.

5.1   Matrix-Matrix-Multiplication

This section will show how the pipelining concept can be used to compute a problem whose memory requirements exceed the device memory. For this, we use a matrix-matrix-multiplication $A \cdot B = C$, where $A, B, C \in \mathbb{R}^{n \times n}$. The size of each matrix is 24576^2 `double` elements, which requires $3 \cdot 4.83$ GB ≈ 14.5 GB in total. We transpose the second matrix so that we can use rows instead of columns for the sub tasks of the multiplication. This results in contiguous storage in memory which is a requirement for the `map` clause.

Since the size of the matrices exceeds the available memory on the device, A and C need to be split into N and B into M parts that can be transferred separately. For the calculation of $A \cdot B^T = C$, the rows of A can be reused for multiple blocks of B and the result is stored in the corresponding parts of C. To minimize data movement the parts of A and C are transferred in `target data` regions. Furthermore, we apply the pipelining concept to B to hide the latency. In theory, we should also be able to apply the pipelining concept to A and C. Unfortunately, this is currently not possible due to some issues in the Intel compiler.

To minimize the data transfers, M has to be as small as possible because matrix B has to be transferred multiple times. For our test, case we chose $M = N = 4$ (i.e., four blocks for each matrix), which has shown to perform best. In theory choosing $N = 2$ fits into the device memory and thus should be beneficial in term of performance. However, this results in stability issues on the device. B could be split into more parts but that does not result in a lower runtime.

In total, the maximum memory usage will be $\frac{4 \cdot 4.83 \text{ GB}}{4} = 4.83$ GB on the device, because we need to store two parts of B simultaneously. For the transfer, we expect $(2 + 4) \cdot 4.83$ GB as B has to be transferred 4 times. In addition, measurements show that the coprocessor needs approximately 1.35 s to allocate each matrix. Based on (2), this sums up to

$$t_{comm} = \frac{(2 + 4) \cdot 4.83 \text{ GB}}{6.7 \text{ GB/s}} + (2 + 4) \cdot 1.35 \text{ s} \approx 4.33 \text{ s} + 8.1 \text{ s} = 12.43 \text{ s}.$$

With the measured runtime of $t_{exec} = 68.38$ s on the device, this leaves

$$t_{comp} = 68.38 \text{ s} - 12.43 \text{ s} = 55.95 \text{ s}$$

for the computation.

Based on (3), we should hence be able to obtain a maximum optimization of

$$o_{max} = \frac{min(55.95 \text{ s}, 4.33 \text{ s} + 8.1 \text{ s})}{68.38 \text{ s}} \approx 18.2 \%.$$

However, as we can currently only apply our concept to B and not yet to A and C we are not able to save more than $4 \cdot (0.72 \text{ s} + 1.35 \text{ s}) = 8.28$ s which would mean an optimization of

$$o_{max} = \frac{8.28 \text{ s}}{68.38 \text{ s}} \approx 12.1 \%.$$

Table 1. Minimum runtime on host and device of 10 repetitions with `dgemm`.

Device	Time
Host device	125.83 s
Target device	68.38 s
w/pipelining concept	61.54 s

Table 1 lists the minimum runtimes on the host and target device. It can be seen that the matrix-matrix-multiplication on the target device (68.38 s) is significantly faster than the host (125.83 s) despite having to transfer the data. Using the pipelining concept yields another improvement of approximately 10% resulting in a runtime of 61.54 s. This is slightly below the estimation, because the model does not account for additional overhead introduced by the pipelining. However, it shows the applicability of the approach.

5.2   Conjugate Gradients Method on Multiple Target Devices

For the evaluation of the pipelining concept on multiple target devices, we implemented a Conjugate Gradients (CG) method. This compute kernel represents a popular and widely used iterative algorithm to approximate the solution for a sparse linear equation system. The computation is dominated by a sparse matrix-vector multiplication (SpMV). In general, the data transfer time for the execution of such a method is low compared to the compute time on a target device, because of the iterative nature of the CG algorithm. However, the amount of memory of a target device is typically small compared to the amount of memory of the host. In order to overcome the size limitation, our implementation of the CG solver can use multiple Intel Xeon Phi coprocessors by distributing the data.

We use a symmetric matrix with a regular sparsity pattern of five non-zero elements per row (except for the first and last few rows). Similar patterns emerge from PDEs with regular discretization. Thus, the decomposition does not require any complex partition algorithms for an adequate load balancing on the target devices. The matrix contains 80 million rows (about 400 million non-zero elements), which results in a memory footprint of about 4.8 GB in a compressed row storage (CRS) format. In addition to the right-hand side vector, the solution vector and temporary vectors (640 MB each) are required by the algorithm. This memory footprint exceeds the memory capacity of a single Xeon Phi coprocessor as used in our setup.

To decompose the data for two devices, we divide the matrix and each vector into two partitions. For all vector-vector operations, local results can be computed. Thus, for the complete solving process no additional data of the matrix needs to be exchanged between the two devices. However, the (partial) matrix-vector multiplication requires the complete intermediate result on each device for each single iteration in order to compute the corresponding (partial) output. Therefore, we need to exchange half a vector from each device in every solving step.

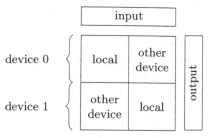

Fig. 3. Partitioning of the matrix, marking parts that are multiplied with local parts of the input vector and blocks that need data from the other device.

Nevertheless, the partial local computation of the SpMV result can be started directly, because the corresponding half of the vector is already present on the device. This enables us the apply our pipelining concept to overlap the transfer of the intermediate result from the other device with the computation that only needs the local part of the vector. After the transfer has completed, the computation can then be finalized with the data received from the other device.

To keep the computation efficient, we already partition the matrix in CRS format on the host: We create four sub-matrices and put each value into the corresponding block as shown in Fig. 3. Thus, it is not necessary to determine which part can be computed with the local part of the right-hand side vector in each iteration.

For the evaluation, we use two different versions of our CG solver: one baseline version that does not overlap the computation and communication, and one improved version that does. In the baseline version, each iteration spends roughly 250 ms for the matrix-vector multiplication which includes exchanging the input vector between the two devices. It first transfers the two parts to the host and then back to the other target device. This can be done concurrently for both devices and hence we assume a communication time t'_{comm} for each iteration based on (2):

$$t'_{comm} = 2 \cdot \frac{\frac{640}{2} \, \text{MB}}{6.7 \, \text{GB/s}} \approx 96 \, \text{ms}.$$

The remaining time is spent for the computation which amounts to

$$t'_{comp} = 250 \, \text{ms} - 96 \, \text{ms} = 154 \, \text{ms}.$$

Based on these expected timings and (3), the upper bound for the optimization is determined by

$$o_{max} = \frac{min(154 \, \text{ms}, 96 \, \text{ms})}{250 \, \text{ms}} \approx 38.4\%.$$

In summary, the presented pipelining concept reduces the computation time of the dominating matrix-vector multiplication by roughly 32%, from 254 s to 173 s.

As in the previous section, the improvement is again lower than the estimated maximum without additionally introduced overhead. Since our concept is only applicable on this most time-consuming kernel, the overall improvement for the total application is lower (about 24%).

6 Conclusion

We have shown how communication and computation can be overlapped when using OpenMP 4.5 `target` directives for a contemporary coprocessor. Besides simplifying programmability, the use of pipelining schemes can improve application performance by effectively hiding communication latencies between the host and the offload devices. It also provides an effective means to offload kernels that require more memory than is available on the device. Our pipelining scheme is portable and increases programmer productivity.

We have evaluated our implementation with two important kernels in HPC, matrix-matrix multiplication, and a sparse Conjugate Gradients solver. Our benchmarks show that overlapping communication and computation effectively reduces the runtime of these kernels by up to 24% for the CG solver. This achievement corresponds to a simple back-of-an-envelope performance model we have presented. The speed-up encourages a deeper evaluation of the profitability of our pattern with different codes.

As future work we plan to investigate the feasibility and profitability of the pattern on current GPUs with, for instance, the OpenACC programming model. We will also perform a performance comparison of the high-level OpenMP or OpenACC implementation with direct low-level implementations like the Intel Coprocessor Offload Infrastructure (COI) or NVIDIA CUDA. This will also include the evaluation how the presented CG will profit from faster interconnects such as NVLink introduced with NVIDIA Pascal.

Acknowledgment. Parts of this work were funded by the German Federal Ministry of Research and Education (BMBF) under Grant Number 01IH13008A (ELP). Simulations were performed with computing resources granted by JARA-HPC from RWTH Aachen University under project jara0001.

Intel, Xeon, and Xeon Phi are trademarks or registered trademarks of Intel Corporation or its subsidiaries in the United States and other countries.

*Other names and brands are the property of their respective owners.

Software and workloads used in performance tests may have been optimized for performance only on Intel microprocessors. Performance tests, such as SYSmark and MobileMark, are measured using specific computer systems, components, software, operations and functions. Any change to any of those factors may cause the results to vary. You should consult other information and performance tests to assist you in fully evaluating your contemplated purchases, including the performance of that product when combined with other products. For more information go to http://www.intel.com/performance.

Intel's compilers may or may not optimize to the same degree for non-Intel microprocessors for optimizations that are not unique to Intel microprocessors. These optimizations include SSE2, SSE3, and SSSE3 instruction sets and other optimizations.

Intel does not guarantee the availability, functionality, or effectiveness of any optimization on microprocessors not manufactured by Intel. Microprocessor-dependent optimizations in this product are intended for use with Intel microprocessors. Certain optimizations not specific to Intel microarchitecture are reserved for Intel microprocessors. Please refer to the applicable product User and Reference Guides for more information regarding the specific instruction sets covered by this notice.

References

1. Aji, A.M., Panwar, L.S., Ji, F., Murthy, K., Chabbi, M., Balaji, P., Bisset, K.R., Dinan, J.S., Feng, W.C., Mellor-Crummey, J., Ma, X., Thakur, R.S.: MPI-ACC: accelerator-aware MPI for scientific applications. IEEE Trans. Parallel Distrib. Syst. **27**(5), 1401–1414 (2016)
2. Beltran, V., Carrera, D., Torres, J., Ayguadé, E.: CellMT: A cooperative multithreading library for the Cell/B.E. In: 2009 International Conference on High Performance Computing (HiPC), pp. 245–253, December 2009
3. Brightwell, R., Riesen, R., Underwood, K.D.: Analyzing the impact of overlap, offload, and independent progress for message passing interface applications. Int. J. High Perform. Comput. Appl. **19**(2), 103–117 (2005). http://hpc.sagepub.com/content/19/2/103.abstract
4. Castelló, A., Peña, A.J., Mayo, R., Balaji, P., Quintana-Ortí, E.S.: Exploring the suitability of remote GPGPU virtualization for the OpenACC programming model using rCUDA. In: Proceedings of the 2015 IEEE International Conference on Cluster Computing, CLUSTER 2015, pp. 92–95 (2015). http://dx.doi.org/10.1109/CLUSTER.2015.23
5. Chen, T., Sura, Z., O'Brien, K., O'Brien, J.K.: Optimizing the Use of Static Buffers for DMA on a CELL Chip. In: Almási, G., Caşcaval, C., Wu, P. (eds.) LCPC 2006. LNCS, vol. 4382, pp. 314–329. Springer, Heidelberg (2007). doi:10.1007/978-3-540-72521-3_23
6. Cui, X., Scogland, T.R., de Supinski, B.R., Feng, W.C.: Directive-based pipelining extension for OpenMP. In: Proceedings of the 2016 IEEE International Conference on Cluster Computing, pp. 481–484 (2016)
7. Hestenes, M.R., Stiefel, E.: Methods of conjugate gradients for solving linear systems. J. Res. Natl. Bur. Stand. **49**(6), 409–436 (1952)
8. Hoefler, T., Lumsdaine, A., Rehm, W.: Implementation and performance analysis of non-blocking collective operations for MPI. In: Proceedings of the 2007 ACM/IEEE Conference on Supercomputing, SC 2007, pp. 52:1–52:10. ACM, New York (2007). http://doi.acm.org/10.1145/1362622.1362692
9. Liu, F., Chaudhary, V.: Extending OpenMP for heterogeneous chip multiprocessors. In: 2003 International Conference on Parallel Processing, Proceedings, pp. 161–168, October 2003
10. Miki, N., Ino, F., Hagihara, K.: An extension of OpenACC directives for out-of-core stencil computation with temporal blocking. In: Proceedings of the Third International Workshop on Accelerator Programming Using Directives, WACCPD 2016, pp. 36–45. IEEE Press, Piscataway (2016)
11. Si, M., Ishikawa, Y., Tatagi, M.: Direct MPI library for Intel Xeon Phi coprocessors. In: 2013 IEEE International Parallel and Distributed Processing Symposium Workshop and PhD Forum (IPDPSW), pp. 816–824. IEEE (2013)

Custom Data Mapping for Composable Data Management

Tom Scogland$^{(\boxtimes)}$, Chris Earl, and Bronis de Supinski

Lawrence Livermore National Laboratory, Livermore, CA 94550, USA
{scogland1,earl2,bronis}@llnl.gov

Abstract. Early experiences with OpenMP 4.0, as well as other directive-based offload models, have shown that deep copy is a key challenge to porting complex applications to offload directives. Without a flexible deep-copy mechanism, pointer-based data structures are at best difficult to manage, particularly when shared memory between the host and device cannot be assumed. Despite the importance of the issue, and the considerable effort expended by vendors, standards bodies and users, no solution has emerged as the clear choice. We propose an approach that combines a restricted compiler-assisted (sometimes called "true") deep copy with a mechanism for users to register their own custom mapping implementations that we call packers. This combination offers the flexibility to address complex cases when necessary while keeping the complexity out of the directives, a balance that serves all cases.

Keywords: Deep copy · Complex data · OpenMP

1 Introduction

Handling hierarchical, and in particular dynamically allocated, data structures has proven to be a significant challenge for offload-based programming models, and directive-based models like OpenMP in particular. Deep copy, the ability to copy not just the surface structure of a hierarchical object but its indirectly referenced children as well, can be difficult even in relatively straightforward host-only code, but becomes seemingly intractable when combined with disjoint memory spaces and device management. The ubiquity of such structures in the form of everything from linked lists to, trees, graphs, and even conceptually simple structures like `std::vector<T>` exacerbates the situation. This complexity has made deep copy one of the most frequently requested enhancements to the OpenMP device constructs.

This work was performed under the auspices of the U.S. Department of Energy by Lawrence Livermore National Laboratory under Contract DE-AC52-07NA27344 (LLNL-CONF-733464).

© Springer International Publishing AG 2017
B.R. de Supinski et al. (Eds.): IWOMP 2017, LNCS 10468, pp. 338–347, 2017.
DOI: 10.1007/978-3-319-65578-9_23

In order to solve this problem, OpenMP must address several particular data mapping challenges:

Composable deep copy Implementing deep copy for a structure s1 that contains a pointer to s2, which already has an implementation, should not require a reimplementation of the work done on s2, including when s1 and s2 share the same source-level definition (i.e., recursive deep copy).

Updates must be safe In order to keep data coherent, the mechanism must support updates; some proposals insufficiently address this requirement due to potential overwriting of host pointers by device pointers.

Performance must be reasonable Deeply copying a nested structure is inherently expensive but an automated mechanism should incur little overhead beyond a manual implementation.

Several proposals and research projects have considered deep copy. Almost all have one of two forms: manual deep copy or compiler-assisted "true" deep copy. In general, the manual options are more verbose and require much more user effort, and result in harder-to-maintain code. In particular, manual deep copy requires the explicit listing of each component to be mapped onto the device at each point where its mapped, effectively requiring code replication.

Compiler-assisted deep copy, in the form of directives that encode the structure and mapping requirements of a type, cleanly separates the concerns of mapping a particular type from its use, allowing a simple map of a variable to invoke the required logic. Such approaches produce cleaner code where a user maps a value, but tend to become extremely complex for data-structures that contain multiple pointers to parts of the same memory or if the dynamically allocated structure contains cycles, as in the case of a circular linked-list or graph.

Both kinds of deep-copy support have advantages and disadvantages, but the complexity and abundant corner-cases in the compiler-assisted approach have so far kept standards focused on implementing only manual deep copy semantics. In particular OpenMP 4.5, with refinements in OpenMP TR4, introduced a top-down attachment mechanism to allow for manual deep copy.

Our proposal extends OpenMP's deep copy facilities with constructs that provide the main benefit of compiler-assisted deep copy, a simple compiler-assisted mechanism to map a value in a user's compute code for easy cases with user-defined custom mappers for the harder cases. By allowing users to handle their own data marshalling and reconstruction, as well as to write their own conditional and computational code to determine how to perform those operations, we avoid many of the pitfalls of previous directive-based compiler-assisted approaches. A solution based entirely on custom implementations from users even for simple cases would be unduly verbose, so we provide an option for strictly top-down hierarchical data structures to leverage the existing manual deep copy functionality to write custom mappers that a compiler expands.

In the rest of this paper, we first present related work in Sect. 2. Our proposed design for a deep-copy extension to OpenMP is presented next in Sect. 3. Finally we discuss the properties of our proposed design in Sect. 4.

2   Related Work

A major challenge for HPC developers is to manage code and data on multiple architectures. OpenMP began to address this challenge with version 4.0, and continues to improve its support in version 4.5 [6]. One of the most common complaints with these versions is the lack of good deep copy support [3]. While composable deep copy solutions have previously been proposed [1], the OpenMP standard does not include one. The most recent technical reports on OpenMP (TR4 [7] and TR5 [8]) provide mechanisms for a restricted form of top-down hierarchical deep copy and a proposed interface for multi-level memory. However, neither really supports arbitrarily complex deep copy.

OpenACC's current standard [5] also only supports deep copy through manual means. Some proposals would allow data re-shaping on transfer (without deep copy capabilities [2]) and to enable deep copy through compiler support [4].

3   Design

Existing proposals to standardize deep-copy discussed in Sect. 2 have largely focused on one of two approaches: type annotations that facilitate compiler generation of mapping code that composes pointer-based structures, or manual attachment that gives the user flexibility but must be replicated throughout the source code. We aim to provide an interface that: allows for composition of mapping functionality; separates concerns between computation and mapping logic; and provides the same flexibility as manual mapping.

We need an interface that is flexible enough to encompass arbitrary data structures and yet is easy to use for simple ones. Figure 1 lists the new directives, clauses and modifications that we claim meet this requirement. We discuss this proposal in greater detail in the ensuing sections.

3.1   Mappers

The `declare mapper` construct defines how to map a given type. Complex data structures, or custom behavior, require the use of packers, which we discuss in Sect. 3.2, but the `declare mapper` construct, without custom packers, can handle simple nested structures with pointers or references and dependent as long as a `sub_maps()` clause is specified. A set of sub-maps on a mapper with the name `foo` serves as a template for how the compiler should expand `map(foo: v)`, similarly to previously proposed annotation-based deep-copy mechanisms. Figure 2 defines a mapper for the `myvec_t` and for `mypoints_t`, which contains both pointers to and an immediate value of type `myvec_t`.

The example illustrates some key features. While the first mapper explicitly lists the variable being mapped in the `sub_maps` clause, the mapper for `mypoints_t` does not. Thus, users can leverage the existing behavior of OpenMP's partial mapping to map a `mypoints_t` without having to pull

```
1    // Mapper
2    #pragma omp declare mapper \
3        type(<type>) \
4        [default] /* if specified, this mapper will be used implicitly */ \
5        [name(<name>)] /* if unspecified, name == type */ \
6        [submap([<map-type allowed>:]<list-items>...)] \
7        [no_<packer stage>]\
8        [can_skip]

9    // OpenMP provided value for submap
10   T     * omp_item; // Pointer to T, where T is of type <type>

11   // [Un]Packers
12   #pragma omp declare map_{packer,unpacker}_{to,from}(<mapper_name>) \
13       expr(<packing/unpacking expression>) \
14       [size(<size expression>)] \
15       [in_place] /* reuse the staging buffer, to == from */ \

16   #pragma omp declare map_{submap,subrelease}(<mapper_name>) \
17       expr(<sub-map mapper/releaser expression>) \

18   // OpenMP provided values for expressions
19   T     * omp_from; // Pointer to T, where T is <type> address of:
20                     //   packer_to: the list-item provided to map
21                     //   unpacker_to: the input buffer on the device
22                     //   packer_from: the buffer used in the target region
23                     //   unpacker_from: the staging buffer on the host
24   T     * omp_to;   // The buffer data is packed, or unpacked, into
25                     //   packer_{to,from}, unpacker_to: a buffer of
26                     //                     size max_size
27                     //   unpacker_from: a pointer to the original list item
28   size_t omp_from_size; // The size in bytes of the buffer in omp_from
29   size_t omp_to_size; // The size in bytes of the buffer in omp_to

30   // Address management
31   #pragma omp target data use_device_addr(<mapped object>)

32   // Extension to map()
33   #pragma omp target... map([<mapper_name>][,<map-type-modifier>...:]...)
```

Fig. 1. Our proposed extension.

in unnamed, and unnecessary, fields. Also, such mappers compose with one-another. The list-item on Line 20 of the example references the mapper for the myvec_t type, expanding the list-item into its component parts, exactly as in the existing map clause.

Unless the sub_maps clause specifies an allowed map-type, its list-items inherit the map-type of the map clause that uses its definition, defaulting to tofrom. For example, an update(to: v) expands all sub-maps with allowed map-types of to or tofrom and updates the device with data from the host as appropriate. While that behavior is generally desired, sometimes some fields should not be updated. The scratch field of mypoints_t is an example. Since it always just holds temporary data, we limit the behavior in which it participates to only the alloc map-type, which also includes release and delete behaviors.

While specifying members in sub_maps covers many real-world use-cases, it suffers from several limitations. This mechanism can only map members that are visible; private fields of classes or structures in C++ for example cannot be listed. Types used by sub-maps are static types, just as with any map clause, so the dynamic type of an object is not considered and values may be sliced as a result.

```
1    typedef struct myvec {
2        size_t len;
3        double *data;
4    } myvec_t;

5    #pragma omp declare mapper \
6        type(myvec_t) \
7        default \
8        sub_maps(*omp_item, omp_item[0].data[0:omp_item->len])

9    typedef struct mypoints {
10       struct myvec * x;
11       struct myvec * y;
12       struct myvec * z;
13       struct myvec scratch;
14       double useless_data[500000];
15   } mypoints_t;

16   #pragma omp declare mapper \
17       type(mypoints_t) \
18       default \
19       sub_maps(/* self only partially mapped, useless_data can be ignored */\
20               omp_item[0].x, omp_item[0].x[0:1], /* map and attach x */  \
21               omp_item[0].y, omp_item[0].y[0:1], /* map and attach y */  \
22               omp_item[0].z, omp_item[0].z[0:1], /* map and attach z */ )\
23       sub_maps(alloc:omp_item[0].scratch) /* never update scratch */

24   // Usage in code
25   mypoints_t *p = make_array_of_mypoints(N);
26   #pragma omp target map(p[0:N])
27   //...
28   // Translates to the following, replicated for all i from 0-N:
29   #pragma omp target map(p[i], \
30       p[i].x[0:1], p[i].x->data[0:p[i].x->len] \
31       p[i].y[0:1], p[i].y->data[0:p[i].y->len] \
32       p[i].z[0:1], p[i].z->data[0:p[i].z->len])\
33       map(alloc: p[i].scratch)
```

Fig. 2. An example of a straightforward mapper with a single child mapper.

Finally, cycles in the data structures being mapped will not be detected, which precludes its use for any kind of cyclic graph or circular list structures. Rather than make the mapper more complex, we introduce packers to address these issues and more.

3.2 Packers

Mappers defined only in terms of their sub-maps work entirely within the mapping semantics defined by OpenMP 4.5. They use partial mapping of structures and pointer attachment, and they expand to separate the mapping of a structure from its use, but they do not fundamentally change the mental model of how mapping works. Packers, on the other hand, change that model.

We model our deep-copy extensions as a serialization/deserialization pipeline, that Fig. 3 represents. OpenMP 4.5 mapping behavior runs along the left-hand side of this figure with an optional bitwise copy from the input buffer to the input data and from the output data to the output buffer. We logically expand the pipeline to include a input phase that packs data on the host and unpacke it on the device and an output phase that reverses the actions. Thus, we can

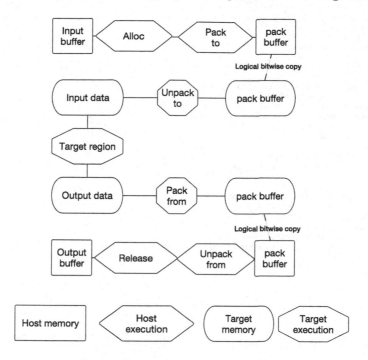

Fig. 3. The conceptual mapping pipeline

perform transformations on the data on each inbound or outbound transfer. The opportunity to transform the data supports the conversion of deep, or otherwise complex, data-structures into a format that can be safely bitwise copied and recreated from the simplified format after the copy is complete.

Packers define provide custom implementations of stages in the pipeline for use in the `mapper` construct. Each stage can be specified separately: the `map_submap`, `map_packer_to`, `map_unpacker_from`, and `map_subrelease` run on the host device and `map_unpacker_to` and `map_packer_from` execute on the target device. A mapper that specifies any packer stage must provide all stages or explicitly list the `no_<stage>` clause on the `mapper` construct (this requirement does not apply to the submap and subrelease stages). Where the `no_<stage>` clause explicitly skips a stage, a bitwise copy logically replaces it, although an implementation may be able to skip one or more these copies.

Each packer takes the name of the associated `mapper` clause as well as a required `expr` clause that implements the appropriate behavior. They may also optionally take: a `size` clause, which takes an expression that should evaluate to the maximum size required for output from that stage or defaults to `sizeof(type)`; and an `in_place` clause, which causes the runtime to skip creation of a staging buffer into which pack the data is packed, and instead uses the input buffer for the packing, or unpacking, space.

```
1    struct list {
2        struct list *next, *previous;
3        size_t data_count;
4        plain_data_t data;
5    } list_t;

6    size_t pack_list(list_t *from, list_t *to) {
7        int n_nodes = 1; // include handle node
8        list_t *cur = from->next; //handle does not store data
9        for (list_t *cur = from->next; cur != from && cur != NULL; cur = cur->next) {
10           to[n_nodes] = *cur;
11           n_nodes++;
12       }
13       to[0].data_count = n_nodes;
14       return n_nodes * sizeof(list_t); // Return the space actually used
15   }

16   void unpack_list_from(list_t *from, list_t *to) {
17       int n_nodes = from->data_count; // include handle node
18       list_t *cur = to->next; //handle does not store data
19       while (cur != from && cur != NULL) {
20           cur->data = from[n_nodes].data;
21           cur->data_count = from[n_nodes].data_count;
22           n_nodes++;
23           cur = cur->next;
24       }
25   }
26   #pragma omp declare mapper type(list_t) no_packer_from
27   #pragma omp declare map_packer_to(list_t) \
28                       size(count_nodes(omp_from) * sizeof(list_t)) \
29                       expr(pack_list(omp_from, omp_to))
30   #pragma omp declare map_unpacker_to(list_t) expr(fix_list_pointers(omp_from)) in_place
31   #pragma omp declare map_unpacker_from(list_t) expr(unpack_list_from(omp_from))

32   // Usage
33   #pragma omp target map(l)
34   {    plain_data_t d = l->next->next->data;
35        //...
36   }
```

Fig. 4. A mapper for a doubly-linked list with custom packers and unpackers.

The example in Fig. 4 shows a mapper for a circular doubly-linked list. This list stores a count and a bitwise copyable structure in each node as data, and uses a node with no data as a handle that identifies the head and tail nodes. Unlike our mapper example in Fig. 2, the mapper for list_t does not use any sub-maps. Instead we simply declare that a packer_from stage is not needed. Since neither a submap nor a subrelease are specified neither is required. The first stage, the packer_to, calls a function to count the nodes in the list to determine the size. Alternatively, if a maximum size is known, a constant could be supplied and the return value of the packer expression will be interpreted as the number of bytes that it used. In our example, the packer copies the contents of each list node into a position in an array of nodes, then stores the number of nodes in the first element. The unpacker on the way into the device is declared in_place so it uses the staging buffer on the device as both its input and its output. Its expression calls a declare target routine that iterates through the array and fixes the next and previous pointers of each element so that the linked-list is well-formed, but leaves the nodes grouped into a contiguous array through the target region. Since the data is already in a packed form, it can be copied back with a bitwise copy, then data is copied from each node in the packed array into the potentially non-contiguous original nodes.

While the code that implements the linked-list mapper in terms of packers and unpackers is not short, it provides a clean interface for users to map a linked-list by its handle. The same packing and unpacking code can map to or from a target device and in update constructs, just like the sub-maps in simple mappers. However, support for these phases can require extra work in some cases. The pack to and unpack from can use unstructured update directives as part of their implementation, particularly for child data, termed sub-maps, that need independent reference counts. This facility supports larger code bases but its use does not provide the OpenMP runtime sufficient information to manage the allocation and release of these sub-maps without user action. Thus, the map_submap and map_subrelease constructs take expressions to increment or decrement the reference counts of associated sub-maps respectively.

Finally, we propose the use_device_addr for data-mapping constructs. While mappers based on sub-maps compose naturally with other mappers, including a sub-map in a packer-based mapper is more complex. However, this functionality is necessary. Since each mapper manages a single reference-counted device-side view of the data, any data for which the lifetimes of pieces of the structure may be different must be mapped in pieces. Thus the use_device_addr clause supplies the address of the corresponding storage on the device for a given host pointer, such that a custom packer can include it in the buffer to be bitwise copied to the device. This clause also offers greater flexibility when interoperating with native interfaces that may require a device address rather than the host handle to device data provided by use_device_ptr.

4   Discussion

Our extension uses user-defined functions to manage data mapping. Alternatively users could combine unstructured data mapping consructs with their own functions. This approach would require fewer, if any, changes to the OpenMP specification. However, our approach has several advantages. First, as with any directives, the compiler can ignore our new constructs and clauses. Second, are approach facilitates compiler optimization of data copies. Third, OpenMP's mapping model checks if variables are present on a device to avoid unnecessary mapping operations. Incorporating packing into this mapping model easiy avoids packing and unpacking overhead in these cases. The equivalent checks in user code can be impractical if not impossible. The remainder of this section discusses how our extensions addresses the challenges listed in Sect. 1.

4.1   Composability

Exclusively compiler-assisted deep-copy mechanisms must provide composability by design. As a result, they often do not support complex cases such as circular data structures. Our solution includes support for manually implemented mappers, which complicate composability. Any mapper implemented entirely with sub-maps automatically uses mappers specified for clause list-items. Thus, like other compiler-assisted mechanism, it supports composability even if those mappers are implemented with explicit custom packers.

Packers can compose in two distinct ways. First, a mapper that uses packers can specify sub-maps, in which case those maps are available before the pack-to stage is executed on the host, and any transfers and unmaps are completed after the unpack-from stage. These sub-maps can be referenced in the packed data structure by embedding the result of the `use_device_addr` clause. Second, the pack-to phase can include `target enter data` constructs to map children, with matching `target exit data` constructs in the unpacker-from stage if the `sub_maps` clause is specified. We require the extra clause because the expression of the pack-to phase may hide the amount of space that the map must allocate, an issue that also complicates updates as we discuss next.

4.2   Updates

Updates through mechanisms like `target update` and `map(always:...)` pose difficulties for deep-copy proposals. Pointer-based data-structures on many devices must use device-specific values for pointer fields. If an update of the structure blindly copies pointers, the device (host) pointers overwrite the host (device) values. As of OpenMP TR4, attached pointers are not brought back to the host and the compiler ensures the error does not occur. While, user-implemented packers may overwrite host pointers with device pointers in the unpacker-from stage, Fig. 4 shows that a correct user implementation can avoid the error or even translate device pointers to the correct host addresses.

Our extension introduces a new issue with updates. Packers that use `sub_maps` for composition must behave differently when space is allocated from when data is only transferred. Thus, we require the runtime to support a boolean `omp_update` variable that indicates the map only transfers data. Thus, packing stages can perform the correct action depending on its value. While this mechanism increases mapper complexity, it supports correct behavior for updates.

4.3   Performance

The performance implications of our extension are complex. If sub-mappers are used, performance is equivalent to a manual deep copy using attachment semantics. The OpenMP `target` implementation in clang currently supports pointer attachment by synchronously copying data and then the pointer to the transfer buffer. When the atttached pointer is part of a larger aggregate buffer, our extension can improve performance with an unpacker-to that assigns all of the pointers in one device kernel instead of using individual transfers for each one. On the downside, if all six stages of the pipeline for a packer-based mapper are implemented and copy the data in each stage and the data is copied both to and from the device, *four* copies are performed as well as the usual two bitwise copies. However, the additional allocations and data movement can be limited to required stages while batch transfers can reduce total data movement cost. Further refinement of the interface may yield additional optimizations. For example, the expansion of an array of `mypoints_t` structures in Fig. 2 is correct but cannot batch the various buffers into a single larger allocation without breaking the requirements of the API. We will explore opportunities for array-based packers and similar optimizations as part of a performance evaluation across various use-cases as part of future work.

5 Conclusions

We have presented a deep-copy extension for OpenMP that combines compiler assistance and user-defined behavior. The user-defined component (packers) exposes a four-stage pipeline to allow the user to customize the behavior on host and target in each direction. This conceptual pipeline supports mapping parallelism as well as data-specific optimizations. Our extension addresses several traditionally challenging issues without requiring the directives to support a complete language. In future work, we will explore this extension in the context of larger applications, and investigate the possibility of bulk-packing operations for arrays of data structures rather than single instances at a time.

References

1. Beyer, J., Oehmke, D., Sandoval, J.: Transferring user-defined types in OpenACC. In: Proceedings of Cray User Group (CUG14) (2014)
2. Hoshino, T., Maruyama, N., Matsuoka, S.: An OpenACC extension for data layout transformation. In: 2014 First Workshop on Accelerator Programming Using Directives (WACCPD), pp. 12–18. IEEE (2014)
3. Karlin, I., et al.: Early Experiences Porting Three Applications to OpenMP 4.5. In: Maruyama, N., Supinski, B.R., Wahib, M. (eds.) IWOMP 2016. LNCS, vol. 9903, pp. 281–292. Springer, Cham (2016). doi:10.1007/978-3-319-45550-1_20
4. OpenACC Standards Committee: Deep copy attach and detach. Technical report TR-16-1 (2016)
5. OpenACC Working Group and Others: The OpenACC Application Programming Interface, Version 2.5 (2015)
6. OpenMP Architecture Review Board: OpenMP Application Programming Interface, Version 4.5 (2015)
7. OpenMP Architecture Review Board: OpenMP Technical Report 4: Version 5.0 Preview 1. Technical report TR-4 (2016)
8. OpenMP Architecture Review Board: OpenMP Technical Report 5: Memory Management Support for OpenMP 5.0. Technical report TR-5 (2017)

Author Index

Printed in the United States
By Bookmasters